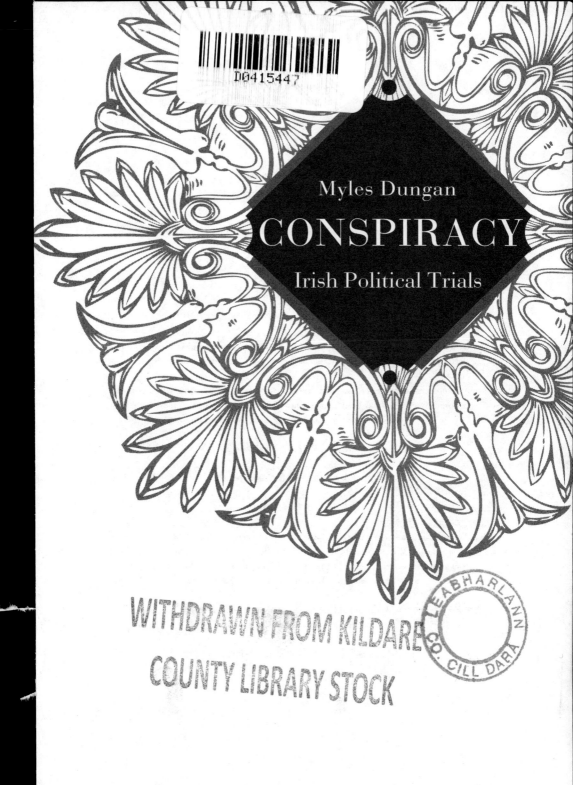

Myles Dungan

CONSPIRACY

Irish Political Trials

Conspiracy: Irish political trials

First published 2009

by Prism
Prism is an imprint of the Royal Irish Academy
19 Dawson Street
Dublin 2
www.ria.ie

The author and publisher are grateful to the National Library of Ireland and the National
Portrait Gallery, London, for permission to reproduce illustrations in this book.

During the production process some illustrations have been retouched or tinted for aesthetic
purposes. Every effort has been made to trace the copyright holders of these items
and to ensure the accuracy of their captions.

ISBN 978-1-904890-58-4

British Library Cataloguing in Publication Data. A CIP catalogue record for this book
is available from the British Library.

Printed in the UK by Athenaeum Press.

10 9 8 7 6 5 4 3 2 1

For my late uncle and aunt, Patrick and Bee O'Reilly of Baileborough, Co. Cavan, who almost enticed me into the legal profession and their sons (my cousins), Pat and Myles, who supervised much of my adolescence.

CONTENTS

ILLUSTRATIONS

All illustrations are reproduced courtesy of the National Library of Ireland unless otherwise stated. Particular thanks are due to their Prints and Drawings, and Ephemera Departments.

ACKNOWLEDGEMENTS

I would like to thank Clare Duignan, Lorelei Harris, Ana Leddy, Peter Mooney and Malachy Moran of RTÉ for the parts they played in bringing this project to fruition.

I am also extremely grateful to Frank Callanan, Justice Patrick McCartan and my TCD fellow student, Maeve Ryan, for reading all or parts of the text and making useful and constructive comments.

To Ruth Hegarty and Pauric Dempsey of the Royal Irish Academy—thank you both for the idea, coffee and validation. To Lucy Hogan—thanks for the apostrophes and the buckets of patience.

As always, to Aonghus Ó hAonghusa and the staff of National Library of Ireland my thanks for a highly professional service and a second home.

And to my darling wife, Nerys, for working around me for months and providing a first home. Once again *diolch yn fawr*.

All trials are trials for one's life, just as all sentences are sentences of death ...[1]

(Oscar Wilde, *De Profundis*)

The government, against which a claim of liberty is tantamount to high treason, is a government to which submission is equivalent to slavery.[2]

(Edmund Burke, *On conciliation with America*)

When the distinguished journalist, jurist and crime novelist, Matthias McDonnell Bodkin, announced his intention to write a book on noteworthy Irish trials, one unnamed barrister advised him to confine himself exclusively to political cases. 'The history of Ireland, for more than a century is written in the evidence and verdicts of political prosecutions', McDonnell Bodkin was told by his colleague.[3] He ignored the distinguished counsel's advice and instead cast his net widely across a variety of civil and criminal cases. This current volume has, however, taken the advice to heart, while recognising its one-dimensional nature. It is as reductionist to parse Irish history since the Act of Union, 1800, through a trail of trials as through a series of failed rebellions. But nowhere are the contradictions and paradoxes of the Anglo–Irish relationship in the 'long nineteenth century'[4] more apparent than in the gladiatorial arena that ranged from Petty Sessions to Commission Courts.

It is not possible in a discussion of seven trials to essay a comprehensive overview of the relationship between the Irish people and English law under the Union. The very act of selection, especially as the choices made here are often based on the dramatic elements of the cases, would leave any conclusions drawn open to legitimate challenge. Nonetheless, when seen in conjunction with a number of other 'political' trials during the 121 years of the Union, some equally celebrated at the time, a pattern can be discerned. This suggests that the law courts became a key battleground in the developing struggle for social equity and Irish nationhood. The constant subtext is the difficulty of reconciling British jurisprudential ideals with the realities of Irish politics so that the notion of a legitimate 'Union' had some meaning. The logic of the political unification of the two 'kingdoms' was that they should have been governed by a, substantially, uniform legal code. Instead, all too often, Ireland simply became John Bull's other jurisdiction. Governance and the application of the law could frequently be colonial in nature. Ireland was more India than it was Sheffield or Surrey.

One of the most resourceful servants of the Crown in nineteenth-century Ireland, the Special Resident Magistrate Clifford Lloyd, came from Burma in 1880 to take on the task of curtailing the activities of the Land League. In his memoir of the period, he wrote of the Royal Irish Constabulary (RIC), upon whose services he greatly relied, that it 'can best be described as an army of occupation, upon which is imposed the performance of certain civil duties'.[5] As for the magistracy of the country, he observed that admission to its ranks required 'absolutely no qualification whatever' and that 'many gentlemen obtained these appointments not on account of their capacity, intelligence or experience, but as a reward for political services rendered to the Government'.[6] It is a surprisingly frank and accurate assessment from someone who might have been expected to depict the infrastructure of Irish law enforcement in a more positive light.

It is undoubtedly the case that 'in spite of the frequent social and political turmoil of Ireland in the nineteenth century, there is much evidence of Ireland's "normality" as a society'.[7] However, this work eschews the mundane or 'secular' criminality to focus on the politically 'sectarian'— overt political crime or criminal acts committed or tried in a politicised context. It can be argued that, at certain times, much of the crime in Ireland dealt with outside of Petty Sessions Courts was politically motivated. Maurice Healy, barrister and nephew of the waspish T.M. Healy, MP, wrote in his memoir of the Munster circuit at the turn of the century that during the 1880s 'apart from political crime, there were practically no cases for the judges to try. Crimes of lust, or greed or dishonesty were non-existent. Crimes of violence were plentiful; and were nearly all political'.[8]

In a society where laws are often framed as instruments of social, cultural or political control, and where a suspicion exists that due process has been contaminated by a political agenda, a trial becomes something other than mere litigation. For this volume, seven trials have been chosen for examination in most of which a case can be made that the establishment sought to subvert its own laws for political purposes. Beginning and ending with Dublin-based insurrections (the Robert Emmet rebellion and the Easter Rising of 1916), the seven trials encompass critical elements of the labours of Irish nationalism, constitutional and revolutionary, against

British rule. They exemplify the atavistic tendency of the governing body politic to protect itself against challenge, the innate sense of superiority and entitlement on the part of the Ascendancy and establishment, and the lack of mutual comprehension between governors and governed. Fair-minded administrators like Under Secretaries Thomas Drummond (1835–40) and Thomas Larcom (1853–68) might have wished, according to Edmund Dwyer Gray, for 'the law in Ireland to have been dispensed on the same principles as in the rest of the United Kingdom' but it was not, nor, from a British perspective, could it ever be.[9] But the fact that Ireland was utterly unlike the rest of the United Kingdom can only be advanced in partial justification for this discrepancy.

In an Irish context the term 'political trial' is self explanatory to some, oxymoronic to others. The notion of a 'political' prosecution was, of course, consistently rejected by the establishment. The British authorities refused to accept that political offenders were 'conscionable prisoners'. There was, as Gray put it, a 'common-law unwillingness to distinguish between political and ordinary crime'.[10] However, many of those convicted of crimes such as high treason, sedition, treason felony and seditious libel were often not treated as fairly as common criminals. The deluxe treatment of the leaders of the Repeal movement, jailed in 1844, 'corresponded with the traditional custom of Great Britain in regard to political offenders', according to Gray, the grandson of John Gray, editor and proprietor of the *Freeman's Journal*, who was one of those imprisoned.[11] Despite the imprisonment of O'Connell and his co-accused for conspiracy, the political nature of their 'crime' meant only a minor curtailment of their freedom. At the other extreme was the exceptionally harsh treatment, admittedly in time of war, meted out to a number of participants (including some of little or no influence) in the Easter Rising of 1916. In a highly political gesture, Patrick Pearse, James Connolly, Joseph Plunkett *et al.* forfeited their lives without the benefit of a public trial by their peers. Gray acknowledged in 1889 that the law did not distinguish between 'ordinary' and 'political' crime. '*That* the law has never done, except indirectly ... [but] ... it was the constitutional custom to supply in practice what was defective in the law.'[12] It appears that exceptionalism could mean anything from incarceration in conditions of relative luxury to summary execution without due process.

In seeking to define a 'political' crime during the period of the Union it is probably prudent to confine the description to offences such as those named above—high treason, treason felony, sedition and seditious libel.

The 'crimes' of Robert Emmet and the 1916 rebels are unambiguously political. There is no more political act than an attempt to overthrow a government. The case of John Magee, editor of the *Dublin Evening Post* is also clear-cut. He was charged with seditious libel in 1813 for a relatively mild attack in his newspaper on the outgoing lord lieutenant. The 'traversers' in the 1844 conspiracy case were not accused of pursuing an illicit objective.[13] Their crime was of conspiring together to achieve a legitimate political goal. The Invincibles, although guilty of a heinous and brutal crime, did not murder Lord Frederick Cavendish and Thomas Henry Burke for their purses but for their politics. The *Times* Commission of 1888–9, while not a formal trial, involved the indictment of an entire political movement. The Maamtrasna murders, which began as an act of mindless criminality, quickly acquired highly politicised overtones.

There are few instances in the cases described, of outright or blatant collusion to subvert natural justice. In many instances, the plainly and unblushingly guilty were punished. This sometimes occurred in a charged atmosphere hardly conducive to the success of retributive justice. But many Irish political trials under the Union are also characterised by the flouting of vaunted procedures and the contravention of some very English notions of fair play. While abuse of process may be politically expedient or unavoidable, it does nothing for the repute of the law other than to reinforce disrespect and disapprobation. Furthermore, these infringements were more systemic than opportunistic. If legal sleight of hand was essential to maintain a modern *pacata Hibernia* occult forces could usually be deployed to achieve a pre-determined conclusion. No conspiracy or even communication was necessary for the disparate elements (executive, judiciary, counsel and jury), to play their allotted roles. It was as natural as the human body warding off infection. Whether operating in retaliation for rebellion or anticipation of dissent, Britannia waived the rules with a degree of regularity and, at times, almost casual efficiency.

Irish revolutionary movements faced nigh on insurmountable odds in any attempt to achieve separation by force. However, given the great pride taken by Britain in the evenhandedness of its legal system, constitutional movements should not have been subject to hostile legal action as so regularly proved to be the case. Had equity prevailed some of the trials discussed in this volume would never have taken place. Others might have had different outcomes. But, where justice deferred to political imperatives, the possibility (and occasionally, the inevitability) of miscarriage or mere retribution was omnipresent. Burke's comment, cited at the opening of this chapter, concerning the British response to democratic dissent in eighteenth-century American colonies is apposite in the case of nineteenth- and early twentieth-century Ireland.

Sir Roger Casement, in his celebrated speech from the dock in 1916, observed of British law in Ireland that it did not enjoy the support of the Irish people: 'but it exists in defiance of their will [in] that it is a rule, derived not from right, but from conquest'.[14] Of course, if one were to substitute the word 'privilege' for 'conquest' British law as it was practised in Ireland was of a piece with the treatment of English dissentient radicalism in the first half of the nineteenth century. Irish agrarianism or militant nationalism could easily be viewed, albeit simplistically, through an establishment prism, as a mere variant of English radical dissent. All three could be rolled up together by reactionaries as manifestations of antipathy towards the status quo, which was characterised by defiance of the law. Working class movements like Chartism, which posed a potential threat to the establishment, were dealt with in a manner not unlike Irish activist organisations.[15] However, other English radical groups, like the Anti-Corn Law League, led by Richard Cobden and John Bright, were treated quite differently to the Chartists. The movements led by Daniel O'Connell and Charles Stewart Parnell were closer in methodology and ethos to that of Cobden and Bright, however, the official response to the activities of the Irishmen was more akin to the treatment of the Chartists.

Not all of the cases presented here are trials in the common understanding of the word—i.e. defence and prosecuting counsel arguing before a jury. Not all were conducted in Irish courts. Not all were capital cases. But even if lives were not at stake, reputations were in jeopardy or legitimate political opposition at hazard. Trial by jury, trial by Commission Court, trial by court martial and trial by special court, these were the methods used in meting out 'political' justice in the 'long nineteenth century' and all are encompassed in the selected narratives.

While special pleading in political cases was *de rigeur* for prosecuting advocates, when it came to the Bench a degree of even-handedness was expected. However, in the cases that follow the rulings, directions and indeed the general demeanour of the presiding judges leave much to be desired. Whether it be Lord Norbury attempting to silence Emmet or Justice Pennefather instructing the jury to convict O'Connell of conspiracy, most demonstrate the veracity of the axiom of the journalist, historian and barrister, R. Barry O'Brien, who observed that 'In England when an advocate reaches the Bench he ceases to be a politician. In Ireland he is always a politician'.[16] As long as the two main English political parties regularly alternated in government the danger of a judiciary entirely dominated by Whigs or Tories could be averted. In Ireland, such was not necessarily the case. No matter what the political stripe of the British government, access to the Irish Bench, especially in the early part of the nineteenth century, was largely confined to Protestants and Unionists.

The first Irish Catholic judicial appointment since the reign of James II was not made until 1835. By the time of the disestablishment of the Church of Ireland in 1869, only half the country's judges were Catholic. Between 1853 and 1900, 60 barristers were appointed to positions on the Bench of the higher courts. More than two-thirds were Protestant.[17] This is not to suggest that Protestant judges were all, by definition, militant or doctrinaire Unionists, or that they were incapable of abandoning whatever political bias they might have had in the pursuit of justice. But there are many examples of judges who acted as if they were front-line defenders of the Union or of landlord privilege.

Take just two judges from the 1880s not discussed in the three cases from that decade presented in this volume. In 1882 Mr Justice Lawson, the object of an assassination plot by the Invincibles, jailed Edmund Dwyer Gray, proprietor of the *Freeman's Journal*, for contempt for publishing a letter by William O'Brien in his newspaper. O'Brien, editor of Parnell's *United Ireland*, had used the correspondence column of the *Freeman* simply to point out that the night before arriving at a guilty verdict in a Co. Clare 'outrage' murder case the hand picked jury had been running riot through the Imperial Hotel and had openly associated with members of the public in the Billiard room.[18] Rather than investigate the antics of the jury, Lawson opted to shoot the messenger instead. Gray was sentenced to three months of which he served six weeks, while continuing to edit his paper from Richmond Prison.

Mr Justice May who presided over the state trial of Parnell and the leadership of the Land League in January 1881, in refusing a motion for a postponement the previous month, took it upon himself to outline the 'facts' of the case in justification of his decision.

> For several months in this country the law has been openly defied and trampled on ... a large portion of the community, urged on by members of this Land League,

> have practiced a system of fraudulent dishonesty in refus-
> ing to pay their just debts. This country has been for
> months in a state of terror. It has been tyrannised over by
> an unauthorized conspiracy ...

And in order to make his meaning perfectly clear, he concluded, 'Let the trial proceed as speedily as possible, and if Mr. Parnell has to complain of anyone it is of himself and of the conduct of those associated with him'.[19] The fact that the lord chief justice was largely correct in his summation of the grip agrarian crime held on the country hardly justifies a speech worthy of an opening address by the Crown prosecutor. Such was the outcry at his remarks that he was obliged to retire from the case and leave it in the hands of Mr Justice Fitzgerald and Mr Justice Barry.[20] The prosecution of the 'traversers', who included Parnell, John Dillon, Joseph Biggar, Thomas Sexton (all MPs) as well as Land League functionaries like treasurer, Patrick Egan, failed.

There were a number of outstanding judges on the Irish Bench, most notable amongst them being Christopher Palles, lord chief baron of the exchequer, who spent more than 40 years as a judge. His elevation to the bench was one of the last acts of William Gladstone as prime minister in 1874—he was appointed on the platform at Paddington Station as the Grand Old Man was on his way to Windsor to return the seals of office to a relieved Queen Victoria. For Maurice Healy, Palles was 'a pattern of all that is great and good; no word could be written in his praise that would be extravagant'.[21] But the Pantheon occupied by Palles was, otherwise, sparsely populated.

Pennefather, whose direction to the jury in the state trial of 1844 (see Chapter 3) did the defendants few favours, proved himself considerably less partial earlier in his career when presiding over the Doneraile conspiracy trial of October 1829. In this instance, the ambitious solicitor general, John Doherty (later a judge in the trial of Smith O'Brien and the other Young Irelanders in 1848), arraigned 22 supposed Whiteboys[22] for conspiracy to murder based on the evidence of two paid informers, Patrick and Owen Daly. Some of those implicated by the Dalys became 'approvers' and gave dubious evidence for the Crown to save their own lives. The accused were defended by O'Connell. The entire affair 'had been conjured into existence by a paranoid establishment'.[23] It was largely through the intervention of Pennefather, who alerted O'Connell to a major discrepancy in the evidence of one of the informers, that most of the accused were acquitted.

Of course, to some extent, and in the latter half of the nineteenth century in particular, Irish Catholics had only themselves to blame for the overwhelmingly loyalist complexion of the judiciary. As former MP William Keogh discovered when he was raised to the Bench, a particular kind of opprobrium was often reserved for Catholics thus elevated. However, Keogh's pre-existing unpopularity, based on his abandonment of the Independent Irish Party in the 1850s to take a government position, contributed greatly to the popular revulsion at his appointment.

The eminent barrister and historian Frank Callanan, has defended the nineteenth-century Irish Bench by contrasting it with a magistracy even less distinguished in its application of equity: 'the Irish bench—while largely unionist in political orientation and protestant in religious allegiance—was prepared in some degree to hold the ring, and to constrain the powers of the Irish executive and the magistracy'.[24] However, to be more impartial than the magistracy is a modest enough recommendation. 'Corruption and inefficiency were believed to be endemic amongst its membership.[25] Most magistrates were drawn from the aristocracy of a local area. Most had a vested interest in the maintenance of the status quo. Most were Protestant grandees, frequently absent in Dublin or London, making crucial decisions affecting the lives of their Catholic neighbours and tenants: 'and the religious divide ... encouraged popular hostility towards a magistracy often suspected of sectarian bias in carrying out its judicial functions'.[26] Before 1836 magistrates had to be qualified barristers. That qualification was removed under the terms of the Constabulary (Ireland) Act, 1836, and 'there were recurring complaints that the resident magistracy was staffed by the relatives and friends of men of influence'.[27]

By 1884, when the legal system had become more 'professionalised' and was no longer in the hands of the local Ascendancy class, half of the country's resident magistrates were former army officers, a further third had been recruited from the higher echelons of the Royal Irish Constabulary. They were an extension of the will of Dublin Castle rather than independent adjudicators of the law. This was clearly the case with the special resident magistrates appointed by the Liberals in the early 1880s. These men, who included the formidable Clifford Lloyd, were afforded quasi-military powers when it came to dealing with agrarian crime and were regarded by nationalists as an offshoot of the police force as much as of the judiciary.

If the Crown prosecutor in a political case could not be assured of assistance from the Bench, he could, depending on his own shrewdness, seek favour in the jury-box. Throughout most of the nineteenth century the practice of 'jury-packing' by the prosecution, was widespread. This was a useful method of retaining some semblance of proper legal form. Justice was seen to be done but it was all an optical illusion. The die was cast from the outset because a skilfully assembled and politically hostile jury was intent on conviction however weak the Crown case presented to them.

In the early part of the century jury-packing was used to ensure guilty verdicts were returned against nationalist agitators of various hues where the evidence presented was not as compelling as the authorities' desire for the incarceration of the accused. Subsequently, juries were often packed to secure verdicts that were more likely to be legitimate but which could not be obtained from a predominantly Roman Catholic jury in the locality in which the crime had been committed: 'jurors were sometimes unwilling to consider evidence from the crown and acquitted the accused'.[28] That unwillingness often stemmed from intimidation by associates of the accused. This applied in equal measure to witnesses. However, sympathy and identification with the objectives of the perpetrators of, for example, agrarian crime, also influenced juries outside of the major urban centres. The practice of moving the venue of trials from the general location of the crime (a rarely invoked eighteenth-century initiative) became an accepted practice under the aegis of nineteenth-century coercive legislation. The policy was pursued, ostensibly, to prevent interference with jurors or witnesses, but all too often the real intention was to circumvent sympathetically inclined local sentiment and pack metropolitan juries in order to secure a guilty verdict.

In the early 1800s the main prerequisite for selecting a jury well-disposed towards the Crown was a knowledge of the jurors' religion. It was almost axiomatic that a Protestant jury in a political case against a nationalist defendant would find in favour of the prosecution. The jury in the trial of John Magee (Chapter 2) and the state trials of 1844 (Chapter 3) are cases in point. During the debate on the guilty verdict on O'Connell and a number of other leaders of the Repeal movement in 1844, the former Whig prime minister, Lord John Russell, hardly an uncompromising champion of Catholic Ireland, commented on the ubiquity of the practice. He observed to the House of Commons:

> It may be said that the laws are the same for both countries—that Ireland has nominally the same law as England—that the trial by jury is the same in both countries. Is it so, in fact? That it was not so, was perpetual

matter of complaint in Ireland. Can we wonder that they
frequently harboured long revenge—that they did not
chuse [sic] to apply to the tribunals of the country for
justice—that when the poorer Roman Catholics saw all
the men of their own religion carefully and systematically
excluded, a distrust of the administration of justice generally prevailed?[29]

Russell concluded by acknowledging that 'Ireland was occupied, not
governed'. While it was the case that 'in name ... the same fundamental
laws existed in the two countries ... [the reality was that] ... in practice they
were so differently administered as to create two widely dissimilar systems
of rule'.[30]

Four years after Russell expressed those sentiments the leadership of
the 1848 rebellion. William Smith O'Brien, Terence Bellew MacManus,
Patrick O'Donohoe and Thomas Francis Meagher stood trial in Clonmel
in connection with the fracas at Ballingarry that was the highpoint of the
1848 rebellion. O'Brien's counsel, James Whiteside, who had defended
O'Connell in 1844, pointed out to Lord Blackburne, the lord chief justice,
that of the 288 jurors empanelled only 18 were Roman Catholics. More
than a quarter of the two previous commission panels in Tipperary had
been made up of Catholics. Whiteside questioned whether the panel had
been 'fairly and impartially arrayed'.[31] Whether or not this was the case it
was the panel from which the jury was chosen. Moreover, O'Brien's
brother, Robert, despite the guilty verdict being handed down on a charge
of high treason, insisted the 'trial was fair and the verdict just'.[32]

The first essential for the successful packing of a jury in the latter half
of the century was good intelligence from the RIC. As Bridgeman states:

What was required was a steady flow of information from
the police on potential jurors ... Since the crown had the
unlimited right to 'stand by' jurors, and was in charge of
the compilation of jury lists, it was hoped that by these
two processes a jury that was not hostile to the crown
would be found.[33]

Some barristers became famous, or notorious, for their ability to select
a jury that would favour the Crown. In the 1880s the barrister Peter
O'Brien, later lord chief justice of Ireland, became so identified with the
practice of challenging potentially unsympathetic jurors that he earned the
nickname 'Peter the Packer'.

Of course jury-packing did not always work. In the 1881 state trials of the Land League leadership, the *Freeman's Journal* recorded the sanguine attitude of Parnell to the proceedings as the verdict approached. 'There sat the Irish leader all day waiting to meet his fate, with the same grave, sweet, tranquil earnestness as if the fate of a nation as well as his own were not in the balance.' [34] Parnell's insouciance was justified. He had already written to Katharine O'Shea anticipating an acquittal on the basis that there were enough Catholics on the jury to guarantee that the 'traversers' would not be found guilty. The jury foreman's wonderful Irish bull to the effect that the twelve men were 'unanimous about disagreeing', when he was asked to deliver a verdict, must have brought a smile to Parnell's lips for a number of reasons. But failure to secure a conviction in the case was a crucial factor in convincing the Liberal government that existing law was inadequate for the pacification of rural Ireland. Coercion legislation followed, *habeas corpus* was suspended and internment without trial reduced the need for malleable juries.

It could be argued that a partisan Catholic jury refusing to convict the clearly guilty was just as sectarian as a packed Protestant jury assembled for political ends and prepared, unblushingly, to follow the dictates of the Crown prosecutor. But in a well-regulated and functioning society governed by consensus there would have been no need to pack juries and no fear of their ignoring evidence, which pointed to the guilt even of 'political' criminals. They would have reached verdicts derived from the facts presented to them, not on the basis of sectarian prejudice. The defining element of jury proceedings is trial by one's peers—not something with which a significant number of *Catholic* accused in political cases would have been overly familiar. A legitimately assembled jury is a group of citizens with a common and vested interest in the maintenance of law and order. Where 'law and order' is not a function of the common good that consensus breaks down and court verdicts become skewed.

It is significant that even in the case of the special juries it was deemed necessary in 1844 to have the leaders of the Repeal movement tried by a packed and entirely Protestant jury. Even Catholics of the same social status as the jurors selected were not considered 'safe' though they might have had a common vested interest in the maintenance of law and order. This was because the 1844 trials were not, in effect, trying a genuine law and order issue. Had the defendants been part of a criminal conspiracy or had they been Chartists intent on social equity or economic redistribution, there would have been no difficulty with placing propertied Catholics on the jury and securing a conviction based on substantive evidence.

The cases selected throw up a veritable rogue's gallery of spies, informers, perjurers and approvers. In cases like the Doneraile conspiracy trials and the Maamtrasna massacre 'investigation', too many ambitious Crown prosecutors demonstrated their willingness to cajole, threaten, bully and coach terrified witnesses to render perjured testimony. This particular netherworld, populated by the likes of James Carey, Anthony Philbin, Thomas Casey and the Dalys of Doneraile was augmented by the mercenary treachery of the likes of Leonard MacNally (see Chapter 1), whose corruption went undetected until many years after his death. With the assistance of informers and approvers the Crown prosecutors regularly demonstrated their readiness to procure convictions of the clearly innocent on the evidence of the avowedly guilty.

The law is required to take its course 'though the heavens may fall'. By fishing for testimony in such murky waters and recruiting amongst the weak and desperate, the Crown was insuring against such an eventuality. Their presence in this narrative underscores the fact that in the landmark Irish political trials under the Union there were no holds barred. queen's counsel may have appeared on both sides but Queensberry rules did not apply.

.1.

THE TRIAL OF
ROBERT EMMET

Oh! Breathe not his name, let it sleep in the shade,
Where cold and unhonour'd his relics are laid;
Sad, silent and dark, be the tears that we shed,
As the night dew that falls on the grass o'er his head.

But the night dew that falls, though in silence it weeps,
Shall brighten with verdure the grave where he sleeps;
And the tear that we shed, though in secret it rolls,
Shall long keep his memory green in our souls.[1]

(Thomas Moore, *Melodies*)

Wild Ignorance
Let loose, and frantic Vengeance, and dark Zeal,
And all bad passions tyrannous, and the fires
Of Persecution once again ablaze.
How had it sunk into thy soul to see,
Last curse of all, the ruffian Slaves of France
In thy dear country lording it.[2]

(Robert Southey, *Written immediately after reading the
speech of Robert Emmet*)

THE VIPER—20 SEPTEMBER 1803

Leonard MacNally had not been Robert Emmet's original choice of advocate. But when John Philpot Curran, the man who had vigorously defended so many doomed United Irishmen in 1798, had thrown up his brief in a fit of anger with the defendant, the young revolutionary was fortunate that MacNally, almost as celebrated, stepped into the breach. Like his client, MacNally was a Protestant and former United Irishman, who had vigorously opposed the Act of Union in 1800. Curran had lauded him for his 'uncompromising and romantic fidelity' to the cause of Irish nationalism.[3]

As Emmet was being escorted from the Commission Court on Green Street, after he was sentenced to die the following day, his distraught barrister stepped forward and embraced the prisoner emotionally before kissing him on the forehead.[4] The gesture was greatly appreciated by many in the crowd who had been impressed by Emmet's dignity and eloquence in his elegant and passionate speech from the dock. MacNally, who would become known as 'The Incorruptible', took many personal and professional risks in his defence of United Irishmen. His success as a defence attorney meant that, after Curran, he was 'the man most obnoxious to the government of that day ... who most hated [the government] and was most hated by them'.[5] His audacity and his acumen were respected in equal measure by opponents of the Union. A physical disability (he had one leg shorter than the other and a pronounced limp) and a very obvious deficiency in personal hygiene may have lulled some prosecution witnesses into underestimating MacNally's prowess in cross-examination. Many who did so paid a humiliating price. They would have been far better advised to have noted his missing thumb instead. It was the result of one of a number of duels he had fought in defence of his honour.

The following day, the morning of Emmet's execution, visiting his client in Kilmainham Gaol, the barrister took it upon himself to break the sad news to Emmet that his mother had died ten days previously. No one had wanted to add to his burdens by informing him of her passing. By way of consolation he reminded the prisoner that he would soon be reunited with her in the next life. Such solace, he might have reasoned, would also be of assistance to Emmet in his forthcoming ordeal. It would help him face his own unenviable fate with equanimity the following day. Emmet was to be brought back to the scene of the abortive uprising that he had masterminded and led. There he was to be hanged and beheaded outside St Catherine's Church on Thomas Street before those citizens of Dublin who chose to witness the event.

The two men talked for some time in a room adjoining Emmet's cell.[6] The high-minded young rebel, according to his counsel, claimed that military help from France was on its way and that had he managed to delay his trial by ten days he might well have avoided the noose, courtesy of Napoleon Bonaparte's troops. He also talked at length of his family and the upbringing which had led to the inculcation of the radical ideas that had proved to be his undoing. He, apparently, had bitter words for one of his prosecutors, William Conyngham Plunket, whose vitriolic closing address to the jury in the treason trial Emmet had taken highly personally. Plunket, he told MacNally, had been a family friend. He referred to him as 'that viper whom my father nourished'.[7] It was the only trace of bitterness

MacNally detected in the young man who was about to face a grim and lonely death. The two friends parted company and Emmet prepared to receive two Church of Ireland ministers who would accompany him to the hastily built gibbet a few hours later.

What the unworldly young idealist did not know, and what none suspected for many years after his death in 1820, was that Leonard MacNally was the most valuable and resourceful spy in the employ of Dublin Castle. Within 24 hours the chief secretary had a detailed account of MacNally's version of the Kilmainham conversation with Emmet. For his egregious betrayal of a personal and professional trust, he would receive a bonus of just over £200.

THE SATURDAY NIGHT REBELLION— 23 JULY 1803

The insurrection in Dublin on 23 July 1803 of a small force of men led by Robert Emmet can be viewed as a fully fledged rebellion in its own right or as unfinished business. In a sense it was a delayed aftershock of the seismic activity of 1798 and cannot be seen in isolation from that rising. 'Emmet's rebellion was a leftover from that of 1798'.[8] It is remembered for the tragic and romantic figure cut by its main protagonist, for the eloquence of his valedictory speech and for the hapless and disorganised nature of its military element. However, while the outbreak of hostilities on 23 July may have been farcical and anticlimactic it, in fact, posed some threat to what proved to be a heedless and complacent British administration in Ireland and its leader was rather more than a mere Byronic star-crossed neophyte.[9]

The rebellion encompassed many of the strands of the uprising of the United Irishmen, with one significant and symbolic aggravating factor. Between 1798 and 1803 Ireland had lost its parliament. The rebellion of Theobald Wolfe Tone, John and Henry Sheares, Vinegar Hill and Boolavogue, had strengthened the hand of the prime minister, William Pitt, in his determination to end the system whereby legislation for Ireland had to pass through an assembly based at Dublin's College Green. An Irish parliament had existed for centuries, though it had been constrained by

Poyning's Law (1494), which meant all legislation had to be sanctioned by the British privy council; and the Declaratory Act of 1720 (the sixth of George I), which empowered the Westminster legislature to make laws for Ireland. That situation had changed in 1782 when a heady cocktail of Protestant patriots, enlightenment idealism and the potential threat of a 100,000 strong force of Volunteers, obliged the Crown to grant Ireland a greater degree of legislative independence. However, this autonomy was significantly circumscribed by the regulatory authority of the Irish executive in Dublin Castle. Grattan's parliament, as it became known to posterity, also lacked democratic legitimacy in being overwhelmingly representative of Ascendancy interests. Some of the principal protagonists of this 'patriot' parliament were unambiguous in their opposition to the repeal of the remaining Popery (Penal) Laws and the extension of further civil rights to Roman Catholics. While Henry Grattan, for example, was a champion of Catholic rights, the other great 'patriot', Henry Flood, was not.

A vital weapon of control in the hands of Dublin Castle, where the patriot parliament was concerned, was patronage. The promise of advancement was regularly deployed to secure the votes needed for the effective maintenance of English rule. A limited, property-based franchise (Catholics did not get the vote until 1793) meant that most of the members of the House of Commons were beholden for their seats to a small number of highly influential figures. Once the bulk of their support was secured the passage of legislation favoured by the castle was assured. This was never more blatantly illustrated than in the recourse to blandishment to ensure that the Irish parliament voted itself out of existence in February 1800. From 1 January 1801 Ireland was to be represented by 100 MPs in the House of Commons at Westminster and 32 peers in the House of Lords. It was an event of enormous psychological moment to the more radical members of the 'the Protestant nation' but, in practical terms, was of lesser political import because, in reality, 'when it really mattered, it was Westminster that called the tune'.[10] The 'Catholic nation' had been courted by Pitt with promises of emancipation (which included the capacity for Catholics to take seats in parliament) and had been largely quiescent in the debate that had raged over the issue.

Despite the opposition of, for example, members of the Orange Order, the parliamentary union secured by Pitt was as much the outcome of renewed Protestant insecurities as it was of Catholic indifference to the fate of an Ascendancy parliament in Dublin. The 1798 rebellion in

Wexford, in particular, with its notorious Wexford Bridge and Scullabogue massacres of Protestant civilians and prisoners, had revived the atavistic fears of the infamous (and much exaggerated) Catholic excesses in Ulster during the rebellion of 1641. The tacit alliance between elements of the United Irishmen and the militant Catholic secret society, the Defenders, had intensified Protestant fears of widespread massacre. Much of the liberal Protestant support, or tolerance, of Catholic demands in 1790s evaporated and after the 1798 rebellion Ireland had reverted to a familiar sectarianism devoid of much of the idealism generated by the American and French revolutions.

In spite of repeated Catholic disavowals, Protestants remained fearful of demands for the restitution of property transferred by plantation or appropriation. Their anxieties on this score were heightened by periodic outbreaks of 'Whiteboy' agrarian violence in opposition to the tithes paid to the established church in certain parts of the country. There were also well-founded concerns about the response of Catholics in the event of French intervention in Ireland. For the most part the minority population relapsed into a garrison mentality that suited the containment objectives of the Westminster government.

In terms of sustained unrest, there might appear to be a degree of continuity between the general rising of 1798 and the much more limited outbreak of 1803. The Wicklow rebels led by Michael Dwyer harassed the authorities for five years after the defeat of the United Irishmen. Orange attacks on Catholics continued in Ulster and thus maintained the phenomenon of 'Defenderism'. Prolonged campaigns of agrarian crime contributed to the impression of an unbroken and persistent conflict. All the more so as they were occasionally used by interested parties to attempt to convince the castle administration that radical political conspiracy continued apace. The suspension of *habeas corpus* remained in place until 1801. Under the terms of the legislation introduced to suppress the rebellion, which also continued in force for some time, 21 men were executed between November 1800 and February 1801.[11]

However, Dublin Castle clearly failed to see any compelling evidence of continuity. In the wake of peace between Britain and France, concluded in August 1801,[12] the authorities had felt secure enough to release a number of United Irishmen and reduce the military establishment in Ireland. The administration of the new lord lieutenant, Lord Hardwicke, was anxious for conciliation rather than renewed confrontation. The former chief secretary, Lord Castlereagh, wrote to Hardwicke in August 1801 congratulating him on 'the present tranquility in Ireland. The Union has already apparently discharged the public mind of a greater portion of the political mischief which has incessantly disturbed it for the last twenty-five years than its most sanguine friend could have expected'.[13]

It was in this context that some of the dislocated elements of the United Irishmen began to reorganise. The reconstructed body was leaner, more elitist and more localised than its predecessor. It consisted, by and large, of an experienced and activist *cadre* that was to form the officer corps in the event of renewed rebellion. It was also based on two presuppositions: that a disenfranchised populace would flock to the ranks when the call to arms came and that assistance would be forthcoming from France. With the renewal of the Bonapartist war in May 1803 the latter eventuality re-entered the realm of possibility. Centrally involved in this covert overhaul was Robert Emmet, younger brother of one of the most prominent United Irishmen, Thomas Addis Emmet.

Robert Emmet, born in 1778, was the youngest son of Dr Robert Emmet, state physician to the viceregal court. His family had originally come to Ireland from Kent and had received land in Co. Tipperary in the wake of the Cromwellian settlement of Ireland. Dr Emmet, infected with the republicanism of the French revolution, would resign his position as a state physician and inspire his sons Thomas Addis and Robert, to adopt his radical ideals. His friend, Henry Grattan, observed sceptically of Emmet *père* that he 'had his pill and his plan; and he mixed so much politics with his prescription that he would kill the patient who took the one, and ruined the country that listened to the other'.[14] Thomas Addis Emmet who was imprisoned after the 1798 rebellion travelled to the Continent on his release before eventually settling in the USA.

Depicted as an intense, shy and diminutive young man, Robert Emmet was, although only 5 feet 6 inches tall, of above average height for his time.[15] If he was as naturally diffident as some have claimed,[16] it did not interfere with his ability to dazzle an audience with his rhetorical powers. As regards his physical appearance one biographer says of him that 'his features were regular, his forehead high and finely formed; his eyes were small, bright and full of expression'.[17] A less flattering description, provided by an ill-disposed Trinity academic to the government for identification purposes, referred to 'an ugly, sour countenance; small eyes, but not near-sighted, a dirty, brownish complexion; at a distance looks as if somewhat marked by the smallpox'.[18]

Emmet, at the age of seventeen, had been secretary of one of four branches of the United Irishmen at Trinity College in Dublin. He was also an orator of note and an outstanding contributor to the proceedings of the college debating club, the Historical Society. His reputation led to his expulsion from Trinity in June 1798 during a purge of 'Republican' elements. In 1799 he fled to France, fearing arrest because of his continued involvement in radical activities and his part in the reconstruction of the United Irishmen. When no charge was laid against him, he returned in October, 1802 and renewed his activities. He quickly established contact with a number of men who had participated in the 1798 rising in counties Wicklow, Kildare and Wexford and who were now quietly living out their lives in relative obscurity in Dublin. Emmet rapidly established a network of committed and proven activists and, in parallel, assembled an arsenal of weapons (fire-arms, explosives and pikes) in storage depots on Patrick Street, Marshal Lane and Thomas Street in Dublin. He was reinforced by the secret return from the Continent of two prominent former United Irishmen, Michael Quigley, a bricklayer from Rathcoffy, Co. Kildare; and, Thomas Russell, an ex-officer born in Co. Cork but residing in Ulster, released from prison after the end of the war with France.

Emmet's plan for a nationwide rising was more comprehensive and detailed than the chaotic and somewhat anarchic nature of the eventual rebellion would suggest. Dublin Castle, the Pigeon House Fort, the artillery barracks at Islandbridge, the Mary Street Barracks and the Custom House were to be seized by a small band of battle-hardened revolutionaries. But even assuming the original blueprint had succeeded in Dublin, what was to happen thereafter was left too much to chance. The Wexford United Irishman, Miles Byrne, who secreted himself in Dublin after the 1798 Rising, was privy to Emmet's plan to extend his rebellion beyond Dublin. 'It consisted in procuring the names and places of abode of those brave fellows in each district who had acquired the reputation of being good patriots in 1798, and who still enjoyed the confidence of the people.'[19] With the assistance of Byrne, Emmet met activists from Carlow, Wicklow and Wexford. They were given three small, marked, ivory counters and told to await the arrival of messengers from Dublin with corresponding counters bearing instructions for 'the general rising *en masse* of the districts organised for that purpose'.[20] In reality Emmet appears to have set too much store by the notion of a spontaneous rebellion in the provinces following on the seizure of the capital and devoted the bulk of his attention to ensuring the success of his own efforts in Dublin.

An inheritance of £2,000 upon the death of his father in December 1802 allowed Emmet to fund preparations for a rebellion himself. The money was invested in the manufacture of pikes, in the assembly of a small arsenal of fire-arms and the securing of premises in which to store the weaponry. Emmet became fascinated with the military potential of the rocket. At least one experiment was recalled by Miles Byrne in his memoirs: a rocket was made fast to a pole 'the match being put to it, it went off like a thunderbolt, carrying the pole along with it, and throwing flames and fire behind, as it advanced, and when it fell, it went on tearing up the ground till the last of the matter with which it was filled was completely consumed'.[21] Emmet's preoccupation with this particular use of gunpowder would prove highly problematic at a crucial point in the preparations for a rising.

Contact was made with the Wicklow rebel, Michael Dwyer, who promised assistance once he was assured that Emmet had secured the city of Dublin. A paranoid and watchful Dwyer spent three anxious days with Emmet and Thomas Russell in early 1803 but his expressions of support were not matched by a practical commitment. He was surprised by Emmet's expressed disinclination to lobby for French support and the young man's antipathy to Bonaparte.[22] Dwyer returned to the relative safety of his Wicklow refuge with serious reservations about Emmet's ability to deliver Dublin into rebel hands.

However, he did make one significant contribution to the cause. His niece, Anne Devlin, was taken on as housekeeper in the establishment on Butterfield Avenue in Rathfarnham where Emmet and his principal associates, William Dowdall, a former United Irishman; Nicholas Stafford, a Dublin baker; and William Hamilton, an Irish officer of the French Army; along with Michael Quigley, planned the rising. The house, near the foothills of the Dublin Mountains, was known to Miles Byrne as 'the Palace'. On at least one occasion as many as 30 rebel leaders sat down to eat in its dining room. Butterfield Avenue was not far from The Priory, the residence of John Philpot Curran. Unbeknownst to the celebrated attorney, Emmet had formed an attachment to his youngest daughter, 21-year-old Sarah.

Although Dublin was the main focus of the rebel's planning Russell and Hamilton were dispatched to Ulster to organise a parallel and simultaneous revolt there. Their efforts were met with a mixture of apathy and outright hostility. Without arms and the promise of French aid, Ulster would not rise along with Dublin.

Emmet's revolutionary template, consisting of a highly compartmentalised command structure rather than a more open national movement vulnerable to penetration, (Dwyer was not told the names of Emmet's associates) was highly successful in concealing his conspiracy from Dublin Castle. He himself did not entirely escape official notice. Leonard MacNally was aware that Emmet was at the heart of post-1798 disaffection but, in a letter to the under secretary, Alexander Marsden, on 19 July 1803 he brushed aside rumours of an impending *coup*. He wrote (over his customary coded signature of 'JW'):

> I daily see different people from the Home Circuit counties, who were implicated in the last Rebellion and the report of them all is that there is neither system nor organisation in the country. They, however, allow that an invasion is expected, in which case they admit a rising would take place whenever the enemy appeared.[23]

The lord lieutenant, Lord Hardwicke, wrote to his brother, Charles Yorke, who was soon to replace the belligerent Lord Pelham as home secretary, 'I cannot find the least apprehension expressed, now that war had broken out again between Great Britain and France, that trouble was brewing among the disaffected in Ireland'.[24]

Official complacency was dented, though not entirely shattered, by an accident in the Patrick Street arms depot. On Saturday, 16 July, an explosion, brought about in the manufacture of fuses for the rockets, ripped through the arms-dump. Although the resourceful Miles Byrne managed to remove most of the surviving weapons before the authorities were fully alerted, the incident forced Emmet to advance the date of the rebellion. He settled upon 23 July for the Dublin rising. Four days after the explosion Hardwicke was less confident in his evaluation of the passivity of the Irish than he had been a week before. He informed the prime minister, Henry Addington, that 'It still appears that there are no leaders of any consequence; but it is equally true, and it is a fact which ought not to be concealed from the Government in England, that agitators are certainly at work'.[25] He also requested the prime minister to allow for the renewed suspension of *habeas corpus* arguing that

> it is better to prevent mischief by detaining those who are preparing for the insurrection, than to trust to their subsequent detection and punishment, and it can hardly be expected that disaffection should have entirely ceased in this country, or that the enemy should not use every means to revive and increase it.[26]

Despite the 'fair warning' provided by the Patrick Street explosion and an abundance of rumours, the government exhibited an inertia for which it would be castigated after the events of 23 July. The castle cause was not helped by the fact that the chief secretary, William Wickham (an acknowledged expert in the art of espionage and intelligence gathering), was out of the country due to illness. Alexander Marsden appears to have had at least a vague inkling of what was about to happen. The under secretary opted to spend the night of 22 July in Dublin Castle itself. But Hardwicke was the epitome of insouciance. He left the castle that night for the Viceregal Lodge in the distant Phoenix Park. The route taken by his carriage brought him close to Marshal Lane, the site of one of Emmet's principal arms-dumps. His presence in the Viceregal Lodge left him exposed, vulnerable and of no assistance the following day to a potentially beleaguered Dublin Castle administration.

For Robert Emmet, who left the Marshal Lane depot on the night of Saturday, 23 July with 100 men, parallels with the 1916 Rising, are inescapable. The secrecy that was the hallmark of Emmet's insurrection was 'its greatest strength (and weakness)'.[27] Emmet's meticulous preparation was too dependent on the absolute sequential execution of his integrated plan. A rumour that the rising had been postponed reduced the numbers of followers available to him. A determined and well co-ordinated surprise attack might well have taken Dublin Castle but failed to do so. Promised support from Michael Dwyer in Wicklow and rebel elements in Kildare failed to materialise. Faced with inevitable defeat, Emmet, like Pearse a century later, opted for the politics of the noble gesture.

The distribution of handbills addressed to the 'Citizens of Dublin' preceded the military action. The population was advised that 'A band of Patriots, mindful of their oath and faithful to their engagement as United Irishmen, have determined to give freedom to their country, and a period to the long career of English oppression'.[28] The rising was planned for 9.00 p.m., close to dusk. The military force commanded by the young revolutionary, himself resplendent in a magnificent green uniform and armed with the only sword available to the rebels, was augmented by drinkers from the public houses around Thomas Street 'bent solely on pillage and murder'.[29] The proclamation of the provisional government was read publicly in order to give political legitimacy to proceedings. 'You are now called on to show to the world that you are competent to take your place among nations', it began.[30] Unfortunately the debacle that followed was to show no such competence.

Realising that the seizure of Dublin Castle was an impossibility, Emmet chose the sensible course of taking his small force to Wicklow and joining forces with Michael Dwyer. The mob element among the rebels decided otherwise. An unfortunate hussar who chanced to ride by Francis Street became the first victim of the rebellion when he was piked to death. By the time the coach of the relatively benign privy councillor and chief justice, Lord Kilwarden[31] was attacked (he and his nephew were killed); Emmet, Quigley, Stafford and other leaders of the insurrection had already left for Rathfarnham. Arriving there at about 11.00 p.m. he received an angry reception from a dejected Anne Devlin. The following evening he and a small band of men escaped to the Wicklow Mountains. Within days Emmet had abandoned this refuge and was lodged in a house at Harold's Cross belonging to Ann Palmer, daughter and sister of 1798 rebels.

Alerted to the chaos in the Thomas Street area, soldiers of the 21st Regiment arrived to quell what amounted to little more than riotous behaviour. Skirmishes were fought with the remaining rebels and casualties ensued on both sides. After the rump of Emmet's force had dispersed members of the yeomanry were sent house to house through the Liberties of Dublin to arrest suspects. It would be more than 100 years before the city witnessed similar skirmishes between Irish Republicans and British soldiers.

Although Emmet would later accept full responsibility for the abject failure of the rebellion he was, at first, not disposed to do so. His quoted response to the anger of Michael Dwyer's niece was 'Don't blame me. The fault is not mine'.[32] Logistics and planning were clearly Emmet's strengths rather than competent military leadership in the field. His abandonment by the auxiliary forces of Wicklow and Kildare, over which he had no personal control, was based on their hard-headed assessments of his chances of success. But, as Miles Byrne pointed out, he was also deserted by one of his own appointees, William Dowdall, who 'could have no excuse to offer for his conduct on this occasion'.[33]

Public reaction to the events of 23 July 1803 was not dissimilar to that which marked Easter Monday, 1916. Dublin Castle was stunned, both at the audacity of the rebels and its own lack of preparedness while much of the population, and not just anxious Protestants, was angered. The young Catholic barrister, Daniel O'Connell, writing to his wife, Mary, observed that 'for my part I think pity would be almost thrown away upon the contriver of the affair of the 23rd of July. A man who could coolly prepare so much bloodshed, so many murders—and such horrors of every kind has ceased to be an object of compassion'.[34] O'Connell was of the opinion that

Emmet deserved to hang. However, as Emmet biographer Marianne Elliott has pointed out, 'even the achievements of O'Connell—undoubtedly the most important politician in the making of modern Ireland—would be swept away in the romantic revolutionism that had Emmet at its centre'. Elliott also observes, however, that in addition to the sympathy aroused by 'Emmet's boyish looks, good stock, eloquence and desperate sincerity', there was considerable anger on the part of many Protestant and Catholic citizens 'at the re-imposition of strict security measures, when there had been a welcome period of mild government'.[35]

The embarrassment and discomfiture of Dublin Castle at being caught completely unawares was exacerbated by its lack of information as to the main motive force behind the rebellion. Emmet was not immediately identified as the lavishly accoutred sword-bearing leader of the semi-disciplined force that had briefly held the area around Thomas Street in the name of the 'provisional government'. As events were still being played out on the streets, Marsden, at 11.00 p.m. wrote to the home secretary, Lord Pelham, in London to apprise him of the news of the abortive rising. He concluded with a display of self-exculpation: 'For some days past we had heard that a rising was talked of, and it was asserted by many that it would take place. Such precautions were taken as the circumstances seemed to warrant, but the mischievous disposition which prevails at present is beyond what was calculated upon'.[36] With flagrant disloyalty he mentioned that while he was at his post in Dublin Castle, the lord lieutenant was in his residence in the Phoenix Park.

Hardwicke was terse, defensive and self-protective in his professional and personal correspondence in the days that followed. To his brother, who would shortly succeed Pelham, much to the lord lieutenant's delight, he observed of the rebels that 'they do not seem to have been ably commanded, and indeed everything shows that this insurrection was the work of a rabble without leaders'. Two days later he wrote that

> it is unfortunate that such a conspiracy should have been formed and brought to such a point without being discovered, and that it should be possible for a secret of such a nature to be so well kept. Some people find fault and affect to blame both Marsden and Wickham for too great a degree of credulity on the state of the country ...[37]

He made no mention whatever of his own credulity. On 2 August his brother warned him:

> I ought not to conceal from you that very insidious
> attempts are making in various quarters to make the
> world believe that the Irish government were surprised,
> that you had no intelligence or paid no regard to it, and
> that no proper military precautions were taken in the
> course of Friday and Saturday morning.[38]

In the House of Commons, on 11 August, under pressure from William
Windham, an ally of the late Edmund Burke and a former secretary of war
(he had resigned with Pitt over Catholic Emancipation), Lord Castlereagh
exonerated the Irish executive. He, 'insisted, that the Irish government were
not surprised; that Dublin was sufficiently garrisoned; and that if it was not
for the murder of Lord Kilwarden, the insurrection in Dublin was not
important enough to be called rebellion'.[39] The debate gave the Irish-born
playwright, Richard Brinsley Sheridan, an opportunity to attack the government on the basis that 'it would be vain to look for harmony in a
country where the minority is to lord it over the majority, and where the
meanest and basest of those professing the religion of the minority, is to
have more political power than the richest and most exalted of those whose
religious belief is different'.

The fact was that English confidence that the Union offered a panacea
for Irish ills and that the savage military setbacks of 1798 suffocated disaffection for a generation had undoubtedly generated a measure of
complacency. The intelligence operation, so capably run in 1798 by the
former under secretary, Edward Cooke, had been allowed to wither. It was
even seen as hearkening back to an era of corruption and jobbery that was,
so the theory went, to be ended by the Union. Thomas Bartlett sums up the
period as follows:

> Allegations of subversion, insurrection, popish plots,
> French emissaries, imminent massacres and the like were
> to be treated with skepticism, if not incredulity ... given
> their evident mistrust of all those who had been involved
> in pre-Union politics, it was probably inevitable that the
> new men in Dublin Castle would miss some clues ...[40]

When it came to the prosecution of the leaders of the rebellion, and
especially Emmet himself, thoroughness was restored and such mistakes
would not be repeated.

Emmet remained at large for a month after the rising (with the help of
the courageous silence of Anne Devlin). During that time he was able to

renew contact with Sarah Curran. The two corresponded while he resided in the Palmer household under the alias of Hewitt. The identity of the acknowledged leader of the rising did not long remain a secret, however, as a police force, under the command of the redoubtable Major Henry Charles Sirr, the man who had arrested Lord Edward Fitzgerald, was searching for Emmet. His presence in the Harold's Cross household was eventually betrayed to Sirr and Emmet was arrested there on 25 August. He attempted twice to escape and was slightly wounded in the process. Taken from him were two unsigned letters from Sarah Curran that would prove crucial in deciding his ultimate fate. She had asked him to destroy both. Initially a paranoid government took the letters to be coded messages related to Emmet's subversive activities. It is clear from his interrogation by members of the privy council that the issue of the letters and the possibility of Sarah Curran being identified as an accomplice dominated his thinking. Also discovered was a letter that Emmet had been writing to the government in which, among other things, he advised that the use of terror to suppress the rebellion would only result in its resurgence.

Having secured its prisoner the government was less than sanguine about the possibility of getting a conviction against him for high treason. Emmet had taken the precaution of disguising his handwriting so that ascribing incriminating documents to him was problematic. There was also unwillingness on the part of potential witnesses to testify against him. Wickham summed up the dilemma in a letter to Charles Yorke's secretary, Reginald Pole Carew:

> if the prosecution against him should fail, it will probably be owing to his act in changing frequently his manner of writing ... He was very much beloved in private life, so that all the friends of his family, even those who abhorred his treasons, will be glad of any pretext to avoid appearing against him, and we shall be left, I fear, to accomplices in his own guilt, who will give most reluctant testimony against the man who was considered the chief of the conspiracy.[41]

So inadequate and circumstantial was the Crown case against Emmet that consideration was even given to the production of one or more of the castle's spies to testify against him in open court. Wickham, a former spymaster himself, conveyed something of his own horror at the suggestion that a productive resource, someone like MacNally, might be voluntarily squandered in this way when he wrote: 'The question of bringing forward secret information has been well considered and discussed, and there is but one opinion on the subject—*viz.*, that it were a thousand times better that Emmet should escape than that we should close for ever a most accurate source of information'.[42]

Although the Crown gathered sufficient evidence to establish a *prima facie* case against Emmet it was the prisoner himself who sealed his own fate. When Emmet was brought before Wickham, Lord Redesdale, the lord chancellor, and Standish O'Grady, the attorney general, for questioning on 30 August, the executive had no idea of the identity of the writer of the two letters found on its prisoner. The stated object of the interrogation sounds strangely innocuous. Emmet was merely, 'informed that he was sent for that he might have an opportunity of explaining what appeared suspicious in his late conduct'.[43] From the outset, Emmet made it clear that he had no intention of co-operating with the process. Asked his name by O'Grady he responded, 'Robert Emmet. Having now answered to my name, I must decline answering any further questions'. He maintained this taciturnity throughout a series of questions about his dealings with France, the various aliases he had used, the identities of his closest associates and the proclamation of the provisional government. However, when the matter of the Sarah Curran letters was put to him he became both agitated and voluble. In a manner which must have alerted the privy councillors to his vulnerability on the issue, Emmet blurted out:

> As to the letters taken out of my possession by Major Sirr, how can I avoid this being brought forward? May I ask if the name of the writer might be mentioned to me? May I know by what means those letters may be prevented from coming forward? Has anything been done in consequence of those letters being taken? May I learn what means, or what has been done upon them? [44]

When O'Grady, sensibly, declined to enlighten him, Emmet, unwisely and naively, continued. 'You must, gentlemen, be sensible how disagreeable it would be to one of yourselves to have a delicate and virtuous female brought into notice'. He then gave the first tentative indication that he would be prepared to bargain his own life away in order to ensure that the writer of the letters was not identified. He may have assumed that Sarah Curran had already been questioned or arrested. 'What means would be necessary to bring the evidence in those letters forward without bringing the name forward?' he inquired.

The attorney general was obdurate. 'The expressions in those letters go far beyond a confidential communication between a gentleman and a lady. There are evidences of High Treason, and therefore their production is necessary.' On hearing this, Emmet raised a white flag. 'Then nothing remains to be done,' he ventured, 'I would rather give up my own life than injure another person.' Later he made it as plain as he could that he was prepared to face death in order to ensure that Sarah Curran was not identified or proceeded against. 'If I have assurances,' he offered, 'that nothing has been done, and nothing will be done, upon these letters, I will do everything consistent with honour to prevent their production ... Personal safety would weigh nothing if the production of those letters could be prevented.' He then relapsed into polite silence when his interrogators continued to seek confirmation of the identities of his accomplices in the insurrection.

But the privy council was now aware that, while it would get no useful information from Emmet, the Curran letters could be used to force him to acquiesce in his own conviction. Emmet, who had been negligent in retaining the correspondence in the first place, compounded his original error on 8 September when he wrote a letter of his own to Sarah Curran[45] and gave it to be delivered to an apparently friendly Kilmainham Gaol warder, George Dunn. It was in Wickham's hands within hours. The following morning Major Sirr arrived with warrants to search the house of John Philpot Curran and interrogate his daughter. This, in turn, set off a chain of events greatly to the advantage of the Crown. Curran, who had been engaged as Emmet's lead counsel but who had been unaware of the prisoner's relationship with his daughter, threw up the brief. He was replaced by the state's most valuable intelligence asset, Leonard MacNally.

The castle was now doubly indemnified against acquittal. For the duration of the trial, the Curran letters remained in full view of the prisoner and in the ten-day period between the resiling of Curran and Emmet's appearance in the Green Street Court-house, the castle was assured of valuable intelligence on the conduct of the defence case. Thanks to MacNally's information and the potency of the Curran letters, Wickham was able to tell Pole Carew on 14 September that 'as I understand, he will not controvert the charge by calling a single witness?' This confidence was based on a letter from MacNally in which he informed the chief secretary that: 'He [Emmet] does not intend to call a single witness, nor to trouble any witness for the Crown with a cross-examination, unless they misrepresent facts'.[46]

On 4 September Emmet actually wrote to Wickham virtually offering to allow the prosecution a free pass. In the letter, which had a profound influence on the chief secretary, he offered himself as sacrificial victim. ' ... let the lives of others be spared: let the documents affecting another person be suppressed, and I will try how far in my conscience, and according to *my* notions of duty I ought to go.'[47]

THE TRIAL OF ROBERT EMMET, 19 SEPTEMBER 1803

The recoil of the government from the indignity suffered on 23 July was swift in its advent and savage in its impact. Many hundreds more than had taken part in the skirmishing on Thomas Street itself, were arrested. Although the rebellion had been largely limited to Dublin and its environs the round up of United Irish veterans was nationwide and extensive.[48] Treason trials and executions followed rapidly. This decisive action on the part of the government was not merely retributive but precautionary. A French invasion was feared. If it were to take place the castle wanted to ensure that there would be no United Irish infrastructure available to augment and assist the Napoleonic forces. Its fears were not unjustified. Soon after the collapse of the rebellion, Miles Byrne had been dispatched by Emmet to France to seek military help.

In the days before Emmet came to trial some minor players in the rebellion, such as John Killeen, Felix O'Rourke and John McKenna were hanged and beheaded in different parts of Dublin. Given the bloody prologue, it was natural that the trial of the man held by the Crown to have been the leader of the rebellion would attract much interest. Presiding over the Commission Court (assisted by Baron George and Baron Daly) was the formidable Lord Norbury, the 'hanging judge' of 1798. All three men had been colleagues of Lord Kilwarden. The portly Norbury (John Toler before his ennoblement) was a dyspeptic figure who, according to the memoirist Jonah Barrington, 'had a hand for every man and a heart for nobody'.[49] Aligned against the prisoner was an impressive legal team led by Attorney General Standish O'Grady and including William Conyngham Plunket, a bitter opponent of the Act of Union, a strong advocate of Catholic rights but a man intent on demonstrating his loyalty to the new, post-Union polity. Emmet's defence was led by Peter Burrowes,[50] a distinguished defender of United Irish prisoners in the past, and Leonard MacNally. At the defendant's behest neither man would be required to intervene to any great effect during the twelve-hour jury trial.

Proceedings began at 9.30 a.m. at Green Street. Emmet was led to the dock in chains and O'Grady, the attorney general, 'a lawyer of limited ability who owed his rise more to his support of the government than to any legal accomplishments',[51] rose to make his opening statement:

> My Lord and Gentlemen of the Jury. It is my duty to state as concisely as I can the nature of the charge, which has been preferred against the Prisoner at the bar; and also, Gentlemen, the nature of the evidence, which will be produced to substantiate that charge. It will require upon your part the most deliberate consideration: because it is not only the highest crime of which at all times the subject can be guilty, but it receives, if possible, additional aggravation, when we consider the state of Europe and the lamentable consequences which revolution has already brought upon it.
>
> Perhaps at former periods some allowance might be made for the heated imaginations of enthusiasts; perhaps an extravagant love of liberty might for a moment supersede a rational understanding, and men might be induced, for want of sufficient experience or capacity, to look for that liberty in revolution. But sad experience has taught us, that modern revolution is not the road to liberty. It throws the mass of the people into agitation only to bring the worst and the most profligate to the surface. It originates in anarchy, proceeds in bloodshed, and ends in cruel and unrelenting despotism.
>
> Therefore, Gentlemen, the crime of which the Prisoner stands charged demands the most serious and deep investigation, because it is in its nature a crime of the blackest dye, and which under all existing circumstances does not admit of a momentary extenuation ...
>
> Gentlemen, upon former occasions, persons were brought to the bar of this court, implicated in the rebellion, in various though inferior degrees. But if I am rightly

instructed, we have now brought to the bar of justice, not a person who has been seduced by others, but a Gentleman to whom the rebellion may be traced, as the origin, the life, and the soul of it. If I mistake not, it will appear, that some time before Christmas last the prisoner who had visited foreign countries, and who for several months before had made a continental tour, embracing France, did return to this country full of these mischievous designs, which have been now so fully exposed. He came from that country, in which he might well have learned the necessary effects of revolution; and therefore if he be guilty of the treason, he embarked in it with his eyes open, and with a previous knowledge of all its inevitable consequences.

But notwithstanding, I am instructed, that he persevered in fomenting a rebellion, which I will be bold to say, is unexampled in any country, ancient or modern. A rebellion which does not complain of any existing grievances, does not flow from any immediate oppression, and which is not pretended to have been provoked by our mild and gracious King, or by the administration employed by him to execute his authority. No, Gentlemen, it is a rebellion which avows itself to come, not to remove any evil which the people feel, but to recall the memory of grievances which, if they ever existed, must have long since passed away, the provocations of 600 years have been ransacked, the sufferings of our ancestors have been exaggerated, our state in former ages, and at various remote times misrepresented, in expectation of extracting from the whole, something like a provocation to justify a revolution, which at the present hour and moment would have no rational foundation ... This gentleman's arrival in this country from France, is the source to which the Rebellion may be traced; and the conduct adopted by him leaves little room to suppose I can be mistaken in this conjecture. He might have found the embers of the Rebellion of 1798, but he shortly blew them into life and animation.

O'Grady went on to outline some of the particulars of the Crown case against Emmet, his use of the aliases Ellis (in Rathfarnham) and Hewitt (in the Palmer house), the establishment of arms depots, his association with the likes of William Dowdall ('a person of much treasonable celebrity'[52]), and his attempted flight when arrested by Major Sirr. O'Grady mocked the composition of the provisional government which had issued the proclamation publicly read on 23 July. He described its members, scornfully, as 'fitting upon the second floor of a malt house, meditating without means, and marshalling armies that they had never enlisted'. Extracts were read from Sarah Curran's letters but, in keeping with the compact with the defendant, they were described as having been written by 'a brother conspirator'. He concluded with a reminder to the jury of their duty to the state:

> if it shall appear, that the Prisoner was the prime mover of this rebellion, that he was the spring which gave it life and activity, then I say, no false feeling of pity for the man, should warp your judgment, or divert your understanding. I know the progress of every good mind is uniform; it begins with abhorrence for the crime and ends with compassion for the criminal; I do not wish to strip misfortune of perhaps its only consolation.
>
> But it must not be carried so far as to interfere with the administration of public justice. It must not be allowed to separate punishment from guilt; and therefore, if upon the evidence you shall be satisfied that this man is guilty, you must discharge your duty to your king, to your country, and to your God. If on the other hand nothing shall appear sufficient to affect him, we shall acknowledge that we have grievously offended him, and will heartily participate in the common joy that must result from the acquittal of an innocent man.[53]

After O'Grady's ostentatiously baroque opening came the mundanity of the prosecution witnesses.[54] They included Joseph Rawlins, the Emmet family attorney, from whom Burrowes managed to extract an admission that whatever Emmet might be he was not a Bonapartist. George Tyrrell, another lawyer, identified Emmet and William Dowdall as the men who had leased the Butterfield Avenue house, Emmet using the alias of Ellis. An ostler named John Fleming, who had done a deal with the Crown, testified as to the workings of the arms depot on Marshal Lane. Patrick Farrell, who had been taken prisoner by the rebels on the night of 22 July and held against his will, was called to identify Emmet as the leader of the rebellion. Questioned by MacNally (who was being prompted directly by the defendant), Farrell admitted that Emmet had protected him from harm during his brief incarceration. Throughout this phase of the trial most of the interventions the defendant allowed his counsel to make related to evidence against his associates rather than testimony designed to incriminate him.

A barely co-operative John Palmer was then placed in the witness-box. Both he and his mother, Ann, could, potentially, face charges of harbouring the fugitive Emmet in Harold's Cross. Reluctantly, to avoid the prosecution of his mother, Palmer recounted how the prisoner had stayed on two separate occasions in Harold's Cross under the name of Hewitt. He claimed to be unable to identify Emmet's handwriting, exposing a significant weakness in the Crown case. Namely that it was unable to establish the provenance of the letter to the government discovered by Sirr in the Palmer house. When formally asked by O'Grady to identify Emmet, the young man was clearly loath to do so until encouraged by a smiling prisoner in the dock. Under Emmet's instructions, Palmer was not cross-examined. It must have been abundantly clear to the jury and all other observers at this point that Emmet had not the slightest intention of defending himself against the treason charges.

The final Crown witness, the capable policeman, Major Charles Henry Sirr, told the court about the arrest of Emmet and his response to a slight wound inflicted on him in the course of his escape attempt. Sirr had, generously, offered an apology to Emmet for his rough treatment to be told 'All is fair in war'. If Emmet saw himself as a soldier the implications were clear. The prosecution also sought to read extracts from the unfinished letter to the government that had been seized by Sirr in Harold's Cross. To his credit Norbury intervened. Pointing out that the prisoner had not been established as the source of the document he refused permission to have it entered into evidence. However, because the defence itself offered no objection the contents of the letter were read.

The prosecution case having concluded at around 6.00 p.m., the next installment of the drama should have involved the presentation of defence witnesses. But there were none to be sworn. Neither, at the insistence of Emmet, were there to be any closing arguments from Burrowes or MacNally on his behalf. MacNally rose and addressed the court. As 'Mr. Emmet did not intend to call any witnesses, or to take up the time of the

Court by his counsel stating any case, or making any observations on the evidence. He presumed the trial was now closed on both sides'.[55]

However, MacNally had reckoned without the determination of William Plunket to have his say. Plunket had been assigned by the prosecution to make its closing address. The once virulently anti-Union barrister was not to be denied this opportunity of expressing his abhorrence, on behalf of the castle, of the treasonable act of Emmet in 'compassing and imagining the death of the King'.[56] Plunket indicated to Norbury that he would go ahead with his address to the jury. When MacNally demurred the attorney general insisted on the right of the Crown to proceed with its closing statement. He maintained that 'The prisoner declining to go into any case, wears the impression that the case on the part of the crown does not require any answer'. Plunket's scathing and highly personalised address would, in part at least, provoke Emmet into making the most celebrated political speech from the dock of any Irish rebel.

In 1800, during the Union debates, Plunket had taken the lead, along with Grattan, in opposition to the measure. With hyperbolic intensity, he had sworn 'to resist [Union] to the last gasp of my existence and with the last drop of my blood'. He had threatened, were the Union to be accepted, to 'like the father of Hannibal, take my children to the altar and swear them to eternal hostility against the invader of my country's freedom'.[57] Watched now by those who would have been supporters or antagonists during that period he rose to his feet to berate and rebuke Emmet while leaving behind the rebellious anti-Union persona of 1800. He addressed the twelve men who had already been listening patiently to argument and evidence for nearly nine hours:

> My Lords and Gentlemen of the Jury. You need not enter-
> tain any apprehension, that at this hour of the day, I am
> disposed to take up a great deal of your time, by observing
> upon the evidence which has been given. In truth, if this
> were an ordinary case, and if the object of this prosecution
> did not include some more momentous interests than the
> mere question of the guilt or innocence of the unfortunate
> gentleman, who stands a Prisoner at the bar, I should have
> followed the example of his counsel; and should have
> declined making any observation upon the evidence. But,
> Gentlemen, I do feel this to be a case of infinite impor-
> tance indeed. It is a case important, like all others of this

kind, by involving the life of a fellow subject, but it is doubly and ten fold important, because from the evidence which has been given in the progress of it, the system of this conspiracy against the laws and constitution of the country has been developed in all its branches; and, in observing upon the conduct of the Prisoner at the bar, and bringing home the evidence of his guilt, I am bringing home guilt to a person, who, I say, is the centre, the life-blood and foul of this atrocious conspiracy.

Plunket then did precisely what he had indicated he would not do and recapitulated the essentials of the prosecution case. Given that the fatigued jury, not to mention the stoic defendant, had only just been released from the demonstration of that case, his arguments were largely redundant. His comments were laced with a thinly veiled contempt for the working-class origins of some of Emmet's associates. They are introduced, as 'Dowdall the clerk ... Quigley, the bricklayer ... Stafford the baker ... the illiterate victims of the ambition of this young man'. His text spoke of a duped supporting cast and a vain, egotistical messianic *bourgeois* who was overseer and conspirator-in-chief. Referring to the underlying Republican philosophy of the United Irishmen, as expressed in the proclamation of the provisional government, Plunket sneered at the notion of the establishment in Ireland of a 'free and independent Republic'.

> There is no magic in the name. We have heard of 'free and independent Republics,' and have since seen the most abject Slavery that ever groaned under iron despotism growing out of them.
>
> Formerly, Gentlemen of the Jury, we have seen revolutions effected by some great call of the people, ripe for change and unfitted by their habits for ancient forms; but here from the obscurity of concealment and by the voice of that pigmy authority, itself created and fearing to show itself, but, in arms under cover of the night, we are called upon to surrender a constitution, which has lasted for a period of one thousand years. Had any body of the people come forward, dating any grievance or announcing their demand for a change? No, but while the country is peaceful, enjoying the blessings of the Constitution, growing rich and happy under it, a few, desperate, obscure, con-

temptible adventurers in the trade of revolution form a scheme against the constituted authorities of the land, and by force and violence to overthrow an ancient and venerable constitution and to plunge a whole people into the horrors of civil war! ...

And how was this revolution to be effected? The Proclamation conveys an insinuation, that it was to be effected by their own force, entirely independent of foreign assistance. Why? Because it was well known, that there remained in this country few so depraved, so lost to the welfare of their native land, that would not shudder at forming an alliance with France and therefore the people of Ireland are told, 'The effort is to be entirely your own, independent of foreign aid'. But how does this tally with the time when the scheme was first hatched; the very period of the commencement of the war with France? How does it tally with the fact of consulting in the depot, about co-operating with the French ...?

Let me allude to another topic: they call for revenge on account of the removal of the parliament. Those men, who in 1798, endeavoured to destroy the Parliament, now call upon the loyal men, who opposed its transfer, to join them in rebellion; an appeal vain and fruitless. Look around and see with what zeal and loyalty they rallied round the Throne and Constitution of the country. Whatever might have been the difference of opinion heretofore among Irishmen upon some points, when armed rebels appear against the laws and public peace every minor difference is annihilated in the paramount claim of duty to our King and Country ...

Gentlemen, I am anxious to suppose that the mind of the Prisoner recoiled at the scenes of murder which he witnessed and I mention one circumstance with satisfaction, it appears he saved the life of Farrell and may the recollection of that one good action cheer him in his last moments. But though he may not have planned individual murders, that is no excuse to justify his embarking in treason which must be followed by every species of crimes. It is supported by the rabble of the country while the rank, the wealth and the power of the country is opposed to it. Let loose the rabble of the country from the salutary restraints of the law, and who can take upon him to limit their barbarities? Who can say, he will disturb the peace of the world and rule it when wildest? Let loose the winds of heaven and what power less than omnipotent can control them? So it is with the rabble, let them loose and who can restrain them?

What claim then can the Prisoner have upon the compassion of a jury, because in the general destruction which his schemes necessarily produce, he did not meditate individual murder. In the short space of a quarter of an hour what a scene of blood and horror was exhibited. I trust that the blood which has been shed in the streets of Dublin upon that night, and since upon the scaffold, and which may hereafter be shed, will not be visited upon the head of the Prisoner. It is not for me to say, 'what are the limits of the mercy of God?' What a sincere repentance of those crimes may effect. But I do say, that if this unfortunate young gentleman retains any of the seeds of humanity in his heart, or possesses any of those qualities which a virtuous education in a liberal seminary must have planted in his bosom, he will make an atonement to his God and his country, by employing whatever time remains to him in warning his deluded countrymen from persevering in their schemes.

Much blood has been shed, and he perhaps would have been immolated by his followers, if he had succeeded. They are a bloodthirsty crew, incapable of listening to the voice of reason and equally incapable of obtaining rational freedom, if it were wanting in this country, as they are of enjoying it. They embrue [sic] their hands in the moist sacred blood of the country, and yet they call upon God, to prosper their cause, as it is just! But as it is atrocious, wicked and abominable, I most devoutly invoke that God to confound and overwhelm it.[58]

On the basis that Emmet had long since run up a white flag and entered his own *nolo contendere*, for many years after the trial Plunket was excoriated for proceeding with the flogging of an already defunct horse. His often snide and personalised innuendo depicting Emmet as narcissistic and self-important was widely deprecated. Clearly designed to obviate the possibility of any personal sympathy on the part of the jurors for the predicament of the handsome, noble, young defendant; Plunket's barbs must have wounded Emmet. One observer noted that when 'the infatuation of his own conduct was alluded to he assumed an air of haughty and offended dignity'.[59]

Because of his aggressive opposition to the Union in 1800, Plunket was dubbed a hypocrite for his steadfast defence of the new status quo in his philippic against Emmet. The suggestion, which he disputed, that he had been a confidante of the Emmet family appeared to add to the extent of his personal betrayal. He had certainly, at one time, been friendly with Thomas Addis Emmet. According to his detractors it was his enthusiastic onslaught on the philosophy, the pretensions and the treachery of Emmet which secured his November 1803 appointment as Irish solicitor general. In subsequent years Plunket steadfastly maintained that 'the times rendered [the speech] necessary' and insisted that his main criticism of Emmet had been that he had abused his position in society by 'endeavouring to dissatisfy the lower orders of labourers and mechanics with their lot in life, and engaging them in schemes of revolution from which they could reap no fruit but disgrace and death'.[60] On more than one occasion he sued for libel when his conduct was criticised in print.

Wickham was certainly well pleased with Plunket's handiwork. He wrote to Pole Carew on the day of Emmet's execution, 'I hope you will have read Plunket's speech with attention. It is not so well given as the Attorney-General's, because of his rapid manner of speaking, which made it more difficult to follow him; but enough appears to satisfy you that it must have been a most masterly performance'.[61] In extenuation, it should be pointed out that it was Standish O'Grady who insisted that Plunket should be allowed to proceed with his closing argument and 'for Plunket to refuse would have been tantamount to expressing approval for the conduct of the accused, something which, in the light of his anti-Union activities, would scarcely be in his interests to do'.[62]

After Norbury's direction to the jury, the twelve Dubliners who had listened patiently to hours of evidence decided they did not need to leave the box in order to reach a verdict. Their decision took no one by surprise.

Emmet was found guilty of high treason. After a brief and futile intervention by MacNally seeking the postponement of the passing of sentence, Emmet was asked by the clerk of the court 'What have you therefore now to say, why judgement of death and execution should not be awarded against you according to law?'[63]

THE SPEECH FROM THE DOCK, 19 SEPTEMBER 1803

Were it not for what followed the name of Robert Emmet might be no more celebrated today than that of Thomas Russell, who made his own, less impressive, speech from the dock prior to his execution in October 1803. Emmet has been mythologised and rendered iconic on the basis of a valedictory speech, no accurate record of which exists today.[64] Until the bicentenary of his death in 2003, little attention had been paid to the notion of the speech as being Emmet's attempt to rewrite a record sullied by Plunket.

While we are clear on the general thrust of Emmet's oration there is no consensus as to the specific text. There is a suspicion that Emmet's valedictory has either been wilfully misquoted or posthumously co-opted. There are 'two strands of tradition to be considered, each with its special bias. These could be called the official and the patriotic versions, of which only the latter has remained current'.[65] One of the earliest 'official' versions, published in the name of one of the prosecution counsel, William Ridgeway, a noted court reporter, is likely to have been sanitised. It excludes, for example, most of the stirring and emotional rhetoric from the 'patriotic' peroration. Ridgeway's version may also have been augmented when it came to Emmet's criticism of the autocratic nature of Bonapartism. Equally, florid *ex post facto* accretions by ideological sympathisers must be treated with extreme caution. R.R. Madden, the nineteenth-century historian who interviewed many survivors of 1798 and 1803, produced a composite text based on the memories of witnesses to the trial. This includes Emmet's famous and emotive conclusion, which inspired subsequent generations of physical-force Republicanism. One of Emmet's most accomplished biographers, Patrick Geoghegan, has suggested that the most accurate account we can hope for is achieved by combining the first part of Ridgeway's version with the latter part of Madden's. The result of such an exercise, including a number of tetchy interruptions by Lord Norbury, follows:[66]

Why the sentence of the law should not be passed upon me, I have nothing to say. Why the sentence which in the public mind is usually attached to that of the law, ought to be reversed, I have much to say. I stand here a conspirator, as one engaged in a conspiracy for the overthrow of the British Government in Ireland; for the fact of which I am to suffer by the laws, for the motives of which I am to answer before God. I am ready to do both. Was it only the fact of treason, was it that naked fact alone with which I stood charged, was I to suffer no other punishment than the death of the body, I would not obtrude on your attention, but having received the sentence, I would bow my neck in silence to the stroke.

But, my Lords, I well know, that when a man enters into conspiracy, he has not only to combat against the difficulties of fortune, but to contend with the still more insurmountable obstacles of prejudice: and that if, in the end, fortune abandons him and delivers him over bound into the hands of the law, his character is previously loaded with calumny and misrepresentation. For what purpose, I know not, except, that the Prisoner thus weighed down both in mind and body, may be delivered over a more unresisting victim to condemnation. It is well: But the victim being one obtained and firmly in your power, let him now unmanacle his reputation. Not, my Lords, that, I have much to demand from you, it is a claim on your memory rather than on your candour, that I am making. I do not ask you to believe implicitly what I say. I do not hope that you will let my vindication ride at anchor in your breasts; I only ask you, to let it float upon the surface of your recollection till it comes to some more friendly port to receive it, and give it flicker against the heavy storms, with which it is buffetted [sic].

I am charged with being an emissary of France, for the purpose of inciting insurrection in the country and then delivering it over to a foreign enemy. It is false! I did not wish to join this country with France. I did join—I did not create the rebellion—not for France; but for its liberty. It is true, there were communications between the United Irishmen and France; it is true, that by that, the war was no surprise upon us. There is a new agent at Paris at this moment, negotiating with the French Government to obtain from them an aid sufficient to accomplish the separation of Ireland from England and before any expedition fails, it is intended to have a treaty signed, as a guarantee, similar to that which Franklin obtained for America. Whether they will do that now, England you may judge. But the only question with the members of The Provisional Government was: Whether France should come to this country, as an enemy? Whether she should have any pretext for so doing? Whether the people should look to France as their only deliverer, or through the medium and control of the Provisional Government attain their object? It is not now, that I discovered, or that the rest of the Provisional Government of Ireland feel [sic] what it is, that binds states together. They well know, my Lords, that such a disposition exists only in proportion to its mutuality of interest; and wherever that mutuality does not exist, no written articles can secure the inferior state, nor supply the means of protecting its independence.

In this view, it never was the intention of the Provisional Government of Ireland to form a permanent alliance with France; well knowing, that if there is between states a permanent mutual interest, more or less, though treaties may be made, yet for the most part, it is not the treaty which binds them together, but a sense of common interest, and where that interest does not exist treaties are soon represented as unjust, they are qualified and interpreted at pleasure, and violated under any pretext. Under these views, it never was the intention to form a permanent treaty with France and in the treaty, which they did make, they had the same guarantee which America had, that an Independent Government should be established in the country, before the French should come.

God forbid that I should see my country under the hands of a foreign power. On the contrary, it is evident from the introductory paragraph of the address of the Provisional Government of Ireland, that every hazard attending an independent effort was deemed preferable to the more fatal risk of introducing a French army into the country. For what? When it has liberty to maintain and independence to keep, may no consideration induce it to submit. If the French come as a foreign enemy, Oh, my Countrymen, meet them on the shore with a torch in one hand a sword in the other—receive them with all the destruction of war—immolate them in their boats before our native soil shall be polluted by a foreign foe. If they succeed in landing, fight them on the strand, burn every blade of grass before them. If they advance; raze every house; and if you are driven to the centre of your country collect your provisions, your property, your wives and your daughters, form a circle around them, fight while two men are left, and when but one remains let that man set fire to the pile, and release himself and the families of his fallen countrymen from the tyranny of France.

Deliver my country into the hands of France? Look at the Proclamation. Where is it stated? Is it in that part, where the People of Ireland are called upon to show the world that they are competent to take their place among nations? That they have a right to claim acknowledgment as an Independent Country, by the satisfactory proof of their capability of maintaining their independence by wresting it from England with their own hands? Is it in that part, where it is stated, that the system has been organised within the last eight months, without the hope of foreign assistance and which the renewal of hostilities has not accelerated? Is it in that part, which desires England not to create a deadly national antipathy between the two countries? ...

But it is said, we must have had it in view to deliver up the country to France and this is not attempted to be proved upon any ground, but that of assertion. It is not proved from our declarations or actions; because every circumstance attending the attempt which took place, shows, that our object was to anticipate France. How could we speak of freedom to our countrymen, how assume such an exalted motive and meditate the introduction of a power, which has been the enemy of freedom wherever she appears. See how she has behaved to other countries. How has she behaved to Switzerland, to Holland and to Italy? Could we expect better conduct towards us? No! Let not then any man calumniate my memory by believing, that I could have hoped for freedom from the government of France, or that I would have betrayed the sacred cause of the liberty of this country, by committing it to the power of her most determined foe.

With regard to this, I have one observation to make: It has been stated that I came from abroad: If I had been in Switzerland, I would have fought against the French; for I believe the Swiss are hostile to the French. In the dignity of freedom, I would have expired on the frontiers of that country, and they should have entered it only by passing over my lifeless corpse. But if I thought the people were favourable to the French I have seen so much what the consequences of the failure of revolutions are, the oppressions of the higher upon the lower orders of the people. I say, if I saw them disposed to admit the French, I would not join them, but I would put myself between the French and the people, not as a victim but to protect them from subjugation, and endeavour to gain their confidence, by sharing in their danger.

So would I have done with the people of Ireland, and so would I do, if I was called upon to-morrow. Our object was to effect a separation from England ...

[The court here interrupted the prisoner.][67]

LORD NORBURY: At the moment when you are called upon to show, why sentence of death should not be pronounced against you, according to law, you are making an avowal of dreadful trea-

sons, and of a determined purpose to have
persevered in them which I do believe has
astonished your audience. The Court is most
anxious to give you the utmost latitude of
indulgence to address them, hoping that such
indulgence would, not be abused by an
attempt to vindicate the most criminal measures and principles, through the dangerous
medium of eloquent, but perverted talents ...
You sir, had the honour to be a gentleman by
birth, and your father filled a respectable situation under the government. You had an
elder brother,[68] whom death snatched away,
and who when living was one of the greatest
ornaments of the bar. The laws of his country
were the study of his youth; and the study of
his maturer life was to cultivate and support
them. He left you a proud example to follow;
and if he had lived, he would have given your
talents the same virtuous direction as his
own, and have taught you to admire and preserve that constitution, for the destruction of
which you have conspired with the profligate
and abandoned, and associated yourself with
ostlers, bakers, butchers, and such persons,
whom you invited to councils, when you
erected your Provisional Government, when
you sallied forth at midnight with such a
band of assassins and found yourself implicated in their atrocities. Your heart must have
lost all recollection of what you were. You
had been educated as a most virtuous and
enlightened Seminary of Learning[69] and
amidst the ingenuous youth of your country,
many of whom now surround you, with the
conscious pride of having taken up arms to
save their country against your attacks made
upon it: and amongst them there may be a

throb of indignant sorrow, which would say—'Had it been an open enemy, I could have borne it; but that it should be my companion and my friend.[70]

EMMET: What I have spoken was not intended for your lordships, whose situation I commiserate rather than envy; my expressions were for my countrymen. If there be a true Irishman present, let my last words cheer him in the hour of his affliction.

[Interruption by the court.]

EMMET: I have always understood it to be the duty of a judge, when a prisoner has been convicted, to pronounce the sentence of the law. I have also understood that judges sometimes think it their duty to hear with patience and to speak with humanity; to exhort the victim of the laws, and to offer, with tender benignity, his opinions of the motives by which he was actuated, in the crime of which he was adjudged guilty. That a judge has thought it his duty so to have done, I have no doubt; but where is the boasted freedom of your institutions—where is the vaunted impartiality, clemency, and mildness of your courts of justice, if an unfortunate prisoner, whom your policy, and not justice, is about to deliver into the hands of the executioner, is not suffered to explain his motives, sincerely and truly, and to vindicate the principles by which he was actuated?

My lords, it may be a part of the system of angry justice, to bow a man's mind by humiliation, to the purposed ignominy of the scaffold; but worse to me than the purposed shame, or the scaffold's terrors, would be the tame endurance of such foul and unfounded imputations as have been laid against me in this court. You, my Lord, are a judge. I am the supposed culprit. I am a man—you are a man also. By a revolution of power, we might change places, though we never could change characters. If I stand at the bar of this court and dare not vindicate my character, what a farce is your justice? If I stand at this bar and dare not vindicate my character, how dare you calumniate it? Does the sentence of death which your unhallowed policy inflicts on my body, condemn my tongue to silence and my reputation to reproach?

Your executioner may abridge the period of my existence, but while I exist I shall not forbear to vindicate my character and motives from your aspersions; and as a man to whom fame is dearer than life, I will make the last use of that life in doing justice to that reputation which is to live after me, and which is the only legacy I can leave to those I honor [sic] and love, and for whom I am proud to perish. As men, my lord, we must appear at the great day at one common tribunal, and it will then remain for the Searcher of all hearts to show a collective universe, who was engaged in the most virtuous actions, or actuated by the purest motives, my country's oppressors or ...[71]

LORD NORBURY: If you have any thing to urge in point of law, you will be heard; but what you have hitherto said, confirms and justifies the verdict of the Jury.[72]

EMMET: My lord, will a dying man be denied the legal privilege of exculpating himself, in the eyes of the community, from a reproach

thrown upon him during his trial, by charg-
ing him with ambition and attempting to
cast away, for a paltry consideration, the
liberties of his country, why then insult me,
or rather why insult justice, in demanding of
me why sentence of death should not be
pronounced against me? I know, my lord,
that the form prescribes that you should put
the question; the form also confers a right of
answering. This no doubt may be dispensed
with, and so might the whole ceremony of
trial, since sentence was already pronounced
at the castle, before your jury were impaneled [*sic*]. Your lordships are but the priests
of the oracle, and I submit, but I insist on the
whole of the forms.

[Here Mr. Emmet paused, and the court desired him to proceed.]

I have been charged with that importance in
the efforts to emancipate my country, as to
be considered the keystone of the combination of Irishmen, or, as it has been expressed,
'the life and blood of this conspiracy.' You do
me honour overmuch; you have given to the
subaltern all the credit of a superior. There
are men concerned in this conspiracy, who
are not only superior to me but even to your
own conceptions of yourself, my lord; men,
before the splendour of whose genius and
virtues, I should bow with respectful defer-
ence, and who would not deign to call you
friend—who would not disgrace themselves
by shaking your bloodstained hand ...

[Here he was interrupted by Lord Norbury.]

What, my lord, shall you tell me, on the
passage to the scaffold—which that tyranny,

of which you are only the intermediate minister, has erected for my death—that I am accountable for all the blood that has and will be shed in this struggle of the oppressed against the oppressor? Shall you tell me this—and must I be so very a slave as not to repel it?

I do not fear to approach the Omnipotent Judge, to answer for the conduct of my short life; and am I to stand appalled here before a mere remnant of mortality? Let no man dare, when I am dead, to charge me with dishonour—let no man attaint my memory by believing that I could have engaged in any cause, but of my country's liberty and independence. The proclamation of the provisional government speaks my views—no inference can be tortured from it to countenance barbarity or debasement. I would not have submitted to a foreign oppression for the same reason that I would have resisted tyranny at home ...

If the spirits of the illustrious dead participate in the concerns of those who were dear to them in this transitory scene, dear shade of my venerated father, look down on your suffering son, and see has he for one moment deviated from those moral and patriotic principles which you so early instilled into his youthful mind, and for which he has now to offer up his life!

My lords, you are impatient for the sacrifice. The blood which you seek is not congealed by the artificial terrors which surround your victim—it circulates warmly and unruffled through its channels, and in a little time it will cry to heaven—be yet patient! I have but a few words more to say—I am

going to my cold and silent grave—my lamp
of life is nearly extinguished—I have parted
with everything that was dear to me in this
life, and for my country's cause with the idol
of my soul, the object of my affections. My
race is run—the grave opens to receive me,
and I sink into its bosom! I have but one
request to ask at my departure from this
world: it is the charity of its silence! Let no
man write my epitaph: for as no man who
knows my motives dare now vindicate them,
let not prejudice or ignorance asperse them.
Let them rest in obscurity and peace, my
memory be left in oblivion and my tomb
remain uninscribed, until other times, and
other men, can do justice to my character.
When my country takes her place among the
nations of the earth, then, and not till then,
let my epitaph be written. I have done.[73]

Despite his peevish interruptions, according to Madden, Norbury, 'after
an address which was pronounced with an emotion never before exhibited
on any former occasion by his Lordship, pronounced the dreadful sentence,
ordering the prisoner to be executed the following day'.[74] Ridgeway, whose
account was the official government version and may have been censored,
makes no reference to the most celebrated line in the speech, 'When my
country takes her place among the nations of the earth, then, and not till
then, let my epitaph be written'. His account has Emmet concluding with
the less memorable phrase: 'Let my character and my motives repose in
obscurity and peace, till other times and other men can do them justice;
Then shall my character be vindicated. Then may my epitaph be written'.
Neither does he give the prisoner the last word. According to the Ridgeway
account, a brief dialogue between defendant and judge followed Emmet's
intended peroration before Norbury pronounced sentence. This did not
suit the 'patriotic' version of events, which gives Emmet the final word.[75]

Whatever the truth of the matter, in terms of the historical 'memory' the
accuracy of Madden's or Ridgeway's version is immaterial. Emmet, had,
after all, been on his feet for twelve hours. Would he have been capable of
such heady rhetoric at that point, especially in the face of the repeated and

hostile interpolations of an impatient Norbury? But posterity and the Irish nationalist narrative had found an unimpeachable hero and a resounding slogan. The imagery of the 'cold and silent grave' and the notion of Emmet's epitaph remaining 'uninscribed' were enhanced by a series of exhumations and interments which resulted in the symbolic, and continuing, uncertainty surrounding the whereabouts of Emmet's grave. The Judas kiss of MacNally, the sacrificial offers by the prisoner of his life, the invocation of his father's memory and the absence of a verifiable corpse added to the messianic symbolism. His 'resurrection' was his reinvention.

On the morning of his execution Emmet entertained MacNally in Kilmainham Gaol and gave him letters to be delivered to Thomas Addis Emmet. These outlined the details of the conspiracy and the blueprint for the rebellion. In his final act of treachery towards his client, MacNally took them to Dublin Castle. MacNally's account of his final conversation with Emmet is not to be trusted. The renegade barrister shared in the embarrassment of the castle at its surprise over the rebellion. He was anxious to rehabilitate himself, and his 'repetition' of Emmet's claim that a French force was on its way served MacNally's own agenda of keeping the authorities on full alert and the secret-service fund topped up.

Emmet was executed on a scaffold erected outside St Catherine's Church on Thomas Street at 3.00 p.m. on 20 September, the day after his conviction. According to the account of Edward Lees, the postmaster general,

> he conducted himself with a degree of hardihood bordering on insanity ... Arrived at the fatal spot where thousands of the populace were assembled to behold the Execution he ascended the platform with the most undaunted resolution and determined resignation to his fate ... It was expected by most people that he would address them—I believe he was prevented—he uttered not a word.[76]

A former college friend Rev. Dr Haydn, standing near the scaffold later told R.R. Madden that he had heard Emmet say 'My friends I die in peace—and with sentiments of universal love and kindness towards all men'. A militia officer, R. Rainey, who had attended the trial, wrote to a friend that 'he behaved with dignified firmness to the last, it was expected he would have made some inflammatory harangue, but he only said, "My cause was a noble one and I die at peace with all the world"'.[77]

Thirty minutes after his body was cut down, he was beheaded and his head held aloft for inspection by the assembled thousands. A legend, already begun with his speech from the dock, was augmented by the mystery of the disposal of his body. His remains were removed to Kilmainham where a death-mask impression was taken. As his mother had recently died, his only remaining family members were his pregnant sister, Mary Anne Holmes, and a sixteen-year-old niece. As a result, no family member claimed the body and he was buried in nearby Bully's Acre in a pauper's grave. Head and body were not interred together. Later, friends of the family exhumed his body and buried it secretly. His final expressed wish, for his grave to remain without epitaph, was respected. There have been many theories as to the whereabouts of his corpse and many fruitless searches but, in essence, as his biographer, Patrick Geoghegan, has observed, 'the failure to find Emmet's body has added to his deification'.[78]

In a poignant postscript to the whole affair the chief secretary, William Wickham, resigned. Although there must be at least some suspicion that he was made a scapegoat for the intelligence failures of Dublin Castle, his avowed reason was the impossibility of continuing to perform his job after reading Emmet's letter to him of 4 September (see above). In his own letter of resignation, he explained his reasons:

> ... in what honours or other earthy advantages could I find compensation for what I must suffer were I again compelled by my official duty to prosecute to death men capable of thinking and acting as Emmet has done in his last moments for making an effort to liberate their country from grievances the existence of many of which none can deny, of which I myself acknowledged to be unjust, oppressive and unchristian. I well know that the manner in which I have suffered myself to be affected by this letter will be attributed to a sort of morbid sensibility, rather than to its real cause, but no one can be capable of forming a right judgment on my motives who has not like myself been condemned by his official duty to dip his hands in the blood of his fellow countrymen, in execution of a portion of the laws and institutions of his country of which, in his conscience he cannot approve.[79]

Was the trial of Robert Emmet fair? Clearly there can be no doubt whatever about Emmet's complicity in the rebellion that, to this day, bears his name. He planned an insurrection, largely financed it himself, and, in concert with others, rose against the state. But what was the purpose and extent of that insurrection? Was Emmet guilty, as the charge of high treason alleged, of 'compassing and imagining the death of the King'?[80] While Emmet had no specific intention of killing George III, the prosecution case was based on 'an offence of constructive treason whereby an intention to imprison, depose or restrain the king was regarded as including an intent to kill him'.[81] Supreme Court justice, Adrian Hardiman, argues that Norbury misdirected the jury on the issue of treason 'where the jury was simply told that if they accepted the evidence of the witnesses the offence of treason was complete'.[82] He goes on to present a complex and sophisticated argument in support of the contention that the government was acting *ultra vires* in putting Emmet on trial for the offence of high treason.[83]

But whether or not the government was acting outside of the law on foot of its indictment, the charge of high treason was not challenged and the case continued. Within the context of what followed was the defendant dealt with fairly? Marianne Elliott, in her biography of Emmet, insists that 'contrary to legend it was a fair trial'.[84] Adrian Hardiman describes the case, as conducted, as a 'show trial'.[85] He claims that the result was rigged and that it was designed to demonstrate that the executive had 'cracked the conspiracy'. Emmet, therefore, was correct in his observation that the 'sentence was already pronounced at the castle before your jury were impaneled [*sic*].'[86]

The castle's embarrassment over, its lack of foreknowledge of the rebellion had already resulted in the speedy dispatch of a number of minor players in the affair when Emmet was delivered into its hands. By then, Hardiman maintains that 'the government desperately needed a prominent, and Protestant, victim on whom the rebellion could be blamed'.[87] Emmet was perfectly willing to take that responsibility upon his own shoulders. In the interests of self-preservation it was imperative for the administration to establish that the primary reason for its intelligence failure was that virtually all advance knowledge of the details of the insurrection blueprint were lodged in the brain of one man. Unlike the United Irish rebellion of 1798, the 1803 uprising could not be readily penetrated by spies and informers.

While it is technically correct to say that Emmet's trial was conducted with a large measure of legal scrupulousness (Norbury's ruling on the letter to the government being a case in point), it is equally the case that the government could afford to observe the legal niceties as long as it possessed the silver bullet of the Curran letters. At all times Emmet was constrained in his defence by the knowledge that the letters of a 'brother conspirator', on display during his trial, could have their real context revealed to the court. There is some evidence that even Norbury was aware of the significance of this correspondence when he advised Emmet that 'if the prisoner wishes to have any other part of these papers read he may'.[88] Was this a subtle reminder from the Bench that Emmet was expected to adopt the line of least resistance?

He certainly did when it came to the ineffectual cross-examination,[89] non-existent rebuttal evidence and the failure to challenge the admissibility of correspondence that had not been established as having emanated from his pen. Once the prosecution was assured that the defence would only put up token resistance there was no compelling reason not to observe the proper forms. Hardiman describes 'the crown's blackmail', probably formalised by MacNally, as 'quite improper'. He goes on:

> As a result of this arrangement the government were [*sic*] able to introduce in evidence without objection highly incriminating documents which they were admittedly unable to prove in the manner required by law. If this had not occurred, then, even on the government's own view, they were liable to lose the case.[90]

Not even this dubious compact with the defendant, which virtually guaranteed a favourable result, was sufficient for the castle. The executive needed an additional advantage, at least one, and possibly two, spies in the enemy camp.[91] In the unlikely event that Emmet was to decide suddenly to jettison Sarah Curran and conduct a robust defence, the Crown would quickly have been informed. It is worth interrogating the manner in which MacNally became Emmet's counsel. When Curran discovered the relationship between his client and his daughter, he was placed in an invidious position. However, had he chosen to do so, he might, albeit with great difficulty, have retained the brief. But he was instructed abandon the case by Hardwicke. It could be argued that this was done in the knowledge that Emmet would instantly approach MacNally to replace Curran. As far as the castle was concerned this was clearly a consummation devoutly to be wished. So while the trial itself may have been conducted in a fair and reasonable manner the entire process was, at the very least, irregular, or, at worst, a flagrant miscarriage of justice.

APOTHEOSIS, 1803+

Every mythical hero, in modern parlance, needs a posthumous champion. Emmet managed to capture the imagination of a number of distinguished apologists. Some legends grow wild, most are carefully cultivated.

Robert Emmet had a number of inspiring qualities but nobility and courage (also demonstrated in abundance by the likes of Thomas Russell) were crucially augmented by a romantic narrative and an early death. His speech from the dock, and especially the stirring peroration, provided a literary focus for an increasingly literate society. The Emmet myth took off almost immediately. 'He fitted easily into a long-standing tradition linking the deaths of successive generations of fallen leaders with that of the ancient mythic hero Cu Chulainn.'[92]

In the years after his execution, Emmet's name was kept before the Irish public by the likes of Walter 'Watty' Cox, proprietor/editor of the irreverent *Irish Magazine*. Cox elevated Emmet's memory by presenting him as a tragic and romantic figure rather than the vainglorious, hapless opportunist of the government narrative. Conscious of the need for a villain, Cox relentlessly pursued Plunket as the serpent in Eden. Later he would be replaced as *bête noir* by Leonard MacNally. But Emmet's true good fortune was probably his early friendship with Thomas Moore. The two attended Trinity College together. Moore's, 'projection of Emmet as tragic romantic hero set the tone for the legend. Emmet himself brooding and rather humourless, was Ireland's perfect romantic hero'.[93] With Moore as elegist and narrator the Emmet legend grew. It was enhanced by the romanticism of the Young Ireland movement and, of course, fed into the philosophy of blood sacrifice espoused by Pearse in 1916. Books, poems, songs and plays in both Ireland and the USA (final home of his brother Thomas Addis Emmet) about this young, nationalist martyr-figure, kept him before the public throughout the nineteenth century. He remained an integral part of popular culture for decades after his death and an established figure in the Irish political/historical pantheon at least until the IRA campaign of the 1970s encouraged a reassessment of his legacy. In the 'post-revisionist' climate of the early part of the twenty-first century, the coincidence of his bicentenary brought him back into a more realistic and less romantic focus. He is as interesting today for the growth of his romantic legend, as he is for any of his own personal achievements and failures.

Such was the appeal of Emmet that, in the early part of the twentieth century, when a fit-up theatre company re-enacted his trial in a rural Irish venue, the hostility of the crowd towards the actors playing O'Grady, Norbury and Plunket was so palpable that when the jury was asked by 'Norbury' to reach a verdict, for reasons of discretion, Emmet was found not guilty.[94] Had that been the actual decision of the jury, he would barely be remembered today. It was the verdict that transformed him into an iconic and articulate martyr.

.2.

THE TRIAL OF
JOHN MAGEE

I never take up a Newspaper without finding something I should have deemed it a loss not to have seen;
never without deriving from it instruction and
amusement.[1]

(Dr Samuel Johnson)

... he should always consider the liberty of the press as
a national evil, while it enabled the vilest reptile to
soil the lustre of the most shining merit, and furnished
the most infamous incendiary with the means of disturbing the peace and destroying the good order of
the community.[2]

(Lismahago to Matthew Bramble, *The expedition of
Humphrey Clinker*, Tobias Smollett)

'A RICH MAN'S BASTARD'

Descended from the illegitimate son of King Charles II and his French mistress, Louise de Kerouaille, Charles Lennox, fourth duke of Richmond,
was one of the most enthusiastic early sponsors of the game of cricket.
Soldier, duellist and first-class wicketkeeper, he was to die of rabies in 1819
as a result of an encounter with a Canadian fox. But in July 1813 he had
just reached the end of his tenure, and his tether, as lord lieutenant of
Ireland and was about to be replaced by his successor, Viscount Whitworth.
The *Dublin Evening Post*, a newspaper not noted for its sympathy with
his administration, issued a parting shot that was even more scurrilous
than some of its previous philippics against his viceroyalty. Using as a
pretext a commemoration at the Dublin statue in honour of King William
on 12 July, the *Post* took issue with Orange identification of the demands
for equality of Catholic citizens with the tyranny of King James II. But the
meat of the article was a direct personal attack on the pretensions and prejudices of Richmond himself.

Your grace is proud of your Stuart descent. We know it.
Your plate and your pictures—your medals, insignia, and
heraldic devices—your motto and your crest—the bar
through the crown emblazoned on your carriage—the

ostentatious display of the silver on your sideboard, evidently show that you adopt an opinion, that it is a prouder and a better thing to be a rich man's bastard than a poor man's heir. The Catholics served your family long; they never received anything from them but injury. They served in various countries under various princes of your house. They never found any of them other than a tyrant ... They share not in the dishonour of the unprincipled king who terminated that regal line, more than you do in the disgrace of the unprincipled, adulterous harlot who commenced your ducal line ... [3]

It was the sort of vituperation calculated to result in a challenge to duel or a libel contest in the courts. Richmond's difficulty, and that of his waning administration, was that the proprietor of the offending publication, a Presbyterian printer named John Magee, was in no position to fight a duel as he was already in jail awaiting trial, charged with an earlier libel on the duke. His case, in which he was being defended by Daniel O'Connell, had been adjourned and was due to recommence in a fortnight. If Magee was hoping for a sympathetic hearing from a compassionate court, he was going about things in entirely the wrong way.

THE COUNSELLOR

Daniel O'Connell, born in 1775, was a member of a large, well to do, Roman Catholic Co. Kerry family that had managed to weather a century of anti-Catholic legislation and retain much of its property and privileges. This achievement had come about as a result of much *legerdemain* and the frequent use of the wild and lightly monitored coastline of his native county for smuggling purposes. From a family of ten, he married a woman with ten siblings and together they had ten children. His education was paid for by his uncle, Maurice 'Hunting Cap' O'Connell, who had made a small fortune trading with Spanish and French merchantmen. (Much of that trade was actually legal and above board.) Trained in the legal profession, O'Connell's reputation as a defence lawyer earned him his first popular nickname 'The Counsellor'.[4] Influenced by some of the enlightenment and radical ideals of the late eighteenth century he became a member of the United Irishmen, but served in the lawyers' yeomanry corps during the

1798 rebellion. His observation of that failed insurrection was to convince him that 'all work for Ireland must be done openly and above board' and that 'in order to succeed for Ireland, it was strictly necessary to work within the limits of the law and constitution'.[5]

The gradual alleviation of the Irish Penal Laws in the eighteenth century had left one major anomaly untouched. Roman Catholics, although now permitted to vote in elections, were not allowed to sit in parliament. They were also excluded from a number of prominent government positions, including that of lord lieutenant and chief secretary. In the early 1800s various Catholic organisations, the Catholic Committee and, later, the Catholic Board, sought to rectify this egregious infringement of Catholic rights. O'Connell played a prominent role in both bodies. A half-promise of Catholic emancipation had been made in advance of the Act of Union. This was done in order to guarantee the acquiescence of the Catholic population in the abolition of the Irish 'patriot' parliament in Dublin that, in effect, represented the Protestant Ascendancy.

The promissory note to the Catholics of Ireland had not been honoured, partly due to the obduracy of King George III. Fears of a consequential transfer of power and influence, as well as suspicions of covert Roman Catholic priestly support for the United Irishmen and the rebellion of Robert Emmet,[6] meant that Ascendancy figures in Ireland were also disinclined to remove this final barrier to full Catholic citizenship. Where the Act of Union was concerned, O'Connell preferred the measure of Irish independence afforded by a Protestant parliament, however circumscribed, to the alternative. In one of his first public speeches in 1800, O'Connell, smarting from the charge made by fellow barristers that Catholics were pro-Union addressed an anti-Union meeting and observed 'that he would rather confide in the justice of his brethren, the Protestants of Ireland, who have already liberated him, than lay his country at the feet of foreigners'.[7]

Post-1800 Catholic grievances went much further than a mere desire for parliamentary representation. The religious reforms of the late eighteenth century had simply not delivered in the manner suggested by O'Connell in his impassioned defence of the College Green parliament. Anti-Catholic discrimination in the distribution of publicly funded positions was still rife. In the years immediately following the Union, of the more than 4,000 offices for which Catholics were eligible, they held fewer than 180.[8] It was this wider sense of disenfranchisement that would underpin a massive popular campaign (in the 1820s) for the achievement of an objective that would be of precious little benefit to most of the agitators. Catholics who had supported the Union and who were encouraged by the return of Pitt (architect of that piece of legislation) in 1804 as prime minister were to be sorely disappointed when he indicated his intention to oppose any measure of Catholic relief. Conversely, the stock of O'Connell, who had opposed Pitt in 1800, rose amongst the small metropolitan *élite* that led the Catholic Committee. Over the next four years he managed to undermine the conservative and pusillanimous leadership of the Committee and gradually take control of the organisation.

The death of Pitt, in January 1806, and the installation of a Whig dominated 'Ministry of all the Talents', led by Lord Grenville and with the sympathetic Charles James Fox as foreign secretary, augured well for the Catholic cause. The duke of Bedford replaced Lord Hardwicke as lord lieutenant (Hardwicke had actually been relatively conciliatory) and a number of relief measures were proposed. Nothing tangible or constructive had been achieved, however, by the time of Fox's death in September 1806, and the dissolution of the ministry the following year.

Bedford was replaced by the duke of Richmond, a vigorous opponent of Catholic Emancipation. The placatory policies of the Whigs went into sharp reverse. The appointment of the secretary of the Grand Orange Lodge to the privy council and of William Saurin, a figure known for his antipathy to further Catholic relief measures, as attorney general, provided an ample demonstration to Catholic leaders of the direction that would be taken by the new administration.

In 1812 when Robert Peel, son of a successful businessman, became Irish chief secretary at the age of 24, no one, least of all the man himself, could have suspected that he would remain in the post for six years. Since the Union the primary occupant of the chief secretary's lodge had changed, virtually, on an annual basis. While the ministry, of which he was a representative, was avowedly open-minded on the subject of Catholic Emancipation, Peel himself was not. He was opposed to the measure and was determined, during his term in Dublin Castle, to crush the Catholic Board and those who agitated for palliative measures for members of the majority religion. His policies would earn him the, rather obvious, soubriquet of 'Orange' Peel. This particular jibe was liberally employed by O'Connell. Peel was, perhaps, fortunate in that his arrival, more or less, coincided with the departure of the duke of Richmond as viceroy and Sir Charles Saxton as under secretary. This allowed him considerable latitude in the formulation of policy. But his impressive acumen and his innate resolve suggests that, even had those more experienced bureaucrats remained in place, he would have dominated the Irish administration.

O'Connell did not take long to unleash his particular line of invective on the young English functionary. He described Peel disparagingly, and memorably, as 'a raw youth squeezed out of the workings of I know not what factory in England, and sent over to Ireland before he had got rid of the foppery of perfumed handkerchiefs and thin shoes'.[9] This, and other sallies, did nothing to endear O'Connell to the future prime minister and their mutual antipathy would grow and fester until O'Connell's death in 1847.

Rather than risk an immediate direct confrontation with the Catholic Board, Peel chose, instead, to take on its champions in the press. In February 1813 Hugh Fitzpatrick, a Dublin printer, was fined £200 and jailed for libel for publishing a pamphlet entitled *A statement of the Penal Laws which aggrieve the Catholics of Ireland*.[10] It had been written, anonymously, by a prominent Catholic Board member and barrister, Denys Scully. The alleged 'libel' would suggest either a degree of administrative oversensitivity or Peel's intention to discourage and suppress even the mildest adverse comment. As the *Dublin Evening Post* explained: 'An unlucky note in this Book charged the Duke of Richmond's Government with partiality, even in the dispensation of criminal justice, and mentioned, that a man of the name of Barry had been hanged, who, if he happened to have been a Protestant, was almost certain of a pardon'.[11] The prosecution of the lawsuit and its outcome, highly favourable to the executive, were intended as a warning to other pamphleteers and newspaper editors who sought to undermine the authority of Dublin Castle or generate animosity towards the administration amongst the Roman Catholic *élite*.

PATRIOTS V PENSIONERS—THE EARLY NINETEENTH CENTURY PRESS

By the early nineteenth century Irish national newspapers, with circulations ranging from mere dozens[12] to, at most, just over two thousand,[13] were either 'independent' or 'castle' in their political orientation. Publications falling into the latter category enjoyed generous financial support from the authorities. The partisan 'patriot' press of the late eighteenth century had either 'dispersed',[14] adapted to the new post-Union political realities, or been suborned by official 'bribes'.[15] According to Stephen J.M. Brown, 'There was, as yet, no Catholic ... press'.[16]

The 'castle' papers (the *Dublin Journal*, the *Correspondent* and the *Freeman's Journal*) were supported and subsidised by the administration to the tune of over £10,000 per annum. Independent titles, like the *Dublin Evening Post* and the *Evening Herald* emerged or returned to the marketplace as dissenting voices when it became, relatively, safe to do so in the years after the 1798 repression. Some papers, like the *Freeman's Journal*, were not entirely dependable in their loyalties. The *Freeman* veered between outright collaboration (during the proprietorship of the so-called 'Sham Squire' Francis Higgins—up to the time of his death in 1802) to a somewhat more qualified and nuanced support supplemented by occasional bouts of independence during the proprietorship of Phillip Whitfield Harvey, himself the beneficiary of a government pension of £200 a year.

For some proprietors, economic reality meant the necessity of state subsidisation. Blatant affiliation to the policies of Dublin Castle generally resulted in relative unpopularity and unsustainable circulation figures— hence the need for Crown bounty to survive. For 'independent' proprietors, any close association with government policies was too high a price to pay. It brought with it a threat of political and commercial irrelevance or outright extinction. However, the loyalties of Irish papers, magazines and periodicals in this period were never set in stone. Not even the most fundamental allegiance to the 'patriot' or 'Unionist' cause was absolutely guaranteed. Even the *Correspondent*, established and largely funded by the castle, bowed to the prevailing *zeitgeist* at one point and spent a period in independent opposition.[17] When its ownership changed in 1812 the *Hibernian Journal,* originally anti-Union, travelled in the opposite direction. In the process it shed most of its readership.

Even the most acquiescent of place-seekers was also susceptible to changes of government in England that, in turn, translated into new political imperatives in Dublin Castle. In 1793 the *Dublin Journal* was acquired from the Faulkner family by the virulent Orangeman and loyal castle supporter, John Giffard. The unpopular and unprofitable *Journal* was claimed by Giffard to be 'held in trust for the government'.[18] It could not have survived without being buttressed financially. But even the *Journal* occasionally found itself at odds with the prevailing wisdom of the administration when policy was being driven by moderate regimes, like the short-lived administration of Fitzwilliam in the pre-rebellion period and that of Hardwicke from 1804–06. The latter fell out with Giffard and removed him from his government job in customs and excise.

The principal control and reward mechanisms employed by the executive involved patronage in the form of direct government transfers (via payment for carrying proclamations and official advertisements) and access to the 'expresses'. The latter was a government courier service that brought London papers to Dublin several hours before the arrival of the regular mails. As most Dublin newspapers consisted of little more than plagiarised English copy, it was a huge commercial advantage to have priority access to the London sheets so that they could be filleted and reproduced under a Dublin masthead in advance of one's rivals. Realising this, under the viceroyalty of the duke of Bedford (1806–07), the *Correspondent* was established by the castle, subsidised to the tune of £1,200 per annum and given exclusive access to the 'expresses'.[19] This ability to 'scoop' its rivals created a unique, if short-lived, publishing phenomenon, a commercially successful 'castle' newspaper. At various times, depending on the ebb and flow of government patronage and imperatives, it was obliged to share this facility with other newspapers, including the *Freeman's Journal*.

If seduction, corruption and bribery failed to keep newspapers in line, the alternative at the disposal of the administration was recourse to the courts or to the exchequer. Recalcitrant newspapers could be taxed into quiescence or insolvency. But if papers proved unexpectedly tenacious and their opposition persisted, the libel laws could be deployed to despatch offending proprietors or editors to jail.

Stamp duty and taxes on advertisements were familiar administrative weapons in the curtailment of political commentary in England, just as bounty from secret service funds was an equally powerful inducement to conformity there. By the time of the Act of Union, English newspapers faced duties of 3½d per copy, putting them out of the price range of all but the wealthy.[20] A similar regime applied in Ireland, though the duty was of the order of 2d per copy.[21] However, in both instances, favoured publications would, in effect, be compensated for this 'tax on knowledge' by means of official subvention.

In the budget of 1810, in response to the defection of the *Freeman's Journal* and the *Correspondent* to the 'independent' camp in light of extreme government unpopularity, the Irish chancellor of the exchequer brought in a controversial 'revenue raising' measure by doubling the tax on newspaper advertisements. As the castle newspapers had much smaller circulations and, consequently, little other than government advertising, the measure had little effect on them. The opposition papers were forced to raise their prices from 4d to 5d and try to withstand the inevitable fall in circulation. The next change of government brought the *Correspondent* back into the castle fold.[22]

The ultimate sanction, however, and one used sparingly in the first decade of the new century, was incarceration for libel. The 1793 Libel Act had, on the face of it, liberalised the entire procedure by transferring to juries the right to decide whether or not an article was libellous. The difficulty, however, lay with the constitution of the juries. The administration, already ensured of the collaboration of the judiciary, simply packed juries with its own supporters when a guilty verdict was required in order to discourage dissent. As a result, by the second decade of the new century 'Newspaper owners and editors lived in constant fear of fines and periods in jail'.[23]

Next to Hugh Fitzpatrick, the other most prominent victim of the libel laws was Watty Cox, editor of the pugnacious *Irish Magazine*. Notwithstanding his claim that 'I do not think that the press in Ireland can do the same mischief to the government that it does [in England]',[24] William Wellesley Pole, chief secretary before Peel, ordered the arrest of Cox in 1811 for an article advocating Irish separatism. On 29 May Cox was fined £300 and sent to jail for a year. He was also sentenced to be pilloried, but seems to have enjoyed this supposed indignity as a large crowd of supporters turned up to see him in the stocks.

Robert Peel did not share Pole's estimation of the opposition press in Ireland. In his dealings with the Irish he was motivated by his belief that 'an honest despotic government would be by far the fittest government for Ireland'.[25] His autocratic tendencies left no room for a dissenting press. With Cox in jail, the most egregious dissentient was John Magee of the *Dublin Evening Post*. Given that the administration was unable to bribe or tax Magee into subservience, Peel chose the coercive option.

Under the proprietorship of John Magee, the *Dublin Evening Post* was a fearless critic of Dublin Castle and of the administration's Catholic policies. Its success in antagonising the ruling *élite* can be gauged from the level of abuse heaped upon it by the castle press. Peel decided to bring the *Post* to heel rapidly and thoroughly. An early opportunity presented itself. On 5 January 1813 the *Post* published a polemic condemning the viceroyalty of the recently departed duke of Richmond. It was written, according to one of O'Connell's biographers, Seán O'Faoláin, either by the ubiquitous Denys Scully or another Catholic Board member, James Finlay. The article noted that

> If the administration of the Duke of Richmond had been
> conducted with more than ordinary talent, its errors
> might, in some degree, have been atoned for by its ability
> and the people of Ireland, though they might have much
> to regret, yet would have something to admire: but truly,
> after the gravest consideration, they must find themselves
> at a loss to discover any striking feature in his Grace's
> administration that makes it superior to the worst of his
> predecessors. They insulted, they oppressed, they mur-
> dered, and they deceived.

Having established that the Richmond administration was no better
than those of the previous two decades, the *Post* went on to itemise the
abuses heaped upon Ireland by some of the former incumbents.

> The profligate, unprincipled WESTMORLAND—the cold-
> hearted and cruel CAMDEN—the artful and treacherous
> CORNWALLIS left Ireland more depressed and divided
> than they found her—they augmented the powers of the
> Government, both in the Military and Civil branches—they
> increased coercion and corruption, and uniformly
> employed them against the Liberties of the People.[26]

In the context of the libel legislation of the time ('a mere mechanism of
political censorship, with cruel penalties being imposed retrospectively for
breaches of an unspecified and unpromulgated code'[27]), Peel was enabled
to take punitive action against the publishers. In April 1813 Magee was
charged with libel.

THE TRIAL OF JOHN MAGEE

The *Post*, in the circumstances, might have been expected to maintain a
low profile in order to improve the chances of a verdict favourable to its
proprietor. Instead it seemed to go out of its way to antagonise the administration even further. The case first came before the King's Bench Court on
31 May 1813 and was adjourned at the insistence of the defence. Three
days later the *Post* railed 'though the government press teems with daily
libels upon the whole population of the country, it is remarkable enough

that not a single state prosecution has been instituted against it'. Of its pro-prietor, the *Post* observed: 'While he lives, though it be in a dungeon, the spirit of the press shall walk abroad, like the air of heaven, the pure impal-pable vehicle of light and life to the community. Hear it, every titled plunderer of the people, for it shall penetrate into the recesses of your crimes.'[28] On 16 July the paper published a far more personal tirade against the duke of Richmond than the alleged libel for which Magee was being prosecuted (see above).

O'Connell, as a Catholic, was not permitted to 'take silk'. Therefore, he appeared for Magee as a junior counsel opposed by a battery of illustrious king's counsel. The legal team acting on behalf of the Crown was formida-ble. Leading the case against the newspaper proprietor was the Irish attorney general, William Saurin. Born in Belfast of French Huguenot stock, Saurin had been appointed attorney general in 1807. He had been MP for Blessington in Grattan's parliament and a bitter opponent of the Union. However, 'after the Union his conduct had been most exemplary, and his reward had been proportionate to his loyalty'.[29] By 1813 he reserved most of his hostility for the cause of Catholic relief and was recog-nised as a 'Protestant zealot and Ascendancy man'.[30] He took considerable personal pleasure at the prospect of the professional task in hand. One of O'Connell's earliest biographers, C.M. O'Keeffe, characterised him as

> a Frenchman in face, a Scotchman in character—an Orangeman by choice ... He was something of a Republican by nature, but fashioned by circumstances into a Tory; moral but not pious; decent but not devout. His passions were violent, and rather covered than sup-pressed ... He was wholly free from vulgarity and quite denuded of accomplishment.[31]

Saurin was briefed by the solicitor general, Charles Kendal Bushe, a future Irish lord chief justice. O'Keeffe describes Bushe as of 'open and sunny character ... conspicuously liberal ... a man of refined manners and of polished if not prudential habits ... of infinitely more use to the aristoc-racy—infinitely more mischievous to the Catholics than Saurin could possibly have been'.[32] Some semblance of mutual regard appears to have existed between O'Connell and Bushe that was absent from the former's relationship with Saurin. In his speech in defence of Magee, O'Connell went so far as to make a flattering reference to Bushe. The solicitor general, though O'Connell's political views were anathema to him, once acknowl-

edged that 'if he had a suit at law, he would certainly employ him'.[33]
Supplementing the impressive legal artillery at the disposal of the Crown
was the judge in the case, Justice Downes. In the words of Brian Inglis the
Irish judiciary was, in effect, 'supernumerary Crown counsel'.[34]

Public interest in the case, which commenced on 26 July 1813, was
enormous. 'Each day, long before the hour when Chief-Justice Downes
took his seat, the Court of King's Bench was crowded to suffocation.'[35]
The *Evening Post* took the lead in highlighting the predicament. 'It was
not merely the prosecution itself, nor the popularity of the leading
counsel and client—the leading articles, which still continued undaunt-
edly in the *Evening Post,* roused the popular excitement to something
bordering on frenzy.'[36] A sense of anticipation built up as a consequence
of two adjournments on 31 May and 7 July, when the defence mischievously sought the attendance of William Wellesley Pole and Sir Charles
Saxton with the avowed intention of cross-examining the former chief
secretary and under secretary.

On 26 July O'Connell sought another adjournment and, when this was
denied, he and the defence team affected to throw up their briefs only to
return when Magee instructed them to allow the case to commence.
O'Connell then turned his attention to the jury. He questioned two
members in particular, Thomas Andrews and Alexander Montgomery,
inquiring of both whether they were members of an Orange society, the
Aldermen of Skinner's Alley. Andrews claimed he had not been a member
for twenty years. Montgomery denied membership but added that he
'respected the body very much'.[37] Another juror, William Walsh, admitted
to membership. O'Connell's challenge to his continued presence on the
jury was denied by Justice Downes. Unable to change the complexion of a
jury he suspected would be universally hostile, O'Connell sat back to listen
to Saurin's opening argument.

> My Lord and Gentlemen of the Jury it is a very painful
> part of the duty of the office which I hold under the
> Crown, to bring before you the present case. This is an
> indictment against the Traverser, John Magee, for a Libel
> on his Grace the Duke of Richmond, the Lord Lieutenant
> of Ireland. It will be my duty to explain to you the
> meaning and motives of this Libel, in order to justify the
> causes and reasons of this prosecution. I must be aware of
> the jealousy which your minds should naturally entertain

for the invaluable privilege of a Free Press; but I trust, I know the value, and venerate that privilege no less than any other man in the community. Within its legal and proper bounds, it is the security of the subject against the Government, and of the Government against Faction in the State. But when it transgresses those bounds, and that to a wide extent, it is peculiarly incumbent on those who administer and dispense the Law, to correct its abuses. If it is then allowed to pass unchecked by those to whom is given the care of enforcing obedience to the rules of the Constitution, the privilege itself will be brought into danger, and the happiness and security of those, for whose welfare it was intended, will be destroyed.

It is the privilege of the subject in this country to use his pen and his tongue, without any previous restraint whatever. Every subject of the land has a right to carry a staff in his hand, but if he will use that staff to commit assault and battery on every man who may excite his enmity, or be the object of his spleen, it is necessary that the law should interfere, not to take away his privilege, but to correct the abuse, punish the offender.

That, Gentlemen being the true liberty of the Press, which it is the duty of us all to preserve inviolate, if every ruffian in the community, who throws off those restraints which a regard to truth imposes on other men, takes upon him to slander and revile, and deal out his Billingsgate upon every character, however exalted, pure, and honorable [sic], which may excite his envy or his malice, or throw obstacles in the way of his factious and revolutionary politics, and through his wickedness the Liberty of the Press is abused, it then becomes necessary to apply the corrections of the law, lest that Liberty of the Press should be turned into an engine of public calamity, and endanger the safety of the State ...

Saurin read the libellous paragraph from the *Post* article before continuing.

Gentlemen, at the end of a long and honourable career, such as the Duke of Richmond's when every good and loyal man is mourning the departure of, perhaps the best

Chief Governor that Ireland ever saw, it is melancholy and afflicting to think that there should exist a faction so desperate and a ruffian so atrocious, who could compose and deliberately publish so malignant a calumny. But I do not conceive that in this part of the libel his chief object is to insult and outrage the feelings of the Duke of Richmond: if he had such an object in view, little does he know the character he was traducing, the armour which honour and integrity threw around him render him as invulnerable as he is insensible to such attacks as these. If the libel related only to him it would have gone by unprosecuted by me. But the imputation is made against the Administration of Justice by the Government of Ireland; and it forms only a part of a system of calumny with which an association of factious and revolutionary men are in the habit of vilifying every constitutional authority of the land ... It has only one object; you must see to whom it is addressed; it is appealing to the religious prejudices of that part of the community, which has been already too far misled by misrepresentation, and calculated to disaffect the population of the Country in their obedience to their lawful Government—to excite in their minds hatred against those whom the laws have appointed to rule over them, and prepare them for revolution, by exciting them to a civil and religious war. I say, no less atrocious are the motive and malignant purposes of this publication.

... in such audacious and seditious language, does this ruffian traduce and vilify the public functionaries of the State, so as to threaten the public peace, and the security of the Government. How can we expect submission to the law, so necessary to the well being of the State, if those whom God and the law have constituted our Governors, are to be held up to hatred and detestation—as prone to every vice, and divested of every private and public virtue? The tremendous licentiousness of the Press calls for the interposition of the law—if it be not applied, it is impossible to say to what extent the mischief may not lead. It is for you, Gentlemen, in the capacity which you fill, to apply the wholesome correction of the law to these baneful libels.

The state of the Public Press, at this day, is beyond the licentiousness of all former times and precedents. We remember the state of the Press in the year which preceded the Rebellion, to the instrumentality of which, in a great degree, that Rebellion must be imputed; and I do most seriously aver, that the Press at this day goes beyond any thing to which the Press of that time went ... I do not shrink from the aspersions of *The Evening Post*; they have no terrors for me. In the discharge of my duty, going steadily forward, I will not betray the Constitution and the law of the country—I will always be, as the whole tenor of my life proves me, an enemy of faction in all its branches, but particularly of that faction which has been labouring in this country in favour of those principles which produced the horrors of the French Revolution, and would rob us of our laws and liberties.

I think it is time that the Public, to whom this Libel is addressed, and whose minds have been abused and misled by misrepresentation, should be undeceived; lest, seeing Libels such as these, going unpunished, they might think such atrocious imputations would not be made if they were not, in some degree, true. They will argue, that the faction which promotes this system of abominable and unexampled libelling is become so strong, that the Government dare not wrestle with it. It is to remove this prejudice and error from the public mind—it is to teach them, that those who publish those Libels are common, and ordinary, and contemptible malefactors, that this prosecution is instituted. They must see them committed to prison to expiate their offence, unpitied and unprotected; and then they will feel they are not altogether to submit themselves to the wickedness of this faction, by whom they are misled and abused, in order to effect their wicked purposes ...[38]

O'Connell listened in silence while his client was described by Saurin as 'a brothel keeper' and 'a kind of bawd in breeches'.[39] The following day as his biographer, Patrick Geoghegan, puts it 'abandoning the caution which characterized much of his legal career, he delivered one of his most vehement attacks on British misrule in Ireland'.[40] As a legal defence of his client the monologue that followed was both flawed and futile. As polemic it was without equal. Seeking an audience well beyond the confines of a largely hostile court-room, O'Connell used his unrivalled rhetorical powers to bludgeon, dazzle and misdirect. Knowing his client stood virtually no chance of exoneration, O'Connell seized the opportunity to indict a tyrannical British legal and political establishment for the crimes of neglect, bigotry and repression. He commenced with some rhetorically inspired personal abuse directed at Saurin.

> I consented to the adjournment yesterday, gentlemen of the Jury from that impulse of nature which compels us to postpone pain; it is, indeed, painful to me to address you; it is a cheerless, a hopeless task to address you; a task which would require all the animation and interest to be derived from the working of a mind fully fraught with the resentment and disgust created in mine yesterday, by that farrago of helpless absurdity with which Mr. Attorney General regaled you: But I am now not sorry for the delay. Whatever I may have lost in vivacity, I trust I shall compensate for in discretion. That which yesterday excited my anger, now appears to me to be an object of pity; and that which then roused my indignation, now only moves me to *contempt*.
>
> I can now address you with feelings softened, and, I trust, subdued; and I do, from my soul, declare, that I now cherish no other sensations than those which enable me to bestow on the Attorney General, and on his discourse, pure and unmixed compassion. It was a discourse in which you could not discover either order, or method, or eloquence; it contained very little logic, and no poetry at all: violent and virulent, it was a confused and disjointed tissue of bigotry amalgamated with congenial vulgarity. He accused my Client of using Billingsgate, and he accused him of it in language suited exclusively for that meridian; he descended even to the calling of names: he called this young Gentleman a

Malefactor, and a Jacobin, and a Ruffian, Gentlemen of the Jury—he called him Abominable, and Seditious, and Revolutionary, and Infamous, and Ruffian again, Gentlemen of the Jury—he called him a Brothel Keeper, a Pander, a kind of Bawd in breeches, and a Ruffian a third time, Gentlemen of the Jury. I cannot repress my astonishment how Mr. Attorney General could have *preserved* this dialect in its native purity; he has been now for near thirty years in the class of polished society—he has for some years mixed amongst the highest orders in the State; he has had the honor [*sic*] to belong for thirty years to the first profession in the world—to the only profession, with the single exception, perhaps, of the military, to which a high-minded Gentleman could condescend to belong—to the Irish Bar ...

Devoid of taste and of genius, how can he have had memory enough to preserve this original vulgarity—he is, indeed, an object of compassion; and, from my inmost soul, I bestow on him my forgiveness and my bounteous pity. But not for him alone should compassion be felt—recollect, that upon his advice—that with him, as the prime mover and instigator, all those rash, and silly, and irritating measures of the last five years, which have afflicted and distracted this long suffering country, have originated with him. Is there not then some compassion due to the millions whose destinies are made to depend upon his counsel?—Is there no pity to those who, like me, must know, that the liberties of the tenderest pledges of their affections, and of that which is dearer still, of their country, depend upon this man's advice?—Yet, let not pity for us be unmixed—he has afforded the consolations of hope— his harangue has been heard—it will be reported —I trust faithfully reported; and, if it be but read in England, we may venture to hope, that there may remain just so much good sense in England, as to induce the conviction of the folly and the danger of conducting the Government of a brave and long enduring People by the counsels of so tasteless and talentless an adviser ...

O'Connell's oratory, scornful and derisive, lofty and grandiloquent, by all accounts, while not completely extemporised, was largely unscripted. C.M. O'Keeffe maintained that 'there were no traces of pre-arrangement; no high-wrought passages smelling of the lamp and forced in for effect ... He passed from one key to another—from the calm to the vehement, from humour to passion, the auditor hardly knew how; yet the transition always seemed natural'.[41] Never one to wield a rapier when he had a cudgel at his disposal O'Connell continued to pummel the hapless, and by now visibly uncomfortable, attorney general:

> My Lord, upon the Catholic Subject, I commence with one assertion of the Attorney General, which, I trust, I misunderstood. He talked, as I collected him, of the Catholics having imbibed principles of a Seditious, Treasonable and Revolutionary nature! He seemed to me, most distinctly, to charge us with Sedition and with Treason! ... I content myself with proclaiming those charges, whosoever may make them, to be false and base calumnies! It is impossible to refute such charges in the language of dignity or temper. But if any man dares to charge the Catholic Body, or the Catholic Board, or any of the individuals of that Board, with Sedition or Treason, I do here, I shall always in this Court, in the City, in the Field, brand him as an infamous and profligate LIAR! Pardon the phrase, but there is no other suitable to the occasion. But he is a profligate Liar who so asserts, because he must know that the whole tenor of our conduct confutes the assertion. What is it we seek?

O'Connell got no further. Justice Downes attempted to intervene but was testily swatted away by the Counsellor. Chastened by the experience, the judge left O'Connell largely to his own devices thereafter.

CHIEF JUSTICE: What, Mr. O'Connell, can this have to do with the question which the Jury are to try?

MR O'CONNELL: You heard the Attorney-General traduce and calumniate us—you heard him with patience and with temper; listen now to our vindication. I ask, what is it we seek? What is it we incessantly, and, if you please, clamorously petition for? Why, to be allowed to partake of the advantages of the Constitution. We are earnestly anxious to share the benefits of the Constitution—we look to the participation in the Constitution as our greatest political blessing. If we desired to destroy it, would we seek to share in it? If we wished to overturn it, would we exert ourselves through calumny, and in peril, to obtain a portion of its blessings? Strange and inconsistent voice of calumny! You charge us with intemperance, in our exertions for a participation in the Constitution, and you charge us at the same time, almost in the same sentence, with a design to overturn that Constitution. The dupes of your hypocrisy may believe you— but base calumniators, you do not, you cannot believe yourselves.

The Attorney-General, 'this wisest and best of men', as his colleague, the Solicitor-General called him in his presence—the Attorney-General next boasted of his triumphs over Pope and Popery. 'I put down,' said he, boastingly—'I put down' the Catholic Committee—'I will put down, at my good time, the Catholic Board.' This boast is partly historical, partly prophetical. He is wrong in his history—he is quite mistaken in his prophecy. He did not put down the Catholic Committee —we gave up that name … Next, he glorifies himself in his prospect of putting down the Catholic Board. For the present, he indeed tells you, that much as he hates the Papists, it is unnecessary for him to crush our Board, because we injure our own Cause so much. He says, that we are very criminal, but we are so foolish that our folly serves as a compensation for our wickedness—we are very wicked, and very mischievous, but then we are such foolish little criminals that we deserve his indulgence. Thus he tolerates offences because of their being committed sillily; and, indeed, we give him so much pleasure and gratification, by the injury we do our own Cause, that he is spared the superfluous labour of impeding our Petitions by his prosecutions, fines, or imprisonments. He expresses the very idea of the Roman Domitian, of whom some of you, possibly, may have read; he amused his days in torturing men—his evenings he relaxed in the humble cruelty of impaling flies. A Courtier caught a fly for his imperial amusement—'Fool,' said the Emperor, 'fool, to give the trouble of torturing an animal, that was about to burn itself to death in the candle.' Such is the spirit of the Attorney-General's commentary on our Board. Oh rare Attorney-General!—Oh best and wisest of men!!!

But to be serious. Let me pledge myself to you that he imposes on you, when he threatens to crush the Catholic Board. Illegal violence may do it—force may effectuate it; but your hopes and his will be defeated, if he attempts it by any course of law. I am, if not a Lawyer, at least a Barrister. On this subject I ought to know something; and I do not hesitate to contradict the Attorney-General on this point, and to proclaim to you and to the Country that the Catholic Board is perfectly a legal Assembly—that it not only does not violate the law, but that it is entitled to the protection of the law; and, in the very proudest tone of firmness, I hurl *defiance* at the Attorney-General—I defy him to allege a Law, or a Statute, or even a Proclamation, that is violated by the Catholic Board. No,

Gentlemen no, his religious prejudices—if the absence of every charity can be called any thing religious—his religious prejudices really obscure his reason—his bigoted intolerance has fatally darkened his understanding, and he mistakes the plainest acts and misquotes the clearest law, in the ardour and vehemence of his rancour. I disdain his moderation—I scorn his forbearance—I tell him he knows not the law, if he thinks as he says; and, if he thinks so, I tell him to his beard, that he is not honest in not having sooner prosecuted us; and I challenge him to that prosecution.

It is strange—it is melancholy to reflect, on the miserable and mistaken pride that must inflate him to talk as he does of the Catholic Board. The Catholic Board is composed of men—I include not myself—of course, I always except myself—every way his superiors—in birth, in fortune, in talents, in rank. What, is he to talk of the Catholic Board lightly? At their head is the Earl of Fingall, a Nobleman, whose exalted rank stoops beneath the superior station of his virtues—whom, even the venal minions of power must respect. We are engaged in a struggle, through the open channels of the Constitution, for our liberties. The Son of the ancient Earl, whom I have mentioned, cannot, in this his native land, attain any of the honourable distinctions of the State, and yet Mr. Attorney-General knows, that they are open to every son of every bigoted and intemperate stranger that may settle amongst us.—But this system cannot last—he may insult—he may calumniate—he may prosecute, but the Catholic Cause is on its *majestic march*—its progress is rapid and obvious—it is cheered in its advance, and aided by all that

> is dignified and dispassionate, by every thing
> that is patriotic, by all the honour, all the
> integrity of the Empire; and its success is just
> as certain as the return of to-morrow's sun
> and the close of to-morrow's eve.

As if the trenchant onslaught against Saurin had not already fatally prejudiced any slim hope of an acquittal, O'Connell then lowered the boom on the jury itself. He claimed that some of its members had recently signed a 'No Popery' petition, and pointed out that 'you would not have been summoned on this Jury, if you had entertained liberal sentiments'. Surprisingly, Justice Downes made no attempt to stifle what must have appeared to the Bench to have been a gratuitous attack on twelve honest (Unionist) citizens. O'Connell continued:

> ... Oh, Gentlemen, it is not in any lightness of heart that I
> thus address you—it is rather in bitterness and in sorrow;
> you did not expect flattery from me; and my Client was
> little disposed to offer it to you; besides, of what avail
> would it be to flatter, if you came here pre-determined; and
> it is too plain that you are not selected for this Jury from
> any notions of your impartiality. But when I talk to you of
> your oaths and of your religion, I would full fain I could
> impress you with a respect for both the one and the other.
> I, who do not flatter, tell you, that though I do not join
> with you in belief, I have the most unfeigned respect for the
> form of Christian Faith which you profess. Would that its
> substance, not its forms and temporal advantages, were
> deeply impressed on your minds—then should I not
> address you in the cheerless and hopeless despondency that
> crowds on my mind, and drives me to taunt you with the
> air of ridicule ...
>
> ... The Attorney-General defective, in argument, weak
> in his cause—has artfully roused your prejudices at his
> side. I have, on the contrary, met your prejudices boldly.
> If your verdict shall be for me you will be certain that it
> has been produced by nothing but unwilling conviction,
> resulting from sober and satisfied judgment. If your
> verdict be bestowed upon the artifices of the Attorney-
> General, you may happen to be right, but do you not see

the danger of its being produced by an admixture of passion and prejudice with your reason. How difficult is it to separate prejudice from reason, when they run in the same direction. If you be men of conscience then, I call on you to listen to me, that your consciences may be safe, and your reason alone be the guardian of your oath, and the sole monitor of your decision.

By now O'Connell had 'effectively alienated all the sympathy of the judges, jury and prosecutor'.[42] Having duly antagonised the jury, while, in the process, making a valid political point about jury-packing by the Crown, O'Connell then went on to deal with the alleged offence. He pointed out that the libel complained of was neither seditious nor a personal slander on the duke of Richmond. It was not even claimed in the indictment to be false. O'Connell observed that if Magee, rather than being an independent and critical voice, had agreed to be a supporter of government policy 'he might libel certain classes of His Majesty's subjects with impunity—he would get abundance of money, a place and a pension ... I am greatly within bounds when I say that at least £5,000 per annum of the public purse would reach him if he was to alter his tone and abandon his opinions'.[43] He then proceeded to read the offending article and defend its accuracy and fairness, inquiring 'Is it a crime not to admire an Administration? Is it an indictable offence not to admire its occult talents?'

> ... Recollect that the Attorney-General told you, that the Press was the protection of the People against the Government! Good God! Gentlemen, how can it protect the People against the Government, if it be a crime to say of that Government that it has committed errors, displays little talent, and has no striking features? Did the Prosecutor mock you when he talked of the protection the Press afforded to the People? If he did not insult you, by the admission of that upon which he will not allow you to act, let me ask, against what is the Press to protect the People? When do the People want protection? When the Government is engaged in delinquencies, oppression and crimes? It is against these that the People want the protection of the Press.
>
> Now, I put it to your plain sense, whether the Press can afford such protection, if it be punished for treating of these crimes. Still more, can a shadow of protection be

> given by a Press that is not permitted to mention the
> errors, the talents, and the striking features of an
> Administration? Here is a watchman admitted by the
> Attorney-General to bé at his post to warn the People of
> their danger, and the first thing that is done to this watch-
> man is to knock him down and bring him to a dungeon,
> for announcing the danger he is bound to disclose. I agree
> with the Attorney General, the Press is a Protection; but
> it is not in its silence, or in its voice of flattery. It can
> protect only by speaking out when there is danger, or
> error, or want of ability.

O'Connell then dissected the offending article and attempted to validate
the *Evening Post* comparison of Richmond's tenure to that of other oppressive castle administrations. In order to justify the contention that the duke's
predecessors included a number of 'murderers' he went back as far as the
earl of Essex and the 'butchery' by Grey of the Smerwick Garrison in 1580
during the Desmond rebellion. To substantiate the reference to the 'artful
and treacherous Cornwallis' O'Connell characterised the former lord lieutenant as 'the Artificer of the Union'. Cornwallis had secured much
Catholic support for the measure with the promise of Catholic emancipation and had resigned when George III had vetoed further discussion of
such a concession. O'Connell expressed his own satisfaction that the promises of Emancipation made at that time have not been fulfilled. The price
had been too high 'when the Catholic trafficked [*sic*] for his own advantage
upon his Country's miseries, he deserved to be deceived'.

Discussion of the Act of Union allowed O'Connell the opportunity of a
highly effective digression. He was enabled to remind the court of the hostility of both Bushe and Saurin to the passage of the Act through Grattan's
parliament. So virulent was Saurin's opposition that he had been accused of
dangerous radicalism and even Jacobinism by his opponents. 'Citizen'
Saurin had once observed that 'debates might sometimes produce agitations
but that was the price necessarily paid for Liberty'. Such a sentiment was
pure manna from heaven to his current opponent.

> Yes, agitation is, as Mr. Saurin well remarked, the Price
> necessarily paid for Liberty [*said O'Connell, to the
> amusement of the court-room*] we have paid the price,
> Gentlemen, and the honest man refuses to give us
> the goods.

From his speech of the 13th of March, 1800, I select these passages:

Mr. Saurin said, he felt it his duty to the Crown, to the Country, and to his Family, to warn the Minister of the dreadful consequences of persevering in a measure, which, the People of Ireland *almost unanimously disliked.*

And again;

He, for one, would assert the principles of the Glorious Revolution, and boldly declare, in the face of the Nation, that when the Sovereign Power dissolved the compact that existed between the Government and the People, that moment the Right of Resistance accrues. Whether it would be prudent in the People to avail themselves of that right would be another question—But if a Legislative Union were forced on the country, against the will of its Inhabitants, it would be a Nullity, and resistance to it would be a Struggle against Usurpation, and not a resistance against the Law.

May I be permitted just to observe, how much more violent this Agitator of the year 1800 was, than we, poor and timid Agitators of the year 1813. When did we talk of Resistance being a question of Prudence? Shame upon the men who call us intemperate, and yet remember their own violence ... Mr. Saurin, in 1800, preached the holy doctrine of Insurrection, sounded the tocsin of Resistance, and summoned the People of the land to battle against it, as against an *Usurpation.* In 1800 he absolves the Subjects from their allegiance, if the Usurpation, styled the Union, shall be carried—and he, this identical Agitator, in 1813, indicts a man, and calls him a Ruffian, for speaking of the Contrivers of the Union, not as Usurpers, but as artful and treacherous men. Gentlemen, pity the situation in which he has placed himself; and pray do not think of inflicting punishment upon my Client, for his extreme moderation.

... the Attorney General ... insists upon punishing Mr. Magee; first, because he accuses his Administration of 'Errors'—secondly, because he charges them with not being distinguished for 'Talents'—thirdly, because he cannot discover their 'Striking Features'—and, fourthly, because he discusses an 'Abstract Principle'. This is quite intelligible—this is quite tangible. I begin to understand what the Attorney-General means by the Liberty of the Press—it means a prohibition of printing any thing, except praise, respecting *the Errors, the Talents, or the Striking Features*', of any Administration, and of discussing any *Abstract Principles of Government*. Thus the forbidden subjects are Errors, Talents, Striking Features, and Principles. Neither the Theory of the Government nor its Practices are to be discussed—you may, indeed, praise them—you may call the Attorney-General 'the best and wisest of men'—you may call his Lordship the most learned and impartial of all possible Chief Justices—you may, if you have powers of visage sufficient, call the Lord Lieutenant the best of all imaginable Governors. That, Gentlemen, is the boasted Liberty of the Press—the Liberty that exists at Constantinople—the liberty of applying the most fulsome and unfounded flattery, but not one word of censure or reproof. Here is an idol worthy of the veneration of the Attorney-General. Yes; he talked of his veneration for the Liberty of the Press; he also talked of its being a protection to the People against the Government. Protection! not against errors—not against the want of talents, or of striking features—not against the effort of any unjust principle—Protection! against what is it to protect? Did he not mock you?—did not he plainly and palpably delude you, when he talked of the protection of the Press? Yes. To his inconsistencies and contradictions he calls on you to sacrifice your consciences ...

Here I should close the Case—here I should shortly recapitulate my Client's Defence, and leave him to your consideration—but I have been already too tedious, and shall do no more than recall to your recollection the purity, the integrity, the entire disinterestedness of Mr. Magee's motives. If money were his object, he could easily procure himself to be patronized and salaried; but

he prefers to be persecuted and discountenanced by the
Great and Powerful, because they cannot deprive him of
the certain expectation, that his exertions are useful to
his-long-suffering ill-requited Country. He is disinterested, Gentlemen; he is honest; the Attorney General
admitted it, and actually took the trouble of administer-
ing to him advice how to amend his fortune and save his
person. But the advice only made his youthful blood
mantle in that ingenuous countenance, and his reply was
painted in the indignant look, that told the Attorney
General he might offer wealth but he could not bribe;
that he might torture, but he could not terrify! Yes,
Gentlemen, firm in his honesty, and strong in the fervour
of his love of Ireland he fearlessly awaits your verdict,
convinced that even you must respect the man whom you
are called upon to condemn. Look to it, Gentlemen.—
consider, whether an honest, disinterested man shall be
prohibited from discussing public affairs—consider
whether all but flattery is to be silent—whether the discussion of the errors and the capacities of the Ministers
is to be closed forever? Whether we are to be silent as to
the crimes of former periods—the follies of the present,
and the credulity of the future; and, above all, reflect
upon the demand that is made on you to punish the can-
vassing of abstract principles.

Has the Attorney General succeeded? Has he procured
a Jury so fitted to his object, as to be ready to bury in
oblivion every fault and every crime, every error and every
imperfection of public men, past, present and future ... Is
there amongst you any one Friend to Freedom—is there
amongst you one man, who esteems equal and impartial
justice? Who values the People's Rights as the foundation
of private happiness, and who considers life as no boon
without liberty—is there amongst you one Friend to the
Constitution, one man who hates Oppression—if there
be, Mr. Magee appeals to his kindred mind, and confidently expects an acquittal.

There are amongst you men of great Religious Zeal of
much Public Piety. Are you sincere? Do you believe what

you profess? With all this zeal, with all this piety, is there any conscience amongst you—is there any terror of violating your oaths? Be ye hypocrites, or does genuine religion inspire ye? If you be sincere—if you have conscience—if your oaths can controul [sic] your interests, then Mr. MAGEE confidently expects an acquittal. If amongst you there be cherished one ray of pure Religion—if amongst you there glow a single spark of Liberty—if I have alarmed Religion, or roused the spirit of Freedom in one breast amongst you, Mr. Magee is safe, and his Country is served; but if there be none—if you be Slaves and Hypocrites, he will await your Verdict, and despise it.

O'Connell's second implicit attack on the jury clearly indicated that he had no illusions as to the probable verdict. Had he harboured any faint hope when he finished his epic address it would have been extinguished by the direction to the jury of the chief justice, in which Downes offered the opinion that 'the Paper in question was a gross and scandalous Libel, and on which, if they believed the Evidence of the Publication, they were bound to find a Verdict of Guilty against the Defendant'.[44] The jury, no doubt bridling at O'Connell's overt hostility, probably needed little encouragement to find against the Counsellor. 'After a short consultation', they brought in a verdict of guilty. Final sentencing was postponed until November and Magee was committed to Newgate Prison.

O'Connell's outraged harangue, amounting to far more than the mere skilled professional advocacy of an attorney, lasted for four hours. It was more an indictment of the government than it was a defence of his client. This would become an issue for Magee in the months ahead. Astonishingly, despite the tangential relevance to the case of many of his most scathing arguments the Counsellor had been allowed to proceed almost unchecked by the Bench. As Seán O'Faoláin describes it, 'the court seems to have listened open mouthed, aghast, silenced, unable to realize that a cowering Catholic, one of the "scum of the earth" had stalked into their courts and flung defiance in their teeth'.[45] O'Connell's caustic abuse was aimed directly at the Irish legal and administrative *élite*, but it was also intended to find an audience in England, where he hoped the case would be reported. The speech travelled even further afield. It was translated into French and Spanish. However, perhaps the primary target was the browbeaten Catholic population of Ireland. Oliver MacDonagh refers to them as the 'shadowy masses ... the Irish Catholic millions whom he was telling not to crouch, not to admit inferiority, not to fear'.[46] O'Connell was, of course, doing much more than telling the cowed Catholic population not to fear, he was, by risking severe sanctions himself, showing them that it was possible to stand up to the apparently overwhelming power of the executive.

An anonymous letter to O'Connell's Merrion Square house, enclosing a guinea, captured the reaction of one observer to O'Connell's rhetoric. It was to be replicated when accounts of O'Connell's speech were published. The correspondent, who signed himself 'E.B.' wrote, with considerable hyperbole, that 'Your language I found, I shall not say convincing, but dazzling and overpowering—and as the soul of man is by nature darting into the sublime region of eternity, I beheld with ecstasy the fire of your soul darting through your eyes while addressing the suppressors of vice, the bible distributors'. However, despite his admiration for O'Connell's advocacy 'E.B' had no illusions about its likely impact. 'Poor Magee! Alas, poor Yorick!' he concluded.[47]

In the introduction to its transcript of the trial, written by Denys Scully, the *Evening Post* lavished praise on O'Connell.

> We are almost afraid, we said, to trust our feelings, in describing the masterly, silencing, *crushing* speech of this splendid Advocate. He just defended Mr. Magee, as Mr. Magee wished to be defended. No flattering, no parley with the Crown Lawyers, the Jury, or the Court. He knew that the bigotry and beastly abuse of the Attorney General was not to be answered, as a King's Counsel would have endeavoured to do. In an evil hour, Mr. Saurin threw down the gauntlet; it was taken up by Mr. O'CONNELL, and dashed contemptuously in his teeth ...

Scully probably added to the severity of Magee's sentence by excoriating the attorney general who he described as

> flattering himself, that his character, as a Member of the Irish Administration, gave him a *charte* [sic] *blanche* to abuse all his adversaries, and to pour a torrent of virulent vituperation upon the Catholics of Ireland—upon the First Press in Ireland, and, upon the Catholic Board; he fancied that no one had the nerve, the presumption, forsooth, to oppose and to repel his Billingsgate invective.

> Mistaken and infatuated creature! how did you feel when
> Mr. O'CONNELL branded you as a Libeller before the
> Court, a Calumniator in the face of your Country, and,
> to your beard, a Liar.[48]

Saurin's reaction to the verbal barrage to which he was subjected must have been, primarily, one of shock. He made no real attempt to bring O'Connell to heel or to staunch his polemical flow. O'Keeffe, paraphrasing Scully's account of the trial, wrote that 'Even his enemies were moved to pity by his visible agony—the writhings of his frame, the contortions of his countenance, the green and livid hue that alternately succeeded the faint flushings of his quivering cheek'. Robert Peel, who attended throughout, sought to reassure the attorney general 'with kind whispers and soothe him with looks of sympathy'. But Peel's intervention does not appear to have been very effective as 'The sweat trickled down his forehead, his lips were as white as ashes, his jaws elongated, and his mouth unconsciously open'.[49] While bearing in mind that this commentary is an exultant Catholic take on Saurin's discomfiture there can be little doubt that the attorney general found the experience quite humiliating.

An incensed Peel, wrote to Whitworth, the new viceroy, that

> O'Connell spoke for four hours, taking the opportunity
> for uttering a libel even more atrocious than that he was
> proposing to defend, on the Government and the admin-
> istration of justice in Ireland. His abuse of the Attorney
> General was more scurrilous and more vulgar than was
> ever permitted within the walls of a court of justice. He
> insulted the jury, collectively and individually, accused the
> Chief Justice of corruption and prejudice against his
> client, and avowed himself a traitor, if not to Ireland, to
> the British Empire.[50]

Making allowance for the obvious value judgements it was as accurate an assessment as any of what had taken place.

The government press responded to O'Connell's prolonged polemic with equal vituperation. Giffard had already acknowledged, in advance of the case, that 'The Protestants of the metropolis are frightened'. The inappro-priately named *Patriot*[51] owned by the chronic debtor William Corbet and supported almost exclusively by the castle, described O'Connell, colourfully but redundantly as 'a bandy-legged dancing-master'.[52] The *Dublin Journal* characterised him as 'a ruffian'. Amongst Catholics the speech had a profound impact. O'Connell had articulated their grievances with a venom which delighted the country's majority population, as well as liberal Protestants. When the *Evening Post* published a pamphlet with an account of the trial carrying a verbatim report of O'Connell's speech 10,000 copies were sold on the first day,[53] an outcome which went some way towards financially compensating Magee for the fine imposed by the court.

How have O'Connell's biographers assessed his performance in the Magee case? C.M. O'Keeffe, an enthusiastic O'Connellite apologist, writing in 1864, commented rather emotively and with undisguised triumphalism that

> The terror and vexation with which O'Connell's defence of Magee overwhelmed Saurin was not confined to that official—it embraced at once the whole of the Irish Orangemen, who shuddered and turned pale at the courage with which O'Connell bearded the insolence of office ... All that class of men who saw with satisfaction the bridges of Dublin, in 1798, garnished with trunkless heads, and the mangled backs of the lacerated 'Papists' bleeding under the lash, apprehensive of retribution for their cruelties, trembled at this outburst of patriotic eloquence, like the white-faced culprit before the black-capped judge.[54]

In *The king of the beggars*, Seán O'Faoláin, while acknowledging that the speech was 'shamelessly irrelevant' says of 'The Counsellor' that 'He fought it with such wild courage that it not only marked him out definitely as the national leader, but defined the attitude of his party, smashed the aristocratic junta, and flung the entire movement into the balance between utter ruin and ultimate success'.[55] Patrick Geoghegan is more measured in his judgement and manages to see the trial from John Magee's point of view. He notes that 'The Magee trials were probably the only time that O'Connell acted as a politician in the courtroom rather than as a lawyer'.[56]

Oliver MacDonagh, while acknowledging that the contemporary wisdom was that O'Connell had sacrificed his client for his own ends, found this judgement 'superficial'. He insists that Magee's fate was sealed 'whatever conventional line of defence was chosen' and suggests that O'Connell was seeking to secure a hung jury. He adds, however, that

Magee's fate was a secondary consideration. O'Connell used the trial first and foremost to assert, in a more public and telling form than had ever been available to him before, that Catholics were fully the equals, rank for rank, of their Protestant counterparts ... This address, magnificently structured and endlessly fertile in invention and allusion, was probably O'Connell's master forensic display. It also marked a new stage of Catholic pretension, even arrogance.[57]

In the *Dublin Evening Post* pamphlet, which exacerbated Magee's already parlous situation, Denys Scully addressed those critics who alleged that O'Connell was negligent in his representation of his client:

With regard to the mode in which Mr. Magee has been defended, he has only to reiterate the assurance he has so repeatedly expressed in his Paper, that the line of defence taken for him, that the topics upon which Mr. O'Connell has insisted, are precisely those he was instructed to adopt. Mr. Magee has identified himself with the Country; and the defence upon which he stood was that which would not only include his own justification, but stand as an argument in favour of this Persecuted Land. For what he may suffer in person, for the ordeal through which he may be destined to pass, he is fully prepared.[58]

If indeed that was Magee's position at the time of the publication of the pamphlet and before his sentencing in November, 1813, he was to change his tune radically.

O'Connell's *ex post facto* justification for his highly politicised and personalised conduct of the defence was that, with a partisan Bench and a packed jury-box Magee's conviction was inevitable. However, in choosing to ridicule and castigate the administration in such a public fashion O'Connell knowingly aggravated the libel for his own political ends and, arguably, for his own personal aggrandisement. Any sight of the travails of Magee, who would go to jail for the greater glory of O'Connell and the cause of Catholic relief, was lost in the gladiatorial arena. However, O'Connell also invited the severest repercussions on his own head. His well-rehearsed, carefully contrived, but nonetheless sincere contempt for the establishment forces arrayed against him could have cost him dearly.

The failure of the Bench to protect Saurin or the jury from O'Connell's invective is, at times, bewildering. His apparent professional 'death-wish', indicated by the level of disrespect he displayed towards the judiciary, is only explicable in a man fully prepared to share the inevitable fate of his client. O'Connell would not have been unique amongst Irish political leaders were he to have believed that his reputation might be enhanced by a sojourn in jail for defying the castle establishment. However, according to his biographer, William Fagan, who observed him in action frequently, O'Connell had a habit of treating judges as he found them. 'If they were haughty, he was proud. If they were malevolent, he was cuttingly sarcastic ... He could not be awed'.[59] He would rarely have encountered a court more worthy of disparagement. The contumely he heaped on judge, jury and advocates might have been as much a function of personal animus as it was of political exigency.

THE INCARCERATION OF JOHN MAGEE

Magee, chastened but not bowed by the verdict, was back before the courts within a short period. The *Dublin Evening Post*, in August 1813, published a series of resolutions passed in Kilkenny, which were critical of the verdict in the original trial. Peel, who had, in the interim, managed to dissuade the Prince Regent from suing Magee for libel,[60] struck again. This time his target was not just Magee and his irritating newspaper but the Catholic Board itself. Peel wanted, through the libel prosecution, to reach out and prosecute the framers of the resolutions themselves. But, as in the case of the Richmond libels, Magee refused to identify the men responsible. They were Denys Scully, author of the resolutions, and chairman of the meeting, Major George Bryan, MP for Kilkenny and a member of the Catholic Board who refused to make himself answerable for the resolutions. Once again Magee took the full force of the Crown campaign on his own head.

The silencing of the *Post* was by now a very personal issue as far as Peel was concerned. His animosity towards the newspaper is evident in his correspondence. In one dispatch, written in 1813, he wrote,

> most of the dissatisfaction in this country arises from the
> immense circulation of that nefarious newspaper the

> *Dublin Evening Post.* It is sent gratuitously into many
> parts of the country, and read by those who can read, to
> those who cannot; and as it is written with a certain
> degree of ability, and a style which suits the taste of those
> upon whom it is intended to work, it does, no doubt,
> great mischief.[61]

Peel sought to clip the paper's wings by taking a number of measures against it, in tandem with the libel actions. Denial of access to the all-important 'expresses', the policy of previous chief secretaries, continued and was augmented by other petty but effective moves.

Peel was also hopeful that the ongoing Magee case might be used to trip up O'Connell. Anticipating the sentence Peel wrote, in November, to his friend, Otway Cuffe, earl of Desart 'I hope the Chief Justice will not allow the court to be again insulted and made the vehicle for treason, but that he will interrupt O'Connell's harangue by committing him to Newgate for contempt'.[62]

The young chief secretary would ensure, with the help of a co-operative judiciary that Magee's continued ability to make mischief would be permanently curtailed. The 'Kilkenny resolutions' trial resulted in a fine of £1,000 and six months being added to Magee's sentence for the Richmond libel. As a consequence, stewardship of the *Post* passed to his brother, James.

On 27 November 1813 Magee was back before Justice Downes, assisted by Justices Osborne and Day, for final sentencing in the Richmond libel case. Facing O'Connell again, Saurin was not about to endure further mortification or embarrassment at the hands of the Kerry junior counsel. He went on the offensive from the outset. Referring back to O'Connell's conduct during the original trial, he complained bitterly and belatedly that 'such an outrage on public decency had not occurred in the memory of man'.[63] He then added a professional slur to personal pique by insisting that O'Connell had abetted Magee's criminality during the trial by aggravating the libel.

Almost languidly, O'Connell rose to reclaim his professional honour. 'I am delighted,' he began sarcastically, 'at the prudence of the Attorney-General in having made that foul assault on me here, and not elsewhere, because my profound respect for the bench overcomes now those feelings that, elsewhere, would lead me to do what I should regret—to break the peace by chastising him.' It took a short time for the import of O'Connell's remarks to sink in. He was clearly suggesting that if Saurin had made his accusation outside of a King's Bench Court he would have horsewhipped him, which would have led, inevitably, to a duel.

Justice Day, not normally the most perspicacious of judges, was first to intervene. 'Chastising! The Attorney General! If a criminal information were applied for on that word we should be bound to grant it.' The famous advocate, John Philpot Curran, had once said of Day that his attempts to understand an even vaguely complex point of law 'reminded him of nothing so much as the attempt to open an oyster with a rolling pin'.[64] But O'Connell's renewed affront to Saurin could neither be misunderstood nor ignored. A splenetic row followed during which O'Connell stood his ground and refused to continue until the imputation that he was an accessory in Magee's criminality was withdrawn. Eventually Saurin was forced to back down.

Having secured a psychological advantage over his opponent O'Connell renewed his abuse of the attorney general. However, retaining an element of caution he did so obliquely and cleverly 'under a thinly veiled vision of the future'.[65] He prefaced his remarks with the disclaimer that he had no complaint to make of the current Bench or Crown prosecutors. But he then went on to invoke a vision of a tyrannical future. 'At such a period it will not be difficult to find a suitable Attorney-General—some creature, narrow-minded, mean, calumnious, of inveterate bigotry and dastard disposition—who will prosecute with virulence and malignity and delight in punishment.'[66] It was clear to everyone in the court that the future was now and that O'Connell was, yet again, insulting Saurin to his face.

He concluded with a further statement of defiance of the attorney general. 'I never will make him any concessions. I do now, as I did then, repel every imputation. I do now, as I did then, despise and treat with perfect contempt every false calumny that malignity could invent, or dastard atrocity utter whilst it considered itself in safety.'[67]

Magee had heard enough. He had already spent four months in jail and was not prepared to have his barrister's spleen condemn him to an increased sentence. He instructed Thomas Wallace, another member of his counsel, to take charge. Wallace, in effect, was called upon to disown O'Connell. Referring to 'the sins and crimes of counsel', he suggested to the court that lead counsel and not the defendant should be held liable for any insults to the attorney general. O'Connell was understandably livid and denied that he had intended to cause offence. In the event, Wallace's intervention had little if any effect. Magee was fined £500 and sentenced to two years in prison.

O'Connell's behaviour drew the ire of the redoubtable 'Hunting Cap'. A fortnight after his tussle with Saurin, Maurice O'Connell wrote to his nephew from Kerry asking that 'you will not suffer yourself to be hurried by hate or violence of passions to use any language unbecoming the calm and intelligent barrister or the judicious and well-bred gentleman, or that may expose you to the reprehension ... of the court'.[68] More than a century later Seán O'Faoláin passed critical judgement on the performance of O'Connell in the Magee case. 'Possibly some will turn from it also in disgust, for there is truly in all this a certain amount of the "bandy-legged dancing-master", the cheap mountebank'. Accusing his subject of 'secretly trying to seize absolute power and push everybody else out of his way'. O'Faoláin contrasts O'Connell's conduct and rhetoric unfavourably with that of Robert Emmet, the Sheares brothers and William Smith O'Brien, before adding 'Everybody, indeed, who regards gracious living, nobility in thought and word and behaviour, must read this demagogue with a curl of distaste ... O'Connell did a great deal to kill gentle manners in Ireland, to vulgarise and cheapen us'. O'Faoláin, however, acknowledged the Counsellor's strategy was justified by pointing out that 'The trouble with gentle manners is that they become the "justification" of injustice'.[69]

In 1814 James Magee was brought before the court for publishing a speech of O'Connell in which the latter had maintained that Catholics received insufficient protection from ubiquitous Orange violence. The *Post*, not unreasonably at this point, waved a white flag. Magee's editor, F.W. Conway, told the court that he had been advised by his proprietor to modify the anti-government tone of the paper. Aggrieved at having to bear the brunt of the administration's gall and, angry at O'Connell for having aggravated the libels in the 'duke of Richmond' lawsuit the Magees had decided that enough was enough. If O'Connell was prepared to sacrifice the liberty of John Magee in exchange for a public platform for his cause, and if a prominent Catholic Board member was not prepared to accept some responsibility for the 'Kilkenny' libel the Magee family was not content to continue lending the support of the *Dublin Evening Post* to the Catholic cause. John Magee's sense of grievance would be more credible had he himself not further provoked the administration in his paper in advance of the 'Richmond' libel case and published the best-selling account of the trial before his unsuccessful appeal in November 1813.

The *Post* continued to represent itself as independent, but thereafter 'the Catholic party regarded it as a Castle newspaper'.[70] It was publicly critical of Bryan and O'Connell for their part in John Magee's imprisonment. Little by little the petty restrictions imposed on the journal were lifted by Peel. The £1,000 'Kilkenny' fine was remitted on guarantees of future good behaviour. By 1818 John Magee was in receipt of annual payments from Dublin Castle. In his survey of the Irish press, Brian Inglis noted that 'The *Evening Post* did not take as sycophantic a line as the *Dublin Journal* ... it continued to follow a moderate and fairly conciliatory policy. But it never regained the influence it had wielded when Peel became Chief Secretary'.[71] The Catholic cause suffered as a result. No editor was courageous enough to take on the castle establishment in quite the consistent manner that Magee had done [72] given the treatment that had been meted out to him. In that sense at least the perfumed youth with thin shoes had prevailed over the pugnacious advocate.

Not unlike another future Tory prime minister, and long-serving Irish chief secretary, Arthur Balfour, Peel, during his reign in Dublin Castle, had the resourcefulness, commitment and ruthlessness to achieve more or less what he wanted. In 1814 the Catholic Board, on foot of government proclamation, was dissolved. The imminent defeat of Napoleon had eliminated any need on the part of the British government to mollify Irish Catholics. For the remainder of Peel's tenure, the struggle for emancipation, while it continued, did so with less intensity. The mutual antipathy that had developed between Peel and O'Connell from the outset of the former's tenure led to the threat of a duel between the two. All of which makes it richly ironic that it was a Tory administration with a rebellious duke of Wellington, as prime minister, and a reluctant Peel as home secretary, that was forced to convince a recalcitrant King George IV to concede Catholic Emancipation in 1829 in the wake of Daniel O'Connell's victory in the 1828 Clare election.

.3.

THE STATE TRIALS
OF 1844

Criminal justice once fished with a hook, she now fishes with a net.[1]

(*The Quarterly Review*)

I am glad I am in prison. There wanted but this to my career. I have laboured for Ireland—refused office, honour, and emolument for Ireland—there was just one thing wanted—that I should be in jail for Ireland. This has now been added to the rest, thanks to our enemies, and I cordially rejoice at it.[2]

(Daniel O'Connell on his stay in Richmond Prison)

The punishment was clearly going to be in inverse proportion to the supposed gravity of the conspirators' crime. Daniel O'Connell and his fellow prisoners had been allowed to choose their own place of incarceration. They had opted for Richmond Bridewell, a prison mainly used to accommodate debtors, on Dublin's South Circular Road. It was a wise choice. Appointment to Richmond's board of superintendents was in the gift of Dublin Corporation, now dominated by the Liberator's supporters. The jail itself was convenient to the city; the quarters were relatively spacious and bright. Not that any of the prisoners would be sharing accommodation with members of the indebted classes. O'Connell and his fellow prisoners would serve their sentences in the comfort of the homes of the governor and deputy governor. In time the entire episode would become known as 'the Richmond picnic'.[3] Hailed by his Roman Catholic fellow countryman as a martyr for the nationalist cause, O'Connell's Richmond experience was, in truth, 'martyrdom de luxe'.[4] Though the detainees were denied their freedom, one of them wrote that 'the imprisonment proved as little unpleasant as a holiday in a country house'.[5]

O'Connell, who was 69 years old at the time of his first (and to many of his enemies, belated) sojourn in jail, was sentenced on 30 May 1844. His fellow accused, John, his son; Thomas Matthew Ray, the 44-year-old secretary of the Repeal Association; Thomas Steele, nicknamed the 'Head Pacificator'; Fr Thomas Tierney, a Roman Catholic priest of Clontibret in Co. Monaghan;[6] and three national newspaper editors, Charles Gavan Duffy of the *Nation*; John Gray of the *Freeman's Journal* and Richard Barrett of the *Pilot*; had also been found guilty of seditious conspiracy.

Their arrival at the Bridewell had been like a religious procession. Flanked by a large force of mounted police the carriages of the 'Repeal martyrs' had been surrounded and followed by thousands of supporters. According to one newspaper account 'O'Connell entered the prison with as buoyant a step as if he were treading the heath, and breathing the air of his wild, native mountains'.[7] Given that he and his son would enjoy the comforts of the Governor's house for the duration of their stay his buoyancy was hardly misplaced.

After the attentions of the highly deferential Governor Purdon, O'Connell was greeted by his daughters, Ellen and Betsey, and Mary, the wife of his son, John. One or other of them would remain in attendance until both men were released. O'Connell's first remark to his children was rather melodramatic: 'Thank God, I am in jail for Ireland'.[8] The other prisoners settled into the house of the deputy governor and awaited the arrival of their wives to take up residence.

As well as their spouses, the prisoners were also allowed their own servants. Food was imported from eating-houses outside the walls of the prison or, more often than not, provided by hundreds of well-wishers. Each prisoner had his own bedroom and sitting-room. Meals were taken communally and shared with distinguished visitors and fervent supporters. The table, in the governor's house, was rarely set for fewer than 30 people and the menu was seldom less than sumptuous. Charles Gavan Duffy, the youngest of the prisoners, recalled that:

> from the first day presents of venison, game, fish, fruit, and the like began to arrive; and after a little they found themselves established in a pleasant country house, situated in the midst of extensive grounds, bright with fair women and the gambols of children, and furnished with abundant means either for study or amusement.[9]

Initially, however, both of the latter were in short supply, not on account of any limitations placed on the prisoners by the authorities but due to their own huge popularity. The *Freeman's Journal* (which continued to be edited from prison by John Gray) reported that the desire on the part of the citizenry to gain access to the prisoners was insatiable. Every day large crowds would gather at the penitentiary gates seeking admission to visit one or other of the prisoners. The *Freeman* reporter wrote that 'We saw gentlemen of the highest respectability content to take their places on the exterior of the crowd, and wait while numerous batches were admitted, until gradually they themselves approached the gate, and obtained the coveted entrance'.[10]

O'Connell quickly put an end to this and the nationalist newspapers made it known that entrance to the prison was restricted (by the prisoners) to the hours of midday to 4.00 p.m. and that no casual visitors would be admitted on Mondays or Wednesdays. Left to their own devices the prisoners went about their business. O'Connell proposed to write his 'Life and times' and 'had a collection of the necessary books of reference set on shelves round his study'. Furthermore, the newspaper editors continued to edit and 'some of the other prisoners did a little amateur journalism'. [11] Both John O'Connell and Thomas Ray wrote pieces for the *Nation*.

For debtors, warders, agitators and editors it was business as usual.

FROM LIBERATOR TO REPEALER: 1830-44

In 1829 Daniel O'Connell and the first coherent, wholly political, mass movement in Irish history, the Catholic Association, had, courtesy of The Liberator's election victory in Clare the previous year, forced the hand of the Conservative government led by Wellington and Robert Peel. Roman Catholics, previously barred from taking seats in parliament, were admitted to the House of Commons when the repugnant Oath of Allegiance was revised. The Catholic Relief Act of 1829 also removed a number of the residual social, political and economic restrictions on Catholics in Britain and Ireland. For O'Connell, as his biographer Oliver MacDonagh explains, 'the next fifteen years saw the confirmation, exercise, and decline of his mastery in Ireland'.[12]

The early years of the post-Emancipation period were, for O'Connell, dominated by the violent agrarian opposition to the payment of levies to the established church that became known as the Tithe War, and the struggle for the democratisation of British politics that culminated in the Reform Act of 1832. The elections of that year returned a caucus of around 40 Irish MPs allied to O'Connell and committed to repeal of the Act of Union. The violent activities of Ribbon organisations and the demands emanating from the newly minted Repealers led King William in his speech to the parliament in 1833 to seek 'such additional powers as might be found necessary in Ireland for controlling and punishing the disturbers of the public peace and for preserving and strengthening the Legislative Union between the two countries'.[13] The following year the House of Commons rejected O'Connell's motion for repeal by 523–38.

This defeat, although embarrassing for O'Connell, had the effect of allowing him to 'park' the issue of the restoration of an Irish parliament and to form a working alliance with the governing Whigs, which held out the promise of improving social and economic conditions in Ireland. The so-called 'Lichfield House compact' of 1835 cemented that alliance and the five-year term of Thomas Drummond as under secretary brought considerable benefits to the country and to its overwhelming Roman Catholic majority. Drummond and the Whigs, driven on by O'Connell, challenged the Protestant Ascendancy in their appointments to the judiciary, magistracy and constabulary. The inauguration of the Poor Law system, including the elective Poor Law Guardians, transformed Irish local government by diverting responsibility for issues like public health, poverty and sanitation away from the hierarchical grand jury system dominated by the landed gentry.

The return to power of the Tories led by O'Connell's intractable foe, Sir Robert Peel, in 1841, put an end to the era of modest co-operation between a, largely, functioning and cohesive Irish Party and the incumbent government. The Tories refusal to treat seriously the new democratic populism of the Repeal Association forced O'Connell to shift his attention from Westminster and to concentrate on domestic agitation in the years that followed. The return of only eighteen Repeal MPs in 1841 had helped persuade O'Connell to make a virtue of necessity. The pre-eminence of Repeal activity, assisting as it did, the diminution of politically inspired violence in rural Ireland, also served to divert the Tory focus away from the country and allow O'Connell to build up a movement which the Peel administration would be forced to take seriously.

The passage, in 1840, of the Municipal Corporation Act, which broadened the franchise in the municipalities, led to the eclipse of the ruling Tory/Unionist element on Dublin Corporation. In the same year that the return to power of Peel closed off opportunities at Westminster, O'Connell was elected Mayor of Dublin, becoming the first Catholic to hold the office since the seventeenth century. In 1843 the new political reality on Dublin Corporation was underscored when, after a three-day debate, a motion in favour of Repeal of the Act of Union was carried by 41–15. It was the first symbolic act in a year that O'Connell had already designated as 'Repeal year'.

The Repeal Association, like later nationalist mass movements, also took upon itself some elements of a parallel administration. It was organised along quasi-military lines with wardens and inspectors responsible for activities at grass-roots level. Its internal disciplinary procedures brought into being a policing and judicial structure, which gave it something of the feel of a 'government in waiting'. According to Oliver MacDonagh 'Repeal police and a Repeal arbitration system for land disputes pointed in the direction of alternative government from below and the supersession, in part at least, of the official agencies of law and order'.[14] These aspects of the movement were to be thrown back at the defendants in the state trials as reinforcement of the charges of conspiracy to subvert the Union.

Where the Repeal movement was also qualitatively different to the Emancipation campaign was in having the support of a weekly newspaper, the *Nation*. Founded by Thomas Davis, John Blake Dillon and Charles Gavan Duffy, it was part-newspaper, part cultural pamphlet. Initially unswerving in its support of O'Connell, though the 'Young Ireland' cohort at the heart of the journal had significant differences with his brand of nationalism, it offered an urban, middle class, intellectual and cultural contrast to O'Connell's rural populism, increasing absolutism and blatant demagoguery. It also injected an additional element vital to the credibility of a movement led by a sexagenarian, that of youthful energy. The newspaper also became the fulcrum of a politico-cultural movement within a movement, Young Ireland. Its numbers would later be augmented by, among others, the militant John Mitchel and the aristocratic MP, William Smith O'Brien, who was a late convert to the Repeal cause.

In 1842, a politically revitalised O'Connell, declared that 1843 would be 'the Great Repeal year'.[15] For the man himself it was to be his 'Indian summer, his final blaze'. Reinforcing the sense of the Repeal movement as an alternative centre of power was O'Connell's stated aim of enrolling 3 million members by the middle of 1843 and having those members select a Council of Three Hundred which would meet in Dublin. MacDonagh asserts 'Clearly, O'Connell was promising the unilateral establishment of a virtual parliament'.[16] The fact that the council was to meet 'spontaneously' as guests of O'Connell and was to be chosen by the nebulous process of 'expressions of confidence' rather than votes, was a purely legalistic construct designed to keep on the correct side of the law. The prospect was greeted by opponents of Repeal as a brazen and defiant statement of intent by O'Connell.

The 'Repeal year' was characterised by a series of extraordinary public demonstrations which the censorious *Times* dubbed 'monster meetings'. The appellation stuck. It can hardly have been unwelcome, despite the source. Forty meetings (O'Connell himself spoke at thirty-one), covering almost every county in Ireland, were attended by millions. Even the decidedly hostile *Times* estimated the attendance at the 'Lady Day' meeting held at Tara on 15 August, at 1 million people, though this is almost certainly an overestimate. Despite the massive attendances at these events they were well marshalled and disciplined. Copies of the key-note speeches were issued beforehand to selected readers for distribution amongst the crowd. A relay system ensured that the crowd furthest removed from the platform was still able to 'hear' what was being said by O'Connell, Steele and others.[17]

Most meetings (they averaged two a week) were held on Sundays or holy days of obligation, and as they were established on the political landscape, they became more festive and elaborate. Groups travelled to the venues from a radius of between 30 to 60 miles. Some arrived up to two days before the speakers. Greenery, in the form of ceremonial banners or boughs, was pervasive. Large delegations were often accompanied by bands. The huge crowds would be marshalled by Repeal Association wardens often wearing hats inscribed with the legend 'O'Connell's Police'. The sway of O'Connell himself and the increasing influence of the Temperance Movement of Fr Theobald Mathew, helped to ensure sobriety. Masses were said at numerous altars on the sites of the meetings. The affairs were models of organisation, crowd control and, when the speeches started, emotional manipulation. 'What impressed—and alarmed—the opponents of the movement was the absence of disorder and the virtually mechanical obedience of so immense and diverse a body.'[18] However, of equal concern to the castle was the support O'Connell garnered from among the burgeoning Catholic middle class, the Roman Catholic hierarchy and priesthood.

In his speeches to the enthusiastic masses O'Connell, ever the crowd-pleaser, tailored his oratory to the occasion, as the novelist and historian Thomas Keneally suggests, it was 'the uttering of violent metaphor a prayer for legislative equity'.[19] The prevailing narrative was a litany of victimhood and a rhetoric of defiance. There were frequent invocations of Ireland's unhappy past and unsatisfactory experience under the Union. His mesmerising hyperbole whipped up the crowd into a nationalistic frenzy but the truth was that O'Connell required only the show of strength implicit in the attendance of hundreds of thousands of devotees of Repeal. The optics were more important than the verbal excoriation of the Peelite administration in Dublin Castle. The message to the authorities from the activation of such vast popular support was *'après moi le déluge'*. The colourful sentiments expressed, though incidental to the main strategy of the Repeal Association at the time, were sufficiently belligerent to provide the basis of the administration's case against the leaders of the Repeal Association and their amanuenses in the nationalist press. Government note-takers diligently captured the speeches from the public platforms while the *Freeman's Journal*, the *Nation* and the *Pilot* as well as the splenetic anti-Repeal press, recorded the sentiments expressed at the meetings and at the banquets that followed.

O'Connell, in order to sustain the impetus of the movement, adroitly left implicit the assumption that, in the absence of Repeal, a more extreme form of activism might be required. At Trim, Co. Meath, on 16 March, he remarked to those attending a celebratory dinner:

> when I stand in your presence, men of Meath, and ask you are you slaves, and will you be content to be slaves, I join in your response, and say to myself, I shall be either in my grave or a freeman ... A man might expect coercion acts, and tithe bills, insulting reform measures, and restricted franchise bills—there is no bill in the catalogue of oppressions that you might not expect; but I would walk to Drogheda and back again to see the man who is blockhead enough to expect any thing except injustice from an English parliament towards Ireland.[20]

At Mullaghmast, Co. Kildare, on 1 October (where he was presented with a 'crown' in a gesture much commented upon in the conspiracy trial), he told the crowd:

> Take it from me, that the union is void. I admit that it has the force of law, because it is supported by the policeman's truncheon, the soldier's bayonet, and the horseman's sword; because it is supported by the courts of law, and those who have power to adjudicate. But I say solemnly it is not supported by constitutional right. The union, therefore, in my thorough conviction, is totally void. I have physical force enough about me today to achieve any-thing, but you know full well it is not my plan. I won't risk one of you—I could not afford to lose any of you. I

˙will protect you all, and I will obtain for you all the
Repeal of the Union.[21]

In his most vehement denunciation of the Union, at Mallow, Co. Cork,
on 11 June, O'Connell overstepped the mark, by suggesting that some form
of martyrdom might be required to force the hand of the British government. The context for what became known as the 'Mallow Defiance' was
the dismissal of a number of prominent Repealers, including O'Connell
and his son John, from the magistracy. While O'Connell may have been
carried away by his own rhetorical exuberance he made certain before the
speech—made at a post-rally banquet—that reporters were aware that his
remarks would be of major significance. He announced:

> I think I perceive a fixed disposition on the part of some
> of our Saxon traducers to put us to the test. The efforts
> already made by them have been most abortive and
> ridiculous. In the midst of peace and tranquility they
> are covering over our land with troops ... Are we to be
> called Slaves? Are we to be trampled under foot? Oh!
> they never shall trample me at least. I was wrong. They
> may trample me under foot; I say they may trample me,
> but it will be my dead body they will trample on, not
> the living man, They have taken one step of coercion,
> and may I not ask what is to prevent them from taking
> another?[22]

Less than two weeks later he executed an about face, withdrawing his
belligerent assertions: 'I am not determined to die for Ireland,' he told his
listeners, 'I would rather live for her (cheering) for one living Repealer is
worth a churchyard full of dead ones.'[23] But, as Duffy observed, 'The language of the Mallow Defiance placed O'Connell and the Government
under obligations which neither could evade with impunity'.[24]

It took some time for Peel to respond to the emergent and activist consensus amongst the members of the 'Catholic nation'. This was despite
urgent appeals from the lord lieutenant, Lord de Grey, for legislation to
ban the 'monster' meetings. Peel had a dilemma. The nationalist agitation
in Ireland mirrored a similar campaign against the Corn Laws, being led,
in England, by the radicals Richard Cobden and John Bright. To ban the
Irish assemblies would invite calls for similar repressive action against the
Anti-Corn Law League. However, the threat of an 'alternative' assembly in

Dublin was a bridge too far. Despite O'Connell's evasiveness on the timing of the initial meeting of the Council of Three Hundred, the government was determined that it would never convene. A pretext was required to arrest the progress of the movement that seemed to be advancing inexorably towards such a logical and unacceptable conclusion. This was provided in notices for a monster meeting at Clontarf in early October that made references to the 'Repeal cavalry'. O'Connell's repudiation of the 'military' terminology of the posters came too late. The meeting was banned and Dublin was reinforced militarily to deal with any opposition to the injunction. The language of the official proclamation, issued by the lord lieutenant and the privy council, foreshadowed the indictment of the Repeal leadership that was to follow.

> Now we, the *Lord Lieutenant*, by and with the advice of Her Majesty's Privy Council, being satisfied that the said intended Meeting so proposed to be held at or near *Clontarf*, as aforesaid, can only tend to serve the Ends of Factions and Seditious Persons, and to the violation of the Public Peace, *do* hereby strictly Caution and Forewarn all Persons whatsoever, that they do abstain from Attendance at the said Meeting: and *we* do hereby give Notice, that if, in defiance of this Our Proclamation, the said Meeting shall take place, all Persons attending the same shall be proceeded against according to Law.[25]

O'Connell reluctantly acceded to the, extremely belated, proclamation of the meeting. The Repeal Association displayed its efficiency by ensuring that word of the cancellation spread fast enough to head off any potential confrontation with Crown forces. Hearing of the decision to cancel the meeting (arrived at unanimously by the Executive Committee of the Repeal Association) Fr James Tyrrell of Lusk, Co. Dublin, left his bed and spent a dreary night ensuring that his parishioners would not make the journey to Clontarf the next day. For his pains, Tyrrell would be indicted for conspiracy along with O'Connell. His exertions on a cold October night may have contributed to his early demise. He was dead before the case finally came to trial. Another of the accused, Thomas Steele, travelled to Clontarf and personally ensured that none of those who had not been informed in time were allowed to loiter at the venue and provoke a military response.

THE STATE TRIALS:
JANUARY–FEBRUARY 1844

There is a myth that the proscription of the Clontarf 'monster' meeting, spelled the immediate end of the Repeal agitation. This was not the case. It simply heralded a new, more reactive, phase in the campaign. Nevertheless, according to R.F. Foster, 'O'Connell's image was badly dented among a public nurtured on extremist rhetoric'.[26] The received wisdom is that the 'Young Ireland' element of the Repeal Association, disgusted at the pusillanimity of O'Connell, split irrevocably from the larger movement and began their plans for the rebellion which, abortively, took place in 1848. Retrospective assessments like that by Charles Gavan Duffy, half a century later, that the Clontarf decision 'deprived the movement in a moment of half its dignity and all its terror'[27] tend to reinforce that notion. In fact most of the Young Ireland bloc, insofar as it was already an identifiable faction in 1843, approved of the cancellation of the Clontarf meeting. Their real and fundamental differences with O'Connell (based on their uncompromising, non-sectarian separatism) would emerge publicly in the wake, not so much of the Clontarf decision, but of O'Connell's manoeuvring after the state trials.

Four days after the proclamation that ended the heady phase of mass participation in the Repeal campaign the government swooped. O'Connell and his associates were charged with seditious conspiracy. The complex indictment (over 100 yards long in one of its printed forms) followed in November and was brought to the Dublin grand jury for consideration. The attorney general, T.B.C. Smith, pressed for an early trial. The defence, citing the 57 pages of charges that had to be answered, sought delay. Eventually the trial was postponed, not to allow the defence sufficient time to prepare its case, but rather because of the need to revise the jury-lists for the city of Dublin, where the trial was to take place.

The Crown chose to have the case heard by a special jury. In mid-century places on special juries were confined to those citizens of exceptionally high status and income. Up to 11,000 householders were entitled, on the basis of their property valuations, to inclusion on the ordinary jury-list, in November 1843. But there were fewer than 400 names on the special jury-list of whom 10% were Catholics. The intention of the castle administration in appointing a special jury to hear the evidence in the state trial was transparently obvious. A largely Protestant jury was likely to be more malleable. However, the official responsible for the compilation of the lists, the recorder, Frederick Shaw, MP for Dublin University, informed the city sheriff that the special jury-list required extensive revision. Although the sheriff, an official appointed by the previous, Unionist dominated, corporation, would have preferred to proceed on the basis of the old list it was thought wiser, for political reasons, not to do so. 'But the officials of the Sheriff's office, who had stuffed panels and packed juries for a life-time,' according to Duffy, 'were not easily baffled.'[28]

The revision, which caused the postponement of the start of the trial to 15 January 1844, threw up a total of 717 possible jurors. The procedure was that 48 of those names were to be drawn out by ballot. All jurors thus empanelled were obliged to attend the first sitting of the Queen's Bench Court. The Crown and defence teams could each object to twelve jurors and the final jury would be selected from the remainder. However, mysteriously, 60 names were omitted from the new list. William Ford, solicitor for the defendants, protested against the use of such a 'mutilated' panel. He alleged that there had been 'an infamous tampering with the list' and that 'the names of many of the best known Catholic gentlemen in the city had been illegally suppressed'.[29] The sheriff (who had refused a copy of the original list to the accused) insisted that there had been no collusion or conspiracy to exclude Catholics and that the 60 names had simply been mislaid and that a page must have been accidentally 'dropped' from the list. An investigation by John O'Connell suggested that this was highly unlikely to have been the case and that, 'the packing was planned and well worked out to the end; regardless alike of truth and shame'.[30]

It can be argued that the loss of 60 names from a list of over 700 was of no great significance. However, this was subsequently found to be of major import by the law lords. Half of the sixty names were those of potential Catholic special jurors. Given the under-representation of Catholics on the special jury-list to begin with the loss of thirty names was of major consequence to the traversers (so-called because they had 'traversed' the indictment). Only 11 Catholics were included among the 48 drawn by ballot to be empanelled. The Crown solicitor, William Kemmis, with twelve peremptory challenges in his arsenal, set about disposing of all of them by arbitrary challenge before the jury was sworn. As he did so, one of the defence attorneys, John Macnamara Cantwell, was heard to mutter 'There goes the first Papist ... another Catholic ... another' until all eleven were gone and the prisoners were faced with the prospect of being tried by an entirely Protestant and, almost by definition, overwhelmingly hostile jury.[31]

The Crown case was in the hands of the attorney general, T.B.C. Smith, a future Irish master of the rolls. One of the defendants, Charles Gavan Duffy acknowledged Smith's 'active intellect' but pointed also to his chronic irritability, brought on by notoriously bad digestion. Like the legal animal that he was Smith was perfectly adapted to his natural environment: 'Surrounded by the trappings and formalities of a court of law where he was much at home,' wrote Duffy, 'Mr. Smith had a certain prim dignity; but he was so meagre, unwholesome, and ghastly that elsewhere he looked like an owl in the sunshine.'[32] Bizarrely, during the course of the trial, Smith was so offended by an assertion made by a member of the defence legal team, Gerald Fitzgibbon, that he was on the verge of issuing a challenge to a duel. His ire and vanity risked the abandonment of the trial as the defence counsel, in such an instance, would have been entitled to throw up their briefs. The row was smoothed over privately by the court.[33]

Smith was assisted by, among others, the solicitor general, Richard Wilson Greene, and the elderly QC, Robert Holmes, 'Father of the Irish Bar'. The appearance of Holmes can only be seen as the Crown's attempt at tokenist respectability for its cause. Holmes was nationalist window-dressing of an iconic kind. As the brother-in-law of Robert Emmet, he had been jailed in 1803. His opposition to the Union had not wavered since then and his protracted career as queen's counsel was owing to his refusal to accept any position of profit from the Castle. His position on the Crown prosecution team was due to the inherent professional flexibility of his profession and, in some measure perhaps, to his resentment at O'Connell's regular criticisms of the United Irishmen, to whose memory he was still attached. When Richard Barrett had supported O'Connell's line in the *Pilot* and attacked the aged barrister personally, the fearsome Holmes had challenged the newspaper editor to a duel. Barrett, wisely, declined the challenge.

It was unlikely that the traversers could look to the Bench for much assistance. One of the four judges, Justice Perrin, was known to be fair-minded and even-handed in his approach to the law. The presiding judge, Chief Justice Pennefather, however, according to the highly partisan Duffy, was:

> descended from a family of Puritan 'Undertakers' gorged
> with lands and offices during the penal times, but still on
> the watch for ministerial favours for his kith and kin, [he]
> had been a fierce politician, and could scarcely regard one
> who questioned English Supremacy or Protestant
> Ascendancy in Ireland except as a personal enemy.[34]

Of the other two judges, Justice Crampton 'had been a vehement Tory at the Bar' while Justice Burton displayed an unfortunate tendency to nod off in the middle of proceedings.

The defence case was placed at a further disadvantage by the refusal of the Crown to supply them with a list of witnesses. This meant that the traversers had no opportunity to investigate the credentials of the witnesses and establish or challenge their credibility. It was the practice in England to furnish such a list. In a recent equivalent case, the prosecution of the leadership of the radical Chartist movement, such a facility had been offered unquestioningly. While acknowledging the English practice the prosecution contended that such a custom did not exist in Ireland. In fact the issue had never been raised in a Queen's Bench Court before because there was no recorded instance in which the witness-list had been requested and that request had been denied. Called upon to adjudicate on the matter, only Judge Perrin ruled that there should be uniform practice as between the two jurisdictions. Pennefather, in his statement of the majority opinion, held that 'their defence, if any defence they have, does not depend on the names of the witnesses, but the nature of the charge ... the defendants would not be a whit benefitted [sic] by knowing whether the names of the witnesses are AB or CD'. As Duffy recollected many years later: 'so it was determined, literally in the face of Europe, that there should be one law for political offences in England and another in Ireland'.[35]

On the first day of the state trial, nationalist Dublin seemed divided in two. Half the city was in Merrion Square to accompany the defendants from O'Connell's home to the Four Courts. The other half was already trying to gain access to the court of Queen's Bench. Barriers of solid oak were used to fence off the court-room from the huge crushing mass of people hoping to gain access. The crowd spilled out from underneath the dome of the Four Courts onto the quays outside and across the bridge to the far side of the river.

In respect of the charges against the defendants, according to Oliver MacDonagh 'in today's terms, it is difficult to see that O'Connell was being charged with more than conducting a massive political campaign: the "crime" consisted of its success in mobilisation and its objectives'.[36] In essence the traversers were being charged with advocating repeal of the Act of Union. The actual conspiracy charges and the evidence presented in justification of the entire proceedings were either highly questionable or utterly risible. In opening the case, Smith, who had promised to reveal 'as wicked and foul a conspiracy as ever disturbed an empire', announced that:

the traversers stand indicted for having conspired and confederated to create disaffection and discontent, and to create hatred against the constitution and government as by law established, and to stir up ill-will among various classes, especially towards her Majesty's subjects in England, to render the army disaffected, and by unlawful means and demonstrations of physical force to alter the laws and constitution of this country as at present established, and by means of these proceedings dissolve the legislative union between Great Britain and Ireland.

It was a pithy distillation of the original Leviathan of an indictment. Smith then went on to define the term 'conspiracy' for the jury.

With respect to the law of conspiracy it was a crime which consisted either in a combination and agreement by persons to do some illegal act or acts, or to effect a legal purpose by illegal means; and a confederacy to effect either an illegal object, or even a perfectly legal object by unlawful means, is, in contemplation of law, criminal, and amounted to a conspiracy. [37]

In seeking to establish that a criminal association existed between all eight men on trial, Smith, on the face of it, was hardly on solid ground. Duffy maintained that some of the traversers did not even know each other while 'some of them existed in a still completer [sic] state of alienation, for they had ceased to know each other'.[38]

However, the allegation of conspiracy, because it was notoriously difficult to defend, had the advantageous effect for the Crown of making the defendants responsible for each other's acts. Once conspiracy was established it made, for example, O'Connell responsible for newspaper reports of his activities over which he had no control and Richard Barrett responsible for the activities of an organisation, the Repeal Association, of which he was not a member. In addition had the Crown simply indicted the defendants for illegal assembly (in the organisation of the monster meetings) it would have been necessary to try the case in the locality in which the alleged offence occurred. This would have impaired its ability to appoint (and pack) a 'tame' special jury.

Smith then went through the history of the Repeal movement from the days immediately after the Emancipation victory and recounted the various attempts by British governments to suppress or discourage the Repeal campaign. In response to the nationalist assertion that the 'monster' meetings were intended to acquaint the British administration with the nature and extent of opposition in Ireland to the Union the attorney general pointed out, by way of demonstrating that they did not have a legitimate constitutional pretext 'that no petition was presented from any of those meetings during the last session of parliament'.[39]

Smith then focused on the cultural wing of the movement, attacking the *Nation* for 'the writing of seditious poetry'. He contented himself with quoting, with evident distaste, merely one popular text, *The Memory of the dead*—which, famously, begins 'Who fears to speak of Ninety-eight?/Who blushes at that name?/When cowards mock the patriot's fate/Who hangs his head for shame?'[40] and observed that, 'more intended to excite feelings of discontent and disaffection amongst the people of this country, could not be found in the works of the same character published in 1797'. [41] After expatiating at length on more prosaic examples of seditious journalism from Charles Gavan Duffy's newspaper, he invoked the 'Mallow Defiance'. Quoting at length from O'Connell's incautious speech of 11 June 1843 he concluded with the rhetorical question 'Gracious God! Was there ever heard such an attempt to create, between fellow subjects of the same empire, the sting of indignation, to be excited against those who were called "our Saxon oppressors?"'[42]

The newspaper avenged itself on the attorney general three days later by assailing the tedium of his interminable speech. With gratifying but ill-advised invective the *Nation* observed that:

> men who had expected a lofty and solemn impeachment soon sickened under the weary monotony with which Mr. Smith read his litany of extracts. Drip, drip, like water from a rusty pump, the familiar facts fell from his lips ... at one of the most important points of the indictment might be seen two of the traversers reading newspapers, one copying documents for his defence, two writing autographs in ladies' albums, one noting a brief and the rest absent from court, while the majority of the junior bar were joking *sotto voce*, the audience cutting sandwiches or chatting—a painter making sketches of the ladies in the gallery—fully half the jury fiddling listlessly with their pens, the other half making painful exertions to do their

> duty—two or three of the counsel for the defence reading
> their briefs, and one of the judges fast asleep.[43]

The judge in question was the somnolent Burton.

As he parsed the speeches of the leaders of the Repeal Association at the various monster meetings around the country the attorney general put his own construction on remarks made by O'Connell, and others, such as 'Will you join me in giving Ireland to the Irish?'[44] and variations thereof. The government argued that these were veiled calls to arms rather than the ambivalent rhetorical flourishes of an impassioned demagogue. O'Connell might have recommended submission to the law but, asserted the attorney general, this was only 'till he was ready to break it successfully'.[45] Professions of loyalty to the Crown[46] made in many of the speeches and resolutions of the meetings were merely a smoke screen. In his account of the meeting at Mullaghmast, chosen, provocatively according to Smith, because it was the site of the massacre of 400 Catholics in 1577, he even seemed to suggest that the Liberator had his sights set higher than Repeal. O'Connell had arrived at the venue clad in scarlet and a golden crown had been placed on his head. It was, perhaps, fortunate that the gesture had not been made at Tara, ancient seat of the High Kings of Ireland.

Smith continued in this vein for two days, speaking for a total of twelve hours. Much as the English attorney general would do almost half a century later in the case of another Irish national movement, the Land League, swathes of material from the speeches and articles of the traversers was quoted in support of the contention that they were conspirators who were intent on using violence or the threat of violence to achieve unwarrantable ends. After two days Smith ended by addressing himself directly to the special jury. He asked them to do their duty, 'firmly and temperately'. In effect, however, he was demanding of them that they refuse to baulk at conviction because of intimidation:

> for in agitated times it is hard to preserve the equable
> balance of the mind. Fear is a corrupting principle, and
> alarm operates in different and opposite directions. In
> such times the influence of panic has led men, I am sorry
> to say, of all classes, to truckle to the insurgents, to
> decline those duties which the administration of justice
> calls for; or, what is worse, to discharge them in a spirit
> of base compromise, in the silly hope of securing what

could never be more than a temporary and precarious safety, or from the abject motive of earning an ignominious popularity.[47]

The first witness called by the prosecution was Frederick Bond Hughes, a government reporter imported from England. He was there to give evidence about a number of meetings (principally Mullaghmast) which he had been dispatched from England to report upon. He was examined by the solicitor general, Richard Wilson Greene

GREENE: You are a short-hand writer?

HUGHES: Yes, I am.

GREENE: You have been constantly in the habit of reporting?

HUGHES: Yes, I have been reporting for the last seventeen or eighteen years.

GREENE: Upon different occasions?

HUGHES: Yes, upon different occasions.

GREENE: Do you remember having come over to this country in September last?

HUGHES: Yes, I do.

GREENE: On what day did you arrive?

HUGHES: On the 29th of September ... on the 30th I mean.

GREENE: On what day of the week?

HUGHES: On Saturday. I never was in Ireland before; I recollect the following day, the 1st of October; I went to Mullaghmast on that day; I think I arrived there about half past twelve o'clock; there were a great many persons assembled about the grounds when I got there, a large number; I should think, about thirty or forty thousand persons, as near as I can guess; I could not see over the whole extent of the ground; I saw persons coming from different places with banners; if you will allow me to refer to my book I shall tell you the inscriptions I took on that occasion, a note or memorandum of what passed; that is, of the speeches; I have it here; I saw the inscriptions; 'Hurrah for the Repeal!' was one of them; 'A Nation of Nine Millions is too strong to be dragged at the tail of any other country;' in the front of the platform was an inscription, 'The man who commits a crime is an enemy to his country,' 'Ireland must be a Nation,' there were several persons in and about the platform, with papers round their hats, and staves in their hands; there was an inscription on the papers, 'O'Connell's Police;' I know the traverser, Daniel O'Connell; I see him in court [Here Mr. O'Connell, who sat at the table immediately under the witness's chair, rose and bowed with a smile to the witness.] Mr. O'Connell arrived at the place of meeting about two o'clock; I am not aware that I saw Mr. John O'Connell on that occasion; there were some of the gentlemen present whose names I learned, Mr. Ray and Dr. Gray, I think I should recollect Mr. Ray [the witness here turned to the traversers' box in which Mr. Ray and Dr. Gray sat, and identified both gentlemen]; I know Mr. Thomas Steele, I saw him at that meeting; I see him now in court; Mr. O'Connell was dressed that day in a sort of velvet robe, scarlet or claret colour; some gentleman proposed that Mr. O'Connell should take the chair; that motion was put and carried; Mr. O'Connell addressed the meeting on his taking the chair ... I heard resolutions proposed at that meeting ... 'We, the gentry, clergy, freeholders, and other inhabi-

	tants of the province of Leinster, here assembled, do declare in the face of heaven and our country, that no power on earth save the Queen, Lords, and Commons of Ireland, can make laws for Ireland;' That resolution was put from the chair and carried.
GREENE:	Who was the chairman?
HUGHES:	Mr. O'Connell was; the resolution was carried; after that I saw some gentlemen come forward and present Mr. O'Connell with a velvet cap; it was a round velvet cap ...
GREENE:	What was done with the cap after that?
HUGHES:	It was placed on the head of Mr O'Connell.
GREENE:	Did he then say anything?
HUGHES:	Yes; he said he accepted the gift with pride and pleasure.

Hughes's matter-of-fact evidence occasioned the first recorded laughter in the case when he quoted a sly barb of O'Connell in reference to the former prime minister (now leader of the House of Lords) the duke of Wellington. O'Connell had managed to turn an oft quoted phrase of the Dublin-born soldier and politician against him. 'The following passage in reference to the Duke of Wellington was received with great laughter: "The poor old Duke! what shall I say of him, To be sure he was born in Ireland, but being born in a stable does not make a man a horse."'[48]

Hughes was the first of a number of reporters and note-takers called by the Crown in order to assign the speeches cited by the attorney general to the various accused. In the course of his evidence it transpired that he had mistakenly identified Richard Barrett as having been in attendance at a number of meetings. When he had alerted the Crown to his error no action was taken to amend the charges against Barrett.

Eight days into the case (Tuesday, 23 January) a Co. Meath magistrate, George Despard, unwittingly captured some of the atmosphere of the great 'monster' meeting at Tara and the reverence and awe of the crowds for the Liberator. He was examined by Serjeant Warren and began by giving an account of following members of the crowd from the nearby town of Trim.

DESPARD: They marched from thence to Tara (six Irish miles). They formed upon the green of Trim, and marched through the town. They marched in ranks four deep. There were bands and carriages. There were some people on horseback. There were persons who assumed command over the others; persons who had wands, and I understood them to be repeal wardens. I heard persons saying to others 'Keep your step, man; keep your rank.'

WARREN: Did all the persons you saw upon Tara come from Trim?

DESPARD: No, nor one-twentieth part of them. I know there were bands there from Kildare, Wexford, Dublin and Westmeath; and a man told me he came from Nenagh. I was some time on the ground before Mr. O'Connell arrived. There were various bands marching from Dublin and other places with flags and banners flying.

WARREN: Can you calculate the number of persons who were present at the meeting of Tara?

DESPARD: It would be almost impossible to form an accurate estimate of the number. I had the assistance of an old officer in making the calculation, and my opinion is that there were one hundred thousand persons at least at the meeting. I calculated that there were about seven thousand horsemen. I counted nineteen bands. I did not see the people upon the hill of Tara commanded as at Trim. I think the procession came up about two o'clock, and when Mr. O'Connell got on the platform the crowd gathered round, and in about an hour and a half there was a sudden movement of the meeting in bodies of about twenty thousand, as if there was some concocted plan ...

I was then standing on the ditch watching the procession. A well-dressed man turned round and said to me, loud enough to be heard by every one—'That it was not gentlemen O'Connell wanted there.' I looked at him for a moment and said—'What does he want?' When he replied—'He wants men of bone and sinew like me, who would be able for the work when it comes.' Mr. Walker, the sub-inspector, was standing near at the time. I then said—'I suppose he wants men like those frieze-coated men up there?' He replied—'Just so.' I continued to ask where he came from, and he told me 'that he came from the barony of Shilmalier, in the county of Wexford, with 2,000 who were joined in Kildare by 3,000 more.'

Mr. O'Connell's procession then passed by, and he turned round and said, 'You did not take off your hat to O'Connell.' I answered, 'I did not,' upon which he said—'Then you do not belong to our party.' I replied—'Certainly not; I do not belong to any party here.' The man answered—'I know by the curl of your lip that you do not' [great laughter]. I continued to say to him, 'That I was glad his eyes told him so much truth; that I was only amusing myself, and did not belong to any party.' He said—'Oh, no matter, we will let you come on the field for all that.' A person then came up and said, 'If you do not know that gentleman, you had better let him alone.' ... Some of them shouted, 'Long life to Mr. Leather Roland,' but I afterwards found out that it was Mr. Ledru Rollin[49] they meant [great laughter].[50]

At the conclusion of the prosecution case, Richard Lalor Shiel, one of the founders of the Catholic Association two decades before, rose to begin the case for the defence. Sheil, a talented playwright, was MP for Dungarvan and a former vice-president of the Board of Trade. One of the most celebrated barristers in the country at the time, Sheil represented John O'Connell. Susceptible to gout he was obliged to address the jury with his hands swathed in flannel bandages. The court might have saved itself the trouble of hearing his opening address as he had already been prevailed upon by friendly newspaper reporters to deliver it to them in advance. Initially disappointed when he told them that 'though he had the speech in his head, nothing but a few memoranda existed on paper', he undertook, however, to render it privately and did so with the inclusion of 'his allusions to the bench and his sarcastic apostrophes to the counsel for the Crown'.[51] Astonishingly, in a *tour de force*, he then delivered the same speech, almost verbatim, to the court.

Sheil began with an obvious but telling observation. Based on the attorney general's indignation at the 'envenomed' language of the monster meetings, he wondered why they had not been suppressed much sooner. ' ... how does it come to pass that no single step was ever taken by him,' Sheil inquired, 'for the purpose of arresting the progress of an evil represented by him to be so calamitous.' He then went on to accuse the government of being, in effect, *agents provocateurs*.

> He told you that the country was traversed by incendiaries who set fire to the passions of the people. The whole fabric of society, according to the Attorney General, for the last nine months has been in a blaze; wherefore then did he stand with folded arms to gaze at the conflagration? Where were the castle fire-engines; where was the indictment? Is there not too much reason to think that a project was formed, or rather that a plot was concocted, to decoy and ensnare the traversers, and that a connivance, amounting almost to sanction, was deliberately adopted as a part of the policy of the government, in order to betray the traversers into indiscretions of which advantage was in due time to be taken? I have heard it said that it was criminal to tell the people to 'bide their time;' but is the government to 'bide its time' in order to turn popular excitement to useful official account? The public prosecutor who gives an indirect encouragement to agitation, in order that he may afterwards more effectually fall

upon it, bears some moral affinity to the informer, who provokes the crime from whose denunciation his ignominious livelihood is derived. Has the Attorney General adopted a course worthy of his great office; worthy the ostensible head of the Irish bar, and the representative of its intellect in the House of Commons?

Is it befitting that the successor of Saurin, and of Plunket, who should 'keep watch and ward' from his high station over the public safety, should descend to the performance of functions worthy only of a commissary of the French police; and in place of being the sentinel, should become the 'Artful Dodger' of the state? But what, you may ask, could be the motive of the right hon. gentleman for pursuing the course he has adopted, and for which no explanation has been attempted by him? He could not have obtained any advantage signally serviceable to his party by prosecuting Mr. Barrett, or Mr. Duffy, or Dr. Gray, for strong articles in their newspapers; or by prosecuting Mr. Steele, or Mr. Tierney, for attending unlawful assemblies. He did not fish with lines, if I may avail myself of an illustration derived from the habits of my constituents at Dungarvan, but cast a wide and nicely constructed trammel-net, in order that by a kind of miraculous catch he might take the great agitator-leviathan himself—a member of parliament, Tom Steele, three editors of newspapers, and a pair of priests in one stupendous haul together. But there was another object still more important to be gained. Had the Attorney General prosecuted individuals for the use of violent language, or for attending unlawful meetings, each individual would have been held responsible for his own acts; but in a prosecution for conspiracy, which is open to every one of the objections applicable to constructive treason, the acts and the speeches of one man are given in evidence against another, although the latter may have been at the distance of a hundred miles when the circumstances used against him as evidence, and of which he had no sort of cognizance, took place.

> By prosecuting Mr. O'Connell for a conspiracy, the
> Attorney General treats him exactly as if he were the
> editor of the *Freeman,* the editor of the *Nation*, and the
> editor of the *Pilot* newspapers. Indeed, if five or six other
> editors of newspapers in the country, had been joined as
> traversers, for every line in their newspapers Mr.
> O'Connell would be held responsible. There is one
> English gentleman, I believe, upon that jury. If a prosecu-
> tion for conspiracy were instituted against the Anti-Corn
> League in England, would he not think it very hard indeed
> that Mr. Cobden and Mr. Bright should be held answer-
> able for every article in the *Chronicle,* in the *Globe,* and
> in the *Sun?* How large a portion of the case of the crown
> depends upon this implication of Mr. O'Connell with
> three Dublin newspapers? He is accused of conspiring
> with men who certainly never conspired with each other.
> For those who know anything of newspapers are aware
> that they are mercantile speculations—the property in
> them held by shares; and that the very circumstance of
> their being engaged in the same politics alienates the pro-
> prietors from each other. They pay their addresses to the
> same mistress, and cordially detest each other.[52]

Sheil trawled through Irish history before pouncing on one of the
central arguments of the case made for the Act of Union, that, as a consequence of its passage many benefits were meant to flow: 'but had those
benefits been realized? Had even the principles and the practice of constitutional law, long recognized in England, been extended to Ireland? Could
such a trial as the present take place there?'[53]

In conclusion, to controvert the Crown charge that the alleged conspiracy had a violent intent, Sheil adverted to the many examples of
O'Connell's condemnation of violence and asked:

> Can you bring yourselves to believe that he would blast all
> the laurels, which it is his boast that he has won without
> the effusion of a single drop of blood; that he would
> drench the land of his birth, of his affections, and of his
> redemption in a deluge of profitless blood, and that he
> would lay prostrate the great moral monument, which he
> has raised so high that it is visible from the remotest

region of the world? What he was in 1798 he is in 1844
... Of the charges preferred against him, am I not right
when I exclaim that his life contains the refutation.[54]

The next six days were taken up with the submissions of the defence
counsel for the remaining prisoners. They were mere prologue to the speech
eagerly anticipated by all observers, that of O'Connell himself, pleading
on his own behalf. When he rose on the eighteenth day of the trial 'He had
laid aside the barrister's costume, and appeared in his ordinary dress'.[55]
O'Connell can have cherished few hopes of reprieve from the expertly
packed and entirely Protestant jury. A career marked, not only by the
triumph of the reversal of the last disabling anti-Catholic laws, but also by
occasional injudicious sectarian provocations, had done little to endear
him to politicised members of the established church.

William Henry Curran, eminent barrister and son of John Philpot
Curran, writing even before Catholic Emancipation, elegantly captured
O'Connell's penchant for antagonising the Ascendancy.

> The admirers of King William [Curran averred, tongue
> embedded in cheek] have no mercy for a man who, in his
> seditious moods, is so provoking as to tell the world, that
> their idol was 'a Dutch adventurer.' Then his intolerable
> success in a profession where many a stanch [sic]
> Protestant is condemned to starve, and his fashionable
> house in Merrion-square, and a greater eye-sore still, his
> dashing, revolutionary equipage, green carriage, green liv-
> eries, and turbulent popish steeds, prancing over a
> Protestant pavement to the terror of Protestant passen-
> gers—a nuisance that in the good old times would have
> been put down by an Act of Parliament—these and other
> provocations of equal publicity, have exposed this learned
> culprit to the deep and irrevocable detestation of a numer-
> ous class of His Majesty's hating subjects in Ireland.[56]

This was the man who rose to make his case to a jury chosen with the
express purpose of ignoring his arguments. With this in mind O'Connell
made it clear from the outset, that, as in his defence of John Magee in 1813,
his remarks were not primarily addressed to the twelve men in the jury-box.

> I do not stand here my own client. I have clients of infi-
> nitely more importance. My clients in this case are the

Irish people—my client is Ireland—and I stand here the advocate of the rights, and liberties, and constitutional privileges of that people. My only anxiety is lest their sacred cause—their right to independent legislation—should be in the slightest degree tarnished or impeded by anything of which I have been the instrument. I am conscious of the integrity of my purpose—I am conscious of the purity of my motives—I am conscious of the inestimable value of the object I had in view—the repeal of the union. I own to you I cannot endure the union; it was founded upon the grossest injustice; it was based upon the grossest insult—the intolerance of Irish prosperity ... I am not here to deny anything I have done, or here to palliate anything that I have done. I am ready to re-assert in court all I have said—not taking upon myself the clumsy mistakes of reporters—not abiding by the fallibility that necessarily attends the reporting of speeches, and, in particular, where those speeches are squeezed up together, as it were, for the purpose of the newspapers. I don't hesitate to say that there are many harsh things said of individuals, and clumsy jokes that I would rather not have said, but the substance of what I have said I avow, and I am here respectfully to vindicate it; and as to all my actions I am ready not only to avow them, but to justify them. For the entire of what I have done and said was done and said in the performance of, to me, a sacred duty—the endeavouring to procure the restoration of the Irish parliament ...

We will now take this conspiracy; let us see whether there are any negative qualities in it as to the evidence produced by the crown. It is admitted by the crown itself in this case, that there *was* no privacy; no secrecy; no definite agreement whatever to bring it about; but, above all, there was no private agreement, no secret society, nothing concealed, nothing even privately communicated; there was no private information; nay, not one private conversation; everything was open, avowed, proclaimed, published. A secret conspiracy! which there was no secret about; all lay openly proclaimed, and openly published; whether in the *Dublin Evening Mail* or *Dublin Evening Post*, for all has been raked out of that secret abyss of all secret channels of communication, the public newspapers! Really, it is quite too harsh a thing for one to be called on to defend himself against a conspiracy so perpetrated, committed in open day, and committed by public announcement, with the ringing of bells ... [57]

O'Connell, who had worked with William Wilberforce for the abolition of slavery throughout the British Empire, digressed slightly to ruminate on the impact of a conspiracy charge against Wilberforce and his supporters, had one been brought against that movement by the government

How would they have started if this doctrine of conspiracy was sooner invented, and the slave bound for ever, till somebody with milk-and-water accents—with mild tea-table talk endeavoured to persuade some one to abolish it [laughter]—until some one went to America and spoke soft things to the owners of the negroes, and, having in as gentle a way as possible insinuated the atrocities practised towards the slaves, then, by-and-bye to coax the owners, and win upon them to consent to the abolition of slavery! Gentlemen, it was the calling down of public indignation—the rousing of all that was virtuous in the public mind, and that Heaven-descended spirit of persevering, open, bold humanity that shook off the fetters of the negro, and re-established him in freedom![58]

As had Sheil, O'Connell highlighted the relative equanimity with which the government appeared to have viewed the Repeal campaign until the Clontarf meeting:

If we were seditious, why did we not get some warning? Why was there not a proclamation issued against these meetings? Oh! but there was a proclamation at length. I don't like to enter upon any angry topic; but that proclamation was immediately obeyed. You have no evidence of any conspiracy in any one of them, no evidence of anything but a ready submission and obedience to the law.

... We left nothing undone to impress upon the minds of those who joined the movement that the man who committed an offence against the law gave strength to whoever might be the enemy of our cause. Such was the principle that we proclaimed. It may be said that it was one that savoured of hostility; but if so, it had only a stronger effect on that account. You have heard again and again of my assertion that the most desirable of all political ameliorations were purchased at too dear a price if they could only be obtained at the expense of one drop of human blood. That is the principle of my political career; and if I stand prominent amongst men for anything, it is for the fearless and unceasing announcement of that principle ... It is my boast that Catholic emancipation, and every achievement of my political life was obtained without violence and bloodshed; and is it fair, I ask you, gentlemen, that you should be called upon at this hour of the day to interrupt a man who has laid that down as the basis of his political conduct, and who at no period of his existence was ever known to deviate from the maxim? Is it right that men of honesty and intelligence should be called upon to brand now as a participator in conspiracy the man who has been preaching peace, law, and order during his whole life, and has invariably deprecated and denounced the idea that the objects of his political life were to be attained by an appeal to violent means.[59]

O'Connell went on to review his own recent political record, citing his rejection of Ribbonism, the support offered by the French left-wing politician Ledru Rollin, his opposition to the radical Chartist movement in Britain and his loyalty to the queen. He expatiated at extreme length on British maladministration in Ireland and on the detrimental economic effects of the Union on the country, before concluding:

Why is not the country prosperous? Did I not read for you of the unheard-of magical prosperity that followed her legislative independence? Did I not read extracts from the writings and speeches of men most adverse to Ireland—of men most anxious to conceal her greatness, as evidence of her increasing prosperity under her parliament? What happened once will surely happen again. Oh, gentlemen, I struggle to rescue the poor from poverty, and to give wages and employment to those now idle—to keep our

gentry at home by an absentee tax, after the example of
the government last year, if by no other means, and
compel them to do duty to their country. I leave the case
to you—I deny that there is anything in it to stain me with
conspiracy—I reject with contempt the appellation. I have
acted in the open day in the presence of the government—
in the presence of the magistrates; nothing was secret,
private, or concealed—there was nothing but what was
exposed to the universal world. I have struggled for the
restoration of the parliament to my native country. Others
have succeeded in their endeavours, and some have failed,
but succeed or fail, it is a glorious struggle. It is a struggle
to make the first land on earth possess that bounty and
benefit which God and nature intended.[60]

Reaction to O'Connell's apologia was mixed and tended to reflect the
fault lines along which the Repeal movement was already dividing. Young
Irelander, Thomas MacNevin, alleged that O'Connell had gone out of his
way to flatter the attorney general and described the speech as 'weak as syl-
labub' in a letter to Charles Gavan Duffy. Duffy himself contended that
the address 'was not eminently successful, the materials were necessarily
borrowed from familiar sources and were not relieved on this occasion by
freshness of treatment or vigour of delivery'. The contemporary historian
R.R. Madden, (who read rather than heard the speech) on the other hand,
wrote to the *Nation* editor suggesting that 'Might not one be almost
tempted to desire that O'Connell's political career closed with that stupendous manifestation of intellectual power'.[61]

After the closing address, made on behalf of the Crown by the solicitor
general, in which he re-iterated that the traversers had sought to accomplish a legal object by illegal means, it was the turn of the chief justice to
direct the jury. It was clear that the proceedings, which had continued for
more than three weeks already, had tried the patience of Judge Pennefather.

They had heard, during this long trial a great deal of
eloquence—they had heard also somewhat of declama-
tion—they had heard great oratorical powers, and powers
of reasoning—they had heard a great deal of what might
be deemed poetic; and he did not mean to say but they
had also heard a good deal of what might be more justly
termed prosaic [laughter]. They had heard observations

made to them which he could not help saying, generally, bordered on the verge of impropriety; but, what was more material, they had heard a great deal which it would be very difficult, indeed, to prove was relevant to the subject they had to consider.[62]

The chief justice then told the jury that, despite the multiplicity of charges against the defendants the entire case boiled down to one primary offence:

> They were, one and all, united in the charge of conspiracy, of which no individual could be by law convicted ... for the conviction of any one or more persons for a conspiracy, the law required that a jury should be satisfied that there was a concert between them either for the purpose of doing an illegal act, or else for the purpose of doing, or causing to be done, an act legal in itself, but to be brought about by illegal means.[63]

Crucially, he then instructed the jury to ignore the defence of publicity. It was not necessary that a conspiracy be conducted in secret, especially, as in this instance the aim of the conspiracy was one of 'spreading terror and alarm amongst the Queen's subjects, by collecting together in the open day large bodies of people'.[64]

A Whig peer, Lord Fortescue, later commented that 'when he came to read the charge [to the jury] in a newspaper he could not persuade himself in the first instance that he was not still reading the Solicitor General's speech for the prosecution'.[65] According to Duffy, Pennefather's 'main purpose was to supply oversights or deficiencies in the case for the Crown, and he applied himself to carry it out without shame or reserve'. In the opinion of far less partial observers, Pennefather's obvious bias laid him open to reversal on appeal, on the basis of misdirection. The jury 'after a little decent delay' found the defendants guilty. Even Fr Tierney, who had only joined the Repeal Association five days before the Clontarf meeting, was convicted on one count. O'Connell was heard to observe that the attorney general had been modest in his aspirations 'as these twelve gentlemen would have made no difficulty in convicting them of ... murder'.[66] A letter in O'Connell's papers contains an allegation from a well informed supporter that Kemmis, the Crown solicitor, may even have been in communication with the jury.[67] Sentencing was put off until the opening of the new legal term.

DECLINE 1844-7

The postponement of sentencing on the traversers had the inevitable effect of moderating reaction to the verdict and the conduct of the trial. Any sort of violent response to the convictions would only have served to justify the stiffest possible sentences. Even the *Nation* counselled caution. Recognising the anger of the nationalist community and the desire to give expression to that anger the newspaper wrote:

> You want to punish those who have ventured to fling the name of crime upon the efforts of your chiefs for liberty. The same thing has been done here and elsewhere to the best men labouring in the holiest causes ... They smiled in bitter resolve. They waited and worked. They won vengeance, victory, and eternal glory.[68]

As far as the newspaper was concerned the revenge of the people should be a dish served cold.

At a meeting of the Committee of the Repeal Association, a cautious O'Connell, concerned that continued agitation, on the part of what might be construed by the authorities and the judiciary as a wider conspiracy, would exacerbate the situation and lengthen the sentences, advised that the association be wound up. A compromise was reached whereby the three newspaper editors among the traversers resigned from the Association so that, at least, potential editorial indiscretions might not impact on O'Connell and the others awaiting sentence.

O'Connell travelled to London where a debate on the trial was already in progress in the House of Commons on a motion introduced by the Whig leader, Lord John Russell. As he entered the chamber, to cheers from the opposition benches (a reception similar to that experienced by Parnell on his vindication almost half a century later) a Liberal member for Belfast, who had been speaking in his defence, declaimed 'Let the House judge by the reception which the head conspirator has just met, whether there be much cause for triumph'.[69] Later in the debate Richard Lalor Sheil complained of the

> mutilation of the jurors [sic] panel, and the sectarian character of the jury ultimately chosen ... Names of the witnesses upon the back of the indictment were invariably given to the accused in England; but in the recent

state Trial at Dublin they had been refused. Above all, a charge of conspiracy was sustained by citations from newspapers, which it was not attempted to prove that the chief conspirator had ever seen or sanctioned. Could any instance of the kind be pointed out in the records of English jurisprudence?[70]

The debate continued for five days culminating in the defeat of the Russell motion, critical of the conduct of the trial, by 334–225. O'Connell, who had a chequered relationship with the Whig grandee, once describing him as having 'a thorough contemptuous Whig hatred of the Irish'[71] observed to Sheil that 'Lord John Russell has behaved exceedingly well respecting these trials'.[72]

On 30 May the traversers were sentenced. O'Connell was given a year in jail and fined £2,000. The others received lesser sentences. To mark the beginning of the period ordained for their incarceration that week's edition of the *Nation* was printed in green ink. William Smith O'Brien, scion of one of the most prominent Protestant families in the country, and a former Conservative MP, who had recently joined the association in disgust at the trial of O'Connell, was left in charge of the Repeal Association and an appeal against the sentence was lodged. O'Connell had delighted in the *coup* of O'Brien's 'providential' accession. 'You are,' he wrote in March 1844, 'by your 'antecedents' and your popular talents and your rank and religion just the *beau ideal* of the person wanted to make the cause of Repeal keep its course against the stream of persecution on the one hand and of otherwise inevitable desertion on the other.'[73]

According to Charles Gavan Duffy, O'Brien had

> none of the gifts which attract the multitude except a tall striking figure and a well-poised head. He was not an orator ... his manners were not genial or winning, and he made few intimacies ... [but] ... he was recognised as a man ... who might be counted on to keep his word with a rigid and even pedantic strictness; who was absolutely free from jealousy, who never uttered ill of anyone and whose lightest word was better security than the sealed bond of ordinary men.[74]

So rigidly correct was Smith O'Brien that in a duel with a brother of the inveterate duellist, The O'Gorman Mahon (James Patrick Mahon), he had advised his would-be assassin, before they commenced firing, that he had inadvertently let the cap fall off his pistol. His was a steady, experienced hand at the helm of the Repeal Association while its ruling cadre was imprisoned.

Not, as has been noted above, that the incarceration was tremendously onerous. For O'Connell, 'His confinement in Richmond Prison must count among the most luxurious and least oppressive in the history of imprisonment'.[75] O'Connell himself wrote to his daughter, Betsey fFrench advising her not to bother curtailing her stay in Derrynane in order to return to her Richmond 'duties', 'We are quite gay and cheerful as larks'.[76]

Once their creature comforts had been secured attention was also paid to the physical welfare of the prisoners. O'Connell claimed to have walked three miles a day around the prison gardens. A gymnasium was set up for further exercise. Duffy wrote of this period, 'It was whispered that the two youngest prisoners[77] ... had foils and masks for fencing, and even horses in one of the great yards for daily exercise.'[78] Little wonder that when the Tory newspapers, the *Morning Herald* and the *Standard* suggested that all except O'Connell should be discharged from Richmond, the other prisoners refused to countenance the notion.

To satisfy the national desire for images of the 'martyrs', an artist's studio and a daguerreotype camera were set up in the penitentiary garden 'to multiply likenesses of the prisoners'. O'Connell also agreed to a new portrait by a rising young artist N.J. Crowley who, according to Charles Gavan Duffy, 'produced an ideal O'Connell, a tribune in the height of his vigour and inspiration, bearing only a distant and fanciful resemblance to the original'. A daguerreotype done at the same time was more true to life: 'it exhibits a man of vigorous frame and commanding countenance, both, however, depressed by age and beginning to be marked by decrepitude'.[79] At this point, O'Connell may already have been in the preliminary phase of the brain disease that claimed his life three years later. His relaxed stay in Richmond Penitentiary, rendering him unable to pursue the punishing schedule to which he was accustomed, may well have extended his life.

One aspect of the incarceration that the public was not permitted to share was O'Connell's growing infatuation with a woman young enough to be his granddaughter. She was a Presbyterian in her early twenties, Rose McDowell, daughter of a Belfast merchant and supporter of Repeal, Robert McDowell. According to some accounts she was 'charming ... lively ... cultivated'.[80] He corresponded with her and may even have proposed to her. He wrote to a mutual friend that 'she is one of the most superior women I ever met, with intellect, sound judgement and facinating [*sic*] sweetness'.[81] According to Gavan Duffy:

> His family were naturally alarmed by this incident, and more so doubtless that the lady, whom he proposed to put at the head of their house, differed from them in race, and in religion, and their feverish anxiety could not fail to react upon him. Their fears were allayed in the end by the lady's persistent refusal to become his wife, but this result was not calculated to restore the composure of O'Connell.[82]

O'Connell's final instructions, to his political and financial manager, P.V. Fitzpatrick, were that his correspondence with Rose McDowell, kept in a desk drawer in Derrynane, should be destroyed, though it 'contains nothing disreputable'.[83]

While O'Connell, Steele, Ray and the others rubbed shoulders with debtors and the newspaper editors busily edited their journals, the appeal moved inexorably towards a conclusion in the House of Lords. O'Connell's attitude to the appeal hovered between apathy and pessimism, as one biographer puts it, 'He could not credit that the Lords would reverse a decision so necessary to government prestige'.[84] As astute an observer as Lord Palmerston agreed, writing to his brother that: 'The case in favour of O'Connell must be strong indeed if the decision is given in his favour. The Court will certainly be against him'.[85]

The writ of error in the appeal (the defence case was led by Sir Thomas Wilde, former Whig attorney general) was comprehensive. There were 34 separate grounds cited but the principal hope of the defence was that the convictions would be quashed on the basis of the flawed special jury-list. The appeal was heard by five law lords, two of whom, Lyndhurst (the lord chancellor) and Brougham, were old Tory adversaries of O'Connell. Some support was hoped for from the two partisan Whigs on the panel, Campbell and Cottenham. The final decision was likely to rest with the fifth law lord, Denman. He was also a Whig but one noted for the independence of his decisions. Denman could be relied upon to make a judgement based on the merits of the case rather than political exigencies or prejudices.

Predictably, Denman's casting vote settled the issue. It did so on the side of the defendants. In a landmark judgement on 4 September 1844, the law lords voted by 3–2 to quash the convictions. Denman's decisive opinion was based on the incomplete jury panel. He argued that, had the full jury list been made available, none of the twelve men who heard the case presented might have become jurors. The jury might, conceivably, have been made up entirely of those who had been omitted. In a stinging rebuke of the legal apparatus of the castle administration, Denman held that, 'if such practices as have taken place in the present instance should continue, trial by jury in Ireland would become a mockery, a delusion and a snare'.[86] Three days later, under a banner headline 'Remember the 30th May, 1844!' (the date of sentencing) the *Freeman's Journal* ran the quote in bold type. [87]

By tradition, in the House of Lords, it is only the law lords who vote in such appeals. However, so angry were some of their lordships at the prospect of O'Connell's release that they sought to exercise their prerogative to vote and negative the narrow law lords majority in favour of release. Only the intervention of Lord Wharncliffe, lord president of the council (a Tory supporter of both Catholic Emancipation and Reform) persuaded the recalcitrant Tory lords to uphold tradition and allow the law lords to decide the issue alone.

Once the decision became public knowledge the 'Race to Richmond' began. It was the era before the arrival of the telegraph so that whoever made the journey to Dublin from Westminster in the shortest time would be the bearer of glad tidings. William Ford, the traversers' solicitor began the journey by train from London. Such was his delight and exuberance that, so the story goes, when the locomotive stopped in Crewe he opened his carriage window and shouted 'O'Connell is out', causing confused travellers to scan the platform awaiting his disembarkation. Unlike Pheidippides, who was at least allowed to impart the news he had carried from Marathon before he died, Ford ruled himself out of the race by prematurely shouting 'O'Connell is free' from the deck of the mail steamer *Medusa* as it approached the harbour of Kingstown (now Dún Laoghaire) and the thousands waiting on the shore for news of the lords' decision. Others would precede him to Richmond with the glad tidings

Ford did have the honour of climbing aboard a ceremonial train which travelled to Dublin carrying flags on the engine that bore the legend 'Triumph of law and justice—the judgement reversed' and the more immediate 'O'Connell is free'. But the honour of delivering the news to O'Connell himself fell to a young Repeal activist, Edmond O'Haggerty whose repeated uttering of the phrase 'I'm first. I'm first', when ushered into the Liberator's presence, must call his priorities into question. O'Connell, however, was not disposed to believe O'Haggerty until Ford arrived with confirmation.

Immediately on receipt of the good news, 'something of the original air of solemn farce-cum-fiesta was immediately restored to the affair'.[88] Purdon, the prison governor, is reported to have fainted; such was his extreme excitement and delight.[89] Even the English-born deputy governor was obliged to leave the room to conceal his emotion. O'Connell himself, according to some accounts, was surprisingly 'clouded and gloomy'.[90] Eschewing any display of triumph or validation he walked home from the prison. According to the Young Irelander, Michael Doheny, 'Mr. O'Connell himself did not seem to share in the nation's pride. His spirit was broken ... It was evident something within him had died'.[91]

As far as the radical Young Ireland element within the Repeal movement, exemplified by the likes of Thomas Davis and Charles Gavan Duffy, was concerned such an anticlimax was an unwelcome and undesirable conclusion to an event that was of enormous propaganda value to the national organisation. There was going to be a reception and a procession whether or not O'Connell approved. He and the other prisoners were prevailed upon to return to the jail the following morning (7 September) and to allow themselves to be fêted and embraced as hero-martyrs. So great was the desire for an appropriate celebration that O'Connell was obliged to refuse a processional escort *from* his Merrion Square house back to Richmond for the re-staged release. Later that day he and his fellow prisoners left the penitentiary, 'at the head of a grand procession, and in a triumphal carriage of fantastic construction. The prison had been graced by O'Connell and his fellow offenders and allowed to play a part in a repeal pageant'.[92]

Whatever O'Connell's mood the previous day he took a full and active part in the pomp and symbolism of, what would be described today as a 'media event'. The caravan of carriages and the accompanying procession took a circuitous route, passing Dublin Castle in order to allow the crowd to jeer and hiss that most potent symbol of English rule in Ireland. When the procession reached College Green, O'Connell ordered that his 'chariot' (complete with grandchildren and a harpist playing airs by Thomas Moore) be stopped. In a silent gesture, repeated many years later by Charles Stewart Parnell, O'Connell pointed to the old Houses of Parliament. It was precisely what the young, radical element of the Repeal movement had hoped for, a moment of pure political theatre. But, as with many such examples of high drama and emotion, it was contrived and largely symbolic. O'Connell's grandiloquent gestures may have pointed towards the home of the pre-Union Irish parliament but his thoughts were veering towards compromise on the issue of Repeal of the Act of Union that had permanently prorogued that institution.

When transmitting the details of the appeal Ford had emphasised to O'Connell that the judgement of the law lords was 'On the merits ... no technicalities at all—nothing but the merits'.[93] Others were not so sanguine. To the Young Irelander, Michael Doheny, an opportunity had been missed and O'Connell had simply been released by the legal appendages of a grateful Whig party. This had been done on the basis of expediency and the unsavoury machinations of the Sheriff's office rather than on the genuine merits of the case:

> throughout that long trial the question which would test
> it was not mooted ... the final issue upon which the judge-
> ment was reversed, was not even remotely connected with
> the main inquiry, whether or not the charge of conspiracy
> was sustainable in point of constitutional law ... the plain
> truth is, the judgement was reversed as an essential move
> in a great party game.[94]

In the House of Commons, Lord John Russell played that game to the best of his considerable ability. He fulminated against the iniquities of Tory manipulation of Queen's Bench procedures:

> it was not a trial by fair jury [cheers], but by a jury elabo-
> rately put together for the purpose of conviction [loud
> cheers], charged by a judge who did not allow any evidence
> of any weight in favour of the accused to come fairly before
> his mind, but charged more violently than the Attorney
> General accused [loud cheers], towards a prejudiced jury, in
> such a manner as to prevent justice being done to the
> people of Ireland as it was to the people of England.[95]

Much of O'Connell's aura of legal infallibility was restored by the appeal verdict. But of more consequence to Doheny and other Young Irelanders was the future strategy of the Liberator. Would he be chastened or emboldened by the whole experience? O'Connell left Richmond to return to the healing surroundings of Derrynane. Doheny recorded in his revolutionary memoir *The felon's track* that it was a wary O'Connell who emerged some time later from his Kerry fiefdom: 'His health was soon restored, but his political vigour never. The first time his voice was heard from that retreat, it was to recommend a compromise; and, for the first time, his advice was openly opposed'.[96] Notwithstanding the sceptical watching brief of the Young Irelanders the rest of the Catholic nation celebrated the liberation of the Liberator. The Sunday following the lords reversal the archbishop of Dublin, Dr Daniel Murray, celebrated High Mass 'in thanksgiving to Almighty God for the deliverance of the beloved Liberator to his country, and his fellow martyrs from unjust captivity'.[97] The recently delivered martyrs sat underneath the pulpit facing a grateful congregation. The ringing sermon ascribed O'Connell's deliverance to the intercession of the Virgin Mary herself.

O'Connell was inclined to give the credit to a source with which he had a more ambiguous relationship, the Whigs. The following day was his first opportunity to outline where he intended to take the Repeal movement given the failure and future impossibility of mass protest. At a meeting in the association's Conciliation Hall O'Connell spoke for two hours but said very little. According to O'Faoláin, 'He vituperated, he denounced, he abused, but still he did not come to the point'.[98] He praised his own policy of alliance with the Whigs, pointing out that, 'had there been no interruption of Tory rule, neither Cottenham, Denman nor Campbell would ever have sat in the Bench'.[99] The only coherent policy he outlined was a campaign for the impeachment of the attorney general and the judges of the Queen's Bench. But that was largely the politics of bile not the articulation of strategy. O'Connell was boxing the compass rather than establishing a specific direction for the movement. While the sojourn in Richmond might have benefited his health, it had done little for his confidence or political resolve.

In truth he had long since given clear indications that he was prepared to compromise on Repeal. A week before the state trial he had written to the Whig MP, Charles Buller, pointing out that

> the slightest shrinking from the Repeal is at the present
> moment impracticable. Even my usual doctrine of instal-
> ments would under existing circumstances have the
> appearance of cowardice or at least of paltry timidity. But
> as I have no notion of keeping up a party at the expense
> of sacrificing any measures useful to Ireland, I will can-
> didly tell you what I think would mitigate the present
> ardent desire for Repeal.[100]

His demands included improvements in the areas of church disestablishment, religious equality, tenants' rights, the franchise and corporate reform.

Duffy, who along with Davis, Smith O'Brien and the other leading Young Irelanders, would soon embark on the revolutionary road, wrote that

> O'Connell had once more silently resolved to accept the largest concessions he could obtain from Parliament in lieu of Repeal of the Union. He was surrounded and solicited by men ready to make liberal promises on behalf of the Whigs, his life was drawing to a close, and he had little reliance on his probable successors. Compromise, which he named 'the doctrine of instalments' was one of his favourite agencies[101]

The first wedge driven between O'Connell and Young Ireland was his dalliance with federalism as an alternative to outright Repeal. The notion of an imperial parliament with additional indigenous assemblies in Britain and Ireland did not appeal to the separatist strain within Young Ireland. The *Nation* criticised this apparent *démarche* but within months O'Connell had recanted and the federalist project, insofar as it was anything other than a chimera, was strangled at birth. But his equivocation on the issue of Repeal, allied to significant cultural differences with the *Nation's* romantic revolutionaries, accentuated the differences between the O'Connells and Young Ireland. This rift would widen still further as a consequence of Peel's adroit attempt to enfeeble the entire movement by a policy of judicious concession. The offer of non-sectarian university colleges in Belfast, Cork and Galway was opposed by the confessional Repealers led by O'Connell and the Roman Catholic hierarchy but supported by the secular Young Ireland. A disastrous debate on the subject in, the inappropriately named, Conciliation Hall, in which Davis was overwhelmed by O'Connell, and O'Brien effected a temporary cessation of invective, signposted the end of the road. 'The Association never recovered', wrote Doheny. Young Ireland largely abandoned the increasingly rancorous and divisive Repeal meetings and established an alternative forum, the '82 Club, harking back to the era of the Volunteers and Grattan's parliament. Young Ireland became more militaristic in its trappings. Preparations began for a military insurrection. It would coincide with the Year of Revolution across Europe, but that coincidence would be its only claim to military credibility.

In the absence of any clear and agreed direction on policy it was disease that dictated Ireland's immediate future. A degenerative brain disease would kill O'Connell within three years of his triumphal journey through the streets of Dublin on his release from Richmond. But it was another disease entirely that dictated the country's direction in the years that followed. In 1845 *Phytophthora infestans*, commonly known as potato blight, appeared in the form of spots on the leaves of the staple food of much of the Irish nation, the potato. The disease had, with tragic irony, most probably been brought from the new world by some of the same ships that would take starving and diseased Irish peasants in their hundreds of thousands in the opposite direction in the years immediately following.

At the defiant meeting in Mallow in 1843 O'Connell had told the crowd 'We were a paltry remnant in Cromwell's time. We are nine millions now'.[102] He may have been out by about 0.5 million or so but by the end of the decade the population of Ireland would be a mere 6.5 million. Half a century later it had declined by 50% from its level at the height of the Repeal campaign. Approximately the same number of people said to have attended the monster meeting at Tara, would die of starvation and disease by 1848. By then O'Connell himself was dead, the movement he had created was in disarray and the dissident Young Irelanders, having had a brief moment of inglorious military farce, were in jail or in exile.

.4.

THE
MAAMTRASNA
MURDERS

The judge and jury have discharged
Their duty with much pain.
The verdict no one could dispute,
The evidence was plain.
Then let us pray that their poor souls
On high may mercy find.
And to the five respited men
Give each a tranquil mind.[1]

(*Lamentable lines on the execution of the Maamtrasna
murderers*)

The figure of this bewildered old man, left over from a
culture which is not ours, a deaf mute before his judges, is
a symbol of the Irish nation at the bar of public opinion.[2]

(James Joyce on Myles Joyce)

In early 1883 warders and inmates in Galway Prison began to report strange sightings of a wraith-like middle-aged man protesting loudly at some perceived injustice. In a society accustomed to regular interaction with a thriving nether world, this incorporeal manifestation was not altogether surprising. Many recognised the restless spirit and well understood his anguish. At least one warder offered as an excuse for arriving drunk for his day's work, the fact that he had needed to fortify himself for his regular encounters with the restless spirit of the man who had been cruelly and ham-fistedly hanged just a few months before. His name was Myles Joyce, a native of the small townland of Cappanacreha on the Mayo–Galway border and, it was common knowledge in the west of Ireland, that he had been executed at the end of a sinister process, on the basis of the dubious evidence of a veritable rogue's gallery of informers and turncoats. His ghost may well have stalked the prison until it was demolished to make way for the magnificent Roman Catholic cathedral that stands on the site today. In such consecrated ground his spirit must surely rest in peace but rehabilitation had begun before he even died at the end of a hangman's rope.

THE LAND WAR 1879–82

The emergence on the Irish political scene in the late 1870s of Charles Stewart Parnell, gave the burgeoning Irish agrarian movement an unlikely champion. Parnell was from a Protestant Co. Wicklow landowning family with something of a nationalist pedigree but the man himself was, on the face of it, emblematic of his class. Parnell was high sheriff for Co. Wicklow, and an officer in the Wicklow Militia who played cricket and rode to hounds. There was little to suggest that he was anything other than an archetypal Tory–Unionist landlord. Still less would he have been expected to ally himself after his election to the tiny radical neo-Fenian wing of the Irish Parliamentary Party.

Parnell's emergence as a militant butterfly from a conformist chrysalis coincided with a new economic and social upheaval in Ireland. Two years of agricultural depression and bad harvests had brought an abrupt end to a period of relative boom for Irish tenant farmers. Western parts of the country, where the holdings were smaller and poorer than the norm, were threatened with famine. Evictions for non-payment of rent rose and the handmaiden of eviction, retaliatory agrarian violence, increased in tandem.

One of the first to respond was a former Fenian prisoner, Michael Davitt, recently released from Dartmoor. A Mayoman, whose family emigrated to Lancashire when he was a child, Davitt was preparing to abandon doctrinaire Fenianism and throw himself into the alliance of constitutional nationalism and the agrarian movement. Davitt's primary objective was the immediate amelioration of social conditions in rural Ireland. His ultimate aim was the elimination of the landlord class and the establishment of peasant proprietorship. Intrigued by Parnell, and seeing him as 'An Englishman of the strongest type moulded for an Irish purpose',[3] he offered Parnell the leadership of a new agrarian movement that he, and others, were creating in Mayo. By October 1879 that grassroots activism had brought about the creation of the Land League. Parnell's assumption of the role of president, vaulted him into the unchallenged leadership of the 'advanced' wing of the Irish Parliamentary Party.

The surprise general election, called by Disraeli (the earl of Beaconsfield) in March 1880, offered Parnell an opportunity to make a bid for leadership of the Irish Parliamentary Party. The death of Isaac Butt in 1879 had come too early for such a bold move and the leadership of the Home Rule Party had passed to Cork banker, William Shaw, a moderate figure who was Butt's political *doppelgänger*. Parnell campaigned vigorously for a slate of candidates who shared his activist approach. Many of the men who would dominate Irish nationalist politics for years and even decades to come were returned with his assistance. Among them were John Dillon, James O'Kelly, Thomas Sexton and T.P. O'Connor. With their support, Parnell had sufficient allies after the election to defeat Shaw and become leader of the Irish Party at Westminster.

The election also swept the Liberals, under Gladstone, back into power. In the first queen's speech of his new administration, Gladstone's government promised not to renew Conservative coercion legislation and to introduce a major measure of tenant relief. Despite these assurances the incidence of agrarian 'outrages' trebled over the previous year and one of those murdered was the highly regarded landowner Lord Mountmorres.[4]

On 19 September 1880 Parnell made one of the most significant speeches of his career in Ennis, Co. Clare. In it he told his audience that the concessions forthcoming in the land bill would be a measure of the efficacy of Irish agrarian agitation that winter. The principal tool he suggested employing, in a campaign of civil disobedience, was the negativing of the policy of eviction by a refusal on the part of the peasantry to take up the land from which a neighbour had been ejected. Anyone who did so was to be subjected to a 'moral Coventry, by isolating him from his kind as if he was a leper of old'.[5] One of the first victims of the policy was the agent responsible for the estates of Lord Erne in Mayo, Captain Charles Boycott. After a number of evictions his servants and employees deserted him, shopkeepers refused to serve him and a detachment of Orangemen had to be despatched from Ulster to harvest his crops. To Boycott went the dubious distinction of lending his name to the new phenomenon.

While Gladstone sought to correct the inadequacies of his own 1870 Land Act, his chief secretary for Ireland, William E. Forster, was practising the darker arts of preparing coercive legislation in response to the upsurge of violence. Forster, a Quaker, had established a reputation as a philanthropist as a result of his charitable work in Ireland during the Great Famine. But the nickname he earned as chief secretary, 'Buckshot', captured the contribution he made to Irish history during his tenure at Dublin Castle. The explosion in 'Ribbon'[6] activity, which paralleled the rise in evictions[7] and the desperation of tenants—especially those in the west of Ireland—had, according to Forster, to be met with a resolute response.

In January 1881, Parnell, seen to have placed himself at the head of an anarchic movement, along with many of his political associates, was tried in Dublin for offences related to the activities of the Land League. The jury was unable to come to a decision and the defendants were acquitted. It was an instructive moment for the Liberal government. Clearly the normal criminal legislative framework was not fit for purpose—that purpose being the defeat of the Land League. At the end of January 1881 Forster introduced the draconian Protection of Persons and Property Bill. It gave the government the power to suspend *habeas corpus* and other civil rights in 'disturbed' areas of the country. Forster told the House of Commons: 'In Ireland the Land League law is supreme, and there is a real reign of terror over the whole country'.[8] People suspected of agrarian offences could be arrested and detained indefinitely without trial.

Later in his speech Forster identified those responsible for 'outrage' as falling into three categories. There were the Ribbon activists, throwbacks to agrarian secret societies of other days. There were Fenians 'who have taken advantage of the present state of affairs'. And then there was a third category:

> there are a large number of men who are the *mauvais sujets* of their neighbourhood. So it not infrequently happens that the most powerful man in a particular district is a contemptible, dissolute ruffian and blackguard, who, his character being known by all his neighbours, is shunned by them all, but who, nevertheless, acts as the powerful and active policeman for the execution of the unwritten law.[9]

What Forster did not seek to do was to roll all three categories into one. However, in many localities, it would become increasingly apparent to special magistrates and the Royal Irish Constabulary, that while the three categories were often distinct, the spectre of the Ribbon/Fenian warlord was not uncommon.[10]

Both the palliative design of the prime minister and the coercive framework of his chief secretary were qualified successes. Gladstone's Land Act brought reductions of 20–25% in rents due to the work of arbitrative land courts. However, such was the level of Liberal veneration of the 'contract' that leaseholders were excluded from the legislation. They were often, as a consequence, left paying higher rates to landlords than neighbouring farmers working holdings of similar size and quality. In addition more than 100,000 tenants were sufficiently in arrears to their landlords that they did not qualify for arbitration.

The violence that continued in spite of the efficacy of Forster's Protection of Persons and Property Act, therefore, was largely prompted by leaseholders, tenants in arrears and militant Fenian/Ribbon elements with a separate agenda. Forster, with the enthusiastic support of the viceroy, Lord Cowper, responded with a venom which earned him the undying animosity of the Parnellites and which gradually eroded his support among the members of the Liberal Cabinet. The endgame, as far as the Chief Secretary was concerned, was the incarceration of Parnell himself and his chief lieutenants. This was finally orchestrated, with the approval and collaboration of Gladstone, in October 1881. Parnell, Dillon, O'Kelly and others were arrested on the basis of allegedly seditious speeches and held, without trial, in Kilmainham Gaol.

The result was the proclamation by the Land League of a No Rent Manifesto and seven months of almost unparalleled strife in rural Ireland. Boycotting, intimidation, maiming and murder became a daily feature of life in the 'disturbed' districts of the country, mainly along the western seaboard. The principal targets were bailiffs, like Joseph and John Huddy, who worked for Lord Ardilaun. Murdered in January 1882, their bodies were found, weighed down in 27 feet of water. Equally vulnerable were agents, like John Henry Blake, an employee of the relentless Lord Clanricarde. Blake, according to the authorities was a man 'on good terms with all the people ... prior to the meetings of the Land League'.[11] If that was indeed the case it offered him no protection. He was shot and killed on 29 June 1882 in broad daylight. The biggest prize of all was a landlord, such as Walter Bourke, who was murdered while coming home from Mass three Sundays before the killing of Blake.[12] Despite this parlous state of affairs the Cabinet baulked at the even more stringent powers being demanded by Cowper and Forster in a new Coercion Bill framed in the spring of 1882. Gladstone preferred to see if the deal done to secure the release of Parnell and his colleagues in the informal compact known as the Kilmainham Treaty[13] would be a more effective vehicle for the curtailment of violence. Reacting to what he saw as a pusillanimous approach, Forster resigned.

But in the near-hysterical aftermath of the Phoenix Park murders of May 1882 (see Chapter 5) the more implacable Cowper/Forster template was followed in the Prevention of Crimes (Ireland) Bill introduced on 11 May 1882 by the home secretary, Sir William Harcourt. This provided for certain serious cases to be heard by three-judge courts; for increased powers of search; and for compensation costs resulting from murder, injury or damage to property to be levied on the jurisdiction in which the crimes were committed (the so called 'Blood Tax').[14] After a lengthy and determined rearguard action by an Irish Party inured to filibustering the business of the House of Commons, the bill became law on 12 July 1882. That summer the country waited for the first arrests and prosecutions under the terms of the new draconian legislation.

It was against this background of a rancorous administration under pressure from a strident opposition and a vengeful British public that news seeped out from one of the remotest regions of the country of the most hideous multiple murder of an often ugly Land War. Although it may well have been an apolitical crime committed outside of even the broadest definition of Ribbon/Fenian violence, it would become one of the most highly politicised of crimes in a decade in which such cases abounded.

The Maamtrasna murders, 17 August 1882

In 1882 Maamtrasna, on the shores of Lough Mask, near the Galway–Mayo border, was an isolated community of 250 or so families eking out a living on largely treeless marginal land under the shadow of the 2,000 foot Maamtrasna Mountain. The people of the region, mainly Joyces, Caseys or Lydons,[15] were Irish-speaking subsistence farmers who struggled to sustain large families in an inhospitable environment. There were no roads in the area and the only bridge had been swept away by a swollen river the previous year. It was a beautiful but forlorn place where, 'abandoned by Church and State, the people were left to their own devices to make their own laws and meet their own crises and feuds. They were left to fashion their own codes, their ethics and morals'.[16] The rugged Galway–Mayo region near Lough Mask, known as 'Joyce Country' because of the dominance of families of that particular surname, was a clannish, violent locality. A number of murders had already taken place there during the Land War.[17] One of these had become infamous. The 1882 murder of Lord Mountmorres, William D. Montmorency, had involved the killing of a man who was seen as an enlightened property owner who refused to resort to eviction. Unlike Lord Leitrim, a notorious landlord murdered around the same time in Co. Donegal who went nowhere without a military escort, he was the softest of 'soft' targets. So too was the family of John Joyce of

Maamtrasna, five members of which were brutally murdered on the night of 17 August 1882.

On Friday, 18 August, John Collins, a tenant farmer, having heard disturbances overnight in the house of his neighbours, the Joyces, went to check if all was well. He must have had some anticipation of what he might find as he brought two other neighbours with him, Mary and Margaret O'Brien. When he walked up to the door of the house he noticed that it was off its hinges. Looking inside he saw the naked corpse of John Joyce. He had been shot to death. Close by him was the body of his wife Bridget who had been savagely bludgeoned to death. Her daughter Peggy, in her mid-teens, and her mother-in-law, Margaret, had received similar treatment. In the only other room in the house lay two seriously injured boys, Michael, aged seventeen, had been shot in the head and stomach. He would later die of his wounds. Beside him lay his ten-year-old brother, Patrick, who had also been assaulted but not shot. Somehow he managed to survive the ordeal and recover.

As local people began to gather around the humble cottage that had housed the Joyce family (another son, Martin was absent, working in service), the police in a nearby temporary police hut at Finney were sent for. The senior RIC man, Constable Johnston, who spoke no Irish, brought Gaelic speaker Sub-Constable Lenihan with him to the crime scene. They managed to interview Michael and Patrick Joyce and were told that the murders had been committed by a group of three or four men. All had their faces blackened and were wearing traditional white-woollen bawneens. Incredibly, nothing was done immediately to assist the two seriously injured young boys. Michael Joyce died in the afternoon of 18 August at around the time that medical aid arrived. In the interim the local magistrate, Newton Brady, took 'dying declarations' from the two boys that coincided with the information they had given to the two RIC constables.

Journalist, Andrew Dunlop, then writing for the *Freeman's Journal* and the London *Daily News*, arrived on the scene 24 hours later. As he describes the scene, nothing much appears to have changed in the interim.

> The peasantry to about the number of about two hundred were gathered on the hill-side, in close proximity to the house, in which still lay the bodies of the murdered family ... The inquest was held in the open air, close to the house, and while it was proceeding the young lad, the sole survivor of the massacre, was carefully carried out and placed, for better air, in an outhouse adjoining.[18]

Not unexpectedly, the national and international reaction to the slaying of almost an entire, defenceless, family was one of utter revulsion. The *Times* report, dated 19 August, observed that, 'it is very much within the truth to say that it has no parallel for absolute barbarity in the modern history, at any rate, of Irish agrarian dispute or vengeance, the only instance that will compare with it in savage brutality as regards the method of perpetration is the Phoenix Park assassination'.[19] The following day the paper spoke for most journals when it commented that,

> no ingenuity can exaggerate the brutal ferocity of a crime which spared neither the gray [*sic*] hairs of an aged woman nor the innocent child of twelve years who slept by her side. It is an outburst of unredeemed and inexplicable savagery before which one stands appalled, and oppressed with a painful sense of the failure of our vaunted civilization.[20]

At around the time that Dunlop was surveying the scene of the crime, the RIC was approached by a cousin of the murdered man, along with his brother and nephew. Anthony, Johnny and Paddy Joyce of Cappanacreha, about three miles from the murder site, were known as the Maolras, after their father.[21] The information they passed to the RIC constables, accustomed to an uncommunicative and unco-operative peasantry—sympathetic towards 'outrage' or intimidated by its perpetrators—was extraordinary in nature.

The 'Maolras' told of an astonishing escapade on the night of 17 August. It was a tale they would repeat on many occasions in different trial venues. The account that follows, a translation from Irish of the evidence of Anthony 'Maolra' Joyce, is taken from the trial of one of the eight men subsequently accused of the murder of John Joyce and his family. Anthony Joyce told the Commission Court in Dublin that

> He was not sure at what hour he went to bed that night. When he had been in bed some time the barking of his dogs awoke him. He got up, and went to the door, and saw six men, whom he did not know at first. He then went round to the back of his house and he saw the six men again there. He then recognised the six men. Their names were—Anthony Philbin, Tom Casey, Martin Joyce, Myles Joyce, Patrick Joyce and Tom Joyce of Cappanacreha. He

had known four of the men since his youth, but two of them lived some distance away from him, Tom Casey and Anthony Philbin. Witness after a time went to the house of his brother, having nothing on him but his shirt, trousers and a flannel vest. He went the 'short cut', his brother and nephew came out. He then observed the six men going to the house of Michael Casey.[22] Witness and his brother and nephew followed them. They went into Casey's house, and on coming out they went the back road. The number of men at this time was ten. The other four were Pat Joyce (Shanvallycahill), Patrick Casey, John Casey, and Michael Casey. Witness saw them coming out of a house and went behind a hedge. Witness went down after them, accompanied by his brother and nephew. The ten men then went towards the lake until they came to the river of Strangalone, when they crossed the river and went towards Maamtrasna. Witness and his companions were following them, no matter where they might go. He knew John Joyce's house at Maamtrasna. He saw the ten men go up to that house, then he heard a noise at the door. At this time witness, his brother, and his nephew were behind a bush. Some of the ten men went in and others remained outside. Witness heard noise like people beating at the door.[23] He heard people in the house shouting and screeching. He could not distinguish the screams of women from those of men. He did not wait after that, but he and his brother and his nephew ran back as quickly as they could to their own houses. Witness stayed with his brother from that time until the break of day. He saw the police next day (Friday) about dinner time.[24]

It was an astonishing tale of amateur detective work, unparalleled in the history of the Land War, and, if true, the Maolras had neatly delivered an unassailable case to the investigating authorities. It was a gift horse that would greatly relieve the intense pressure on the Royal Irish Constabulary and the magistracy to identify the murderers and enable society to take swift vengeance. The authorities had no inclination or reason to question the detailed evidence of the three witnesses, thereafter classified as 'independent' or 'unimpeachable'—the ten men named were duly rounded up and brought before the magistrates in Cong. There the Maolras faced their accusers, recounted their adventure, and were allowed to be questioned by the men they had accused of one of the most brutal crimes in Irish legal history.

Curiously, four of the men named by the Maolras were, like the victims of the Maamtrasna murders, cousins of theirs. Myles Joyce, Martin Joyce and Patrick 'Paudeen' Joyce were known as the 'Seáns', after their own father—brother of Maolra Joyce. Tom Joyce, was a generation removed, he was the son of Paudeen Joyce. However, relations between the 'Maolras' and the 'Seáns' were characterised less by blood ties than by blood feud. All five families lived in relatively close proximity and issues of trespass as well as accusations of sheep-stealing from the mountain commonage on which all local farmers grazed their herds, divided them and regularly set them at each other's throats. Encounters between the 'Maolras' and the 'Seáns' often ended in violence; Myles 'Seán' Joyce had been jailed for assaulting Anthony 'Maolra' Joyce the previous year. He had opted to spend a month in Galway Prison rather than pay a fine of £1.

The other six men named by the 'Maolras' included brothers-in-law, Anthony Philbin (recently returned from Northumberland) and Tom Casey. Both were from the Cappaduff/Glensaul area on the shores of Lough Mask just south of Tourmakeady. The townlands were located about four to five miles from the homes of the 'Maolras' and the 'Seáns' in Cappanacreha. Three more of the accused, Pat Casey, John Casey and Michael Casey (all related), came from the townland of Derry, located about halfway between Cappanacreha and Maamtrasna. It was Michael Casey's house from which, according to the Maolras, the lethal attack had been launched. The final alleged attacker was Pat Joyce from Shanvallycahill, a townland south of Cappanacreha. He was unrelated to any of the 'Maolra' or 'Seán' Joyces. Pat Joyce had a reputation in the neighbourhood for being at the heart of much of the violence and disorder that took place in the area.

No motive has ever been definitively established for such a hideous crime. Nor for the reasoning behind the wholesale slaughter of an entire family other than the need to dispose of witnesses. The RIC investigation was offered a number of different theories. The one that most appealed to a Dublin Castle administration anxious for further justification for the Crimes Act (and for an early judicial coup under its aegis) was that John Joyce had been a member of a local secret society, one of the many informal Ribbon/Fenian 'enforcement' groups which proliferated during the Land War. Information was forthcoming that he had been treasurer of the group, that he had embezzled funds, and that he and his family had been duly punished. Another story suggested that it was his mother who had been the target of the raid. She was said to have given information to the RIC on the location in Lough Mask of the bodies of the missing Huddy brothers. Another claim was that Peggy, the teenage daughter of John Joyce had been seen consorting with admirers from within the ranks of the RIC—a crime punishable by death under the rules of a remote society dominated by Ribbonism.

However, a more plausible explanation—particularly if the case assembled by the state against most of the ten men named by the Maolras is retrospectively challenged—is that John Joyce, in common with many of his neighbours, was a sheep-stealer. The sheep population of the valley grazed on common land in the hills above Maamtrasna. Most feuds, disputes and enmities in the neighbourhood revolved around the theft of livestock. Sheep were the easiest target for those driven by desperation for any means to feed their families. If John Joyce had been embezzling the funds of a local secret society then there was little evidence that he had been spending the proceeds to improve the lot of his family. When the lord lieutenant, Lord Spencer, visited the Maamtrasna murder home a month after the slaughter he wrote to his Cabinet colleague, Lord Granville, that, 'I could not have believed that six human beings could have lived in such a hole'.[25] Controversial evidence would emerge after Dublin Castle had closed the file on the crime, that someone had been so irked by John Joyce's sheep-rustling, that they had engaged the services of local ruffians to kill him.

A week after the murders the ambitious Crown solicitor, George Bolton, was appointed to lead the investigation and to oversee the preparation for proceedings that would take place in Galway prior to a full trial before the Commission Court in Dublin. Under the terms of the recent Crimes Act, it had become more or less mandatory to remove both the accused and witnesses from their own environment and to try capital cases in an urban centre like Dublin. The authorities traditionally experienced difficulties in assembling 'viable' juries in rural Ireland where the population was sympathetic or, at the very least, neutral, when it came to the activities of those involved in agrarian 'outrage'. Dublin could provide a steady stream of propertied, middle-class juries, often disproportionately Unionist in composition, and offered greater security to nervous prosecution witnesses.

The Maamtrasna trials, November 1882

The trials of the ten accused men began in front of Lord Justice Barry on 1 November 1882, in Green Street Court-house. Leading for the prosecution was Irish attorney general William Moore Johnson, assisted by James Murphy, QC, and a future Irish lord chief justice, Peter O'Brien.[26] The prosecution counsellors were briefed by George Bolton. Leading for the defence was George Orme Malley; the defendants' solicitor was Henry Concannon of Tuam. Neither spoke Irish, the language of the bulk of their clients. When Justice Barry ascertained the fact that the accused were Gaelic speakers he insisted on an interpreter. One was provided, a Constable Evans, by the RIC. The prisoners were remanded to Mountjoy until 13 November.

It is distinctly possible that George Bolton's choice of a potential informer from among the ranks of the accused was dictated by linguistics. The best English speaker among the group was Anthony Philbin, brother-in-law of Tom Casey, who had spent a number of years working in England. Philbin insisted that he had been nowhere near the scene of the murder on the night of 17 August. He had been at the wake of a man called Quinn and could produce alibi witnesses. As two of the Maolras[27] had already testified that Philbin had been a member of the murder gang, to have accepted this claim of innocence would have fatally undermined the state case. Instead Bolton managed, in return for a promise of immunity, to extract a 'confession' from Philbin (who was, it would later emerge, almost certainly completely innocent of involvement in the crime). Philbin claimed to have been a member of the group and to have watched as Pat Joyce, Pat Casey and Myles Joyce went into the Maamtrasna house to kill the family of John Joyce. Philbin, in turning state's evidence, had become, in the vernacular of the period, an approver. He would later be joined as a state informer by his brother-in-law, Tom Casey, and both men would be called as prosecution witnesses in the November trials.

The question might well be asked, what was the necessity of accepting Philbin's state's evidence in the first place? The evidence of the Maolras, if it stood up in court, would be sufficient to secure a conviction of all ten accused. It must have become clear to Bolton that Philbin's entire 'knowledge' of the events of the night was based on the eye-witness reports of the Maolra Joyces which he had heard at the Magistrates' Court in Cong. He had no personal details to add to the evidence of the 'independent' witnesses. His usefulness was based entirely on his willingness to perjure himself when it came to identifying the actual killers. That was Philbin's sole function.

As the perceived ringleader of the murder gang, the first of the accused to be put on trial was Pat Joyce of Shanvallycahill. He was bilingual and so had some understanding of what was happening around him as he stood in the dock. The *Freeman's Journal* court reporter described him as a 'thick-set man of about middle height with a somewhat hard expression of countenance ... almost throughout the entire of yesterday's long sitting, he maintained a calm and unexcited demeanour'.[28]

One of the first prosecution witnesses, Constable Johnson, was a useful reminder (and intended as such) to the jury[29] of the awful savagery that had been visited on the family of John Joyce. He told the attorney general:

> I was stationed on 18 August at Finney, a temporary station. About a quarter past nine some of the villagers of Maamtrasna came to the station, and, from what they told me, I went to John Joyce's house. I found John Joyce, whom I knew well previously, lying on the floor, his head towards the fire and his feet towards the door. He was dead and cold. There were two bullet marks on his body—one on the right breast and another on the right side. The wife of John Joyce was lying in the bed. I examined her body. There was a large wound on her forehead over the right eye. Her skull was broken; she was dead. Michael Joyce was lying beside her; he was alive, but weak, and scarcely able to speak. He had one bullet wound under the right ear and another in his right side. I spoke to Michael through an interpreter and he answered. He appeared to be choking. I got him a drink, after which he spoke a little better. I went to the inner room, and saw, lying on the bed, the old woman. She was stripped and dead. Her left arm was hanging down beside the bed. The flesh was off it from the elbow down to the hand ... She was lying partly on her face, her head slightly upturned. I examined her, and found a large wound over her ear, in somewhat the same place as on John Joyce's wife. There was a large pool of blood about her head. Her skull was broken in. In the bed, lying behind her, was the young girl,

her granddaughter. Her head was a little raised and was beside the old woman's feet. Her skull was also broken in, and her brains were flowing out. She was also in her night dress. I saw the little boy Patsey in the same bed. He was alive, in a very weak state, and greatly frightened. I raised him, and spoke to him. His eye was closed. There were two wounds on his head—one over the eye and another above the ear. He was naked. There were two dogs in the room, and I had great difficulty to put them out. One ran under the bed, and I could not get it away for some time. When I spoke to Patsey he answered me. When I returned to the kitchen I found a small bullet—a revolver bullet—beside the body of John Joyce. There were two bullet marks on the wall over the bed in the kitchen, one at the head of the bed, the other at the foot.[30]

Three revolvers had been used in the attack. A total of nine shots had been fired, four had found their targets. The bullets had been used on the two eldest males. The brutal bludgeoning had been reserved for the unfortunate women and the youngest boy. The three women had been beaten almost beyond recognition. One salient fact that Constable Johnson failed to mention, or was not allowed to, was the substance of the conversation he had had on the morning of 18 August with the two young survivors in which both had mentioned the fact that their assailants had been wearing traditional white 'bawneen' sweaters and had blackened faces. To have done so would have been to undermine the testimony, yet to come, of the Maolras. All three at various times had referred to the murder gang as having worn dark clothes. In addition, had they blackened their faces before engaging on the work of the night it would have been impossible to identify them.

The evidence of the Maolras was spread over the first two days of the trial of Pat Joyce. All three insisted on testifying in Irish through the RIC interpreter. This was in spite of the fact that it was suspected their level of knowledge of English was more than adequate. The consequent drawn out nature of their direct evidence and cross-examination allowed the three men plenty of time to think about their answers and made it extremely difficult for Malley to discommode them in any way by changing the rhythm of the questioning. All three, in essence, stuck to the story first heard in the Magistrates' Court in Cong.

With the Maolras as prelude, it was left to the approver to secure the state case against Pat Joyce. James Murphy, QC, took Philbin through the testimony that would send the Shanvallycahill man to the gallows. The understandably tense witness began:

> I live at Cappaduff, County Mayo. I have been at various times in England. The last time I was there for nine or ten years. I lived chiefly in the county of Northumberland. I came back to Cappaduff four or five years ago. I have a brother in law, Tom Casey, living at Glensaul. On the night of the murder my brother in law met me a little distance from my own house. I had gone on the evening of that day to a wake, and after my return I remained a short time in my house. I then went out to look if there were any trespassers on my land, and soon afterwards met Tom Casey. I had known the prisoner [Patrick Joyce]. On the night of the murder I met Tom Casey in the second field from my house, about eighty yards from my house. I live about five or six miles from Maamtrasna. On the way to Derry we met three men as we crossed the river at Cappanacreha. The three men were Myles Joyce, Patrick Joyce and his son, whom I did not know then, but whose name I have since learned to be Tom.

MURPHY: Did the five of you go on together then?

PHILBIN: We did sir, for a short distance.

MURPHY: Did you meet any other man?

PHILBIN: Yes, Martin Joyce.

MURPHY: Where were you when you met Martin Joyce?

PHILBIN: Some short distance away from my house; I don't know the land as I was only there once before.

MURPHY: Could you say at what hour of the night it was when you six met together?

PHILBIN: It would be eleven o'clock anyway; between eleven and twelve o'clock, I dare say.

MURPHY: What distance was it from Casey's house to where Martin Joyce had joined you?

PHILBIN: I do not know. It was some distance. We were six in number going up to Casey's house. The five men did not remain long in Casey's house. I joined them again when they came out, I then took notice of four other men.

MURPHY: Who were the four other men whom you noticed?

PHILBIN: Patrick Casey, John Casey, Michael Casey and Patrick Joyce.

MURPHY: ... When the men came out of Casey's house, you being ten in number, where did you go?

PHILBIN: We went down under Casey's house. I crossed a ditch and into a field. I asked Martin Joyce then where they were going to?

MURPHY: ... Tell us, where did you all go to?

PHILBIN: They went away until they came to a street and a house, which I did not know.

MURPHY: Did you all go together?

PHILBIN: Sometimes they would be together and sometimes they would not be together. When going over a ditch or a drain they would scatter.

MURPHY: When you were all going on, were you in the front, or the middle, or behind?

PHILBIN: I was behind.

MURPHY: Who was with you chiefly?

PHILBIN: The one who chiefly kept my company was young Tom Joyce.

MURPHY: Had you any arms?

PHILBIN: No, sir.

MURPHY: Did you see any arms with anyone?

PHILBIN: I saw some when we got to the street and the house which I did not know.

MURPHY: What arms did you see there?

PHILBIN: I saw a revolver with one of the prisoners.

MURPHY: With whom did you see the revolver?

PHILBIN: With Patrick Joyce, the prisoner there.

MURPHY: When they came to the street and the house you have spoken of did you see them going to the door.

PHILBIN: I did, sir.

MURPHY: What was done to the door?

PHILBIN: They broke it in.

MURPHY: Where were you exactly when they were at the door?

PHILBIN: We came out of the garden by the side of the gable, and I was the hindermost. There was a little wall and we got out in front of the door. There were two or three men between me and the men who broke in the door.

MURPHY: Who broke in the door?

PHILBIN: Patrick Casey of Derry, Myles Joyce of Cappanacreha, and Pat Joyce, the prisoner there.

MURPHY: Did you see those three men you have named go into the house?

PHILBIN: I did, sir.

MURPHY: Are you able to state whether any others went into the house?

PHILBIN: I did not see any others going in.

MURPHY: After they entered the house did you hear any noise from inside?

PHILBIN: I heard screeches.

MURPHY: Anything else?

PHILBIN: I heard a shot fired.

MURPHY: What did you do when you heard the screeches and the shot?

PHILBIN: I got frightened, I turned around and went away.

MURPHY: Did you go away by the same way you had come?

PHILBIN: No, the nearest road I could find I broke into.

MURPHY: Did you hear more than one shot?

PHILBIN: When I was a few yards off from the 'street' I heard another shot and I went away as fast as I could ...

MURPHY: Where did you make for?

PHILBIN: I went home without waiting for my brother-in-law or anyone of the party. I made off as soon as I could. I saw none of them again that night

MURPHY: ... From the night of the murder, up to the present, have you spoken to Anthony Joyce, or to his brother John, or to John's son Pat?

PHILBIN: I spoke a word to Anthony the night I was arrested.

MURPHY: Was that when you heard them giving their evidence before the magistrate?

PHILBIN: Yes.

MURPHY: Did you put them some questions yourself then, after you heard them swearing?

PHILBIN: I did, sir.

MURPHY: Was that the only time you spoke to them?

PHILBIN: Yes.

MURPHY: On the night of the murder, after you left
                   Casey's house, did you notice any persons at
                   all following you?

PHILBIN: No sir, I did not.[31]

Murphy's concluding questions were designed to establish that Philbin
could not have concocted his story in concert with the Joyces in any
grandiose state plot to secure convictions against the accused. He was
aware that the defence team would suggest to Philbin that he had not, in
fact, been present on the night of the murders and was simply going
through a well-rehearsed fiction in order to save his own life.

Philbin's narrative was necessarily vague as he had probably never
been near the murder house, or indeed that of Michael Casey. His evidence was such as to preclude any questions on details of the interiors
of either dwelling. It is noteworthy that at all times as he spoke he used
the pronoun 'they' as opposed to 'we', indicating his distinctness from
the rest of the group. He was always behind the others ('hindermost') on
the way to Maamtrasna. He was not armed and claimed ignorance of
what was intended. This also arose out of his 'decision' to remain
outside the house of Michael Casey while a council of war was being
conducted inside. Had he actually remained where he claimed to have
positioned himself, as it happens, he would have been standing exactly
where the Joyces also claimed to have been. This fact, missed by the
defence team, was later established by Timothy Harrington, the Irish
Party MP (see below). Furthermore, his mad dash away from the scene
of the crime at the sound of the first shots would have caused him to
collide with the three Maolra Joyces concealed behind their bush observing proceedings. They, it will be recalled, claimed to have remained *in
situ* until a number of shots had been fired, though they heard the shots
as a series of dull thuds.

When Malley, the leading defence QC, got to his feet he sought
straightaway to undermine Philbin's contention that he had been a par-
ticipant in the slaughter. The subtext of his cross-examination was that
the witness had not been present, knew nothing about the physical location in which the murder had taken place and had been coerced by the
state into a series of inventions and evasions in return for his life and a
pecuniary reward.

MALLEY: You were brought before the magistrate?

PHILBIN: I was sir, at Cong.

MALLEY: And when you were brought before the magistrate you heard Anthony Joyce, John Joyce and Patrick Joyce tell this story?

PHILBIN: Yes.

MALLEY: The whole of this story of going from Derry to Maamtrasna?

PHILBIN: I did not hear them tell the whole of the story. They did not tell all that I knew.

MALLEY: Did they tell that they saw you going along to the murdered family's house?

PHILBIN: They did, but they did not tell the truth when they said that they saw me going with the six men into the house. I do not know [his] house.

MALLEY: ... They could not, then, have told the truth if they said you came out of the house with the ten men?

PHILBIN: I was below the house. It was there I joined them.

MALLEY: How far was that?

PHILBIN: Not many yards—not much more than ten.

MALLEY: Did you keep that distance from them all the way to Maamtrasna? [Pause] Do you understand what I am saying?

PHILBIN: I do, sir.

MALLEY: And why don't you answer? Why don't you answer?

PHILBIN: I was up with them sometimes and behind them four or five yards. We passed over a few ditches.

MALLEY: Where did you cross the river?

PHILBIN: I am not acquainted with the land there. When we went to Casey's house they went in, and I went around behind the house.

MALLEY: Do you know the house next to the house of the murdered man?

PHILBIN: I took no notice of it.

MALLEY: Where were you exactly standing when the men broke in the door?

PHILBIN: About three or four yards behind them, and then I moved out fornent the door.

MALLEY: Did you remain below the house?

PHILBIN: When the men broke into the house I broke and advanced away.

MALLEY: Had the men gone into the house before you went away?

PHILBIN: They had. As soon as I came into the street before the house they broke in the door, and when I heard the screams and shot I went the nearest way. I got frightened.

MALLEY: What do you call the nearest?

PHILBIN: Any way that it was my advantage to go.

MALLEY: ... Was that the way you came?

PHILBIN: I went through other fields to take the nearest way.

MALLEY: ... Now you know what the three men Joyce proved against yourself, that is if their story be true?

PHILBIN: I heard them swearing.

MALLEY: When you were present before the magistrates did you cross-examine them?

PHILBIN: I asked them a few questions.

MALLEY:	Was not that to show that you were not at Maamtrasna at all?
PHILBIN:	I only asked them how long they knew me.
MALLEY:	Was that not to show that you were not there at all? ... Was it not to defend yourself that you put those questions?
PHILBIN:	Everybody was asking questions.
MALLEY:	Was it not to defend yourself that you put those questions? [Pause] Answer the question.
PHILBIN:	Every man was asking questions and we were told to do so.
MALLEY:	On your oath, were you not afraid that you would be punished for the crime?
PHILBIN:	To be sure I was afraid.
MALLEY:	And was it not because you were afraid you swore against that man in the dock, and to clear yourself?
PHILBIN:	It was because I had nothing to do with it myself. I did not do any harm.
MALLEY:	When you met your brother-in-law, Tom Casey, how far were you from Derry?
PHILBIN:	About three miles.
MALLEY:	What brought you those three miles?
PHILBIN:	Tom Casey told me he wanted me, and said he wanted to see the boys.
MALLEY:	Was it mere curiosity that brought you to see him—to accompany him?
PHILBIN:	I did not know what business he wanted of me.
MALLEY:	Did you know when he said that the boys wanted you what he meant?

PHILBIN: I did not know what business he had.

MALLEY: Had you any talk with him?

PHILBIN: I said it was a very strange thing going so far such a dark night.

MALLEY: ... Were you trembling when the Joyces were telling the story?

PHILBIN: Of course; such a charge against anybody would frighten them.

MALLEY: Did you not tell me at first you were not afraid, and say 'Why would I be afraid?'

PHILBIN: Why would I be afraid when I did nothing wrong?

MALLEY: You saw no way of getting out of it except by turning against the others?

PHILBIN: Would I be punished for another man's doings?

MALLEY: Did you not go that night upon your own free will?

PHILBIN: I would not have gone if I knew they were going to murder the man. I went with the men for company.

Later Philbin was put into the anomalous position of having to contradict alibi evidence that would have worked in his favour had he been one of the group still accused of murder. On the night of the murder he had been at the wake of a man named Quinn and some of the mourners had indicated that he had been there until the early hours of the morning. Two of them, a neighbour called Cusack and a relative of the dead man, Thomas Quinn, were even prepared to say that they had accompanied him home. Philbin, however, claimed to have left the wake at nightfall. At that time of the year it would have grown dark at around ten o'clock. Philbin's timing of his departure was crucial to the state case. Had he remained on at the wake for a few more hours he could not possibly have been in Maamtrasna at the time of the murders. In answer to a number of questions from Malley, Philbin denied that he had met his mother at the wake and that he had been accompanied home by Cusack and Quinn:

MALLEY:	Why did you leave the wake so early?
PHILBIN:	I thought it was time for a respectable man to go home, unless he intended to stay till morning.
MALLEY:	Was it because it was time to go home that you left?
PHILBIN:	To be sure.

Philbin was followed into the witness-box by his brother-in-law, Tom Casey, who had offered to turn state's evidence only the day before. His testimony, in essence confirmed that of Philbin. On the third day of the trial the jury took precisely eight minutes to bring in a verdict of guilty against Pat Joyce. He was sentenced to be hanged at Galway Prison on 15 December. The *Freeman's Journal* described Pat Joyce's reaction to the verdict thus: 'The prisoner replied "Not Guilty" raised his left hand, and for a moment pressed his cheek against it; but almost immediately relapsed into complete self possession'.[32]

Pat Joyce was followed into the dock by Pat Casey, 'a middle aged man', most of whose trial took place on 16 November. A template had been laid down in the first trial that was followed faithfully in the two subsequent cases. The Maolras and the approvers repeated their evidence. Defence counsel, despite the occasional stumble, was unable to shake their stories. The jury in the trial of Pat Casey took twelve minutes to reach a guilty verdict. Donning the iconic black cap in passing sentence, Justice Barry observed, with considerable emotion, that

> if ever there was a case in which a combined sense of horror at the crime and the necessity of duty ought steel [to] a man's nerves against emotion or distress, that case is the present. I shall add no words to make you feel conscious of the position in which you stand. You have no mercy to expect in this world. I ask you to turn to that God whose dictates and precepts you have so dreadfully disobeyed.[33]

It is unlikely that Casey understood much of the judge's remarks though he must have been conscious of the meaning of the symbolic black cap.

Fifteen minutes after sentence had been pronounced on Casey, the third prisoner identified by Philbin and Tom Casey as having actually committed the Maamtrasna murders was brought to the dock. Myles Joyce was 'older than either of the previous men[34] who have been tried. He was dressed in older garments, but, unlike them, he did not appear to have the slightest knowledge of the language in which his trial was being conducted'.[35] On the basis of the sensational newspaper coverage of the previous cases, George Orme Malley, QC, moved that the trial of Myles Joyce be postponed. His application was denied, a new jury was sworn, and the curtain went up on a new production of the most gripping piece of theatre of the day. The dialogue was similar, the outcome was the same. After deliberating on the evidence for six minutes the jury brought in a verdict of guilty in the case of Myles Joyce.

The prisoner did not react to the clerk's intoning of the verdict 'and seemed like a man who had only the vaguest notion of what was going on'. Constable Evans intervened and translated the decision of the jury for the impassive man in the dock.

> A change then came upon the prisoner. He showed a little fear, and clutched the bar of the dock, but, looking upwards with a fervent expression and attitude of invocation, spoke in Irish. The interpreter rendered it as follows: 'He leaves it to God and the virgin above his head. He had no dealing with it, no more than the person who was never born, nor had he against anyone else. For the last twenty years he had done no harm, and if he had, might he never go to heaven. He was as clear of this as the child yet to be born ...' Though exhibiting considerable emotion, the prisoner did not lose his self control in the slightest degree. The scene was very painful, and it scarcely added to its solemnity to observe the many ladies who were amongst the audience, and the obtrusive manner in which the thronged court-house gazed with the curiosity of interest, rather than of feeling, upon the condemned and sorrowful looking man.[36]

There remained five prisoners whose fate was still to be decided. All had pleaded not guilty. After a conference between Malley and the Crown prosecutors the defence counsel approached Henry Concannon and advised the men's solicitor that the state was willing to offer commuted sentences if all five of the accused pleaded guilty. Otherwise preparations for a gibbet with eight ropes would continue in Galway Prison. Initially, only one of the men, Michael Casey (who later admitted to complicity in the crime) was prepared to acquiesce. The other four, three of them kin to Myles Joyce, like him, continued to protest their innocence. Only after the intervention of their parish priest, Fr Michael McHugh, were all five persuaded that they would suffer the same fate as the three condemned men if they put the Crown to the effort and expense of five more trials.

Subsequently, when a concerted campaign was under way to rehabilitate four of those five men, as well as Myles Joyce, McHugh rationalised his stance:

> in the interests of the prisoners I considered it the wiser course to plead guilty. I was by no means clear at the time that they were innocent. I was certainly inclined to the belief that they were, but I had no grounds for such a belief, but their own declarations to me. I argued with myself thus—if the men were guilty their plea of guilty can do them no harm, and will save their lives; and that if they were innocent I felt that the truth would leak out, as from my knowledge of the locality and the people I believed such a huge wrong could not continue ... This was the argument I made use of to the men themselves in the cell of Green Street Courthouse; and I daresay it was the argument which induced them to withdraw their plea of 'not guilty' and enter a plea of 'guilty' ... I rather believed they were innocent.[37]

All five pleaded guilty. All five were duly sentenced to death by Justice Barry, though the absence of the black cap in pronouncing sentence indicated his awareness of the fact that an agreement had been reached between Concannon and Bolton which would save the men's lives.

However, nobody appears to have informed or consulted the lord lieutenant, Lord Spencer, in advance. On 23 November the 'Red Earl' wrote to the home secretary, Sir William Harcourt, in a manner that suggested he had yet to make up his mind as to the fate of the five men whom the Crown considered to be accessories to the Maamtrasna murders:

> The conclusion of the Maamtrasna case is, on the whole very satisfactory, but I dread the next stage, the question of the degree of moral guilt of men all equally guilty by law will be very difficult to settle. What weight do you attach to men pleading guilty in a capital case?

I gather from what the judge said that although he left the case free for me, he considered that the 5 men having pleaded guilty should make me commute their sentences. He purposely delivered sentence without assuming the black cap that is an outward form, but I do not know what interpretation is put on it. He must have done it with a meaning.

It is conceivable that the most atrocious murderer may plead guilty from repentance at the last moment before trial, but that would not necessarily carry with it commutation of the capital sentence and it would be wrong that it should. Until I know the actual part taken by these 5 men it is difficult to say whether they are as deeply guilty as the three convicted. In this country the effect of any act connected with a sentence on juries themselves is so much more considered than it would be in England. In this case it is argued that as the fact of pleading guilty confirmed and strengthened the verdict passed by the juries, it did a service to the independence of future juries which ought to be recognised and that a commutation would encourage other men to plead guilty.

As far as I have gone yet in my ideas about this I am inclined to let the settlement rest much more on the degrees in which the men are implicated and the circumstances connected with each other rather than on the fact of their having pleaded guilty. I should like to hear your opinion.

Harcourt was happy to oblige with an opinion, one that would have offered little consolation to the five men whose fates had still to be decided. He replied to Spencer the following day to the effect that 'the simple fact of a plea of guilty is no ground for commutation ... I should therefore be anxious to discern a distinction of moral guilt in the laws which would justify a discrimination in the punishment'.[38]

Ultimately Spencer opted for clemency. He then had to explain his decision to an exasperated queen, who did not appear to want the Crown to be cheated of five nooses. His explanation offers an insight into the process by which he had been given little choice in arriving at his decision:

Lord Spencer would have wished to have considered the degree of guilt of these men, and had he been at liberty to do so, would probably have allowed the law to take its course, in the case of one man who, although he did not enter the house and with his own hands kill the victims, yet allowed the men to assemble at his own house. He was no doubt aware of what was to take place. Lord Spencer however found the Law Officers, although they had not pledged him, had allowed the idea to prevail both with the Counsel for the prisoners and the Judge, that the death sentence would not be carried out, if they pleaded guilty.

The Judge acted on this and most earnestly pleaded for mitigation of sentence. Lord Spencer felt constrained to follow his advice. Had he allowed any of these men to be hung after what took place there would have been such an outcry in the country, and the idea would have been spread that the men were made, on a false representation to plead guilty, that Lord Spencer felt that the harm of this would have outweighed every other consideration for a different course.

Lord Spencer regrets the necessity for this decision as he would have desired to show these deluded people that if they assist at a murder under orders of a secret society or otherwise, they must take the consequences of their act. The three men who actually killed the family will now be hung, and the others will be kept in penal servitude for life. The Queen will understand that Lord Spencer had no share in what was done in Court, but could not disregard the result.

Lord Spencer cannot of course allow these reasons to be made public, but he wishes to lay them before Your Majesty. He must run the risk of his decision being attacked and misunderstood by the Public. The Law Officers acted on the highest motives but Lord Spencer regrets that they were not more guarded.[39]

Spencer had one further crucial decision to make before the executions of the three condemned men proceeded. Two days before their scheduled hangings Pat Joyce and Pat Casey, after some cajoling, were prevailed upon to make statements admitting their guilt and declaring that Myles Joyce was completely innocent of any involvement in the killings. Witnessed by George Mason, the governor of Galway Prison and Richard Evans, the chief warder, Pat Joyce's 'dying declaration' read:

Myles Joyce is as innocent as the child unborn of the crime
of murder of the Joyce family. Seven persons were present
at the time of the murder in the house. Namely, myself,
Michael Casey (prisoner); Pat Casey (prisoner); Thomas
Casey (approver); and three now at liberty and I don't like
to mention their names. Thomas Casey used three revolvers
and it was he who did all the shooting. Two of the three
men, now outside, had a hammer and used it to kill out
those Joyces not dead after receiving the pistol shots.

Anthony Philbin was not present, and I never seen him
in the neighbourhood for the last three years. The Joyces,
who swore against us, did not, nor could not, have seen
us the night of the murder. There was no meeting whatever at Michael Casey's house. The meeting took place in
the house of one of the men who is out, and is a farmer.

The Murder was not the work of a Secret Society, but
was caused by this man (the farmer) who is outside, for
spite. I asked Thomas Casey (approver) when he shot at
John Joyce, the man of the house, what was the cause for
it? He said if I did not hold my mouth, he would soon let
me know as I was not doing anything to help him.[40]

With this statement, and an independent confirmatory declaration from
Pat Casey, the authorities were probably as close to the truth about the
Maamtrasna killings as they would ever be. However, was Earl Spencer to
accept the two prisoner statements, he would be leaving a number of his
officials, George Bolton in particular, open to the accusation that they had
coerced Philbin and Casey into perjuring themselves in order to confirm the
evidence of the three 'independent' witnesses.

It was a step that Spencer, despite personal misgivings, was not prepared
to take. On 19 December he wrote to Justice Barry outlining what had happened. He referred to the receipt of the two statements from Galway:

I went carefully through these statements with the Lord
Chancellor, the Attorney General and Mr. Bolton. They
all disbelieved the statement, and said it was quite inconsistent with the evidence, which you believed as well as
they. There was evident mixture of truth in what they said.

After a long conference, I came to the conclusion that
if no new feature were reported, I would not on these

statements respite Myles Joyce. I felt bound to believe the
evidence, on which the jury convicted him, and of which
you approved. It is noteworthy that no movement whatever was made on his behalf until the 13th, and then it was
not put forward by Concannon or the Priests. I did not
get the Governor's statement until 1 p.m. on the 14th.

I need not tell you what great anxiety these statements
caused me: I may now have made a mistake, but I do not
think I did. I have written you a very imperfect account of
the last episode in this dreadful business. I think no advantage will be gained by any official statement.[41]

Presented with two alternative murder scenarios, in consultation with
one of the officials who had had a controlling hand in the version outlined
to the court and conscious of the political damage that would be done by
acknowledging the validity of the Casey and Joyce confessions, Spencer
baulked. The two statements were quietly buried and the hanging of Myles
Joyce was allowed to proceed. It was a harrowing experience for all concerned. Some time later the nationalist MP, Timothy Harrington, wrote a
second-hand account based on interviews with witnesses to the hanging:

Myles Joyce turned to every official of the jail he met, as
he passed to the scaffold, and, with all the fiery vehemence
of the Celt, declared, in a language which nearly all those
who surrounded him were strangers to, that 'he was innocent. He feared not to die. But he felt the indignity of
being put to death as a murderer.' The scene on the scaffold itself was shocking beyond description. Even with the
cap drawn over his eyes, and the executioner standing,
rope in hand, to hurl the three wretched men together into
eternity, Myles Joyce still declared his innocence; and, as
if eager that his very last breath on earth should be a
protestation to that God whom he was so soon to meet,
he turned again in the direction of the few by-standers,
and 'called God to witness that he knew no more of the
murder than the child unborn;' and with that solemn declaration on his lips he sunk from view. His last effort had
somewhat displaced the arrangements of the executioner.
The rope caught in the wretched man's arm, and for some
seconds it was seen being jerked and tugged in the

writhing of his last agony. The grim hangman cast an
angry glance into the pit, and then, hissing an obscene
oath at the struggling victim, sat on the beam, and kicked
him into eternity.[42]

The hangman at the centre of this Gothic scene, William Marwood,
would later insist that everything had gone according to plan. So would the
Dublin Castle administration. The execution of the three men caused only
minor tremors in the body politic. To most observers, even those utterly
opposed to British administrative practices in Ireland, an ugly boil had been
lanced with the execution of the three men most responsible for a shameful
and vicious murder. Matters might well have remained in that state were it
not for the bizarre altar-rail retraction of the approver, Thomas Casey.

RETRACTION AND REHABILITATION, 1883-5

Casey and Philbin had returned to their homes in Joyce country, albeit
under constant RIC guard. Casey had problems both inside and outside
the walls of his house. The antagonism he felt from neighbours was paralleled by that of his wife. She blamed him for the implication of her brother,
Anthony Philbin, in the entire affair. Casey was also experiencing financial
difficulties. On 8 August 1884 he finally cracked. In a move apparently
orchestrated by the resourceful parish priest of Partry,[43] Fr James Corbett,
uncle of the future world heavyweight boxing champion, 'Gentleman' Jim
Corbett, Casey made a dramatic appearance in the Church in
Tourmakeady at the annual Confirmation ceremony. The archbishop of
Tuam, John MacEvilly, a prelate not noted for fervent nationalism, was
officiating and had been prepared by Corbett for Casey to make a theatrical confession before his family, neighbours and former friends. Casey's
admission (supposedly made at the foot of the altar while clutching a
candle) confirmed most of the contents of the dying declarations of Pat
Joyce and Pat Casey. Predictably he downplayed his specific role in the
killings (others had used the three revolvers) but he also claimed that his,
truthful, confession to George Bolton had been rejected and that he had
been ordered to reconstruct his narrative. He was only accepted as an
approver when he confirmed Anthony Philbin's version of events. As his

police guard was present to witness this epiphany, Dublin Castle was rapidly made aware that the carefully wrought fabric of the official Maamtrasna narrative had begun to unravel.

That the disintegration of that official version of events continued was largely down to the persistence of the nationalist MP for Westmeath, Timothy Harrington. From a journalistic background, Harrington painstakingly pursued the truth with a mixture of dogged leg work, the co-operation of at least one disillusioned official and some good fortune. Within a relatively short period he had learned of the dying declarations of Pat Casey and Pat Joyce, which had exonerated Myles Joyce, and discovered the eye-witness evidence of the victims, Michael and Patrick Joyce, which utterly discredited the identification evidence of the Maolras. On the basis of his research, collected in a pamphlet, *The Maamtrasna massacre: impeachment of the trials* he told the House of Commons that 'the authorities had in their possession at the time of the trial, evidence which would have completely proved the story of the Joyces to be a fabrication, and that they chose to suppress this evidence rather than discredit the testimony of those so-called independent witnesses'.[44]

In his pamphlet, Harrington pointed out a number of crucial anomalies in the evidence of the Maolras. This ranged from the impossibility of Anthony Joyce having seen anybody walking on the boreen near his house from his own front door[45] to the implausibility of their recognising anyone on what had been a moonless night. In a Holmesian moment, he also questioned why John Joyce's dogs did not bark, thus alerting the killers, when his brother Anthony reached his house. Harrington congratulated the Maolras on their evasive cunning in the witness-box: 'It is difficult to refrain from admiring the skill with which they deal in generalities and the manner in which they avoid the specific statement of any particulars that might involve disagreement or contradiction'. His *coup de grâce*, however, was his revelation of the evidence not heard by any of the three juries, of the blackened faces of the killers and the fact that they all wore bawneens. In order to confirm this evidence he had visited the young Patrick Joyce in the industrial school in Artane, where he was in the care of the Christian Brothers. An apparently thriving young boy had repeated to Harrington the statement he had made to Constable Johnson. On the basis of this new evidence Harrington and the Irish Parliamentary Party called for an inquiry in the hope of exonerating Myles Joyce and bringing about the release of the four innocent prisoners serving life sentences in Galway Prison. 'Earl Spencer may refuse inquiry,' Harrington wrote, 'he may not deem the life of a Connemara peasant and the lifelong liberty of a few others of sufficient importance to put his official satellites to the trouble of an inquiry. But it is beyond his power and theirs now to conceal the truth any longer'.

Harrington went even further in his own personal investigation. With the assistance of Fr Corbett he located Thomas Casey and interviewed him at length. In the course of their conversation (published in his pamphlet), Casey identified the three men still at large (whom Pat Joyce and Pat Casey had refused to name), one of whom had been the prime instigator of the killings. He also gave a detailed explanation of how he had been pressurised into perjuring himself in Green Street Court-house in November 1882:

CASEY: On the night of the murder I joined the party at the house of big John Casey, of Bun-na-Cnic.

HARRINGTON: Is that the man by whom you say the murder was planned?

CASEY: Yes ... when I reached big John Casey's house at Bun-na-Cnic, his son, John Casey, jun., met me outside, and gave me a white bawneen to put over my head going in, to make sure that no one would see me passing through the kitchen.

HARRINGTON: ... Were there any persons there before you?

CASEY: Yes, the two John Caseys, father and son, and Pat Leyden. The men that came in after me were Pat Casey, Michael Casey, and Pat Joyce, of Shanvallycahill. They were brought in separately, and had their heads covered.

HARRINGTON: Were there any more in the party that night?

CASEY: No.

HARRINGTON: Did the seven of you remain in the house for any time?

CASEY: Yes, they took a good deal of drink. I was the only one who did not take any drink.

HARRINGTON: ... Did you know what purpose you were called for?

CASEY: I did. I knew it was to carry out the murder
                           we had planned.

Casey went on to tell Harrington that three members of the group were
chosen to do the actual killings. Like Pat Joyce before him he distanced
himself from the actual murders. Joyce had alleged in his dying declaration
on 13 November 1882 that it was Tom Casey, armed with three revolvers,
who was responsible for all the shots that were fired in the house that night.
Casey claimed to have hung back outside the door and alleged that Joyce
himself, John Casey Jr and Pat Leyden had carried out the killing.
Harrington pressed him on the issue:

HARRINGTON: Were you not the greatest stranger in the
                           party; did you not live furthest away, and why
                           were you not asked to go into the house?

CASEY: Well John Casey asked me to, but I would
                           not go.

HARRINGTON: But as you were the greatest stranger, why
                           did they not press you, or why did you not
                           go yourself?

CASEY: Sure they were all strangers, sir.

HARRINGTON: How could they all be strangers; did not
                           some of them live close to the house of the
                           murder?

CASEY: They were all strangers for they had black-
                           ened faces. I had no disguise only a soft hat
                           tied down over my face, for I had a longer
                           distance to go home than any of the others.
                           But they were all blackened. It was young
                           John Casey blackened them with polish
                           [blacking] in his father's house. Pat Joyce had
                           his hat tied down over both his cheeks to
                           cover his beard, and his face was black also.
                           I had a stick in my hand. Two or three of the
                           others had revolvers.

HARRINGTON: What position did you take at the house of
                           the murder?

CASEY:	I stood outside at the gable of the barn, and Michael Casey stood there with me. Five men went into the house, and big John Casey held the light while the other four were killing them.
HARRINGTON:	... This man is still living at Bun-na-Cnic?
CASEY:	He is, and his son also.
HARRINGTON:	He has the name of having a good deal of money?
CASEY:	He has, he is well off, and he lends money to some of the neighbours.
HARRINGTON:	The whole seven of you who were present at the murder were Caseys except two men?
CASEY:	Yes, all except Pat Joyce of Shanvallycahill, and Pat Leyden.
HARRINGTON:	None of the Joyces of Cappancreha knew anything about the murder?
CASEY:	No sir, not one of them knew anything about it.
HARRINGTON:	They were not at your first meeting?
CASEY:	No, they never knew anything of the business.
HARRINGTON:	... You have already stated that you received money from John Casey of Bun-na-Cnic at these meetings?
CASEY:	Yes.
HARRINGTON:	Now, when you all met and arranged this murder, was there no other charge made against Joyce, the murdered man, except sheep stealing?
CASEY:	Yes there was. Himself and Casey had quarrels about sheep, and were at law with one another. But John Casey said that John Joyce

made three attempts to shoot him, and that he could not live in the country with him.

HARRINGTON: Was there not some Ribbon society among you?

CASEY: Yes [hesitatingly].

HARRINGTON: Is it true that John Joyce, the murdered man, belonged to it?

CASEY: He did; they said he was their treasurer, but I did not know much about it, as I was only three months home from England.

HARRINGTON: Who was the head of the society?

CASEY: Pat Joyce, of Shanvallycahill.

HARRINGTON: How did you come into it when you were only a short time at home?

CASEY: Pat Joyce knew me in England.

HARRINGTON: Had this society any connection with any other society in Ireland?

CASEY: No, I knew nothing of any society in Ireland, but we used meet one another in England.

HARRINGTON: Was there anything said about his not accounting for some money he had?

CASEY: Pat Joyce said so.

HARRINGTON: This Pat Joyce was, what you call, I believe, 'a bad boy' here?

CASEY: Well indeed, he was not very good.

HARRINGTON: ... Can you tell me whether Anthony Joyce belonged to the society?

CASEY: I never heard that he did.

HARRINGTON: Must he not have heard something about your first meeting?

CASEY: Perhaps he did, but very little he knew.

HARRINGTON: How do you account for his hitting on some of the right men?

CASEY: He put in the names of all those men because they were always quarrelling with him and his brother.

HARRINGTON: But you had no quarrel with him, how did he come to make the charge against you?

CASEY: Oh, I'll explain that. I asked him in Irish before the magistrates at Cong, the first day. 'Why do you swear all this against me, Anthony Joyce. I never did anything to you?' He said—'Let you hold your tongue, Tom Casey. You have no need to talk, for I saw Pat Casey going over for you in the evening. He went over across the Slieve barefooted.'

HARRINGTON: I suppose he knew that Philbin and you were related?

CASEY: He did; he knew well that Philbin was my brother-in-law, and I suppose that is why he mentioned his name.

HARRINGTON: Was Philbin in the society?

CASEY: He never was, sir, and never knew no more about the murder than the child unborn.

HARRINGTON: Now, I want from you, as clearly as you can, the full story of your interviews with Mr. Bolton. Did anything happen with regard to your information's before you wrote the note to Mr. Bolton on the 11th November?

CASEY: Yes. Several days before that—I think it was on the 6th—Philbin and I were put together into a yard. There was no warder with us. He had written to Mr. Bolton at this time, and Mr. Bolton was after being with him that day. If I remember rightly, that is what Philbin told me ... The Chief Warder said, when he was putting us into the yard—'Go in there and have a talk together.' I was surprised and asked Philbin why we were allowed there together. He said it was that we might give evidence. We were more than an hour in the yard together. No one came near us all that time. Philbin was trying to get me to make a statement. He was all the time saying that I knew all about the murder and I denied it.

HARRINGTON: How did he know that you were anything more guilty than himself?

CASEY: He must have suspected it from seeing me whispering with the other men when we got together, or were going in or out in the van ... One of the warders told me the next day that Philbin had turned. No friends were coming near me, and I was getting afraid. On Friday or Saturday after this I wrote the note to Mr. Bolton asking him to come and see me. I was brought out to the office to see him that day ... There was no clerk in the room, and the Governor and any other person was not there except Mr. Bolton. The warder came as far as the door with me and then stood at the door while I was in. Mr. Bolton was sitting down with his shoes off, warming his feet to the fire. He said, 'Well, Casey, are you going to make a statement' or something like that. I made an effort to save those that were in. I said 'The men that did the murder are outside yet, and these men in here are innocent.'

He said he had more than that from the Joyces and from my brother-in-law, Philbin, that Philbin swore I went to the house for him and that he met me in the field. I am not sure whether it is then Mr. Bolton read Philbin's statement for me, I am quite certain that he read it for me. He would not accept my statement, as I would not make it agree with my brother-in-law, and he called the warder and sent me away. The trial was to come off on Monday ... When we were going into the van I saw Philbin going away in a cab. The other men went into the van. I was the last to go in, and I then said to the Governor that he might speak to Bolton. I had not given him an answer the night before. We were then brought to the court. The nine of us were in the back room of the dock, and my name was called ... I was brought a few yards to the right, to a little room where Mr. Brady,[46] Mr. Bolton and the Governor of the jail were. Mr. Bolton was the first who spoke. He said, 'Now, Casey, are you going to make a statement?' He pulled out his watch, and said I had only a short time. I said, 'I'd like to give evidence fair.' He replied that I 'had only twenty minutes to consider my neck.' Bolton asked, 'Who are the three men that went into the house?' I did not answer fast enough. I did not know who to say. Mr. Brady then said, low across the room to Bolton, 'I know them—Pat Joyce, Pat Casey, and Myles Joyce.' Then I knew what names I should say.

HARRINGTON: ... Out of the ten men sworn against by Anthony Joyce and his brother, only four, you say, had any knowledge of the murder?

CASEY: Only four, Pat Joyce of Shanvallycahill, who was executed; Pat Casey, who was also executed; Michael Casey, who is now in penal servitude, and myself.

HARRINGTON: Now, I want you to name the men accused who were innocent?

CASEY: Myles Joyce, the man who was executed; his two brothers, Pat and Martin, who are in

> penal servitude; Tom Joyce, Pat's son, who is in penal servitude; and little John Casey of Cappanacreha, who is also in penal servitude.

HARRINGTON: Of the seven men who did know of the murder, and took part in it, three are still at large, besides yourself?

CASEY: Yes. One is in England, and the other two are here in the country.

HARRINGTON: Then there are four innocent men in jail and one guilty?

CASEY: Yes, sir.

HARRINGTON: And of the three who were hanged, one man was hanged in the wrong?

CASEY: Yes, sir. Myles Joyce knew no more of that murder than you did, but sure you may say they were all hanged in the wrong, for the evidence against the guilty as well as the innocent was all a lie.[47]

In September, 1884 a Dublin barrister, Edward Ennis, visited Tim Healy with a bundle of papers. He told Healy that

> He had gained access to a room where Crown briefs were carelessly thrown after trial, and found the brief held in the Maamtrasna case by Peter O'Brien, Q.C. (afterwards Lord O'Brien, Chief Justice). Taking the printed 'informations' from it, he gave them to me ... The Prosecution not only suppressed it, but did not produce as a witness the sole survivor of the tragedy.[48]

The brief, which was given by Healy to Harrington, clearly indicated that the Crown prosecutors had no intention of putting the only survivor of the Maamtrasna murders, young Patrick Joyce, on the stand. His evidence was deemed to be of no value. In fact, it would have greatly prejudiced the Crown case. However, the information had been put into the public domain at the time of the murders in newspaper reports so defence counsel must still bear some responsibility for not demolishing the Maolra identification testimony. Malley could also have tried harder to establish a malign motive for the Maolra testimony against their cousins. It might have been difficult for a middle-class Dublin jury to accept that three men would swear away the lives of their blood relations over a few impoverished fields but, as the local curate, Fr McHugh wrote to Harrington, 'there was nothing too wicked or too devilish for Anthony Joyce'.[49]

Harrington introduced all this material in a House of Commons debate on Maamtrasna in October, 1884—but to no effect. The Parnellites sought the posthumous exoneration of Myles Joyce and the release of his innocent brothers and nephew. Though the Irish Party had some Tory support, from the likes of Randolph Churchill for example, the government won the vote by a margin of 48. There would be no release for the four innocent imprisoned men. The collapse of the Gladstone administration in 1885 and a brief Tory *interregnum* allowed the Irish Party to revive the controversy. Churchill and the former chief secretary for Ireland, Sir Michael Hicks Beach, were among those supportive of a motion that would have the effect of embarrassing the previous government and re-opening the case. This was just one element of a potential rapprochement between the Irish Party and the minority Conservative administration of Lord Salisbury. The Liberal Rottweiler, Sir William Harcourt, referred to the flirtation between the Irish and the Tories as the 'Maamtrasna alliance'. But the lord lieutenant, Lord Carnarvon, was not prepared to second-guess the decision of his predecessor, Earl Spencer, just for the sake of discommoding Gladstone's party. The only concession made was another Commons debate on the subject, as L.P. Curtis puts it, 'the Liberals interpreted the Maamtrasna debate as tangible proof of an alliance between Conservatives and Parnellites. A new "Kilmainham Treaty" it seemed, was in the making, with Churchill filling the role formerly played by Chamberlain'.[50] Once again nothing came of the debate that was of any practical value to the innocent prisoners or to the memory of Myles Joyce.

Michael and John Casey did secure early releases from captivity but only through premature death. Michael Casey died in 1895 and John Casey followed him five years later, dying of tuberculosis. The Joyces were finally released in October 1902 after completing twenty years of penal servitude. They were put on a train to Ballinrobe and walked the last eighteen miles home. Young Tom Joyce soon left for America. Martin Joyce succumbed to tuberculosis within four years of his release. Paudeen Joyce died in 1911 at the age of 75.

Twenty years of their lives had been taken from them by Dublin Castle imperatives. These included a need to demonstrate the effectiveness of the Crimes Act and to remind potential malefactors of the omnipresence of the informer and approver in the fight to maintain law and order. In the event that not even the legal structures available were adequate to secure a conviction, unscrupulous or over-enthusiastic functionaries had resorted to threats and intimidation to bend and twist evidence into a persuasive frame. Because the thesis advanced by the Crown was not challenged too robustly by ill-prepared defence counsel it had passed muster. In a memorable but functionally ironic phrase from a century later what transpired to be a similar state of affairs was described by an incredulous Lord Denning as 'an appalling vista'—in the case of defence allegations that the Birmingham Six had been convicted on the basis of concocted evidence.[51]

Like Lord Spencer and the Gladstone administration before him, Lord Denning denied even the possibility of such a scenario. But it was the last vista beheld by Myles Joyce before he was strangled to death in 1882.

A month after the passage of Harcourt's Prevention of Crime (Ireland) Act, the Arrears of Rent (Ireland) Act had also passed through the Commons and the Lords. This measure gave 120,000 tenant farmers substantial relief. Those in arrears were obliged to pay a maximum of a year's rent, the government accepted liability for half of the remainder and the landlord learned to live without the rest. The measure did not end agrarian agitation overnight (there were still thousands of leaseholders outside the ambit of the remedial legislation) but it did, to the great satisfaction of Parnell, rein in the stampeding horse of violence in rural Ireland and slow it to a canter: 'the comfortable majority of farmers quietly settled for the benefits of the 1881 Act, with Parnell's tacit encouragement'.[52] Despite entrenched British prejudices and preconceptions to the contrary, radicalism did not sit well with the more substantial peasants of rural Ireland. The members of the small town *bourgeoisie*, who had, in many instances, led the Land League campaign, were even less comfortable with sustained extremism of any kind.

Furthermore, a start had been made, inadequate and halting as it was, to the process that would eventually end land agitation twenty years later, with the first steps in a programme of land purchase. This would accelerate under the Tories in the latter half of the decade. The prospect of a more contented and acquiescent peasantry and a loss of patience with recalcitrant Irish landlords found the British government delivering on the Land League slogan of 'The Land for the People'. This may have had the effect of restoring levels of rural passivity undreamt of during the Land War but it also permitted the leadership of the Irish national movement, stripped of much of its Fenian adherents, 'to look for new wars to fight'.[53]

.5.

THE
PHOENIX PARK
MURDERS

It presents a blood red page in the history of our country ...[1]

(John Adye Curran, Crown prosecutor)

Lord Frederick Cavendish, Chief Secretary, and Thomas Henry Burke, Under Secretary assassinated in the Phoenix Park at 7 o'c in the evening: by it is supposed 4 men, the most desperate deed that has ever stained the annals of our unfortunate country. It is shrouded in mystery, not known whether it is political or not. I do not know what use our Police or Detectives are, there is one thing certain if the assassins were Irishmen they would have been discovered long ago, in fact they would never have left the Park. God Save Ireland from her enemies.[2]

(Diary entry of Joseph Mullet, member of the Invincibles)

It was a tight and uncomfortable pair of new boots that played the crucial role in one of the most savage political crimes in Irish history. The feet being pinched by the recently purchased footwear belonged to Superintendent John Mallon of 'G' Division of the Dublin Metropolitan Police (DMP). The tall, bearded policeman walked from his office in Dublin Castle on a pleasant Saturday evening in early May 1882 for a belatedly scheduled meeting in a busy Phoenix Park. Little subversive activity taking place in the capital city escaped the attention of the resourceful Ulster Catholic detective. With his extensive underworld contacts Mallon was an invaluable asset to the DMP.[3] He had been selected in October 1881 for the delicate task of arresting Charles Stewart Parnell and conveying him to Kilmainham Gaol without causing a riot. This he had managed to accomplish successfully, albeit with the gracious co-operation of the Irish Party leader.

Mallon, who had a unique talent for intrigue and an educated nose for intriguers, had received a message from an informant named John Kenny who wanted to meet him at about 6.30 p.m. near the Viceregal Lodge (now Áras an Uachtaráin). He was on his way to the *rendezvous* when he encountered a plain clothes 'G' Division colleague. Mallon told the detective that he was on his way to meet Kenny. He then intended to double back and make for his home on the North Circular Road. He was advised against it. His colleague had spotted a number of well-known subversives in the park and had grown alarmed when he saw Mallon. He suspected the most celebrated, most admired and most reviled detective in Dublin was about to walk into a trap. The superintendent was handed a revolver and advised to make his way directly home. Mallon prevaricated before agreeing to leave Kenny to his own devices. The annoyingly painful boots were as much a factor in that fateful decision as any fears of a Fenian ambush.

Had Mallon continued on his journey, perhaps accompanied by his colleague, forewarned and well-armed, events might have taken a very different course on that sultry and sanguinary evening.

To Kilmainham and back:
October 1881–May 1882

Political events in Ireland were heading inexorably towards a climactic clash between the Liberal government and the Land League in the autumn of 1881. The tempo of agrarian violence had not been greatly reduced by Gladstone's Land Act of that year and Parnell, often playing to an extremist gallery in the USA, had gone out of his way to provoke the prime minister. Gladstone had responded in kind. On 7 October 1881, in a speech in Leeds, the Grand Old Man had hinted broadly that the leaders of the Land League would soon be jailed when he pointed out that 'the resources of civilisation were not exhausted' when it came to dealing with the Irish agrarian movement. [4] Parnell responded two days later in Wexford, characterising the man who had piloted the two most significant pieces of Irish lend legislation through the House of Commons as 'a masquerading knight errant' who was supporting the landowners of Ireland by means of 'bayonets and buckshot'.

Parnell was well aware that he was throwing down a gauntlet that the British administration would be obliged to take up. He, famously, speculated later that night, that, were he to be arrested, 'Captain Moonlight will take my place'. By invoking the euphemism for agrarian crime he was acknowledging that the Land War was entering a new phase. He was sending a signal to the extremist forces of the Land League to intensify their activities while, simultaneously, diminishing their relevance in the political resolution of the land question that must follow. An end to the phenomenon of exacerbated agrarian unrest could only be achieved through political negotiation. Ultimately the government would have to bargain with him, directly or indirectly. We can speculate that his motive in appending his signature to the No Rent Manifesto that emanated from Kilmainham Gaol was equally nuanced. He must have known that it would be opposed by most moderate forces and would expose the outer limits of Land League efficacy. Both moves were calculated to underscore the indispensability of his more measured and conservative approach to politics. It was a policy of brinkmanship that had been used successfully by Daniel O'Connell in his day.

At the outset of his incarceration, Parnell had written to Katharine O'Shea that 'Politically it is a fortunate thing for me that I have been arrested, as the movement is breaking fast, and all will be quiet in a few months, when I shall be released'.[5] After six months of his vacation at Her Majesty's pleasure Parnell must have wondered whether he had miscalculated. Instances of agrarian violence showed little sign of abating, in spite of the robust and coercive approach of the chief secretary, William E. Forster, who was compelled to admit to the House of Commons that 'his policy had failed, that he had underestimated the forces with which he had to contend'.[6]

Observing the degree to which militancy held sway in the Irish countryside, Parnell might well have echoed the sentiments of his nemesis. He was fortunate that the combination of an act of pragmatism on the part of Gladstone and some of his ministers, radical distaste for coercion and the coincidental intervention of the husband of his mistress, rescued the Irish leader from a boat that was shipping a dangerous amount of water. The self-serving, often clumsy but nonetheless expedient diplomacy of Captain William Henry O'Shea, a desire for a restoration of his pre-coercion credibility on the part of radical leader, Joseph Chamberlain, and the instinct of Gladstone that Parnell was actually a conservative force in Irish politics, led to an accord rapidly dubbed the 'Kilmainham Treaty' by advocates and opponents alike. Under its eminently deniable terms (no paper trail led to or from Gladstone) tenants in arrears of rent would be allowed to benefit from the rent-fixing Land Courts already working under the aegis of the 1881 Land Act. In return Parnell and his associates would do their best to turn off the tap of agrarian violence.[7] The implication was that, in this event, the special powers vested in the Dublin Castle administration under Forster's Coercion Acts, would be allowed to lapse.

Parnell and his principal lieutenants, John Dillon and James O'Kelly were, after the informal accord came into effect, released from Kilmainham Gaol on 2 May, 1882. Their liberation coincided with the resignation of Forster and the consequent removal from the Cabinet of one of the principal obstacles to any *rapprochement* between the Irish Party and the Liberals. To take his place Gladstone selected the inoffensive husband of his niece, Lord Frederick Cavendish—who also happened to be the brother of the leader of the Whig faction of the Liberal party, Lord Hartington. Cavendish made his way almost immediately to Dublin and was in position by 6 May. His arrival promised to usher in a new era of peace and collaboration between the highly constitutional Parnell and a highly co-operative Liberal administration.

Sweet harmony became cruel discord via the surgical knives of an unknown group of Republican vigilantes, a murder gang who had grandiosely awarded themselves the name of The Irish National Invincibles. They would prove to be anything but. Nonetheless, they managed to achieve permanent notoriety by demonstrating their murderous efficiency.

THE CREATION OF THE INVINCIBLES

The reaction of the extreme Republican Fenian movement to the rise of the Land League was anything but monolithic. This was to be expected in an organisation that had been riven by factionalism since its inception in 1858. The more dogmatic members of the IRB considered any parliamentary struggle for palliative social measures to be counter-productive. To Fenians like Charles Kickham it was axiomatic that a contented peasantry was not a revolutionary peasantry. However, some former or neo-Fenians like Joseph Biggar, Patrick Egan, Thomas Brennan[8] and P.J. Sheridan threw in their lot with parliamentarianism, in the case of Biggar, or popular agrarian agitation in the case of the others. They were joined by large numbers of active members of the organisation, though without the formal imprimatur of its Supreme Council. The likes of Egan and Sheridan (respectively treasurer and paid organiser with the Land League) never unambiguously severed their ties with their former Fenian associates (as had Michael Davitt for example) but concentrated on exploiting and directing the radicalism of the rural popular movement. The Irish Republican Brotherhood, led by the uncompromising Kickham, was, in comparison with the Land League, an *élite* organisation with long-term goals from which it declined to be diverted. The Land League was a highly effective mass movement with more limited objectives and one in which the participants had a greater stake, in terms of process and potential outcome, than had those of previous political organisations such as the Catholic Association or the Repeal Association.

The Irish National Invincibles came into being largely as a consequence of disaffected Fenianism. Its existence did not necessarily imply an actual disaffection with Republicanism itself. The 30 or so members of the short-lived faction appear to have been motivated more by the perception that separatist nationalism was losing ground to a rural radicalism, which was too closely allied to reformist constitutionalism. However, it is difficult to divine the precise motivation of many of those involved in this cabal. Its history is 'riddled with doubt and untruth, vagueness and confusion'.[9] Much of the information about the Invincibles which came into the public domain in the 1880s did so via approvers and informers. This was added to by a highly self-serving account of the group written by fugitive Invincible P.J. Tynan[10] in the 1890s.

The Invincibles were, in essence, a murder gang. Just as the doctrinaire Fenians refused to engage with a constitutional political movement so too did they distance themselves from any involvement in a campaign of murder.[11] One of the men instrumental in the demolition of the Invincibles, John Adye Curran, acknowledged as much in his *Reminiscences*. It had fallen to Curran to interrogate many of the 'usual suspects' in a trawl for information in the early part of 1883. While the core membership of the gang consisted of active Fenians,

> Many of the leading Fenians who came before me expressed what I knew to be genuine horror at the crime, and as a matter of fact I derived very material assistance from them in the course of my inquiry ... They became, so to speak, an excrescence upon the original body, and were at the time of which I write altogether outside its rules and objects.[12]

But with so many mansions in the Fenian household it was almost inevitable that at least one faction would emerge, mirroring that of the irreconcilable O'Donovan Rossa in the USA, intent on direct action of a lethal nature. Much of the impetus for the creation of this fringe group within the ranks of the IRB came from Frank Byrne, secretary of the Land

League of Great Britain. Most of the finance is likely to have come from a source even closer to the centre of the constitutional movement, Patrick Egan, treasurer of the Land League who, in late 1881, was disbursing its funds from the safety of Paris.[13] At least some of the organisational muscle, it is suspected, was provided by P.J. Sheridan. On the run from the authorities, the imaginative Land League organiser met with a number of Invincibles, in the guise of a Roman Catholic priest, the iconically named 'Fr Murphy'. It is not entirely clear whether he did so under the aegis of the Land League, the IRB or the Invincibles. Subsequent attempts by P.J. Tynan to link the Invincibles directly to the Irish Parliamentary Party can safely be dismissed as mischievous and self-aggrandising. However, it is possible that MPs, Joseph Biggar and John Barry, were involved in preliminary discussions that led, ultimately, to the establishment of an *élite* group intent on assassination.[14]

With some cajoling and assistance from the UK, in the form of a Middlesborough-based Land League organiser John Walsh—an emissary from Frank Byrne—the Invincibles grew out of a four-man Directorate in Dublin. All were current or former Fenians. Edward McCaffrey had spent six months in jail for Fenian activities. James Carey, a successful businessman, pious and pietistic Roman Catholic and slum landlord, had acted as an 'enforcer' for the IRB, charged, ironically given his subsequent career, with rooting out informers. James Mullett, a Kickham loyalist, was a Dublin Fenian 'centre',[15] who owned a public house in Lower Bridge Street. Daniel Curley, also a 'centre', was a Dublin carpenter. In late December 1881 the four men swore a blood oath to the effect that 'I of my own free will and without any mental reservation whatsoever will obey all orders transmitted to me by the Irish Invincibles, nor to seek nor to ask more than what is necessary in carrying out such orders, violation of which shall be death'.[16] With Parnell and most of the Irish Party leadership safely in jail and virtual chaos reigning in the country-side, the object of the Directorate was simple; fill the political vacuum with spectacular murders. The four men, along with other recruits, were to engage in the assassination of prominent government officials, beginning with the lord lieutenant, Lord Cowper and the chief secretary, William Edward Forster. Walsh left £50 to fund ongoing activities, promised the creation of more branches and £10,000 of Land League money, and returned to Middlesborough.

Daniel Curley was the most successful recruiter for the organisation (he brought in a young Fenian activist, Joe Brady, amongst others). Carey brought his brother Peter on board as well as a number of his employees.

The least enthusiastic founder member appears to have been Mullett. He may have regretted his betrayal of Kickham or feared that he had become involved in an enterprise which might suddenly career out of control.

Frank Byrne provided the burgeoning terrorist group with the tools of assassination. With the assistance of a sympathiser, Dr Hamilton Williams, a medical doctor, he obtained a dozen surgical knives of the type normally used in amputations. These were brought to Dublin by Byrne's heavily pregnant wife. At around that time Byrne also arranged that his communications be brought to Dublin by an apparently innocuous and anonymous figure, a neighbour of his named Patrick J. Tynan, who, 'was short, plump, round faced and bewhiskered, and he wore a pince-nez perched on his nose. But he had a romantic soul and a vivid imagination'.[17] Tynan was known to the other Invincibles as 'Number 1'—a code name open to misinterpretation and an appellation that he would use to endow himself, retrospectively, with a more central role in the conspiracy once he fled to the USA in 1883.

The first setback for the Invincibles was the arrest of James Mullett on suspicion of involvement in the murder of a police informer. Like most of the members of the group he laboured under the disadvantage of being well known to the police, and to Mallon in particular. He was replaced on the Directorate by Joseph Brady, a Dublin corporation employee. Brady, and another new recruit, his young friend Tim Kelly, were an altogether different breed from the older artisans of the initial Directorate. They were tough and ruthless working-class nationalists and were to become the backbone of the fledgling assassination squad.

On Byrne's instructions, relayed via Tynan, preparations were made for an attempt on the life of 'Buckshot' Forster, the unpopular chief secretary and principal architect of the Liberal government's policy of coercion. Despite assistance with his identification and other valuable intelligence from a Dublin Castle workman, Joseph Smith, and despite elaborate preparations on numerous occasions, the Invincibles never managed to get close enough to Forster to make a credible attempt on his life. Details of the plot against Forster would emerge in 1883, either in open court or in depositions taken from former Invincibles who had been 'turned'. One of those was Robert Farrell, who gave 'G' Division detective, Inspector Kavanagh a detailed account of two bungled efforts:

> The first attempt at assassination was to have been ...
> carried out at the Metal or Queen's Bridge, at Stapleton's
> or Sinnott's corner. His carriage was to have been stopped

there. The orders were given by Dan Curley. Joe Brady
and Tim Kelly were to do the work by forcing open the
carriage door, and then stab Mr. Forster with knives. This
was to be done when he would be coming from the Park
to the Castle in the mornings. The approach of the carriage was to have been signalled by Carey to Mr. Rowles,
a tailor, of Fishamble Street, who was stationed at the
Esplanade, by holding up white handkerchiefs, that those
at the bridge might know that the carriage had passed.
Carey was stationed up near the Park gate. Rowles did
not hold up the handkerchief when the carriage passed,
so the attempt failed.

There was to be another attack in the evening when
Forster would return to the Park, and it was arranged to
take place on the quays at Ireland's, opposite John Street,
and the same parties were to be involved. The reason that
this attempt also failed was that Carey made a mistake in
the cab that Mr. Forster got into at the Castle. They had
scouts about the Castle. Afterwards the police were too
much on the alert.[18]

After Forster's resignation the organisation's attention shifted to the
under secretary, Thomas H. Burke. A rarity in the Dublin Castle administration, Burke was a Catholic who was, in effect, head of the Irish civil
service. He had begun his career at the very bottom of the ladder, as a young
clerk. Scion of a Galway landholding family, Burke, a single man in his early
fifties, had become associated with the punitive policies of his political superior. He had held the post of under secretary since 1869 and had served
under governments led by those two great Victorian antagonists Gladstone
and Disraeli. A conscientious bureaucrat he was now the servant of increasingly unpopular masters. He was a figure who 'left on all the impression of
upright coldness and correct detachment as well as devotion to duty'.[19]

At about 6.40 p.m. on the evening of Saturday, 6 May Burke left his
office in Dublin Castle and took a cab to his Phoenix Park residence.
(Today what was the under secretary's lodge is the Phoenix Park Visitors
Centre, in 1882 Burke lived there with his sister.) About 100 yards past
the newly erected Gough Monument (later blown up by the IRA) Burke,
to his intense surprise, spotted a figure with whom he had just become
acquainted. The new chief secretary, Lord Frederick Cavendish, had

decided to take advantage of the fine evening to walk from Dublin Castle to his lodge (now the US ambassador's residence). Burke offered to give Cavendish a lift or to accompany him on his stroll. The chief secretary sealed both their fates by choosing the latter option. Burke alighted from his cab and they continued their journey towards the Phoenix monument. They were due to meet again that night at the Viceregal Lodge for dinner with Earl Spencer.

As Burke and Cavendish approached the Phoenix Monument they were passed by two tricyclists and two men in a cab. At the polo grounds nearby, a game had just finished. The evening, although fine, had been marked by a number of showers and Cavendish carried an umbrella that he had brought with him from the castle. Up ahead a cab loitered. A group of men approached but parted to allow Burke and Cavendish through. Both men continued on their way. They did not see a number of the men they had passed wheel around and approach them menacingly. Burke was the first to be hacked at with the sharp surgical knives. Cavendish, bravely but futilely, came to his colleague's defence. Despite some dubious *ex post facto* attempts by Tynan to suggest that the attack was explicitly designed to eliminate both men, it is morally certain that the knife-wielding Invincibles had no idea who Burke's defender was. Cavendish was killed either because he chose to involve himself in the affray, or because he was an inconvenient witness. The attack took place within sight of the Viceregal Lodge. In fact what was assumed to have been a drunken brawl had actually been witnessed from Spencer's residence.

A few minutes later the two cyclists who had passed the now stricken men, returned to the spot where they lay dead or dying. Thomas Foley and Patrick William Maguire, were first to chance on the murder scene. Cavendish lay in the middle of the road, Burke on the footpath. Maguire cycled off rapidly to seek assistance while Foley remained behind to offer what help he could. But both victims of the most notorious political crime in Irish history were beyond help. As he stood over Burke, Foley recorded that 'I took hold of his left hand which was lying across his heart, to see if his pulse was beating, and he just gave his last breath into my face and the blood oozed up from his neck'.[20] Burke's throat had been cut and he had an additional wound through the base of the heart. Cavendish had 'a wound in the right lung and a wound in the neck which must have proved instantly fatal'.[21]

The first indication as to the identity of the two victims came when two military aides from the Viceregal Lodge. Colonel Forster and Colonel

Caulfield, attracted by the hubbub, came to inspect the scene for themselves. Caulfield had actually witnessed the altercation from the lodge. Their horrified recognition of the victims changed entirely the nature of the investigation that began with the swift arrival of the police, summoned by Maguire. Spencer was one of the first to be informed. His first thought, not unnaturally, was 'What will I tell the Prime Minister?'[22]

Superintendent John Mallon had not long divested himself of his irksome shoes when his Saturday evening was interrupted with the grisly news. He immediately ordered that all RIC constables within range of the city of Dublin be called in to assist the Dublin Metropolitan Police. Detectives were despatched to the ports and to every railway station in the city. Anyone left was sent to scour the hotels and boarding houses of Dublin. It was essential for the reputation of the DMP that the killers be caught swiftly. Two of the three most senior government office holders in the castle administration had just been brutally murdered within a few hundred yards of the headquarters of the Royal Irish Constabulary, the Viceregal and Chief Secretary's Lodges, and an army barracks. Furthermore they had been allowed to walk, unarmed, in a public park without a single bodyguard to protect them. Just a few hours before, Earl Spencer himself had ridden across the same ground, but he had been flanked by four mounted horsemen. Against knife-wielding assailants even a single armed detective might have been able to save at least one of the two august victims.

Late that night black-edged cards were deposited in the letter-boxes of the Dublin Sunday papers. They read 'This deed was done by the Irish Invincibles'.[23] Within 48 hours posters offering a reward of £10,000 were placed around the city seeking anyone prepared to give information leading to the arrest and conviction of the assassins.

HUE AND CRY: MAY 1882–JANUARY 1883

Initial reaction to the news of the murders was of stupefaction and profound shock. The first information conveyed to London (from a misinformed Spencer) was that Cavendish had survived the assault and was fighting for his life. Mary Gladstone, the prime minister's daughter, calling on her cousin Lucy Cavendish, found her parents and Lord Hartington, already there before her. 'Lucy had borne it wonderfully,' she wrote in her diary, 'at first thinking it was not fatal and that he w[oul]d recover ... "Oh, I know he will live, he is so well, only I must go to him directly".'[24] When the awful truth emerged political consternation followed in its wake. Parnell was so distraught that he felt constrained to offer Gladstone his resignation from political life. The prime minister, sensibly, declined to accept the gesture. Even the normally vituperative *United Ireland*, propaganda organ of the Parnellites, in the issue following the murders, replaced its customary front page political cartoon with an empty box bearing the legend 'In token of abhorrence and shame for the stain cast upon the character of our nation for manliness and hospitality by the assassination of Lord Frederick Cavendish, Chief Secretary for Ireland, and of Mr. Thomas Burke, Under Secretary, in the Phoenix Park, 6th May, 1882'.[25]

In Dublin itself, according to the *Freeman's Journal,* 'Astonishment amounting almost to stupor seemed to have seized the minds of all'. The newspaper's columns bore black borders. Issues of a special midnight edition of the *Evening Telegraph* were snapped up. The *Freeman's Journal* captured the scene:

> Groups assembled in all parts of the city, and by the light of the street lamps men were everywhere seen reading aloud to others the details of the frightful affair. Conjectures of the most extraordinary and conflicting character were formed as to the cause of the murder. The almost universal belief is that the crime could not have been perpetrated by an Irishman.[26]

Michael Davitt, pointing to the use of knives, a weapon not favoured by Irish revolutionaries, was also one of those who clung to this hope.

The *Times*, however, was in no doubt that it was Irishmen who bore responsibility for the murders. Its editorial on 8 May, advised the government that the time had come for retribution:

> The atrocious double murder which closes for the present the long catalogue of Irish crimes must bring home to all but the victims of political fatuity the necessity for prompt resort to measures of a more thoroughgoing and energetic kind than have yet been employed for the vindication of the law. Only wilful blindness can now fail to see that behind the agrarian agitation, behind the 'social revolution' which is Mr. Gladstone's latest but still imperfect

> diagnosis of Irish disorder, there is a political revolution
> inspired by implacable hatred to English rule, and shrink-
> ing from nothing that may seem to further its ends or
> even gratify its passions. The assassination of the Chief
> Secretary and Under Secretary is a contemptuous defiance
> flung back in the face of a Government which has just put
> a severe strain upon the allegiance of its supporters by a
> nearly unqualified surrender to Irish ideas.[27]

Some hostile public reaction might have been expected in England and Irish MPs took steps to protect themselves against possible retaliatory attacks, Tim Healy amongst them. 'The Londoners, however, with their solid good sense and traditional instinct, remained calm,' he wrote many years later.[28]

A sombre House of Commons convened on Monday, 8 May. At 4.15 p.m. Gladstone rose to move for the immediate adjournment of the House. The prime minister did not require the fulminations of the *Times* to per-suade him to introduce an augmented stringency in dealing with crime in Ireland. New legislation was promised later that week. But Gladstone's speech, although laced with intimations of retribution, was free of invective and laden with emotion. Acknowledging the importance of Burke to the governance of Ireland he then added that 'the hand of the assassin has come nearer home'. The MPs may have wondered was this a personal ref-erence to his own familial connection with Cavendish. Though he

> felt it difficult to say a word, yet I must say that one of the
> very noblest hearts of England [Hear, hear] has ceased to
> beat, and has ceased at the very moment when it was just
> devoted to the service of Ireland, full of love for that
> country, [Hear, hear] full of hope for her future, full of
> capacity to render her service.[29]

After a contribution from the Conservative leader in the House, Sir Stafford Northcote, Parnell rose to express his 'unqualified detestation of the horrible crime'. According to Tim Healy when the Irish Party leader got to his feet 'something like a groan arose from a small section, but the vast body of the House angrily suppressed it and listened to him with respect. The sunlight suddenly shot in and made the scene less sad'.[30] Fearing the legislative reprisals that lay ahead,

> he did not deny that it might be impossible for the
> Government to resist taking measures such as had been

mentioned by the Prime Minister. But he wished to express his belief that the crime had been committed by men who absolutely detested the cause with which he had been associated [hear, hear] and who had devised that crime and carried it out as the deadliest blow in their power against his hopes and the new course which the Government had resolved upon.[31]

Pressure on the Dublin Metropolitan Police for a rapid apprehension of the killers was intense. Initially Mallon pursued an investigation along conventional lines. Witnesses were questioned and potential leads were followed. Passenger lists on cross-channel shipping were consulted. An artist's impression of a number of men who had been seen driving away from the scene was widely circulated. It all led nowhere. Gradually the trail grew colder.

Mallon's first breaks in the case came belatedly and largely as a consequence of his exploitation of his own unique skills and knowledge. Publican, James Mullett, Invincible conspirator since the end of 1881, had been on remand since early March 1882. He had been arrested during the investigation of the murder of a police informer, on 25 February, and held on suspicion of being a Fenian organiser. Six weeks after the Phoenix Park murders he was still in jail and his business was in terminal decline. In late June he sent a message to Mallon that he wanted to trade information for his release. What he told the superintendent was the first indication of the existence of an assassination squad composed of renegade Fenians. Mullett named James Carey, Daniel Curley and a cab driver, James 'Skin the Goat'[32] Fitzharris, as the probable perpetrators of the Phoenix Park murders. Mullett was duly released and replaced in Kilmainham by Carey and Curley.

Mallon was the beneficiary of a further stroke of luck in July when a tenant of Carey's, John Fitzsimons, led the DMP to a loft in one of the prisoner's tenement buildings. Fitzsimons had seen Carey enter the loft and, consumed by curiosity, had made a search of his own. He showed the police what he had found. Two long, sharp surgical knives and a Winchester repeating rifle. Forensic examination indicated the presence of mammalian blood on the knives but it was impossible to establish definitively that it was of human origin. The 'blood' later turned out to be rust. It was also impossible to tie Carey directly to the knives as Fitzsimons had seen a number of other people entering and leaving the loft.

In September a frustrated Mallon was forced to release Curley and Carey for lack of evidence. Then, as his biographer puts it, 'at once the reign of terror was re-established'.[33] On 27 November, an attempt was made on the life of a Dubliner, Denis Field, who had served on a jury that had condemned Galwayman Michael Walsh to death for the murder of an RIC constable. A second major attempted *coup*, foiled by an alert body-guard, gave Mallon a further opening that he exploited to the full.

Under the Crimes Act legislation introduced by the Liberal home sec-retary, Sir William Harcourt, in the wake of the Burke/Cavendish murders, a Special Commission Court had been established in Dublin to facilitate the removal of capital cases from localities in which the securing of convictions would be difficult (see Chapter 4). Justice Lawson, the judge who officiated at the first capital trial, that of Francis Hynes for the murder of a neighbour in Co. Clare,[34] had made himself unpopular by ignoring pleas for a mistrial on the basis that the jury had been improperly sequestered. He had also committed the editor and proprietor of the *Freeman's Journal*, Edmund Dwyer Gray, MP, to jail for contempt for adverse commentary on the case. In the process Lawson, already a hugely unpopular figure among nation-alists, had become an Invincibles target.

One of the men selected, at the end of October 1882, with the task of shadowing and killing Lawson was Patrick Delaney, a carpenter who worked for Carey. He would later tell the *Times* Special Commission that he deliberately botched an attempt on the judge's life in the first week in November 1882 in order to save him from assassination.[35] The attack had actually been forestalled by one of Lawson's bodyguards who had wrestled Delaney to the ground when he advanced threateningly on the judge. Mallon, who knew Delaney, believed that he himself had been one of the prisoner's targets some weeks before. This suspicion was later confirmed by Delaney under interrogation.[36]

In his colourful (and often unreliable) hagiography of Mallon, the jour-nalist, Frederick Moir Bussy, recounts the policeman's sense of frustration at his inability to prevent this rash of attacks taking place when he believed that a legal remedy was immediately to hand. 'Mallon became humiliated and despondent. Outrage after outrage was taking place on the very thresh-old of his sphere of duty, and he was utterly powerless. He confessed to me that he was "ashamed and vexed" and at last he was constrained to take his courage in both hands.'[37] What Mallon did was to appeal to the com-missioner of police, Samuel Lee Anderson, to use the full rigours of the

Crimes Act. Under Section 16 of Harcourt's coercion legislation a magistrate could be appointed, with draconian powers, to investigate a crime. He was entitled to question witnesses or suspects, on oath, who would have no recourse to legal counsel. Refusal to give sworn testimony could result in summary imprisonment. Anderson took Mallon's appeal to Earl Spencer who agreed to the full utilisation of the legislation. At the behest of Mallon the magistrate appointed to investigate, in the first instance the attack on Field, was John Adye Curran. The shackles had been loosened.

Writing in the 1890s about the wider investigation into the activities of the Invincibles, P.J. Tynan, who was never actually questioned by the man, described Curran as 'the Grand Inquisitor'[38] and a 'suave Mephistopheles'.[39] The impression is conveyed of a ruthlessly efficient interrogator with the odds stacked in his favour. But, as his final report reveals, Curran was less than optimistic when he took on the task handed to him by the Commissioner.

> At the outset I may here remark that the manner in which the evidence in the several investigations held by me unfolded itself and gradually slowly but surely inculpated and brought to justice the vast majority of those who were actually concerned in the transactions of the 6th May and 27th November, 1882, seemed to me almost miraculous ...[40]

However, the successful breach of the Invincibles conspiracy had less to do with divine intervention than with Curran and Mallon's doggedness, attention to detail, knowledge of human nature and some elements of good fortune.

Mallon was under no illusions that, intimidated by the prospect of swearing under oath, any one of the dozens of suspects questioned would collapse under the strain. What he had in mind was a shrewd psychological ploy. He hoped

> to induce an informer to come forward—to suggest by the subtlety of the questioning and the amplitude of the details at his command that he was completely advised as to the constitution and the methods and movements of the 'Invincibles'. It was by this means that he hoped to impress upon some one of the more highly placed of the 'Invincibles' that the game was up—that there was some-

body 'peaching'—that the safest course was to vomit the whole wicked business and become a Government pensioner under an assumed name, rather than risk the potentialities of the rope or prolonged imprisonment.[41]

In this he would prove to be spectacularly successful as one Invincible after another chose to become an 'approver' rather than face the morose William Marwood on the scaffold.

Mallon had a happy knack of being able to 'read' suspects with the skill of a latter day psychologist. In the case of the peripheral figure of Robert Farrell (see above), Mallon and Curran brought him in for interrogation on a Sunday, just after he had attended Mass and received Holy Communion. Farrell had been uncommunicative but Mallon, taking advantage of his own Catholicism, had appealed to Farrell's conscience and reminded him of the nature of the sacrament he had just received. For his part, Curran made sure to demonstrate to Farrell an in-depth knowledge of elements of the Invincibles conspiracy. Farrell, unaware that much of Curran's information was based on inspired guesswork and conjecture, as well as some solid intelligence, clearly persuaded himself that someone within the wider Fenian organisation had already turned informer. On 3 January, he presented himself to Inspector Kavanagh and recounted what he knew. His knowledge did not extend as far as the identity of the Phoenix Park murderers but his statement identifying James Carey, Dan Curley. Joe Brady and Tim Kelly was enough to allow Curran to go to the lord lieutenant and obtain permission for mass arrests and prolonged detention on 13 January 1883.

In the period between his two arrests Carey had been elected to the Dublin City Council so his appearance at Green Street Court along with twenty others on 20 January, provoked considerable press interest. Among those appearing in court were Robert Farrell, Joe Brady, Edward McCaffrey, Tim Kelly, Daniel Curley, James Mullett, Michael Fagan, a 24 year old blacksmith, and Joseph Hanlon, a 23 year old carpenter.

Farrell was separated from the corralled prisoners and put in the witness-box to testify against them, to their initial consternation. His evidence was tantalising but hardly compelling. The stakes were high for castle officials who had promised a successful conclusion to the Phoenix Park murders investigation before. Farrell was able to implicate Curley, Carey and others in attempts on the life of Forster but he had no direct knowledge to offer about the park murders. The *Freeman* commented that

> If the authorities succeed at last in unearthing any plots worthy of the name, their success may go far to excuse the strenuous and sweeping means which they have resorted to. If, on the contrary, they have discovered merely a mare's nest, they cannot escape the odium of a stringent and arbitrary line of procedure for which clear and striking proof of their charges only can indemnify them.

The newspaper was clearly unimpressed with Farrell's evidence and, implying that the suspects were innocent, pointed out the '*sang froid* of the central principals in the drama enacted—the men in the dock'.[42] As Farrell's evidence had continued, the prisoners had become visibly more relaxed. The Crown had established a case but it was a long distance from proving it.

But for the suspects the fear remained that Farrell would be the first of many approvers as evidence built up against the minor players in the drama. The remand appearances of the suspects were switched to the Magistrates' Court in Kilmainham where the Crown piled up the evidence designed to secure the committal of the prisoners for full trials at Green Street. Journalist, Tighe Hopkins, while noting that, in general, the prisoners 'maintained a front which was not merely cool but defiant' in the dock, also observed 'with what care the prisoners counted their numbers when they were placed in the dock in the morning—the dread of betrayal by an informer, which is the poison in the heart of every Irish conspirator'.[43]

In the weeks that followed cab-drivers, James Fitzharris and Michael Kavanagh, were added to the group of Kilmainham suspects along with a 26-year-old labourer Thomas Caffrey; Dublin Castle workman Joseph Smith; and the man jailed for the attack on Justice Lawson, Patrick Delaney. Over the course of a number of court appearances by the suspects in distinct combinations, accused of different crimes, the Crown produced a series of cogent witnesses and credible identifications but no smoking gun. Curran and Mallon were racing against time to crack the conspiracy from the inside. They sought a plausible informer. In the nick of time Mallon managed to dupe two conspirators into betraying their comrades.

The first to crack was 'sick, frightened, drink-sodden'[44] Michael Kavanagh. Mallon had already heard everything Kavanagh was prepared to relate, and more besides, by placing the cab-driver and James Carey's brother, Peter, in a corridor together in Kilmainham while they awaited a medical examination. Both were on the verge of informing and began to talk about the park murders. Mallon had secreted himself in an oak panel outside the surgery and eavesdropped on the conversation.[45] He was later able to terrify Kavanagh into becoming an approver by telling the prisoner the names of the men he had ferried to the park on 6 May 1882. On 10 February in the court adjacent to Kilmainham Prison Kavanagh described how he had driven Joe Brady, Tim Kelly, Patrick Delaney and Thomas Caffrey to the park. There he had seen Fitzharris in another car with the rest of the gang. He had waited near the entrance to the Park with James Carey and Joseph Smith who had been charged with the task of identifying Burke. Curran and Mallon were getting closer to convictions but still needed corroboration of Kavanagh's evidence and identification of the men in the Fitzharris cab. That came by dint of another demonstration of the enterprising Mallon's artifice and trickery.

The superintendent managed to insinuate himself into the confidence of James Carey. He exploited the vanity of the Invincibles ringleader while simultaneously playing an ingenious psychological game. Placing Carey next to an empty cell he arranged that the grille of the city councillor's door be left open. Carey was able to observe a number of imposing looking visitors make their way into the adjacent cell. Among them, bearing paper and pen, was the instantly recognisable Crown solicitor, George Bolton. When Carey casually inquired as to the identity of the occupant of the neighbouring cell he was told that it was Daniel Curley. He was, of course, expected to make the assumption that Curley had turned queen's evidence. He was then expected to send for Mallon and to seek to jump the approver's queue. He lived up to both expectations.[46]

Many years later, in his *Reminiscences*, Curran revealed that he had been opposed to Carey being taken on as informer. He was of the opinion that the Crown already had enough evidence and that Carey was not deserving of clemency as 'he was one of the leaders and paymasters of the gang'. He was, however, in this instance, overruled for primarily political reasons. 'Counsel for the Crown took a different view—I do not say wrongly. They were of opinion that the fact of a man of Carey's position turning King's [*sic*] evidence would be a warning to all who might in future engage in similar conspiracies.'[47]

Carey's assumption that he had barely beaten Curley to the punch prompted his opening remark when he was escorted to the stand in the preliminary hearing in Kilmainham, to the utter consternation of the defendants, on 17 February 1883. 'Ah! I was before ye's, after all, Dan', he muttered, almost taunting an incredulous Curley as he spoke from the sanctuary of the witness-box. Journalist, J.B. Hall, was one of the many reporters covering the Kilmainham trials. The strongest reaction, he noted, came not from Curley but from Brady. 'Had Joe Brady, who glared at him and stretched forward towards him, been able to reach him, I believe he would have been torn to pieces, for Brady was a powerful young fellow, and for the moment he was for all the world like a tiger on the spring.'[48] Bussy describes

> a yell of execration and despair ... wild and simultaneous, it came from the throats of more than a score of desperate wretches brought suddenly face to face with inexorable retribution. A loud wail of terror at the eclipse of a last ray of hope, distinct, yet inseparable from a howl of rage and hate accompanying the realisation of impending, irresistible destruction ...[49]

In contrast, the *Freeman's Journal* observed, matter of factly, that 'The prisoners did not appear to manifest as much surprise as might be expected'.[50]

Carey, who regularly had to be asked by defence counsel and the magistrates to speak up, took the court on a journey through the secret archive of the Invincibles. He discussed the group's foundation, the attempts on the life of Forster, the acquisition of the knives and, finally, the park murders. The *Freeman's Journal* editorial, although excoriating Carey himself as 'a villain of unexampled depravity' accepted that 'the evidence incontestably discloses the existence of a conspiracy of the foulest character for the most atrocious objects'. Gladstone's secretary, Edward Hamilton, wrote in his diary that 'his evidence ought to be conclusive not only for a committal but also for a conviction'.[51]

Hamilton was unerringly accurate in his assessment of the impact of Carey's testimony, although he, like the government for which he worked, exhibited no scruples whatever concerning the source of the evidence that sent the trials from the Magistrates' Court in Kilmainham to the Commission Court at Green Street. The home secretary himself, Sir William Harcourt, revelled in the fact that so self confessedly prominent a subversive (furthermore one who was a nationalist city councillor) had become an informer. He wrote to the queen that it would 'strike the deepest terror into all the ramifications of the secret societies'.[52]

Carey's evidence meant that the Crown could now move to the trials of the men identified as having assassinated Cavendish and Burke. The centre of activity shifted from Kilmainham Court-house to the Commission Court at Green Street where proceedings were monitored by the cadaverous Justice William O'Brien, known to Bar and Bench as 'hatchet face'. The first trial was that of the man adjudged to have been the leading Invincibles activist, Joseph Brady. The case for the prosecution was opened by the Irish attorney general, Andrew Marshall Porter. Brady seemed unperturbed at the blood curdling allegations being laid out against him. He 'listened with apparent unconcern, occupying himself at intervals picking his teeth with the stump of a pencil'.[53] Porter walked a fine line in his references to Carey. He could not afford to undermine his credibility as a well-informed witness central to the conspiracy. At the same time he did not want to draw too much attention to the Crown's association with such a thoroughly disreputable character. 'Carey was undoubtedly as thick in the assassination business as any one of the others,' the attorney general accepted, 'and it is a matter of public notoriety that he was one of the most actively concerned in the murderous conspiracy.'[54]

Once again the star prosecution witness, as at the Magistrates' Court, was the approver, James Carey. The dark, bearded informer, almost ascetic in appearance, created just as great a sensation at Green Street as he had at Kilmainham. Journalist, J.B. Hall, wrote:

> with a reputation for ostentatious piety, there was something indescribable in the effect his presence produced and with every head stretched forward, and breath almost held, the scene was striking, indeed. He spoke slowly and calmly as he had done at the preliminary hearing. During his evidence he had occasion to look straight at Brady, and their eyes met, and I can never forget the look of scorn, contempt and hatred with which the prisoner fixed his piercing eyes on the informer. Carey quickly shifted his position and looked at him no more until leaving the table he was brought face to face with him and received the same appalling and loathing look.[55]

Although heavily dependent on the evidence of Carey and the other informers the Crown could not be totally reliant on approvers in so important a case. Their testimony would need to be independently confirmed by untainted witnesses who swore to having seen Brady and the others in the park on 6 May 1882. Without this corroboration the nationalist press, and even elements of the British press, would excoriate the castle for the inevitable executions based, constructively, on the word of informers. As Curran wrote 30 years after the event 'Judges ... warn juries not to convict on the uncorroborated testimony of informers alone. I had at least by independent witnesses to place the men in the Park on the afternoon of May 6, and then let the informers tell what happened'.[56]

Public reaction, which might have been expected to be almost universally hostile to the alleged perpetrators of the atrocity in the Phoenix Park, was, because of the traditional Irish revulsion towards informers, broadly sympathetic to the prisoners, especially to the young and cherubic Timothy Kelly. In many nationalist quarters the castle was seen to be resorting, yet again, to debatable tactics (jury-packing was expected to be added to the list of transgressions) in order to secure unsafe convictions. The sympathy of the public was further engaged on the defence side by the behaviour of the judge, William O'Brien, who, according to Maurice Healy, nephew of Tim, 'regarded the doctrine of fair play for prisoners as mere sentimentality'.[57] Much of the first morning was taken up with a wrangle between O'Brien and the newly appointed defence counsel, Dr Webb, who had sought a 24-hour adjournment in order to study his brief. Only a threat by Webb and his two juniors to throw up the brief and the intervention of the attorney general persuaded O'Brien to 'ungraciously' grant the requested postponement.

The following day, clad in a long frieze coat Brady watched as Carey was sworn in. Taking him through his evidence was James Murphy, QC, who had assisted for the prosecution in the Maamtrasna trials the previous year:

MURPHY: Were you ever a member of a secret society or body of men having the name of the 'Invincibles'?

CAREY: I was.

MURPHY: Did you know the prisoner Joe Brady to be a member of that same body?

CAREY: I did.

MURPHY: Were there any number of persons holding higher positions than others in it?

CAREY: There were.

MURPHY: How many were there?

CAREY: Four.

MURPHY: How were the others chosen?

CAREY: ... By one of the four.

MURPHY: ... Who were the four that were first head of the society when it was first established?

CAREY: James Mullet ... Edward McCaffrey, Daniel Curley and myself.

MURPHY: ... After James Mullet's arrest who became chairman?

CAREY: Daniel Curley.

MURPHY: ... Who were the four then when James Mullet was gone?

CAREY: Daniel Curley, Edward McCaffrey, Joseph Brady and myself.

MURPHY: What was the object of that society of which he was one of the four you mention ... ?

CAREY: In the first place to make history, and in the next place to remove all the principal tyrants in the country.

MURPHY: What do you mean by removing?

CAREY: Of course to put them to death.

MURPHY: About what time was that society or organi-sation first established?

CAREY: About the first week in December, 1881.

MURPHY: Who was the man that first established it here?

CAREY: A man named Mr. Walsh was the first man.

MURPHY: Who next took his place?

CAREY: A gentleman who I afterwards learned to be Captain McCafferty.[58]

MURPHY:	And did any other person then direct its movements in place of McCafferty?
CAREY:	Next we had a visitor, and then next was No.1.
MURPHY:	The man you call No.1 but whom we know very well.
CAREY:	Yes.
MURPHY:	Do you recollect having gone out any day to the Phoenix Park, near the Chief Secretary's Lodge, with any member of that society?
CAREY:	I do.
MURPHY:	What was the first day that you went out there?
CAREY:	About a week after this being started in December.
MURPHY:	... Can you tell me who were the persons with you there on the first occasion you went out?
CAREY:	Mr. Walsh was one. I and Daniel Curley went by ourselves. We met Walsh, Mullett, and Edward McCaffrey there.
MURPHY:	When did you next go there?
CAREY:	I went there in April myself, on two occasions.
MURPHY:	... Has the prisoner Joseph Brady been there with you and the others?
CAREY:	I have seen him there.[59]

Discussion of the preparations for the killing of Forster quickly moved on to an account of the events of 6 May. Carey testified to accepting delivery of the knives used for the murders. He recounted how the various members of the Invincibles assigned to commit the crime had gathered in the Phoenix

Park, ferried there in the cabs of Michael Kavanagh and James 'Skin the Goat' Fitzharris. Joe Smith had been delegated the task of identifying Thomas Burke, and when he spotted the under secretary, Carey and Smith were driven by Kavanagh to where Daniel Curley, Michael Fagan, Joseph Hanlon, Joe Brady, Tim Kelly, Tom Caffrey and Patrick Delaney were gathered near the Viceregal Lodge. In Carey's narrative, it was Joe Brady who was in charge of the operation. As Carey spoke the prisoner was seen to be taking detailed notes of his evidence.

MURPHY: And whom did you first speak to when you got to the place where the number of Invincibles was?

CAREY: When the car stopped, Curley and Joe Brady walked over to the side of the road, and Joe Smith at that moment then said 'Mr. Burke' says he 'is the man with the grey suit' and I got down and the car went on a little.

MURPHY: And the car went on a little further?

CAREY: Yes; then we had a conversation the three of us, as we were the three in charge.

MURPHY: That is Brady, Curley and you—the three that were in charge—you say?

CAREY: Yes. The first thing I wanted to know was what I should do with Smith. He sat on the car, and I was told to 'let him get the hell out of that'.

MURPHY: Who told you?

CAREY: Joe Brady. And I went and told him to go home.

MURPHY: ... Well, and what further directions were given to you—was anything said as to what you were to do yourself?

CAREY: I looked round and I seen these two gentlemen coming up, and I said, 'what part am I to take' and 'you go home too' was the answer, or 'you may go away too, you are not wanting here.'

MURPHY: Who said that to you?

CAREY: Joe Brady.

MURPHY: Did you at that time see any of the weapons?

CAREY: I did not.

MURPHY: ... Did you then go away from the group?

CAREY: We had a few words then about the matter, and as I was going away the last words I made use of were with reference to the man in the grey suit, and that was the man that Smith said was Mr. Burke. When I walked away, and when I got a few a few paces off I looked at my watch again and it was seventeen minutes past.

MURPHY: Seven?

CAREY: Yes.

MURPHY: And did you look back again after that time?

CAREY: Yes, when I was about two hundred yards off I looked back, and I seen [sic] the group of seven men on the footpath meeting the two gentlemen.

MURPHY: Now when the seven men on the footpath approached the two gentlemen how were they—were they in twos or threes or how?

CAREY: First three, then two, then another two.

MURPHY: Who were the first three?

CAREY: Curley, Fagan and Hanlon.

MURPHY: Did they proceed to walk towards the gentlemen who were coming up?

CAREY: They were walking towards them.

MURPHY: And who were the next to those three?

CAREY: Timothy Kelly and Joe Brady.

MURPHY: And after them?

CAREY: Delaney, and Tom Caffrey.

MURPHY: And when the gentlemen came up did they pass them by or pass through them?

CAREY: They passed through them.

MURPHY: After they passed through them did you see any of the seven do anything?

CAREY: I lost sight of the first three altogether, they went off towards the road and I did not see them, but I saw the space between the two men and the four, and I seen the four men turn then just right about front.

MURPHY: So as to come after the gentlemen who had come through them?

CAREY: Yes, to follow them.

MURPHY: And when they turned right about, in what order did they come up to the gentlemen—who were the two that came first?

CAREY: Joe Brady was the one in front in the right about movement.

MURPHY: And did you see either of them coming up to either of the two gentlemen?

CAREY: I seen [sic] the two front-rank men closing on the two gentlemen.

MURPHY: Was that Kelly and Brady?

CAREY: Yes, and then I saw only one closing on the two.

MURPHY: And who was that one?

CAREY: Joe Brady.

MURPHY: Did you see which of the gentlemen he closed on first?

CAREY: Well, the gentleman in the grey suit: the gentleman in black was most discernible, and I noticed him; the other was nearest to Brady.

MURPHY: How do you mean—say that again?

CAREY: One of the gentlemen was in black; of course we didn't know who he was—none knew who he was, and I watched the gentleman in the grey suit, but I seen the other also.

MURPHY: Did you see Brady going up to the gentleman in the grey suit?

CAREY: I seen [*sic*] him coming on him, so that there was no space at all between them.

MURPHY: Did you see anything that happened after that—did you see either of the gentlemen fall?

CAREY: I did not.

MURPHY: Where did you make for then?

CAREY: Islandbridge.

MURPHY: When you saw Brady coming up to the gentleman, in the grey suit, so that you could see no space between them, did you see him do anything?

CAREY: I seen a motion of a hand lifted, and at that time I was 250 yards away, and I seen no more.[60]

The participation of Smith in the killing, although peripheral, was of psychological importance to the Dublin Castle administration. He worked in the castle as a labourer and could, therefore, be seen to have infiltrated the administration's stronghold. While the damage he was capable of doing was limited, given the nature of his employment, he had been, nonetheless a potential security threat. The previous December Curran had been waiting to interview witnesses in the Police Court in the Lower Castle Yard when, 'a man came in to nail down the carpet on the floor. The next time I saw that individual was in the dock at Kilmainham as Joseph Smith'.[61] To save his life, Smith too had offered to turn queen's evidence. Mallon had agreed to allow him and James Carey's brother, Peter, to become approvers.

The accretion of evidence from Carey, Kavanagh and the others, when combined with testimony from a park ranger, George Godden, who claimed to have seen Brady on the get-away car, was enough to convict Brady. The jury took 40 minutes to reach its verdict. O'Brien condemned Brady to hang in Kilmainham Gaol on 14 May. 'When sentence of death was pronounced on him,' wrote J.B. Hall, 'Brady, bowing to his counsel (Dr. Webb and Mr. Adams), thanked them. Brady's father was in court and was deeply afflicted, and a pathetic figure in the front of the gallery was a gentle-faced young girl, said to be his sweetheart, and whose tearful eyes were riveted upon him to the end.'[62]

Cleaving to what it apparently saw as an Invincibles hierarchy (although one shorn of their own star witness, James Carey) the Crown next chose to arraign Daniel Curley. His trial began on Monday 16 April. According to the reporter for the *Freeman's Journal*, the prisoner looked

> quite collected and self possessed. He is a remarkably fine
> looking man, of about five and thirty, with a splendid
> physique and features of almost perfect mould. He wears
> a brown moustache and beard, and his hair is carefully
> brushed back from his forehead, which is large, well con-
> structed and indicative of much intelligence. He was
> dressed in a light tweed suit, and present the appearance
> of a very superior type of artisan.[63]

Contemporary photographs reveal a man who bore an extraordinary resemblance to his principal accuser, James Carey. Called upon to repeat his evidence, although the approver 'tried to assume his usual air of self sufficiency and insolent coolness, he looked somewhat browbeaten and careworn'.[64]

But Carey was not nearly so care-worn when repeating his direct evidence as he would be when cross-examined by Curley's counsel, the testy Dr Webb, QC, who essentially, accused the Crown witness of being a murderer. Carey protested that he had not wielded a knife in the Phoenix Park assassinations nor had he ever killed anyone. He referred to his activities as 'playing at soldiers'. Webb also attacked Carey's celebrated pietism as rank hypocrisy. How, he inquired, could you be a sodality member while conspiring to murder? Hoping to damage Carey's credibility with a new jury, Webb attacked one of his vulnerable points, his involvement in the many abortive attempts on the life of W.E. Forster:

WEBB: Will you admit that you were a party to twenty attempts on Mr. Forster?

CAREY: Yes.

WEBB: For the purpose of assassinating him?

CAREY: Just of course.

WEBB: Were there twenty attempts made on Mr. Forster, for the purpose of assassinating him?

CAREY: Yes.

WEBB: And you called that merely playing at soldiers?

CAREY: Well it turned out that.

WEBB: What was your intention; not what was the result—I ask you was it your intention to murder him?

CAREY: Well, I would not call it murder at all, but to remove him.

WEBB: You would not call it murder at all—but to remove him?

CAREY: No.

WEBB: That's your definition, to remove him?

CAREY: Yes.

WEBB: And while these things were going on you were a member of a religious sodality?

CAREY: No, not the whole of it.

WEBB: When did you cease to be a member of the religious sodality?

CAREY: Of course, that's your stand point.

WEBB: Don't sir, dare to address me ... When did you cease to be a member of the sodality?

CAREY: When I was arrested.

WEBB: When was that?

CAREY: On the 12th of January, 1883.

WEBB: Then you were a member of the sodality during the entire year of 1882?

CAREY: Well I had nothing to do with them after the affair happened. Of course, you are aware of that.

WEBB: Didn't you swear in the former trial that you were assisting at the holiest mysteries of your religion at the time you were steeped to the lips in blood?

CAREY: No, I was never steeped to the lips in blood ...

WEBB: But on every occasion you went?

CAREY: No, I don't think I was at the whole of them.

WEBB: Was that the very time these twenty attempts were made on the life of Mr. Forster?

CAREY: No, there were some of them made in March.

WEBB: ... And how did you make history, come?

CAREY: By making so many futile attempts on a man that I had very little compassion for, and a perfect stranger to fall in for what others deserved. That's making history.

WEBB: And do you swear there, speaking in the presence of God, under the solemn sanction of an oath, in a question of life and death, do you say that Mr. Forster deserved to be assassinated in your opinion?

CAREY: He deserved—I say deserved no great love from many Irishmen in any way for his treatment—

WEBB: Did he deserve to be assassinated?

CAREY: I don't care what was done with him.

WEBB: Did he deserve to be assassinated?

CAREY: Oh, you're not going to—

WEBB: I want to press you, I want to know what your moral opinion is; I want to know what your oath is worth. Did he deserve to be assassinated?

CAREY: You don't want me to approve of assassination.

WEBB: I want to know whether you approve of it or not?

CAREY: Well I would not cry much after him at all events.

WEBB: Did Mr. Forster in your opinion, speaking under the solemn sanction of an oath, did he in your opinion deserve to be assassinated?

CAREY: As I have answered you before, I would not cry at anything that would happen him. I wouldn't like to see him going to heaven though.

WEBB: And would you prosecute your vengeance to him even to the next world?

CAREY: I wouldn't care.

WEBB: You didn't care?

CAREY: About him.

WEBB: ... And you wouldn't like him even to be safe in the next world?

CAREY: Well I wouldn't like anyone to be lost.

WEBB: And didn't you say you wouldn't like him to go to heaven?

CAREY: Well, I wouldn't like to meet him there.

WEBB: ... Do you think that Mr. Burke deserved to
                be assassinated?

CAREY: Well, no, I think not.

WEBB: Was he one of the tyrants that you gave your
                vote for the removal of?

CAREY: Well he had the name of being as bad as—

WEBB: As Forster?

CAREY: Yes, only for him Forster wouldn't get all the
                information.

WEBB: And didn't they, or rather did you think that
                Mr. Burke deserved to be assassinated?

CAREY: I had no thinking about it. We got the word
                to go and execute the orders from Number
                One, and it had to be done.[65]

The following day Carey's brother Peter gave evidence that Curley had become (justifiably as it transpired) concerned about the reliability and fidelity of Michael Kavanagh. Peter Carey alleged that Curley had spoken aloud about the need to murder the coachman in order to pre-empt any possible defection on his part. This added a certain piquancy to the evidence of Kavanagh himself who followed Carey into the witness-box and testified to the defendant's involvement in the plot and presence in Phoenix Park.

Reflecting a prevailing unease with the weight being ascribed to the evidence of Carey on the penultimate day of Curley's trial, the *Freeman's Journal* eviscerated what it called the 'approver in chief' yet again and cast doubt on the justice and efficacy of the proceedings:

> he is, by his own profession, so callous a ruffian; he is, by his own approvership [*sic*], so deeply and diffusedly and infa-mously dyed an instigator of assassins, that the best to done with him is to ignore and try to forget him ... We do not for a moment minimise the guilt of whomsoever brutally mur-dered Mr. Burke and Lord Frederick Cavendish, but our desire is to have that atrocious crime expiated in such a way

as to improve, not deprave, the moral feeling of the people,
and be free from the suspicion of impurity or vengeance.[66]

In due course Curley became the second conspirator found guilty of
murder. In his case, the jury took 45 minutes to come to their conclusion.
In a dignified speech from the dock Curley continued to deny his guilt:

> There are several matters, of course, which I wish to make
> mention of—but owing to the fact that there are other
> people awaiting their trial—people who will, of course,
> meet the same fate as me—I expect so anyhow—I don't
> like to go into them—not that I fear death—but I never
> courted it. I deny the charge. Between me and my God—
> between me and my conscience—I deny the charge ... I do
> not pray for pardon—I expect none from the British gov-
> ernment or England, they are my avowed enemies, I tell
> you that my Lord ... I admit myself, I candidly admit, I
> was sworn in a member of the Fenian organisation about
> twelve years ago, when I was 21 or 22 years of age. From
> that time to the present I have worked confidentially in
> that organisation, and I was let into a great many of their
> secrets. That was the first oath I ever took, and that I will
> bring to my grave, faithfully and truthfully. I shall never
> deceive my fellow man—no, never. If I had a thousand
> lives to lose I would lose them before I would deceive my
> fellow man. No man will ever be able to point the finger
> of scorn at me, and say a word against my character,
> moral or otherwise ... 'For it is better to die than live /
> When foul dishonour only life would give.'[67]

Curley was sentenced, by Mr Justice O'Brien, to be hanged four days
after Joe Brady, on 18 May. Timothy Kelly followed him into the dock
almost immediately. It would take three trials to convict the fresh-faced
former choir-boy. Two juries were unable to reach a verdict. An issue
arose as to whether the Crown should pursue the case against him a
third time. Earl Spencer, who was called upon to make the decision, consulted Mallon as to the probable extent of the youth's guilt. Mallon told
the lord lieutenant that Kelly had admitted to his part in the crime but
had refused to plead guilty or to inform on any of the other prisoners.[68]
Spencer decided to proceed with a third prosecution. The crucial evi-

dence in the final trial of Kelly proved to be that of the previously silent Joseph Hanlon, one of the seven men indicted by Carey and himself the final approver. Just over a week after the execution of Brady, in May 1883, a third jury took just 27 minutes to consign the young Dubliner to the same gallows.

This was despite the fact that more than one of them had been seen to be moved to tears by the closing address of Kelly's counsel, D.B. Sullivan, QC. But as he watched the jurors return, Kelly 'narrowly scrutinised the twelve men as they made their way back to their places, then, leaning over to the warder, he said with a smile ... "I'll bet you a bob this lot hangs me". Within little more than three minutes he had been sentenced to death'.[69] According to J.B. Hall:

> Kelly was extremely youthful and simple-looking, and had an air of bewildered anxiety. He was known to have borne a very good character, and it was with profound dismay and astonishment that those who were acquainted with him learned that he was associated in any way with the 'Invincibles' ... The unhappy boy had been a chorister in one of the Dublin Catholic churches, and I was told by the Governor of Kilmainham that the night before his execution he sang in his cell Wallace's pathetic song 'The Memory of the Past.'[70]

The verdict and the execution of Kelly lacked popular support and helped bolster the growing sentiment in favour of the Invincibles. 'The authorities were made to seem unduly persistent and vindictive in their pursuit of the youth.'[71]

Michael Fagan, another of the seven Invincibles cited by Carey as having been part of the gang that surrounded Burke and Cavendish, suffered a similar fate. In his case, the defence was compelled to admit that he had been in the park on 6 May 1882 but contended that he had not been in the vicinity of the scene of the crime at the time of the murders. He had, in fact, been detailed to 'see there was no interference by any escort, or police protectors'[72] as the conspirators had assumed Burke would come through the park by cab, flanked by bodyguards. The defence case failed to impress a jury that took little over half an hour to condemn Fagan.

James Fitzharris, the cabman, originally from Wexford, must have expected a similar fate when his trial began on 30 April. Certainly the precedents were not in his favour. Four men had been tried; four men had been condemned to hang. According to J.B. Hall, Fitzharris

> presented a most remarkable appearance. Although plain to the point of ugliness, there was something almost comical in the expression of his rugged face, and he had a habit of winking to friends whom he recognised in the Gallery, or even to strangers who happened to catch his eye. One of the English newspaper correspondents, describing his countenance, said it presented the appearance of having at some remote period been 'badly battered by contact with a traction engine.' He had the reputation of being an honest, decent type of cabman, quite incapable of being a blood-thirsty conspirator.[73]

As there was no independent evidence of the cabman's presence in the park it was left to the approvers to convict him. A certain vagueness crept into much of the testimony, including that of Carey, and Fitzharris was acquitted of murder, though later tried and convicted as an accessory.

The last two members of the group of seven named by Carey faced trial on 2 May. Both Patrick Delaney (already in jail for the attack on Justice Lawson) and Thomas Caffrey pleaded guilty. Delaney admitted to having been a member of the gang but insisted that he had taken no part in the murders of Burke and Cavendish. He also claimed, once again, to have saved the life of Justice Lawson. O'Brien, who had presided over Delaney's earlier trial, was unrelenting. Sentence of death was passed. Delaney, however, must have known that the information he had given the authorities while in custody would save his life. The death sentence was later commuted. Caffrey, on the other hand, had not collaborated with the Crown prosecutors. He was, according to Bussy 'a somewhat soppy, careless, self-neglectful kind of fellow, who would be anything according to the company he was in ... In fact, he was a fairly average specimen of the Irish "omadhaun" and was so regarded by his companions'.[74]

Caffrey, too, was sentenced to death. There was to be no commutation in his case, despite his plea of guilty. Bussy maintained in his biography of Mallon that the authorities were in possession of information concerning Caffrey which made such a development unlikely. 'Caffrey,' he alleges, 'would never have been hanged for the crime to which he pleaded guilty, had it not been for other offences of which he was never openly accused and for which he was not put on trial.' Bussy further alleges that the weapons used in the murder of the agent, John Henry Blake in Loughrea (see Chapter 4) had been supplied by Curley and brought west by Caffrey who might then have assisted in that or other crimes. Michael Fagan had, according to Mallon, been involved in a similar outrage.[75]

THE FATE OF THE APPROVERS

The Crown managed to secure fifteen convictions in all.[76] But while the hangings of the five men convicted of capital murder failed, understandably, to arouse anything like the antagonism that would later greet the executions of the leaders of the 1916 Rising, there was, nonetheless, a measure of disquiet as Brady, Curley, Kelly, Fagan and Caffrey were hanged over a period of three weeks. The attenuated process of retribution helped to ensure, according to P.J. Tynan, that 'the villains became heroes, and the nationalist press risked English censure by referring to them as "brave, self-sacrificing, misguided", writing of their audacity and fortitude'.[77]

The first to hang, on 14 May 1883, was Joseph Brady, described by Tighe Hopkins as 'the most sympathetic personality in the group'.[78] Hopkins goes on to describe how 'The staunchest of the Invincibles died without a tremor. His cheek had the colour of life, his huge frame had not diminished by the weight of an ounce'.[79] Hopkins spoke to a witness to the execution who had overheard the hangman, William Marwood, in discussion with the Kilmainham Gaol doctor.

> The hangman was positively jubilant [according to the witness], rubbing his hands and exclaiming, 'The eyes of the whole civilised world are upon us this morning, doctor. This is the grandest execution of the nineteenth century' ... When Marwood had adjusted the rope, he literally danced around his victim; and just before pulling the bolt he said, 'Now then, hold back your head, and you'll die easy'.[80]

Curley followed four days later, Fagan on 28 May. Caffrey met his end on 2 June and, the last to go, Timothy Kelly, his fate left in the balance by two failures to convict, was hanged on 9 June 1883. The bodies of the five men were interred below the scaffold where they died in a small prison yard in Kilmainham Gaol. In the cases of Caffrey and Kelly there had been concerted efforts to secure reprieves. Earl Spencer had remained obstinately opposed to the commutation of the sentence of either man. Given the evidence adduced that Kelly had been one of the principals in the assault, even the *Freeman's Journal* was adamant that there was 'no quarrel with the justice which declined to stop short of his execution'.[81]

Two days after the hanging of Caffrey, Earl Spencer had written to Queen Victoria about the process of retributive justice.

> The execution of the men convicted of the Phoenix Park murders has passed off quietly ... There has been but little pressure to obtain commutation of the death sentences. Letters from those who oppose capital punishment, or from others, who considered that leniency would produce a beneficial effect on this country have been sent to Lord Spencer, but not in large numbers ... The only case in which Lord Spencer thought it necessary to alter the sentence was that of Delaney. He had constantly offered evidence and though he was not taken as a witness, some evidence which he gave was used, which probably secured the conviction of one of these men. This having been done it would not have been possible to carry out the sentence of death ... The successful issue of the Prosecution has already had a great effect in Dublin and throughout Ireland, and it is hoped will have a lasting influence in stopping the evil influence of secret societies ...[82]

The Crown may have divested itself of five conspirators to murder but, in the aftermath of the trials, it was faced with the question of what to do with the six approvers who had sent them to the gallows. Three, Kavanagh, Hanlon and Smith, were sent to Australia on board the steamer the *Pathan*. Unfortunately for them the authorities in Melbourne, their ultimate destination, became aware of the intention to dump the three approvers in Victoria and all three ended up being repatriated. Hanlon and Smith managed to escape into comfortable obscurity. Kavanagh, according to Tighe Hopkins at any rate, was not so fortunate: 'He died at twenty-three, poisoned by drink, in a lunatic asylum in London'.[83] Their arrival in the antipodes coincided with what must have been, for them, disheartening news.

James Carey remained in protective custody in Kilmainham for some weeks after the conclusion of the murder trials. Eventually he was told that he was to be shipped to safety in the colonies (in his case the destination was South Africa). In preparation, he changed his appearance. According to Frederick Moir Bussy, who met Carey before his departure with his wife and six children,

> He was clean shaven, and his kinky hair was cut short and parted at the side instead of being divided down the centre as of old. He was a forbidding, objectionable-looking person, with repulsively low forehead, on which the hair grew almost down to his eyebrows, and a large, besotted, red nose. The removal of moustache and beard had disclosed a peculiarly animal mouth that added to the sinister, cut-throat suggestiveness of the whole.[84]

Using the name of Power, Carey and his brood sailed for the Cape of Good Hope on board the *Kinfauns Castle*. The destination, as it transpired, was inappropriately named where the infamous approver was concerned. On board the ship Carey befriended a fellow Irishman, Patrick O'Donnell. As J.B. Hall recounts, their friendship was to be short-lived:

> At Cape Town, O'Donnell was shown a portrait of James Carey the informer he recognised it at once as that of his acquaintance 'Mr. Power.' Carey sailed in the *Melrose* for Port Elizabeth. So did O'Donnell, and while the two men were in the refreshment saloon together, O'Donnell drew a revolver and fired three shots into Carey's body killing him almost instantly.[85]

'The killing of Carey had evoked no feeling of pity anywhere,' according to Michael Davitt. He continued:

> The popular conscience voiced a unanimous verdict of 'Serve him right'. But the fact that he was thus killed, while virtually under the protection of the law he had served in order to save his own neck, created a profound sensation, and begot the impression that he had been deliberately tracked by an avenging executioner so as to carry out the decree of some branch of the Invincible body.[86]

Ten years later, from the safety of the USA, P.J. Tynan enthusiastically and mischievously canvassed this notion. In his florid and highly polemical history of the Invincibles he claimed that O'Donnell had tracked Carey all the way from the UK at the behest of the revolutionary movement. Tighe Hopkins pointed out that O'Donnell had booked his passage to South Africa a month before the Dublin Castle authorities had even decided where to dispatch their asset/liability. Tynan's treatment of the overwhelmingly positive response in Ireland to the assassination of Carey is appropriately pompous and magisterial: 'In Dublin the unthinking element of the people burst into ecstasies of joy; bonfires were burnt, and they seemed to think it an occasion to make glad over. At best his taking off was a melancholy duty, a sad necessity'.[87]

United Ireland could hardly be described as an 'unthinking element' but the newspaper took an almost pornographic delight in the murder of Carey. In addition to triumphalist coverage of the killing, the paper included representations of his assassination as well as a drawing of his death mask.[88]

O'Donnell was returned to Britain where he was tried and hanged. The final victim of the blood-letting of 6 May 1882 in the Phoenix Park was defended by Sir Charles Russell. His claim that O'Donnell had killed Carey in self defence was but a short step from the defence most of his fellow countrymen would have entered, that of justifiable homicide. The latter would have stood no chance of success, neither did the former. O'Donnell was executed in London on 17 December. A marble monument was erected in his honour in Glasnevin Cemetery.

AFTERMATH

Six years after the execution of the leadership of the Invincibles, Patrick Delaney was granted a further day in the sun. He was produced as a witness by the Times in its attempt to 'convict' Parnell of guilt by association with the Invincibles (see Chapter 6). In order to justify its campaign the Times needed to establish the complicity of Patrick Egan in the birth and funding of the organisation. Back in 1883 Carey had, obligingly, implicated Frank Byrne and P.J. Sheridan but had gone no further than hint that the source of the Invincibles' funds was Land League money disbursed by Egan. In his 1883 deposition, referring to a sum of fifty sovereigns left as start-up funding by Walsh in December 1881, Carey said 'I never saw anything at all like that coming into the organisation while it was solely the Fenian organisation'.[89]

Five years after the murder of Carey, Delaney testified to the content of alleged conversations with the city councillor. He claimed that Carey had been encouraged by Egan in his run for a seat on the corporation. 'Mr. Egan urged him on to it—sent letters from Paris to him—that he would pay all expenses in connexion with it'. Delaney claimed that Egan's motive was that 'one of the principal Invincibles in Dublin would be Lord Mayor of Dublin'.[90] Parnell's counsel, Sir Charles Russell objected to the hearsay nature of the evidence but the defence accepted the authenticity of a letter from Egan to Carey sent around the time of the inception of the Invincibles. In the letter, he encouraged Carey to stand and concluded conspiratorially 'Don't say much in reply as my letters are liable to be opened, and don't give your address or name in your letter, only the initial J'.[91]

Russell tried to undo the damage in his cross-examination of Delaney. The distinguished advocate put it to the witness 'that as regards these three men, Egan, Brennan and Sheridan, they had nothing to do with hatching the Invincible conspiracy?' Delaney's response would have been more detrimental had he established himself as a truly credible witness. 'They were the recognised leaders of it,' he said, 'When I was brought into the Invincible party ... they were represented to be the head of it.' He acknowledged, however that he had never actually met them at an Invincibles' meeting. When Russell alleged that he had come to the conclusion they were involved because of what others said to him Delaney's rejoinder was 'It is not my conclusion. It is the conclusion of the leaders of the Invincible party and the leaders of the Fenian organisation'.[92]

The spy, Henri Le Caron, who infiltrated the highest ranks of Clan na Gael in the USA, was of some assistance to the newspaper in connecting the dots that linked Egan to the killers of Cavendish and Burke when he testified at the *Times* Commission (see Chapter 6). In his 'tell-all' memoir, written a year after the death of Parnell, Le Caron referred to the arrival in the USA of 'Egan, Sheridan, Frank Byrne and other Invincibles "on the run"'.[93] Le Caron prevailed on an obliging Egan to describe how he had evaded the clutches of the law when the net was widened in the wake of Carey's apostasy.

According to the well-placed British agent,

> Within twenty minutes of the order being issued of the warrant for his arrest, he knew of the fact. He was at his office at the time, and at once proceeded to his house and packed his satchel ... He destroyed a number of docu-

ments which he had in the house, some of them pertaining to his connection with the Irish Republican Brotherhood, and also some letters of James Carey.[94]

Egan later made his way from Belfast, with some assistance from a Scottish friend in the flour trade, to Rotterdam, via Manchester and Hull. The evidence of Egan's complicity in the conspiracy is compelling if not overwhelming. However, it didn't seem to be of too much concern to his new hosts. Some years later the former Land League treasurer was elevated to the post of US minister (ambassador) to Chile.

For some time it looked as if the admirable policeman, John Mallon, might never be raised to the exalted heights to which he also aspired. Mallon was forced to share much of the credit for bringing the killers of Burke and Cavendish to justice with others. John Adye Curran[95] certainly never understated his role in the investigation and in his autobiography *Reminiscences* is less than generous in his estimate of Mallon's contribution. Almost ten years on the ageing policeman had not benefited in any obvious way from his dogged pursuit of the Invincibles. With a new Liberal government in power in 1892, committed to reintroducing Home Rule legislation, Tim Healy was surprised by a visit from Mallon. The story he told was of others taking the lion's share of the credit for his hard work. 'I had not met him before,' wrote the Irish MP, 'and noted the humility with which he bore himself. He told me the usual tale of the boycotting of Catholics by Dublin Castle, and said he had been shut out from advancement.' He now sought a vacant assistant commissionership. '" … unless I get it under a Home Rule Government, who knows what king will reign in a few years' time?" John Morley then was Chief Secretary, and gave Mallon the post he ambitioned.'[96]

He had earned it. His efficient and often inspired police work had laid bare the entire conspiracy. He was fortunate in that the Invincibles did not lie low for long enough after the Phoenix Park *coup* but his penetration of the organisation was still an example of masterly detective work. As contemporary journalist, Tighe Hopkins, observed, 'He had a memory that never slept, a patience without end, a terrible skill in piecing evidence together, and a complete disregard of danger … those who were to hang shook him by the hand on the eve of execution'.[97]

The Phoenix Park murder trials unpacked and laid bare a vicious conspiracy that was not unique to the Dublin artisan class from which the

Invincibles sprang. Never numbering more than 30 members, and with the homicidal impetus coming from an even smaller governing cadre the Invincibles were, in essence, an urban Ribbon organisation. Like many other Ribbon/Fenian groups it drew its membership from the ranks of the IRB and its inspiration from the *vendetta*. The murders themselves, and the high profile trials that followed, reinforced British notions of Irish savagery, encapsulated in the iconic *Punch* cartoon of the Irish Frankenstein. The association made between bloodthirsty terrorists and the, avowedly, constitutional agitation of the Land League, not to mention the Irish Parliamentary Party was to prove difficult to dispel. It would later be exploited by the *Times* in its indictment of the Irish Party.

James Carey, it was constantly pointed out, was a political figure whose campaign for a seat on Dublin City Council had been supported by *United Ireland*. He had implicated in the genesis of the Invincibles Frank Byrne and P.J. Sheridan, both associated with the Land League and with Parnell himself. When those suspicions were added to the beginnings, in 1883, of a dynamite campaign in Britain, funded from the USA, it was inevitable that the promise implied in the Kilmainham Treaty of an improvement in Anglo–Irish relations would be put on hold. T.D. Sullivan, nationalist MP and former Lord Mayor of Dublin, wrote in his political memoir that 'The immediate effect of the Phoenix Park outrage was to darken the political skies, and blot the vision of peace and friendship that a moment before had looked so fair. Social and party strife went on no less fiercely than before'.[98]

But the murder trials also hinted at the lengths to which the defenders of law and order in Ireland were prepared to go to pacify the country. In more recent Irish history we have seen the role of non-jury courts and informer evidence in the withdrawal by elements of a community of its consent to be governed. While the Liberal government of the early 1880s was able to justify its extreme coercion policies to its home constituency, legislation like the Crimes Act antagonised a militant and motivated Irish population. The use of informers was almost as culturally sensitive an issue in mutinous Ireland as the use of animal fat in cartridges in mutinous India.

Accused by William E. Forster in the House of Commons (February 1883) of having 'planned or perpetrated outrages or murders', Parnell, speaking in his defence, suggested that the former chief secretary might like to return to his previous posting 'to help Lord Spencer in the congenial work of the gallows in Ireland'.[99] To many moderate Irish nationalists the reluctance of the lord lieutenant to review or second-guess the outcome of capital cases smacked of a policy of *pour encourager les autres*. If enough heads could be, metaphorically, placed on stakes in full public view, calm would be restored to the country-side. And if one or two of those heads had once been attached to the bodies of blameless men that was a regrettable and unintended consequence. In reality, Spencer's correspondence shows that he did not resort to such cynical political expediency. The acceptance of Carey as an approver illustrates that the administration sought to strike fear into the hearts of potential wrong-doers but not by executing innocent men. That, however, particularly in the wake of the Maamtrasna affair, was not the perception. What was certainly the case was that Dublin Castle was reluctant to admit to mistakes and offer pardons where appropriate.

Unlike the Maamtrasna case, there is little doubt about the guilt of those executed for the Phoenix Park murders. Yet by the time Tim Kelly had been hanged, the conduct of the case by the Dublin Castle administration had managed to dissipate much of the Irish nationalist sense of horror, revulsion and the need for reparation over the killing of Burke and Cavendish. Kelly's execution 'was the occasion for a nation-wide display of emotion'.[100]

As with Maamtrasna, the Crown had relied on a combination of informant and independent testimony. However, Curran's investigation was scrupulous to a fault when measured against that of Bolton in the case of the Joyce killings. Furthermore the evidence of Mallon's approvers and eye-witnesses was a model of rectitude when set against that of Bolton and Brady's use of Philbin, Casey and the 'Maolra' Joyces. When the Phoenix Park murder trials took place the controversy that arose in 1884 over the Maamtrasna verdicts was still some months in the future. The work of Timothy Harrington had not yet exposed the potential danger of employing dubious informer evidence. Thus the use of the likes of Carey, Hanlon and Kavanagh to implicate their co-conspirators aroused merely a sense of unease and revulsion rather than of anger or outright opposition. The main nationalist daily, the *Freeman's Journal*, repeatedly criticised the practice, reserving its particular scorn for James Carey. The newspaper's proprietor and editor, Edward Dwyer Gray, because of his own experience of the Commission Court in August 1882 would have felt entitled to express some scepticism as to the conduct of justice in Ireland under the aegis of the Crimes Act.

As with the Hynes case—which had led indirectly to Gray's brief incarceration—there was more than a suspicion that the Crown had 'packed' the

juries in the Phoenix Park murder trials. Of the 72 jurors who had participated in the process, 50 were Protestant and only 22 Roman Catholic.
However, two things must be borne in mind. Although such a ratio was
hardly proportionally reflective of the religious divide in Dublin, it reflected
the composition of jury-lists when property qualifications are taken into
consideration. In addition, two 'safe' Protestant juries refused to convict
Tim Kelly on the evidence presented to them and a third only did so on the
basis of the clinching testimony of the final approver, Joseph Hanlon.

The passage of the Crimes Act at a time of high tension and emotion,
undoubtedly, enabled the Liberal government to secure convictions in the
Phoenix Park murder trials. Without the 'Star Chamber'[101] process, permitted under the legislation, initiated under Curran and abetted by Mallon
it is possible that the Invincibles infrastructure would have remained intact,
though some attrition might have been expected were the organisation to
have been in a position to continue its activities. But, put in twenty-first
century terminology, Dublin Castle's success came at considerable cost in
terms of public relations and civil liberties. As Tom Corfe describes it:

> The strict letter of the law having proved so inadequate to
> cope with a hostile country in a revolutionary mood,
> justice was in this instance not seen to have been done;
> justice had been achieved, in fact, but only at the cost of
> severely straining the law. It was an ominous precedent ...
> the Castle added five more martyrs to the Irish pantheon
> of heroes, and 'lion-hearted Joe Brady' was remembered
> not as a vicious criminal but as a defiant victim.[102]

Four years later the *Times* and an entirely new British government
would establish some more ominous precedents in attempting to indict an
entire political movement. They would, however, signally fail to add any
further martyrs to the cause.

.6.

PIGOTT
V
RUSSELL:
THE
PARNELL
COMMISSION

I am tending to the conviction that there are three conditions only requisite for the success of any great project of
reform—namely, a good cause, persevering advocates, and
the hostility of the *Times*.[1]

(Sir Charles Russell, quoting Richard Cobden)

All the acts that were done were done in furtherance of a
concerted and preconceived conspiracy with definite
objects, with definite aims, and the only way in which that
conspiracy could be carried out, the only way in which
the conspiracy or organisation could do the work which
those who are mixed up in it intended it should do, was
by the commission of crimes ... without crime this conspiracy, this organisation, never could have succeeded. [2]

(Sir Richard Webster, attorney general, *Opening address
to the Special Commission on Parnellism and Crime*)

It was 30 October 1889 only the seventh day into what promised to be a
lengthy tribunal and already interest was beginning to wane. A monoto-
nous five-day uninterrupted anti-Land League harangue by the attorney
general had not succeeded in sustaining the interest of the spectators in
Probate Court Number 1. The first *Times* witness in its case against the
Irish constitutional nationalist movement, a rural police constable who had
spoken throughout his evidence in a barely distinguishable, heavily
accented mumble, had emphasised to the accused, counsel, press and audience that this exercise might prove to be more dreary and debilitating than
enlightening or entertaining. Constable Bernard O'Malley was expected
back in the witness box the following morning and those obliged to attend
anticipated another day of tedium. There was some surprise when Parnell,
not the most precise timekeeper, was in his place a quarter of an hour
before proceedings were due to begin.

When Sir Richard Webster announced the insertion of a surprise
witness it became clear what the Irish Party leader had found so potentially
interesting as to cause him to change the habits of a lifetime. The attorney
general announced that, because of business commitments on the
Continent, Captain William O'Shea was being called, well ahead of the
Times schedule, to give his evidence. Sir Charles Russell, Parnell's counsel,

objected and was overruled. The portly former MP, who had been out of the public eye since his resignation from parliament at the time of the defeat of the Home Rule Bill in 1886 (he had been one of the few abstentions in the House) was called to the stand and sworn in. Observed with almost palpable hostility by Parnell, Michael Davitt and Joseph Biggar, O'Shea was clearly nervous at first, but soon hit his stride under the courteous direct examination of the attorney general. The watching *Times* executives, who had been assiduously courting the Captain and by whom he had been subpoenaed, had good cause to be delighted by his evidence.

The *coup de grâce* by the vindictive former friend and ally of Parnell came when Webster produced a number of incriminating letters, in the possession of the *Times* and allegedly signed by Parnell, which seemed to suggest the Irish leader's close affiliation with political violence and, specifically, with the perpetrators of the Phoenix Park murders. O'Shea was the first witness called who was obviously familiar with the Irish leader's signature. His evidence as to the signature on the letters would be highly significant.

WEBSTER:	Will you look, if you please, at that signature? [Handing a document to witness.] Look at the signature on this letter, this paper dated 15th May 1882. You see the signature?
RUSSELL:	That is the Phoenix Park letter, is it not?
WEBSTER:	It is the one which was published.
RUSSELL:	I mean the facsimile.
WEBSTER:	It is the letter which was published?
O'SHEA:	Well, I know nothing about signatures; I am not an expert.
WEBSTER:	I am not saying you are an expert in handwriting. Whose signature do you believe that to be? The signature?
O'SHEA:	I believe it is Mr. Parnell's handwriting.
RUSSELL:	You believe it to be in Mr. Parnell's writing, the signature?
O'SHEA:	The signature, not the letter.
WEBSTER:	Will you look, if you please, at the two letters

> dated the 16th June? Look at the signature to
> those. Whose do you believe it to be?

O'SHEA: I believe it to be Mr. Parnell's signature.[3]

Given that it would be four months before any contradictory evidence
emerged to challenge O'Shea's assertion it was game and first set to the
Times in its attempt to lay responsibility for Irish political and agrarian
violence at the door of Parnell and his entire political movement.

THE *TIMES* V PARNELL,
MARCH 1887–OCTOBER 1888

The 1881 Land Act, William Gladstone's second attempt to sort out the
social and economic mess that was Irish land tenure, was not as flawed a
template as his 1870 scheme. However, by the latter half of the decade any
element of consent achieved in Ireland by conciliatory government policies
was fraying at the edges. The 1881 Land Act better secured that all-important alliterative framework of fair rent, free sale and fixity of tenure.
Unfortunately it had also left hundreds of thousands of Irish tenant farmers
outside its scope by excluding tenants in arrears and leaseholders (as
opposed to the more obviously vulnerable 'tenants at will').

In addition, the debate was about to move on. Land Courts, which
mediated between landlord and tenant to establish a fair rent, a successful
feature of the 1881 legislation, were all very fine but within a few years
of the enactment of Gladstone's legislation discussion in Ireland had
switched to the elimination of the landlord–tenant relationship entirely.
Tenant purchase or peasant proprietary was to provide a final solution to
a decades old conundrum—how to satisfy the demands of mutually
antipathetic entities.

Agitation and agrarian violence, better known to a spluttering British
polity and press as 'outrage', continued and even intensified as the decade
waned. With the Conservatives in power after the defeat of the 1886 Home
Rule Bill, the iron fist was noticeably steelier and applied with little com-
punction or Liberal-style soul-searching. But the velvet glove of the chief
secretary for Ireland, Arthur Balfour (nephew of the prime minister, Lord
Salisbury and a future prime minister himself) was softer and smoother
than that of the conflicted Liberals. Palliative measures accompanied

repressive legislation in a concerted policy of coercion and conciliation. For example, alongside the introduction of a Criminal Law Amendment Bill in 1887, which made it easier to incarcerate the organisers of boycotts and rent strikes, Balfour agreed to the inclusion of leaseholders within the terms of the 1881 Land Act.

Continued economic depression meant that in some parts of the country even the judicial rents established in 1881/2 by the Land Courts were beyond the reach of many tenants. Widespread evictions resumed. The overt reaction was the 'Plan of Campaign' led by MPs William O'Brien and John Dillon (though shunned by Parnell). The covert response was the moonlighting activities of agrarian secret societies. Tensions mounted in parts of rural Ireland in a vicious spiral of retaliatory violence. The quasi-military activities of the Royal Irish Constabulary earned Balfour the nickname 'Bloody'. The crisis reached its zenith in September, 1887 when the police fired on a crowd in Mitchelstown, Co. Cork, gathered to offer support to William O'Brien as he faced trial in the town. Three men were killed and Gladstone thereafter fulminated against Tory policy with the slogan 'Remember Mitchelstown'. The arithmetic nature of political polarisation became geometric.

The *Times*, which, from its base on Printing House Square, was virtually the in-house organ of the Tories and Liberal Unionists,[4] managed to bring some fresh kindling to the fire on 7 March 1887, with the first in a promised series of articles under the title 'Parnellism and crime'. The 'newspaper of record' sought to connect Irish MPs and agrarian activists with complicity in rural 'outrage'. The initial articles were long on rhetoric and indignation but short on specifics. But the lack of excitement generated by the series was rectified on 18 April as the new Coercion Bill faced its second reading in the House of Commons. In that day's edition of the newspaper the *Times* published what purported to be the facsimile of a letter signed by Parnell which connected him to the murder of Chief Secretary Lord Frederick Cavendish and Under Secretary Thomas Burke in the Phoenix Park in May 1882. The letter, to an unknown recipient,[5] if genuine, would end Parnell's political career and set the Irish nationalist cause back by decades. It read:

> Dear Sir,
>
> I am not surprised at your friend's anger but he and you should know that to denounce the murders was the only course open to us. To do that promptly was plainly our best policy.

But you can tell him and all others concerned that though I regret the accident of Lord F. Cavendish's death I cannot refuse to admit that Burke got no more than his just deserts.

You are at liberty to show him this, and others whom you can trust also, but let not my address be known. He can write to House of Commons.

Yours very truly,

Chas. S. Parnell[6]

Such was the reputation of the *Times* for rigour and accuracy that, despite vehement Parnellite protestations to the contrary, it would not have occurred to most readers that the letter might be a fake. This notion was reinforced when Parnell failed to sue the newspaper for libel. He was advised against a defamation action on the basis that were he to sue in London the unpopularity of the Irish cause would guarantee failure while the assured success of a Dublin lawsuit would not offer any realistic vindication.

The facsimile letter was the first in a stream of correspondence published by the *Times*. It conveyed an impression to the reader of an Irish political organisation that could turn the tap of agrarian violence on and off at will. In essence it confirmed many of the latent prejudices of a disapproving British *bourgeoisie* and political establishment. The series also offered validation for the repressive Irish policies of Balfour's regime and emboldened the Conservative administration in its conduct of Irish policy. The consternation and embarrassment of the Liberal allies of Parnell was a bonus for the Tories and the recently sundered Liberal Unionists. The radical leader, Joseph Chamberlain, now had justifiable cause for his personal animosity towards Parnell, other than pique over past slights.[7]

The impact of the 'Parnellism and crime' articles was allowed to dissipate somewhat in the months after the publication of the 'facsimile' letter. Parnell, never one to agonise greatly over English assessments of his character, was adamant that the letter was a forgery and that it was the product of a Tory–*Times* conspiracy to discredit Irish nationalism. The storm had, more or less, blown itself out when the issue was revived by a maverick Irish politician.

Frank Hugh O'Donnell, a former Irish Parliamentary Party MP, was an ally of Parnell's in the mid-1870s when the Irish leader had been a member of a small minority of Isaac Butt's Home Rule League that had scandalised his own party and the House of Commons by resorting to the tactics of the filibuster. The young Wicklow squire, MP for Meath, along with former Fenians, Joseph Biggar and John O'Connor Power, as well as O'Donnell, frustrated by an inattentive Disraeli administration, slowed the progress of government bills to a crawl by a policy of 'obstruction'. Later, the egotistical O'Donnell, always the hero of his own political narrative, fell out with the upstart Parnell and abandoned politics. However, in July 1888, he decided that, arising out of a correspondence related to 'Parnellism and crime', he had been libelled by the *Times*. He sued and lost in spectacular fashion. In so doing he revived the entire controversy.[8] Lead counsel for the *Times* in defending the libel action was, the 'plump, indus- trious and somewhat obtuse Attorney General',[9] Sir Richard Webster. Although a serving attorney general was well within his rights in continu- ing to accept briefs, Webster was criticised for associating himself so closely with such a highly politicised case. His participation contributed to a growing belief that the government and the *Times* were acting in tandem.

The case afforded the *Times* an opportunity to score into an undefended goal. O'Donnell never even took the stand to advance his case. Moreover Webster was enabled to introduce more incriminating letters by reading them into the court record, thus allowing the newspaper to publish them. The letters had, apparently, come into the possession of the *Times* too late for inclusion in the original series, and appeared to incriminate the Land League treasurer, Patrick Egan, and James O'Kelly, MP, both men with strong Fenian backgrounds, as well as Parnell. Not much commented upon at the time, but of crucial significance later, were some misspellings in the correspondence, most notably the word 'hesitancy' spelt as 'hesitency' in a letter allegedly written from Kilmainham by Parnell to Patrick Egan on 9 January 1882 in which he appeared to be calling for drastic action from nationalist militants.

Thanks to O'Donnell's gratuitous intervention Parnell was obliged to attempt, finally, to lay the matter to rest. He sought an investigation of the *Times* allegations by the House of Commons. His favoured vehicle was a Commons Select Committee in which he, and other members of his party, would face the interrogation of their peers—as would their accusers. The Conservative government, egged on by their vindictive Liberal Unionist ally, Joseph Chamberlain,[10] chose an entirely different forum, a Royal Commission. Salisbury's government introduced Special Commission legis- lation to examine, not only the authenticity of the *Times* 'facsimile letter', but the veracity of the newspaper's thesis that the Irish Parliamentary Party and its agents in the Irish National League were felon-setters and conspirators responsible for co-ordinating a campaign of violence against landlordism in Ireland. In effect, the Salisbury administration was putting constitutional Irish nationalism on trial in an attempt to establish that it was anything but constitutional. It was, in other words, employing 'parliamentary machinery for a quasi legal purpose'.[11] The commission was designed, as Margaret O'Callaghan states, 'to render the Irish parliamentary party constitutionally impotent, since it established them all as criminals'.[12]

It was, in effect, an attempt by the Tories to demonise an entire constitutional political movement by raking over its alleged past associations with a form of sophisticated and co-ordinated agrarian and political violence. The Liberal Party would be, implicitly, guilty by association should it choose to pursue an alliance with the Irish Party if the *Times* allegations were substantiated. The upside for the Tories was that either Gladstone and his party would be utterly discredited, or that Home Rule, with its implied threat to the sanctity of the empire, would be off the agenda for a generation.

The Conservative majority in the Commons was sufficient to override vehement Irish and Liberal opposition to the ploy. But even some government supporters were distinctly uncomfortable. That most recalcitrant of Tories, Randolph Churchill, who had resigned in December 1887 as chancellor of the exchequer, attacked the commission as a 'revolutionary tribunal'.[13] The government appointed three experienced Judges, Sir James Hannen (who would be commission president), Mr Justice John Day and Mr Justice A.L. Smith to preside over the state trial and left it to the *Times* to prove its case.

Further support for the suspicion that the Tories were acting in concert with Printing House Square was provided when a reluctant Sir Richard Webster was railroaded by Salisbury into leading for the *Times*. As a consequence, the administration publicly identified itself with the newspaper's cause. Privately, government resources were put into assembling the evidence required to prove the *Times* allegations. Police records, notes of speeches, note-takers and RIC officers were put at the disposal of the newspaper. Many years later a disillusioned former resident magistrate, William Henry Joyce, claimed that he had directed a covert but officially sanctioned operation in Dublin Castle which actively sought out appropriate cases to funnel towards the *Times* for use in establishing its case.

The Irish Party too worked together to prepare its defence. Parnell was convinced that the letters had been fabricated by a group of conspirators and *agents provocateurs* led by his nemesis, Captain William Henry O'Shea, erstwhile colleague and husband of his mistress, Katharine O'Shea. Although sharing Parnell's antipathy towards the conspiratorial captain, some of his colleagues, like Irish Party MP, Timothy Healy, thought differently. Healy was convinced that the most likely forger was a disreputable Dublin journalist, Richard Pigott, a suspected blackmailer and pornographer. Pigott had spent time in jail for pro-Fenian articles published in his newspapers, the *Irishman*, *Flag of Ireland* and the *Shamrock*, but the financial demands of his large family and his perennial insolvency had long since negated any semblance of political idealism that might once have lurked in his complex psyche. By the late 1880s Pigott was a reprobate and a renegade, prepared to offer his journalistic services to anyone who would pay him and suspected of turning society gossip and scandal into opportunities for extortion.

To test his hypothesis Healy persuaded the radical MP, Henry Labouchere, to identify Pigott as the forger of the facsimile letter in his publication *Truth*. Labouchere was a man of considerable means who could afford to run the risk of a defamation payout. A letter ensued from Pigott seeking a retraction but, tellingly, it was not followed by a libel writ.

As was so often the case, help also came from America. The former Land League treasurer, Patrick Egan, had fled there at around the time that John Mallon had broken the Phoenix Park murders case. Given the frequency with which his name cropped up in the *Times* letters he took more than a passing interest in the commission. It was the release of the unpublished letters at the time of the abortive O'Donnell libel action that confirmed Egan's suspicion of Pigott's central role in the affair. Egan was familiar with the journalist's pedigree. He had been the object of a blatant attempt at extortion by Pigott in 1881 (see below) and had been intrigued by similarities in the phraseology of the *Times* letters with phrases in an extensive correspondence of his own with Pigott, which he had retained. In addition to the wheedling extortion letters, Egan had a lengthy correspondence available to him entered into with Pigott when Parnell had purchased the *Irishman*, *Flag of Ireland* and the *Shamrock* for £3,000 in 1881. These titles became the basis of Parnell's press mouthpiece, the weekly *United Ireland* newspaper. Egan, as the man with the Land League chequebook, had done most of the negotiation.

He passed on his evidence and suspicions to Henry Labouchere. In December 1888, a few weeks after the formal sessions of the Commission had begun, he wrote to the radical MP: 'I hope you will be able to squeeze the truth out of Pigott ... as I should dislike terribly to see him profit in any way by his villainy'.[14]

There was additional assistance from closer to home. The Roman Catholic archbishop of Dublin, William Walsh, a prelate known for his strong nationalist sympathies, approached the Parnellites with details of a correspondence of his own. It had begun with an unexpected and unsolicited letter from Richard Pigott just three days before the *Times* had unleashed the 'Parnellism and crime' series in March, 1887. What Walsh showed Parnell's barrister, Sir Charles Russell (a former nationalist MP and celebrated queen's counsel), would become one of the most destructive weapons in the Parnellite arsenal.

THE SPECIAL COMMISSION ON PARNELLISM AND CRIME, OCTOBER 1888–MARCH 1889

While it was hardly the first occasion on which the British establishment had faced either self-appointed or elected representatives of Irish nationalism in the surroundings of a court-room, the Special Commission on Parnellism and Crime was unique in the intervention of a major national newspaper as the prosecutorial force. While the Conservative government of Lord Salisbury stood to benefit politically from any judicial denunciation or sanction of the Irish Party the onus of proving the connection between the parliamentarians and agrarian crime fell, ultimately, on the shoulders and the pockets of John Walter, proprietor of the *Times*. The newspaper might expect and would receive the co-operation of the apparatus of government in Ireland but the financial burden would be borne by the *Times* alone.

Journalist John Macdonald, who covered the commission for the *Daily News*, conveyed a sense of some of the issues at stake and the cultural conflict at the heart of the tribunal in a long piece for his newspaper on the opening day:

> On the morning of Monday, the 22nd of October, 1888, the New Law Courts presented an unfamiliar aspect. Some centuries on the way, they were here at last—the van of a multitude of Irishmen (and Irishwomen) about to assist at a unique operation of historical stock-taking.

Witnesses from every class of society, the Paddy of *Punch's* shop windows, in the flesh, in his traditional costume. He wears knee-breeches and woollen stockings. The style of his tall hat is unknown in Piccadilly. His starchless collar of blue-striped cotton fall round his lean, weather-beaten neck loosely as an aesthete's; and the swallow-tails of his baggy dress-coat of greyish brown shaggy frieze impinge upon his calves. Just as he appears at mass, or on market-days—say at Galway or archiepiscopal Tuam—while he waits, mutely, through the irresponsive hours, straw rope in hand, beside his pig.

Peasant women from the West and South. Some, alas! in the feathered hat of fashion. Others in the more picturesque head-gear, resembling the Scotch Highland *mutch*. One or two display the deep rich red of the Galway petticoat. For outer covering some wear the heavy woollen shawl, broad-striped in whitish grey, and dark brown. But the favourite garment is the long, wide, hooded cloak of deep blue. Seated, silently, with their hoods drawn over their heads, on the side benches of corridors, these peasant women look as if they were at somebody's wake.

The Irish priest, improved, apparently, since Thackeray sketched him, but still with his downcast introspective look, feels his way among the crowd.

At the corners of passages stand little groups of stalwart men, erect, brushed, polished, in dark green helmets and uniforms. Soldiers, of a sort, are they, though they have never taken the Queen's shilling. They are of the 'Peeler *mor*' [sic], big police, of Celtic Ireland, in contradistinction to the 'Peeler *beg*' [sic], little police—to wit, Her Majesty's troops. They are men of the Royal Irish Constabulary, the finest *gendarmerie* in the world. When they return to Ireland they will fall into the old ways of a country in military occupation. They will be seen on guard at barracks; or, rifle armed, tramping in their sounding boots on the platforms of lonely country stations, and glancing sharply into the compartments of passing trains; or on the march to storm a 'fort'.

> There are landlords, and their agents, and district mag-
> istrates, and Crown lawyers, and inspectors and their
> deputies, and some of the unfortunate race of informers.[15]

When the 'greatest political trial in English history' began its public hearings in October 1888, in Probate Court, No. 1, it was assumed that the *Times* would seek immediately to justify its publication of the 'facsimile' letter and copper-fasten its case against Parnell himself. Instead it produced a dismal litany of quotation from supposedly incendiary political speeches and a parade of witnesses who offered as much of an insight into the petty neigh-bourhood squabbles of Irish rural life as into any illicit activities of the Land League. The only relief came with the early appearance in the witness-box of O'Shea (see above). Observers keenly anticipated his cross-examination. It was in the course of his questioning that Sir Charles Russell laid down some significant markers. Parnell's QC had asked the former MP was he acquainted with a number of named individuals. Many were dubious *soi disant* Fenians and murky *agents provocateurs* with whom O'Shea was all too familiar.[16] But reference to one name in particular would have indicated to the *Times* that the Parnellites might be aware of the source of the published letters. O'Shea was asked was he familiar with Richard Pigott. The captain claimed to have no personal knowledge of Pigott, although he admitted to knowing him by reputation. It was the first reference to the suspected forger in evidence to the commission. He would not be mentioned again for four months.

The apparent reluctance of the *Times* to deal with their most sensa-tional allegation may have emanated from a growing uneasiness over the provenance of the cache of 'incriminating' letters from which the newspa-per had quoted so liberally. The documents had initially been brought to the *Times* by Edward Caulfield Houston, a young anti-Parnellite and sec-retary to a landlord/Unionist organisation called the Irish Loyal and Patriotic Union (ILPU), described in the *History of the Times* as 'a body of whose formation to fight Home Rule in Ireland *The Times* had emphasised its approval'.[17]

As a young journalist, Houston had covered the Phoenix Park murder trials for the *Times*, though only as deputy to the paper's Dublin corre-spondent, Dr George Valentine Patton. That experience, and the flight of Egan and Frank Byrne, had convinced him of Parnellite complicity in agrar-ian crime. The newspaper, delighted with this opportunity to inflict damage on Parnell, had not questioned Houston very thoroughly on the prove-nance of the letters. It was only when it became necessary to establish their authenticity that Houston revealed his source. He acknowledged that the letters had been procured for him in three separate caches over the period of a year by Richard Pigott. The more the *Times* editor, George Buckle, discovered about Pigott the less he liked.

Finally, in late February 1889, after presenting the testimony of dozens of victims of agrarian crime, the *Times* was ready to explain to the commission the history of its acquisition of the documents which formed the basis of its case . Under examination Edward Caulfield Houston recounted how he had paid Pigott for writing a number of pamphlets 'exposing' the activities of the league. Through this association he had come to learn of a bag containing incriminating letters that might be available for purchase. He had authorised and paid Pigott handsomely to acquire the letters. The money had come from ILPU funds. It was clear from his evidence that he was so intent on damaging the nationalist cause that he had not sought to test Pigott's credibility. The *Times* manager, J.C. MacDonald explained how the newspaper had recompensed Houston for the expenses incurred in the acquisition of his treasure trove and had published the letters without any serious research into their origins.

Houston managed to convey the impression to the thronged courtroom that while he had been content to make use of Pigott's expertise and reward him for his efforts, he was unhappy to be associated with such an unsavoury individual. Houston had sought to obliterate the trail that connected him with the Dublin journalist by burning their correspondence. The former newspaper proprietor, who up to that point had been an obscure figure, was mentioned so often in the testimony of Houston and MacDonald that his own evidence was eagerly awaited.

Pigott V Russell, 20–2 February 1889

Richard Pigott took the stand on 20 February 1889. He was a small portly individual, white-haired, and, though almost completely bald, sporting a white beard extraordinarily bushy even for an era of often ostentatious hirsuteness. John Macdonald, covering the Commission for the *Daily News*, highlighted his 'big, somewhat irresolute mouth, big fleshy nose, and smallish eyes, far apart. "A benevolent-looking person," one spectator remarked. "Might be a church deacon," observed another'.[18] Watched as he was by the likes of Parnell, Davitt, Biggar and Healy he was palpably nervous. He informed the commission that he was 54 years of age and that he resided at 11 Sandycove Avenue in Kingstown (now Dún Laoghaire). He was a widower, who had lost his wife in August 1886.

In his examination of Pigott, Sir Richard Webster took the witness through his own past associations with the Fenian movement and asked him to describe how he had come by the letters.[19] Pigott claimed that through a former contributor to the *Irishman* newspaper, Eugene Davis,[20] a Fenian who was then living in Lausanne, he had been told of a number of incriminating letters, in Paris, written by Parnell and the Land League treasurer, Patrick Egan. One of these, he was led to believe, tied Parnell closely to the Invincibles, the shadowy group responsible for the Phoenix Park murders. Having already made the acquaintance of Edward Caulfield Houston he had informed Houston of the existence of the documents and had been told by the ILPU Secretary to attempt to secure them. 'Next', as John Macdonald put it acidly, 'followed the story of Pigott's marvellous luck.'[21]

His efforts to locate the letters were assisted, in the course of a trip to Paris at the beginning of April 1886 (paid for, as were all Pigott's jaunts, by Houston); while there he had a chance encounter with a former employee, a compositor by the name of Maurice Murphy, now an agent of the Irish–American Republican organisation, Clan na Gael. Upon discussing old times and revolutionary matters, Pigott recounted his conversation with Davis. As Pigott described it, three or four days later, 'Murphy' informed his old employer that he had made inquiries and, miraculously, could source the letters for the sum of £500. Pigott, having satisfied himself as to the authenticity of the documents (he was familiar with the handwriting of both Parnell and Egan from the time of the sale of his newspapers to the Land League) secured authorisation from Houston to purchase the contents of the bag. But, as these transactions are never straightforward, he first had to make a preparatory journey to New York (also funded by Houston) to obtain permission for the sale from an American Fenian he named as John J. Breslin. After this transatlantic *sortie* and the 'approval' of Breslin the stage was set for the transfer to take place.

This was achieved with great theatricality in the Hôtel Deux Mondes on the Avenue de l'Opera in Paris in July 1886. Houston himself was prevailed upon to participate. While he waited in his room upstairs, Pigott met 'Murphy' downstairs and was given the letters and a set of old accounts. These he brought to the animated young Unionist. Houston studied the documents and, satisfied with the significance of his purchase, handed Pigott a £500 cheque drawn on the Thomas Cook office in Paris and £105 as his personal commission. Pigott told the attorney general that he had then accompanied 'Murphy' to the Thomas Cook office, cashed the cheque, handed the money to the compositor and never saw him again.

The next time he saw the letter that was the most treasured item in the collection was in the *Times* on 18 April the following year. Pigott told Webster that two further batches of incriminating letters had serendipitously come into his possession once word had got around Parisian Fenian circles that he was in the market for Parnellite memorabilia. A second collection of letters was sold to him by a man named 'Tom Brown' and a third by someone who didn't even bother to leave an unlikely name. Asked directly by the attorney general if he had forged the letters himself Pigott acknowledged that he was aware that he had been accused of so doing by others, but he absolutely denied the charge.

Were he to be believed by the commissioners, Pigott's narrative was damaging enough but what followed was potentially embarrassing, not just for Parnell, but for his political ally, Henry Labouchere. The Tory attorney general gleefully took Pigott through an encounter with the Northampton MP in the latter's London house the previous autumn. Pigott had just been subpoenaed by Parnell's solicitor, George Lewis. Concerned that he was about to be exposed, while simultaneously tempted by the prospect of further financial rewards, Pigott had been inveigled to travel to London at around the time of the commencement of the commission's proceedings in October 1888. He had been invited to meet Labouchere at his house near Victoria Station. What followed demonstrated that had Pigott, a man well accustomed to double-crossing his associates, been dealt with more deftly, he would probably have betrayed the cause of the *Times* months before he was put on the stand.

When giving his evidence Pigott, naturally, represented himself as having been working in the interests of the *Times* throughout the series of interviews that followed. When he got to Labouchere's house, he told Webster, the Northampton MP was not alone. Also present was Charles Stewart Parnell. The Irish Party leader began immediately to browbeat the Dublin journalist. He maintained that he had unimpeachable evidence that Pigott was the forger and that if he took the stand at the commission he would be ruthlessly exposed as such. Later George Lewis arrived to hector Pigott and to offer him a deal. He would be given immunity from prosecution if he testified that he had forged the letters. In the course of the harangue,

Labouchere had, according to Pigott, taken him outside and offered him £1,000 to testify to that effect. The radical MP had insisted, however, that Parnell was not to know anything of the financial inducement.

The following day, George Lewis came to Pigott's London hotel to take a statement from the journalist. After first ascertaining that Labouchere's offer still stood, Pigott told Lewis a version of what he wanted to hear. He would not admit to forging the correspondence. Instead he modified the tale he had told Houston. In this new version of events he had still 'acquired' the letters but, far from confirming the authenticity of the documents, he claimed that 'I did not believe them to be genuine'.[22] He was prepared to betray the *Times* without admitting his own culpability. Because of Pigott's refusal to admit that he had personally forged the letters Lewis concluded that there was no point in pursuing the negotiations and had brought them to an end.

When the notes taken by Lewis of the conversation were later read into the commission record, Pigott challenged their accuracy. He denied that he had told the London solicitor that he had no faith in the authenticity of the letters. This was for the benefit of his *Times* sponsors. He wished to disabuse them of the suspicion that their star witness had, at the very least, toyed with the idea of abandoning their cause for his own profit and to avoid an appearance at the special commission.

But Pigott's revelation of an apparent attempt by the Parnellites to suborn a key *Times* witness was just one of the issues that needed to be addressed by Parnell's counsel in cross-examination.

The interrogation of Richard Pigott by Sir Charles Russell began just after the lunch-break on the afternoon of Thursday, 21 February. The witness had appeared out of sorts and uncomfortable during the gentle probing of Webster during his direct evidence. At one point, in describing his encounters with Lewis, as the *Birmingham Daily Post* correspondent, Alfred Robbins, observed 'his fingers twitched, and his voice was so broken and husky that water had to be brought'.[23] The levels of stress he had experienced in offering unchallenged testimony would be greatly elevated under cross-examination.[24] Robbins further noted 'when Pigott told these tales of mystery and imagination, his body and spirit alike bowed under the strain, all realized that the great moment of the Commission was close at hand'.[25]

Pigott's adversary was formidable. In 1889 Sir Charles Russell, a future lord chief justice and a former MP, was an advocate at the height of his powers. Ironically he had long held a general retainer from the *Times*. This he had given up in the wake of the 'Parnellism and crime' articles. Even more ironic was the fact that he, essentially, agreed with the *Times* charges against the Land League which he held to be 'a lawless, a rebellious, a violent movement'.[26] Furthermore, he had no great liking for his client either, whom he considered to be 'a selfish fellow. He thinks only of himself'.[27] The principal focus of Parnell was not the *Times* case against the league but the issue of the letters bearing his alleged signature. The popular verdict on the authenticity of those documents would be decided by the outcome of the battle that was about to take place. Parnell, a man accustomed to exercising absolute control over his own affairs, was now dependent on the skills of Sir Charles Russell.

R. Barry O'Brien, journalist, barrister (he had once devilled for Russell) and biographer,[28] was concerned about the state of mind of his former master in the week prior to what everyone knew would be the pivotal confrontation of the entire commission. He need not have worried. O'Brien, describing the scene, wrote:

> At about twenty minutes past two Pigott stepped jauntily into the box,[29] and Russell rose. I never saw such a sudden metamorphosis in any man. During the whole week or more he had looked pale, worn, anxious, irritable, at times disagreeable. Even at luncheon, half an hour before, he seemed to be thoroughly out of sorts, and gave you the idea rather of a young junior with his first brief than of the most formidable advocate at the Bar. Now all was changed. As he stood facing Pigott, he was a picture of calmness, self-possession, strength; there was not a trace of illness, anxiety, or care; a slight tinge of colour lighted up the face, the eyes sparkled, and a pleasant smile played about the mouth. The whole bearing and manner of the man, as he proudly turned his head towards the box, showed courage, resolution, confidence.[30]

Russell was a man in his element. Pigott was clearly not in his. The opening gambit was unexpected and confusing both for the witness and spectators.

RUSSELL: Mr. Pigott, would you be good enough, with my Lord's permission, to write some words on that sheet of paper for me. Perhaps you

	will sit down in order to do it? [A sheet of paper was handed to the witness.] Would you like to sit down?
PIGOTT:	Oh, no, thanks.
PRESIDENT:	Well, but I think it is better that you should sit down. Here is a table upon which you can write in the ordinary way, the course you always pursue.
RUSSELL:	Will you write the word 'livelihood'. Just leave a space. Will you write the word 'likelihood'. Will you write your own name, leaving a space between each. Will you write the word 'proselytism,' and finally (I think I will not trouble you at present with any more), 'Patrick Egan' and 'P. Egan' underneath it—'Patrick Egan' first and 'P. Egan' underneath it. There is one word more I had forgotten. Lower down, please, leaving spaces, write the word 'hesitancy' with a small 'h'. [The witness wrote the words requested.] Will you kindly give me the sheet? Do not blot it please.[31]

As Russell handed the sheet of paper to one of his associates, Frank Lockwood, QC, the latter was heard clearly to exclaim triumphantly, 'We've got him'.[32] As anticipated by the defence counsel, Pigott had just scrawled a telling hostage to fortune.

Russell began his cross-examination by establishing that Pigott had entered into correspondence with Parnell and Egan at the time of the sale of his newspapers. This would be of crucial importance later in the cross-examination. He also sought to establish that Pigott had attempted to sell information on militant nationalism to various viceroys and chief secretaries since the early 1870s. Although Pigott denied any such contact it was clear that Russell was attempting to establish that Pigott would betray in private a cause he championed in public.

Then Russell adverted to Pigott's correspondence with Archbishop Walsh. The journalist had implied in his direct evidence that he had written to the archbishop in the wake of the publication of the facsimile letter by the *Times* and that he had asked to be put in contact with Parnell with a view to countering the effect of the newspaper's campaign. This was patently untrue. The correspondence had begun four days *before* the first salvo in the *Times* 'Parnellism and crime' campaign. Pigott was acting on the assumption that Walsh, who had returned much of the correspondence, would not have retained any of the letters. He was not to know that Walsh was co-operating with the Parnellites. In order to cover himself, however, against the production in evidence of some of the letters, he had advanced the ludicrous thesis, under direct examination by Webster, that the correspondence was subject to the Roman Catholic seal of the confessional. This would have meant that the archbishop was, therefore, obliged to keep it confidential. The interchange that followed (somewhat abridged here) was the first occasion on which Russell got to close quarters with his quarry:

RUSSELL: You are a Catholic are you?

PIGOTT: I am.

RUSSELL: Had you any correspondence with Archbishop Walsh which you say was under the seal of the confessional?

PIGOTT: I had.

RUSSELL: You had?

PIGOTT: I had of course.

RUSSELL: Correspondence?

PIGOTT: Correspondence.

RUSSELL: In writing?

PIGOTT: In writing.

RUSSELL: In which he wrote to you letters, and you wrote him letters?

PIGOTT: Yes.

RUSSELL: And under the seal of the confessional?

PIGOTT: Quite so ... if you will permit me to explain.

RUSSELL: Certainly, I shall not stop you.

PIGOTT: I wished to have advice and instruction.

RUSSELL: Go on?

PIGOTT: Under the seal of perfect confidence with the Bishop as if he were my confessor, and I wrote the first letter asking him would he accept such confidence, and his reply was, certainly he would. Then the correspondence continued, and when it had concluded, in order to keep faith with his undertaking to me, he returned me my letters, and copies of his own letters, lest they should fall into other hands.

RUSSELL: Did this matter upon which you sought his advice relate to the publication of incriminatory material relating to Mr. Parnell and others?

PIGOTT: Yes.

RUSSELL: Did that incriminatory material include letters?

PIGOTT: Yes.

RUSSELL: The letters in question?

PIGOTT: The letters in question—or one of them at least.

RUSSELL: Which of them?

PIGOTT: The published one.

RUSSELL: The one which has been called the facsimile?

PIGOTT: Quite so.

RUSSELL: You knew then, at that time what the charges were to be advanced against Mr. Parnell and his colleagues, or his leading colleagues?

PIGOTT: I really think I should not be asked questions about that correspondence, under the circumstances.

RUSSELL: Well I am afraid Mr. Pigott I cannot oblige you ... The first publication of the articles 'Parnellism and Crime' was on the 7th of March?

PIGOTT: I do not know.

RUSSELL: Well you may assume that is the date?

PIGOTT: Yes, I suppose it is.

RUSSELL: And you were aware of the intended publication of that correspondence?

PIGOTT: No, I was not at all aware of it.

RUSSELL: What?

PIGOTT: No, certainly not, that is that I was aware of the intended publication of a series of articles called 'Parnellism and Crime'.

RUSSELL: Yes?

PIGOTT: Certainly not.

RUSSELL: I do not say that you were aware of what the name was to be or anything of that kind?

PIGOTT: No, I did not know anything at all about it.

RUSSELL: Is that your letter, do not trouble to read it: tell me if it is your letter. [Same was handed to the witness.] Do not trouble to read it?

PIGOTT: Yes, I think it is.

RUSSELL: Have you any doubt of it?

PIGOTT: No.

RUSSELL: My Lords it is from Anderton's Hotel and it is addressed by the witness to Dr. Walsh, Archbishop of Dublin. The date, my Lords, is the 4th of March, 1887, three days before the first appearance of the first series of articles 'Parnellism and Crime'.

'Private and Confidential

Anderton's Hotel, Fleet St., London

March 4, 1887

My Lord,

The importance of the matter about which I write will doubtless excuse this intrusion on your grace's attention. Briefly, I wish to say that I have been made aware of the details of certain proceedings that are in preparation with the object of destroying the influence of the Parnellite party in parliament.'

RUSSELL:	What were the certain proceedings that were in preparation?
PIGOTT:	I do not recollect.
RUSSELL:	You swear that, writing on the 4th March, stating that you have been made aware of the details of certain proceedings that are in preparation with the object of destroying the influence of the Parnellite party in parliament, less than two years ago?
PIGOTT:	Yes.
RUSSELL:	You do not know what that referred to?
PIGOTT:	I do not, really.
RUSSELL:	May I suggest to you?
PIGOTT:	Yes, you may.
RUSSELL:	Did it refer to the incriminatory letters, among other things?
PIGOTT:	Oh, at that date. No, the letters had not been obtained, I think, at that date, had they—two years ago?
RUSSELL:	I do not want to confuse you at all, Mr. Pigott?
PIGOTT:	Would you mind giving me the date of that letter?

RUSSELL: The 4th March, 1887?

PIGOTT: The 4th March, 1887.

RUSSELL: Is [it] your impression the letters had not been obtained at that date?

PIGOTT: Oh yes, some of the letters had been obtained before that date.

RUSSELL: Then, reminding you that some of the letters had been obtained before that date, did that passage that I have read to you in that letter refer to these letters amongst other things?

PIGOTT: No, I rather fancy they had reference to the forthcoming articles in the 'Times'.

RUSSELL: I thought you told us you did not know anything about the forthcoming articles?

PIGOTT: Yes I did. I find now that I am mistaken, that I must have heard something about them.

RUSSELL: Then pray try and not make the same mistake again, Mr. Pigott ... There is the letter and the statement. 'Your Grace may be assured that I speak with full knowledge and am in a position to prove beyond all doubt and question the truth of what I say.' Was that true?

PIGOTT: It could hardly be true.

RUSSELL: Then did you write that which was false?

PIGOTT: I suppose it was in order to give strength to what I had said.

RUSSELL: You thought ... ?

PIGOTT: I do not think it was warranted by what I knew.

RUSSELL: You did not think it was warranted by what you knew?

PIGOTT: No.

RUSSELL: But you added the untrue statement in order to add truth to what you had said?

PIGOTT: Yes.

RUSSELL: Designedly an untrue statement?

PIGOTT: No, I do not think it was actually untrue.

RUSSELL: What?

PIGOTT: Not designedly.

RUSSELL: Accidentally?

PIGOTT: Perhaps so.

RUSSELL: You believe these letters to be genuine?

PIGOTT: I do.

RUSSELL: And did at this time?

PIGOTT: Yes.

RUSSELL: 'And I will further assure your Grace that I am also able to point out how the designs may be successfully combated and finally defeated.' How, if these documents were genuine documents, and you believed them to be such, how were you able to assure his Grace that you were able to point out how the design might be successfully combated and finally defeated?

PIGOTT: Well, as I say, I had not the letters actually in my mind at that time; as far as I can gather I do not recollect that letter at all. My memory is really a blank as to the circumstance.

RUSSELL: You told me a moment ago, after great deliberation and consideration, you had both in your mind?

PIGOTT: I said it was probable I did, but as I say, the thing has completely faded out of my mind. I have no recollection of that at all.

RUSSELL: That I can understand.

PIGOTT: I have not the faintest idea of what I referred
               to particularly.

RUSSELL: I must press you. Assuming the letters to be
               genuine, what were the means by which you
               were able to assure his Grace that you could
               point out how the design might be success-
               fully combated and finally defeated?

PIGOTT: I cannot conceive really.

RUSSELL: Oh try. You really must try.

PIGOTT: I cannot.

RUSSELL: Supposing for instance you could point to
               another, that the letters had been concocted,
               I presume you would say that would be a
               mode in which ... ?

PIGOTT: As I say, I do not think that letter refers to
               the letters at all.

RUSSELL: You know you have more than once told me
               that it did?

PIGOTT: I can only give you my opinion as I say I have
               no recollection.

RUSSELL: We will drop the letters for an instant, and
               come back to them. What were the means by
               which you were able to point out how the
               design might be successfully combated, and
               finally defeated?

PIGOTT: I do not know.

RUSSELL: You must think, please; it is not two years
               ago. Mr. Pigott, had you qualms of con-
               science at that time, and were afraid of the
               consequences of what you had done?

PIGOTT: Not at all.

RUSSELL: Then what did you mean?

PIGOTT:	I cannot tell you, really.
RUSSELL:	Try?
PIGOTT:	I cannot.
RUSSELL:	Try?
PIGOTT:	It is no use.[33]

What does not come across from the transcripts of the cross-examination, published in 1890, is the physical effect on the witness of Russell's unremitting pressure. Many of the advocate's questions were followed by long pauses as the forger, like an uncertain chess-player, assessed the consequential damage of any response he made. As the day went on, his voice became less audible and he was asked to speak up on a number of occasions. Alfred Robbins, observing for the *Birmingham Daily Post*, noted how 'the smooth smile disappeared, the brows knitted, the face flushed and the figure drooped ... his body and spirit alike bowed under the strain'.[34]

For the remainder of Thursday afternoon, Russell continued to pursue Pigott relentlessly in an attempt to force an admission from him that his correspondence with Walsh indicated that he had been preparing to sell out the *Times* cause to the Parnellites. The witness, though frequently relying on fallible recollection and contorted logic as Russell harassed him, had conceded nothing except his credibility by the time the commission adjourned for the day.

Alfred Robbins described how the prospect of the renewed confrontation between the two men on Friday, 22 February, caused a frenzy of anticipation. When the court-room opened on the morning of the second day of the crucial cross-examination, 'Spectators packed themselves in the gangways; sat in the witness-box; invaded even the bench; while the corridor was thronged by eager ticket-holders fighting to secure that much-prized rarity, a vacant place'.[35]

As it would transpire, Pigott had only had a vague earnest of what was to come. Right from the outset of the renewed cross-examination, Russell was at his forensic best. In addition to ensnaring the witness in a web of contradictory detail he employed scepticism, disbelief and subtle mockery to undermine Pigott's fading confidence and waning credibility. He began the day by producing yet another of Pigott's letters to Archbishop Walsh, one that plunged the journalist ever deeper into a mire of his own making. Walsh had responded to Pigott's first letter with a firm refusal to get involved as an intermediary with the Irish Party.

RUSSELL: Is that your letter, Mr. Pigott? [Handing letter to the witness.]

PIGOTT: Yes.

RUSSELL: My Lords, this is dated 12th March, 1887, Hotel St. Petersburg. I am reading all I have.

'My Lord,

I am much honoured by your Grace's reply to my letters. I have no doubt at all that your Grace is right in what you say with reference to the subject of them. My notion was that the evidence I heard of, which is both documentary and personal, would produce a bad effect if published, seeing that it is an artful admixture of what I believe to be true with what I suspect to be false: and that it might be forestalled and rendered harmless by publicly exposing the discreditable means by which it was obtained, and by which further testimony is being sought on which to found a criminal prosecution. Moreover I thought that such a course would forearm the parties concerned with the knowledge of what precisely they would be charged with, so that they would be prepared to meet it.

However, your Grace puts the matter in so clear a light that I now perceive I was quite astray in my calculations as to the effect of the coming publication and prosecution; and it remains but for me to repeat my apologies to your Grace for having troubled you, and my grateful thanks for your Grace's reply.'

RUSSELL: What do you say now?

PIGOTT: ... I think I should be allowed to explain my position. When I communicated with the Archbishop, I had obtained, as I knew, letters which were very seriously compromising, and also I had heard that other publications in support of these letters or in connexion with the letters were being prepared, consequently I was considerably nervous, because when I came to think the matter over I found that although I had an undertaking that I would have no responsibility in the matter, nevertheless, in the event of legal proceedings, the entire burden of proof would naturally fall upon me, therefore I was considerably alarmed; and moreover, at the time I was in very distressed circumstances, and I was receiving no money from Mr. Houston, and my other work had been neglected, and I had lost some of it attending to these matters. That was an additional reason which urged me to write to his Grace, in the hope that he would bring me into communication with the Parnellites, or some of the leading members, perhaps Mr. Parnell himself, with the object of inducing them to provide me with means to leave the country. That is in return for the information that I would give in telling them what I knew as regards the letters and how they were procured; that they would, in return for that, provide me with a sum of money to leave the country, and I should also state that when I did actually obtain the letters I was under the impression that they were not to be published, that they were simply to be held in reserve to be produced in subsequent legal proceedings for libel, consequent upon their publication, not the publication of the letters themselves.

RUSSELL: ... Is there anything more you wish to add?

PIGOTT: Nothing just now occurs to me.[36]

Russell then turned to Pigott's correspondence with erstwhile Fenian, Patrick Egan. In February 1881 Pigott had written to Egan in Paris with a story clearly fabricated to extort a form of 'protection' money from the Land League treasurer.[37] According to the witness he had been approached by two men, whom he claimed not to know but had reason to believe were agents of Dublin Castle. The mysterious visitors had offered him £500 to publish an article on Land League funding that, Pigott suggested, would be severely damaging to the organisation. The piece, allegedly, contained details of payments of 'funds to defend parties accused of complicity in "outrages" and for the support of the families of evicted tenants; and, on the other, curt and emphatic reprisals'. Pigott assured Egan that he considered the entire document to be 'an outrageous libel from beginning to end' but that he was 'in desperate straits. I must have money somehow or throw up the sponge at once. I cannot afford to let so lucky a chance pass for saving myself literally from ruin'. The sum he sought to release him from the necessity of publishing the document was £300. On 11 March Egan replied in the negative insisting that 'Whenever any such accusations are made we will know how to defend ourselves'.[38] Pigott wrote back to inform Egan that, in an act of supreme self-sacrifice for the nationalist cause, he had already decided himself not to accede to the blandishments of the two mysterious strangers before he had received the Land League treasurer's letter.

Although in no doubt that the entire affair was an elaborate figment of an extortionist's imagination, Russell chose to bring a piledriver to bear on Pigott's already shattered credibility. The resulting rapid fire exchange, in which Russell toyed with his prey, approached and often surpassed the level of high farce.

RUSSELL:	Now, I want you to throw your mind back. You were visited by two mysterious strangers?
PIGOTT	Yes.
RUSSELL:	Old or young?
PIGOTT	Middle-aged; one middle-aged and one young.
RUSSELL:	Tall or short?
PIGOTT	I do not know. I cannot say.
RUSSELL:	Dark or fair?
PIGOTT	That I could not tell you.
RUSSELL:	Did they give any name?
PIGOTT	No name.

RUSSELL: Did you ask for one?

PIGOTT No.

RUSSELL: They refused?

PIGOTT I say I did not ask.

RUSSELL: Oh, you did not ask for one?

PIGOTT No.

RUSSELL: Ever seen them before?

PIGOTT Never saw them before.

RUSSELL: Ever seen them since?

PIGOTT No.

RUSSELL: Did they wear masks?

PIGOTT No, they did not.

RUSSELL: Blackened faces?

PIGOTT I simply did not know them.

RUSSELL: Disguised?

PIGOTT I did not know the men.

RUSSELL: Disguised?

PIGOTT No.

RUSSELL: Then these two mysterious strangers came to you one day?

PIGOTT Yes.

RUSSELL: That is very suspicious?

PIGOTT Yes.

RUSSELL: What time one night?

PIGOTT In the evening. Perhaps not in the night; in the evening.

RUSSELL: What time in the evening?

PIGOTT That I could not say.

RUSSELL: Before dinner or after dinner?

PIGOTT   Oh, I think it was after dinner.

RUSSELL: You think it was after dinner?

PIGOTT   Yes.

RUSSELL: Any refreshment did you give them?

PIGOTT   Oh, I might, and I did.

RUSSELL: Had you taken any refreshment yourself before they came?

PIGOTT   I cannot tell you.

RUSSELL: You cannot tell me Mr. Pigott?

PIGOTT   I cannot tell you I say.

RUSSELL: Mr. Pigott, is this absurd story the creation of your own brain?

PIGOTT   It is perfectly true.

RUSSELL: You swear that solemnly before my Lord?

PIGOTT   I do.

RUSSELL: Did you take any steps to try and identify these mysterious strangers?

PIGOTT   No, I did not; certainly not. I had no motive. What motive could I have in proceeding to trace them?

RUSSELL: Pray do not ask me that. I will make an answer by and bye, Mr. Pigott. Do not force me to do it now. Did you take many steps to trace them?

PIGOTT   No I did not.

RUSSELL: To identify them?

PIGOTT   No.

RUSSELL: Did you form any opinion from whom they came?

PIGOTT	I had an idea afterwards that one of the men was a man of the name of O'Sullivan,[39] who had acted as Land League Secretary ... in its early days; a former Secretary.
RUSSELL:	What do you mean by early days?
PIGOTT	At the very outset; the very commencement.
RUSSELL:	1879–80?
PIGOTT	1879 I think.
RUSSELL:	Do you recollect his Christian name?
PIGOTT	I think it was Michael, if I do not mistake.
RUSSELL:	Or Malachi, or Michael Malachi, perhaps a combination of both?
PIGOTT	No, I fancy it was Michael.
RUSSELL:	The man you thought might be O'Sullivan, did he speak with a brogue?
PIGOTT	Oh, I do not know. I tell you I did not know him personally.
RUSSELL:	Did he speak with a brogue is my question?
PIGOTT	I do not know. How can I know when I do not know him?
RUSSELL:	I am talking of the two men who visited you, one of whom you suggest was O'Sullivan. Did he speak with a brogue?
PIGOTT	No, I do not think he did.
RUSSELL:	It would be very hard to find a man of the name of O'Sullivan who did not, would not it?
PIGOTT	Possibly.
RUSSELL:	Did the other man speak with a brogue?
PIGOTT	No; either of them did not. They were both very respectable men.

RUSSELL: And you thought it was a respectable propo-
            sition?

PIGOTT   Yes, certainly.

RUSSELL: That you should for money payment be
            made the medium of publishing statements
            that you believed to be fabrications?

PIGOTT   Well I did not believe them to be fabrications.

RUSSELL: Then you wrote a lie to Egan when you said
            so?

PIGOTT   It was not strictly accurate. I had reason
            afterwards to know that the statements those
            men wished me to publish were absolutely
            true in every respect.

RUSSELL: I may take it it was not any sense of virtue
            that made you recoil from this offer to
            publish?

PIGOTT   No, I suppose not. I do not pretend to be very
            virtuous.[40]

Russell then drew the attention of the witness to a sheaf of correspondence relating to the sale of his three newspaper titles to the Land League.
Pigott had been hoping, not simply to sell the titles but to be kept on the
staff of the newspaper or papers that would emerge from the purchase.
Parnell had insisted not only that his services would not be retained but
that Pigott would undertake not to establish any rival publication within
a two-year period. The extensive correspondence, which included letters
from Egan, Parnell and Pigott, as already noted, had been provided to the
defence team by Patrick Egan.

After reading a number of the letters into the record, Russell asked the
increasingly rattled witness to account for the striking similarities between
phrases used by Egan and Parnell in their correspondence and phrases that
recurred in the published and unpublished *Times* letters. Pigott was forced
to admit that the coincidence was 'very remarkable indeed; so very remarkable as to be extremely improbable'.[41] In the unlikely event that the
implications of his line of questioning were not apparent Russell then
changed tack. He paused, helped himself to a pinch of snuff and, waving

a brown pocket handkerchief in the air, proceeded to pepper the witness with a series of hypothetical questions about the art and the act of forgery.

RUSSELL: I would like to ask you, Mr. Pigott, supposing you wanted to forge a document would it at all be any help to you to have the genuine letter of the man whose letter it was intended to forge before you?

PIGOTT: Of course it would. There can be no mistake about that.

RUSSELL: How would you use it?

PIGOTT: As a copy, of course.

RUSSELL: How would you proceed to use it?

PIGOTT: I cannot say.

RUSSELL: I mean just give me your best idea?

PIGOTT: I do not pretend to have any experience in that line, so I cannot say.

RUSSELL: I mean, just see now how you would begin to use it. Just fancy yourself called upon to forge one of these letters, how would you proceed?

PIGOTT: I decline to put myself in that position at all.

RUSSELL: Theoretically, let me press you?

PIGOTT: I do not see the use of discussing the theory of the question at all. I thought you wanted facts.

RUSSELL: Let me suggest, would you put delicate tissue paper over it and trace it?

PIGOTT: Yes, but how would you proceed then, supposing you had the copies?

RUSSELL: We will get along; I do not know?

PIGOTT: Well, I cannot tell either, you know.

RUSSELL: With your help, Mr. Pigott, we may get to the end of the matter. Supposing, for instance, you had a genuine letter, and you wanted to copy a sentence out of it. Supposing you put delicate tissue over it; that, at all events, would enable you on the delicate tissue to trace the character and outline of the document you wished to forge?

PIGOTT: That is the way you would do it, of course.

RUSSELL: How would you do it?

PIGOTT: I fancy I would trust myself to ...

RUSSELL: Imitation?

PIGOTT: To imitation.

RUSSELL: It would require a little expertness of hand to do it without the paper?

PIGOTT: Yes.

RUSSELL: A more advanced stage?

PIGOTT: Yes.

RUSSELL: The tissue paper which I ignorantly suggest would be far clumsier?

PIGOTT: Your way is much easier certainly.

RUSSELL: You think the way I suggest is much easier?

PIGOTT: I do.

RUSSELL: Why do you think it is much easier, have you tried?

PIGOTT: No, I have not tried. Of course, apparently, it would be much easier; that is apparent to anybody.

RUSSELL: I just want to follow that out a little, it would be much easier to imitate that. Is Mr. Parnell's signature a difficult signature to imitate?

PIGOTT: I cannot tell you.

RUSSELL: What do you think?

PIGOTT: It is a peculiar signature.

RUSSELL: What you would call a strongly marked signature?

PIGOTT: Yes.

RUSSELL: Do you think it was a kind of signature more easily or less easily imitated?

PIGOTT: Really, I do not feel competent to give an opinion. It is a matter of opinion. I do not know what your opinion is upon it.

RUSSELL: I am very anxious to have yours?

PIGOTT: I really have not one.

RUSSELL: Would you say off hand that it was a signature difficult or easy to imitate?

PIGOTT: Considering the peculiarity of the writing I should say it would be difficult.

RUSSELL: You would say it would be difficult?

PIGOTT: Yes.

RUSSELL: More difficult than a free flowing signature?

PIGOTT: Oh yes, I think so.

RUSSELL: ... You were good enough yesterday, Mr. Pigott, to write down the spelling of certain words for me, and amongst others the spelling of the word 'hesitancy'. Is that a word you are accustomed to use?

PIGOTT: I have used it.

RUSSELL: You notice that you spell it as it is not ordinarily spelt?

PIGOTT: Yes, I fancy I made a mistake in the spelling of it.

RUSSELL: What was the spelling of it?

PIGOTT: Using an 'a' instead of an 'e' or vice verse; I really cannot say which.

RUSSELL: You cannot say what was the mistake, but you have a moral consciousness that something was wrong?

PIGOTT: Yes, something wrong.

RUSSELL: I will tell you what was wrong according to the received spelling; you spelt it with an 'e' instead of an 'a'. You have spelt it thus: 'h-e-s-i-t-e-n-c-y'. That is not the recognised spelling?

PIGOTT: I believe not.

RUSSELL: Have you noticed the fact that the writer of the body of the letter of the 9th of January, 1882, the alleged forged letter beginning 'Dear E' spells the word in the same way?

PIGOTT: I have heard that remark long since about the letter, that there was a word misspelt in it; and my explanation of misspelling it was that having that in my mind I got into the habit of spelling it wrong.

RUSSELL: Your attention was called to that a long time ago—that in the alleged forged letter of the 9th January, 1882, beginning 'Dear E' that the word 'hesitancy' was misspelt?

PIGOTT: Yes.

RUSSELL: And you fancy that having had your attention called to the fact that it was so misspelt, it so got into your head: that accounts for your misspelling it yesterday?

PIGOTT: I suppose so. I heard so much discussion about it, and everyone spells it differently. I never met anybody who could spell the word correctly scarcely.

RUSSELL: It had got into your brain?

PIGOTT: Yes, somehow or other.

RUSSELL: Who was it called your attention to the mis-spelling?

PIGOTT: Several people; it was a matter of general remark; I heard it frequently.

RUSSELL: Then you think but for the fact of your attention being drawn to it you would probably have spelt it rightly?

PIGOTT: Yes, but for that I daresay I would.

RUSSELL: It had got into your brain somehow or other?

PIGOTT: Yes.

RUSSELL: And came out at your finger's ends?

PIGOTT: I suppose so.

RUSSELL: This letter purports to be the 9th January, 1882?

    [Russell is referring to the forged or Times letter of that date which was published, with the word 'hesitancy' misspelt.]

PIGOTT: Yes

RUSSELL: You have already told me that this letter is yours, just look at it again and see if there is any mistake [handing the letter]??

PIGOTT: Oh yes, that is all right, that is my letter.

RUSSELL: You did not become possessed of this valuable letter of the 9th January 1882 until the summer of 1886?

PIGOTT: Yes.

RUSSEL: No, I suppose not.

RUSSELL: Up to that time?

PIGOTT: No.

RUSSELL: It began to operate at that time?

PIGOTT: No, I say spelling is not my strong point; I do not pretend to be a good speller.

RUSSELL: Perhaps not. Have you noticed that in this letter you have spelt 'hesitancy' in the same way?

                      [The letter in question was a genuine piece of correspondence between Pigott and Egan at the time of the sale of the former's newspapers.]

PIGOTT: No, I did not notice that.

RUSSELL: ... How do you account for it?

PIGOTT: I cannot.

RUSSELL: You cannot account for it from the disturbance of your brain theory?

PIGOTT: No, certainly not.

RUSSELL: Does it strike you as being a remarkable coincidence or not?—

PIGOTT: No, I do not think it is very remarkable.[42]

Pigott was probably the only person in the room who did not find the coincidence remarkable.

Before the end of the second day of cross-examination Russell produced a lengthy correspondence between Pigott and the former Liberal chief secretary for Ireland, William E. Forster. In a series of begging letters, Pigott had appealed to the chief secretary, in the wake of a number of pro-government articles in his newspapers, for an annual salary by way of reward. Forster had turned him down officially, but the Quaker politician, who could be soft hearted on a personal level in contrast to his hard-line political *mien*, made numerous donations to the impoverished journalist and was rewarded on every occasion on which he did so with further importuning. Gradually the requests had metamorphosed into shrill demands and, finally, into an attempt at blackmail.

As letter after letter was produced (one is tempted to assume that Pigott was unfamiliar with the tendency of eminent personages to hang on to every scrap of correspondence), the effect on:

the densely packed audience in court was wrought up to the highest pitch of amusement and excitement. The Court Usher had long since ceased to cry out 'silence'. The merriment was irrepressible, and almost continuous. The judges themselves were unable to repress their feelings. A loud ringing roar of merriment broke forth, as Sir Charles Russell read Pigott's next letter containing an application for £200 to enable him to proceed to Sydney, and some hints as to the pressure which was being brought to bear on him to publish the Forster letters. Mr. Justice Day, bending forward, reddened and shook with laughter.[43]

The only people not joining in the general hilarity were the representatives of the *Times* and Pigott himself. As Macdonald puts it, 'Poor Pigott looked as if he would prefer even the grave to the witness-box. He changed colour; the helpless, foolish smile flickered about the weak, heavy mouth; his hands moved about restlessly, nervously'.[44]

The final letter produced was an inept attempt at blackmail. It definitively removed any possible shred of doubt about the character of the witness. The documentary evidence of his depravity, however amusing to the onlookers, was also compelling. Pigott had written to Forster indicating that he was disposed to reveal to the public how the chief secretary had bribed him to write a series of tracts favourable to the policies of the castle administration. According to John Macdonald, 'The notion of Pigott's appearing in the character of injured innocence set the audience off, once more, into a fit of laughter'. At that point the wretched Pigott was, temporarily, released from his acute misery 'in the uproar and confusion Pigott descended from his box, smiling foolishly, as he brought down the fabric of *The Times* "letters" case in ludicrous ruin'.[45] Michael Davitt, who had watched the entire proceedings, and whose detective work had been invaluable in the embarrassment of a number of *Times* witnesses, described the cross-examination as 'a process of slaying the slain'.[46]

As Pigott left Probate Court No. 1, Parnell peremptorily and presciently observed that such a thoroughly discredited witness might not return for further questioning the following Tuesday. Turning to his solicitor he said 'Mr. Lewis, let that man be watched. If you do not keep your eye on him you will find that he will leave the country',[47] As it transpired an unmonitored Pigott remained in London for two more days in the course of which he tested the Labouchere option one last time. In a desperate attempt to secure enough money to flee the jurisdiction he confessed to having forged the letters, in a statement witnessed by the distinguished journalist George Augustus Sala. Despite a subsequent retraction it was the thrust of this statement that was read out in court when it re-convened, in the absence of the star witness. On Tuesday, 26 February, when Pigott failed to appear a warrant was issued for his arrest.

The fugitive was already in Paris by then. From there he sent a letter to the commission accepting sole responsibility for the counterfeiting of the entire *Times* cache.

> The circumstances connected with the obtaining of the letters, as I gave in evidence, is not true. No one, save myself, was concerned in the transaction. I told Houston that I had discovered the letters in Paris, but I grieve to have to confess that I simply myself fabricated them, using genuine letters of Mr. Parnell and Egan in copying certain words and phrases by putting the genuine letter against the window and placing the sheet on which I wrote over it.[48]

The method was much as Russell had suggested. 'The second batch of letters was also written by me,' he continued in the letter, 'Mr. Parnell's signature was imitated from that published in the "Times" facsimile letter.'

When the secretary to the commission finished reading Pigott's written confession 'there was an awkward pause'.[49] Then a chastened attorney general rose to respond:

> I desire to say nothing respecting that witness except that I presume everyone will agree that no one ought to attach any weight to any evidence he has given ... I will now, on behalf of those whom we represent, ask permission to withdraw from your consideration the question of the genuineness of the letters which have been submitted to you, the authenticity of which is denied, with the full acknowledgement that, after the evidence which has been given, we are not entitled to say that they are genuine.[50]

From Paris, Pigott fled south to Madrid where he spent a short time under the pseudonym of Roland Ponsonby.[51] His desperate search for funds finally betrayed him. A telegram to London alerted the authorities as to his whereabouts. The Spanish police were dispatched to arrest him. The *Times* described the last moments of the man who had perpetrated an outrageous hoax on the newspaper in dramatic style. Arrested in his hotel Pigott had asked to return to his room before being taken away. While there, watched by detectives he reached for a bag, 'which lay upon a chair. The Inspector seemed to divine Pigott's object and sprang forward to seize him. It was too late. Pigott had a big revolver in his hand, placed the muzzle against his mouth, drew the trigger, and fell to the ground a horribly mutilated corpse'.[52]

By an odd coincidence, perhaps altogether too odd to have been genuine, one of the last people to see Pigott alive was the man who had given early evidence to the commission and left for Spain on business. Captain William O'Shea was dining in the Café Ingles in Madrid on the evening of 28 February when two men entered the restaurant. Despite having earlier told Russell in his commission evidence that he was not acquainted with the journalist O'Shea identified one as an interpreter and the other as Richard Pigott. The visitor, clearly ill at ease, asked for and was handed a paper. This he quartered and began to read, O'Shea wrote to Chamberlain the following week:

> his hand trembled, then he looked around the café through an eyeglass, rose suddenly, touched the inter-preter on the shoulder, and left hurriedly. I mentioned the matter to the President of the Chamber and other friends whom I met in the course of the evening, and hearing of the suicide a few minutes after it occurred the next day, I had no doubt of the identity.[53]

This strange incident has fuelled conspiracy theories that Pigott had fled the relative safety of Paris in order to meet O'Shea in Madrid. It certainly lends some credence to Parnell's suspicions that the malevolent captain, aware that he was being cuckolded by the Irish Party leader, was involved in the forgeries. However, while there is some circumstantial evidence to connect O'Shea to Pigott[54] there is no documentary evidence of his complicity.

The fallout from the humiliation of Pigott and the mortification of the *Times* would have been more significant had it not been followed within ten months by the petition of Captain William O'Shea for divorce from his wife, naming Parnell as co-respondent. In the interim, the Irish Party capitalised on the severe embarrassment of the Salisbury government. The opposition was exultant, relieved and grateful and Parnell, over whom a Damoclean sword had been suspended for some time, was lionised by the Liberal establishment and press.

Irish Unionists, as exemplified by the thoroughly discredited but unapologetic Houston, languished in denial about the entire Pigott affair for some time. There was a belief in Unionist circles that, in withdrawing all the letters, the *Times* had panicked unduly. This was articulated by Houston in a letter to O'Shea a week after the humiliation of Pigott's non-appearance at his resumed cross-examination: [55]

> We are in a perfect muddle over here, and I have the honor [*sic*] and glory of being one of the best abused men in town. 'Our friends the enemy' have overdone Pigott however, and they have sickened the Britisher with the endless reference to his name to such an extent that the opinion of the ordinary man in the street is now beginning to veer round to a belief in some of the letters. My idea is that the first batch were genuine, and that the facsimile letter wh[ich] was amongst them was a bona fide document.
>
> But of course the truth will never be known & whatever chance existed of such a desirable condition of things was entirely removed by the panic stricken lawyers withdrawing the whole of the documents. There have been many lamentable features connected with the case but this has been worst of all. [56]

Despite Houston's chagrin at the 'panic' of the *Times*, the hasty and expeditious jettisoning of the letters is perfectly understandable. Finding themselves in a deepening hole, the *Times* had opted to stop digging. The resources of government and the 'newspaper of record' had been poured into an ill-advised essay into judicial character assassination. The cost of the exercise (£200,000 and a libel settlement of £5,000 on Parnell) crippled the *Times* for a generation. The newspaper's own history pouted with resentment against having had to bear the entire cost 'of what was virtually a State prosecution under Act of Parliament'. [57] The description was appropriate. Although the commission can be seen as the logical outcome for the *Times* of the 'Parnellism and crime' series, it had been visited upon the newspaper by a government determined to undermine and, ultimately, to discredit an entire political movement and, by extension, the British political party with whom the Parnellites were aligned.

But the house had been built of straw, based as it was on the *bona fides* of a deceitful and untrustworthy Dublin journalist. The fabric woven by the attorney general and his legal team, which had Parnellite complicity in agrarian outrage stitched into it, was unravelled by the inability of the *Times* to establish the authenticity of the incriminating letters. Despite months of often compelling (if highly repetitive) testimony designed to implicate the league in the encouragement of sedition and violence, the *Times* case still stood or fell on its ability to prove that Parnell had signed a letter connecting him to support for the actions of the Invincibles. That it failed to do so and was similarly unsuccessful in locating any other 'smoking guns' after a year of evidence over 128 sessions, had political as well as commercial consequences. For once a British government had been hanged on a gibbet of its own construction. Having ostentatiously dispatched the parties into a highly visible and contentious forum and relied, as on so many previous occasions, on the testimony of a classic 'informer' figure, the chagrin of the Tories was intensified. A malleable select committee, shorn of the theatrics and the incisiveness of a Sir Charles Russell,[58] might have been a more appropriate forum after all. The advantages of a victory might have been more muted but failure would have been far less consequential.

The report of Justices Hannen, Day and Smith, which might have proved embarrassing to the Irish Parliamentary Party and the Irish National League, landed like a well-padded package on a deep pile carpet. It appeared in February 1890 and 'preserved a balance so exact as to allow each side to claim victory'.[59] Parnell and his co-defendants, most of the members of the Irish Parliamentary Party, were exonerated of all charges of complicity in violence. The commissioners found, however, that 'the respondents did enter into a conspiracy by a system of coercion and intimidation to promote an agrarian agitation against the payment of agricultural rents, for the purpose of impoverishing and expelling from the country the Irish landlords, who were styled the "English Garrison"'.

As Parnell observed it was, more or less, the verdict he would have arrived at himself. Few would have been shocked, for example, at the Commission's finding that Davitt and certain members of the Irish Party 'joined in the Land League organization with the intention by its means to bring about the absolute independence of Ireland as a separate nation'.[60] That was, after all, the thrust of the New Departure. For most, the findings of the Commission were little more than a statement of the obvious. Nationalists might claim that the violence of the Land War had been spontaneous and uncontrollable. But most of them accepted that it was only because there had been a measure of orchestration of the agrarian outrage of the early 1880s that it had been politically effective.

Conservatives and Unionists could point to hundreds of hours of uncontroverted testimony of Irish political complicity in mayhem and outrage. The Commission, seen as a huge Tory mistake by many contemporary and modern observers, largely because of the Pigott fiasco, can just as easily be viewed as having vindicated the insistence of the Salisbury government in such a root and branch investigation. In essence, Margaret O'Callaghan argues in *British high politics and a nationalist Ireland*, 'the role of the commission was systematically to demonstrate that a criminal conspiracy was, in fact, precisely what the National League had always been. In this it succeeded'.[61] There was ample evidence of the direction of militant agrarianism by extreme nationalist elements from within the leadership of the Land League. It can be argued that the *Times* managed to establish a *prima facie* case that Parnell profited politically from his association with neo-Fenians like Patrick Egan and P.J. Sheridan.

Those findings of the commission critical of the Land and National Leagues were used by Balfour to deprecate the political credentials of the Irish Party and to justify sustained repressive measures. While the resulting coercive regime itself was of much *personal* consequence to many members of the Irish Party, who spent lengthy periods in jail for a variety of political transgressions, the prevailing philosophy that informed it was of less importance. The Irish Party had long since written off the Tories when it came to what had become their fundamental objective by 1889, Home Rule.

But, from a Liberal perspective, the language employed in the commission report, although exploited by the Tories, was not sufficiently disparaging to justify ending the Parnellite alliance. Too much had been invested by both the newspaper and the government in the demolition of Parnell himself. The, often harrowing, evidence alluded to by the commission in its condemnation of the indicted Irish parliamentarians, could be dismissed by the Irish Party as mere prologue and window-dressing undermined by the forensic destruction of the *Times* case by Russell in his confrontation with Pigott. But while Russell may have successfully discredited the documentary evidence for much of the *Times* case against Parnell, Egan and O'Kelly, he, in the course of the other 126 days of evidence, failed to destroy its central thesis of a dysfunctional rural Irish society where agrarian violence was at the service of political forces. Between 1887–9 as the *Times* sought to establish its case, this was hardly a startling revelation. Furthermore, by then the bulk of the Irish Party, and Parnell in particular, was either intent on disassociating itself from agrarianism or having it moved off the political agenda by effectual palliative measures.

The Salisbury government, in seeking to deflect the inexorable rise of Home Rule sentiment, was intent on demonstrating that Irish parliamentarians were unfit to govern. Through a process, which had often amounted to little more than provocation and response, the Irish Party and the Liberals (shorn of the Liberal Unionists) had arrived at a consensus. The Tories, who had not been involved in this, often bitter, evolutionary process, were outside of that consensus. They refused to recognise the implicit statute of limitations on 'criminal' association that underlay the Irish–Liberal alliance. The Liberals had managed to get past the Phoenix Park murders. The Irish had moved beyond Maamtrasna. But the Tories had been peripheral to Liberal England's accommodation with Irish nationalism. They saw no reason why Irish parliamentarians should not be retrospectively 'punished' for 'crimes' that were no longer relevant. In some sense, in the wake of the 1886 Home Rule Bill, they were actually being punished for the threat they posed to the integrity of the empire.

The Great Imperialist, Rudyard Kipling, was unimpressed with the findings of their lordships. His anger found poetic form in *Cleared—in memory of a commission*, one verse of which went:

> They only paid the Moonlighter his cattle-hocking price,
> They only helped the murdered with counsel's best advice,
> But—sure it keeps their honour white—the learned Court believes,
> They never give a piece of plate to murderers and thieves.[62]

Kipling was, no doubt, reflecting the anger of British Unionists that Parnell and his associates had been let off the hook. The Tory establishment had sought to inflict irreparable damage and obloquy on the Irish nationalist cause by means of the full weight of a special commission dissecting the entire movement and holding up the entrails to careful scrutiny. What was, in effect, a vast procedure designed to criminalise an entire political movement, though not the dismal failure it is often represented to be, fell well short of its original intentions. That failure would be rectified less than a year later in a civil court. Whatever advantage accrued to the Irish Parliamentary Party from the *faux pas* of the *Times* and the Salisbury administration would soon be obliterated by the results of the O'Shea divorce case.

.7.

1916:
THE COURTS MARTIAL
AND THE TRIAL OF
SIR ROGER CASEMENT

Right proudly high over Dublin Town they hung out the
    flag of war
'Twas better to die 'neath an Irish sky than at Suvla or
    Sedd-El-Bar
And from the plains of Royal Meath strong men came
    hurrying through
While Britannia's Huns, with their long range guns sailed
    in through the foggy dew[1]

                                     (*The foggy dew*)

The University was changed for me now—new associations, new affiliations. Some of the boys had been 'out',
and had escaped arrest; others who had been in the
country had not received orders. I reconstructed my world
slowly. We were being hammered red-hot in the furnace of
the spirit and a spark was bound to fly and disclose us to
each other, with a word, a look, a chance remark.[2]

              (Ernie O'Malley, *On another man's wound*)

He was wearing a lounge suit, white spats and sporting a cane when
arrested with Thomas MacDonagh, Eamon Ceannt and 120 rebel soldiers
near the Jacob's Biscuit Factory on Bishop Street beside Dublin's Liberties.
Major John MacBride, estranged husband of Maud Gonne and the
'drunken, vainglorious lout' of the W.B. Yeats poem *Easter 1916*, was about
to be 'transformed utterly'.[3] Although a prominent member of the Irish
Republican Brotherhood before emigrating to the USA, the once legendary
Boer War veteran, now working, incongruously, as a water bailiff for Dublin
Corporation, was not a member of the Irish Volunteers. He had simply
joined the rebel force before it had occupied the biscuit factory on Easter
Monday, 24 April. He had been on his way to lunch with his brother, for
whom he was due to be best man two days later. But instead he offered his
services to MacDonagh, commandant of the 2nd Battalion of the Volunteers
and, on the strength of his military experience in command of the Irish
Transvaal Brigade fighting against the British Army in the Second Boer War,
was made second-in-command of the battalion. This was despite the fact
that, 'his famous drink problem set him apart from the puritanical new
republicans'.[4] MacDonagh, however, was pragmatic enough to realise that
he was going to need all the experienced help he could get.

Six days later the military action, which MacBride knew was doomed to failure when he decided to abandon his brother's wedding, was over. Patrick Pearse, James Connolly, Thomas Clarke, Seán MacDermott and Joseph Plunkett, from their headquarters in the GPO, had surrendered and issued instructions to other units to lay down their arms and avoid further needless bloodshed. MacDonagh, apprised of the capitulation when the surrender document, signed by Pearse, was presented to him, 'did not obey the order as it came from a prisoner'. He continued, 'I was then in supreme command of the Irish Army, consulted with my second in command and decided to confirm the order. I knew that it would be inviting my death and the deaths of other leaders'.[5]

And so it proved. The almost casual nature of MacBride's involvement in the insurgency of Easter 1916 was not matched by any similar detachment on the part of the British authorities after his capture. There must be something more than a suspicion that the execution of MacBride had as much to do with his spirited resistance to English imperialism in the Transvaal in 1900 as with any threat to the empire he posed in Dublin sixteen years later.

MacBride faced a Field General Court Martial in Richmond Barracks, Inchicore (now St Michael's, Christian Brothers' School), on 4 May 1916. At dawn the previous morning, three of the signatories of the Proclamation of the Provisional Government of the Irish Republic, Pearse, Clarke and MacDonagh, had been shot by firing squad. The executions and the number of death sentences handed down during the first two days of the courts martial suggested that the new military commander in Ireland, General Sir John Maxwell, intended to mete out summary justice to the rebel leadership. However, if any authority figure amongst the captured insurgents was entitled to clemency surely it had to be MacBride. He had not been a signatory to the proclamation, nor had he been a battalion commander or even part of the organisational structure of the Volunteers. MacBride himself was convinced that he faced a term of imprisonment; he even told another rebel, William T. Cosgrave, future leader of the Irish Free State, that he was concerned he might lose his Dublin Corporation job.[6]

MacBride faced the charge that he 'did take part in an armed rebellion and in the waging of war against His Majesty the King, such act being of such a nature as to be calculated to be prejudicial to the Defence of the Realm and being done with the intention and for the purpose of assisting the enemy'.[7] The first witness called to testify against him was Major J.A.

'Jimmy' Armstrong of the Royal Inniskilling Fusiliers who had taken part in an action designed to force the surrender of the Jacob's Factory garrison as the conflict was winding down on 30 April. MacBride had some previous experience of fighting against Armstrong's regiment, in South Africa in 1900. The commander of the two British Army battalions involved in the attack on Jacob's Factory had, ill advisedly, led his troops into St Patrick's Park, beside the Church of Ireland cathedral. Volunteer snipers had a field day until the British troops found cover. Armstrong told the court about the subsequent surrender of the members of the 2nd Battalion of the Volunteer force:

> I was present at St. Patrick's Park on 30 April. The British troops were fired upon and there were several casualties. The fire came from the neighbourhood of Jacob's Factory. I was present when the prisoners from Jacob's Factory surrendered at 5pm. I recognise the accused as one of them. He gave his rank as an officer.

In the absence of defence counsel (none were permitted by General Maxwell), MacBride attempted a desultory and inconclusive cross-examination of the officer. He declined to question the second witness who identified him, 2nd Lieutenant S.H. Jackson of the 3rd Royal Irish Regiment.

The sole defence witness was a Mrs Allan from Glenageary. She told the court martial that she remembered MacBride leaving her house on Easter Monday morning dressed in civilian clothes. She testified that MacBride's brother was travelling up from Castlebar to meet him at the Wicklow Hotel near Grafton Street. MacBride had told her he would be back by 5.00 p.m. She concluded by pointing out that 'I have never seen him in uniform nor has he got such a thing so far as I know'. Her evidence was, presumably, designed to establish a lack of treasonous intent on MacBride's part when he had left Glenageary on the morning of Monday, 24 April. He had planned to be home for tea, not to be defending a biscuit factory against the forces of the Crown, in the name of the Irish Republic.

When asked by the prosecuting counsel was there anything he wished to say on his own behalf MacBride told the court that while waiting to meet his brother

> I went up as far as St Stephen's Green and there I saw a band of Irish Volunteers. I knew some of the members personally and the commandant told me that an Irish

Republic was virtually proclaimed. As he knew my rather advanced opinions and although I had no previous connection with the Irish Volunteers I considered it my duty to join them. I knew there was no chance of success, and I never advised or influenced any other person to join. I did not even know the positions they were about to take up. I marched with them to Jacob's Factory. After being a few hours there I was appointed second-in-command and I felt it my duty to occupy that position. I could have escaped from Jacob's Factory before the surrender had I so desired but I considered it a dishonourable thing to do. I do not say this with the idea of mitigating any penalty they may impose but in order [to] make clear my position in the matter.

MacBride's tale of spontaneity and serendipity did not have the effect of 'mitigating any penalty'. The three court martial judges, a brigadier general and two lieutenant colonels sentenced him to share the fate of his Bishop St commandant, Thomas MacDonagh, death by shooting. The sentence was confirmed by General Maxwell and the veteran of Ladysmith and Colenso died in a hail of bullets in the old stone-breaker's yard in Kilmainham Gaol at 3.47 a.m. on 5 May 1916.

'AS DOWN THE GLEN ONE EASTER MORN ...'
DUBLIN—24-30 APRIL 1916

Primarily because of an enduring folk memory, as well as its pivotal place in modern Irish history, the military insurrection in Dublin during Easter Week, 1916, is, today, the most familiar act of defiance in two centuries of nationalist rebellion. Events of recent Irish history have ensured that it has also been the most contested. What was hugely controversial at the time, but whose proceedings were not so familiar until quite recently, were the trials by military courts martial of almost 200 men adjudged by the British military authorities to have taken a lead in the Rising. Ninety were sentenced to death, of which fifteen were executed. The consequences of the extreme British reaction are well known and do not need to be rehearsed. What have only emerged within the last decade are the actual records of the courts martial. They are, in the main, flimsy documents but in that respect are probably reflective of the cursory nature of the tribunals themselves. They do not always tally with the memories, memoirs and memorials of those who took part in the process but their release in 2001 adds a crucial element to the, often contradictory, narrative of one of the most momentous weeks in the history of Ireland under the Union.

The established facts of a rebellion undertaken by many of its leaders as a token military gesture, but which developed into a surprisingly successful rearguard action, are well known. The rising was planned by a cabal within the revolutionary Irish Republican Brotherhood and carried out by elements of the Irish Volunteers and the Irish Citizen Army (ICA). A dominant IRB element within the Volunteers, comprising, in the main, of members of the IRB Supreme Council (Pearse, Plunkett, Clarke, Ceannt and MacDermott), had, in 1915, begun intense planning for a rising. The strategy pursued was founded on the familiar philosophy of 'England's difficulty, Ireland's opportunity'. With Britain and France locked in a stalemated struggle with Germany, Joseph Plunkett travelled there to negotiate assistance for the rising. Sir Roger Casement, a leading member of the Volunteers, but not of the IRB, also went to Germany to seek aid. The Irish Volunteers chief of staff, University College Dublin, History Professor Eoin MacNeill, was not aware of the IRB plans and was (along with certain prominent members of the IRB itself, like former Supreme Council member, Bulmer Hobson[8]) kept out of the loop.

When the group expediting the plans for the Rising, the Military Council of the IRB, became aware that the much smaller, socialist, Irish Citizen Army, led by James Connolly and Countess Constance Markievicz, was threatening an insurrection of its own, it intervened. Connolly was 'kidnapped' and made aware of the IRB plans and persuaded to collaborate with the Volunteers efforts, scheduled for Easter Sunday. With the assistance of John Devoy in the USA, an enduring presence in Republican conspiracy for more than half a century, arms were procured from Germany.[9] That least likely of revolutionary conspirators, the former British diplomat, Sir Roger Casement, was permitted by the German authorities to attempt to recruit an Irish brigade to participate in the rebellion from among Irish POWs in German prison camps. The result of his efforts was disappointing. With a few dozen exceptions, Irish POWs remained loyal to the army in which they had enlisted. In early April a German arms ship, the *Aud*, sailed for Kerry while, almost simultaneously, Casement, sailed for Ireland in a German U-boat. Disillusioned by the

German response to pleas for assistance, his intention was to persuade the leaders of the incipient rising to abandon their plans. These were to exploit the scheduled Volunteer manoeuvres to begin on Sunday, 23 April. They would be used as cover for the seizure of key points in Dublin City and other parts of the country.

When Eoin MacNeill finally became aware, on 20 April, of what was in prospect, he only agreed reluctantly to co-operate after being informed that an arms shipment was on its way from Germany. When, on Good Friday, 21 April, it became known that the *Aud* had been scuttled by its own crew after detection by the British navy and that Casement had been arrested in Kerry, MacNeill, seeing the plans for the Rising as folly, took immediate action. He issued the infamous 'countermanding order' calling off the planned manoeuvres on Easter Sunday. The resulting confusion guaranteed a reduced turnout of Volunteers on Monday, 24 April, the new date assigned by the IRB Military Council for the insurrection to take place. On Easter Sunday night the Proclamation of the Provisional Government of the Irish Republic was printed in Liberty Hall, headquarters of the Irish Citizen Army, and signed by Pearse, Clarke, Connolly, McDermott, MacDonagh, Plunkett and Ceannt. Its compelling opening paragraph evoked rebellions of previous generations and exhorted the populace to rise along with the small band of rebels. 'Irishmen and Irishwomen: In the name of God and of the dead generations from which she receives her old tradition of nationhood, Ireland, through us, summons her children to her flag and strikes for her freedom.' However, it was the buried reference to support from Germany ('our gallant allies in Europe') that was to have as much significance for the leadership of the rebellion in the days after its final collapse.

The military action, begun by the Irish Volunteers with an abortive attempt to seize a lightly guarded Dublin Castle, came just in time for the IRB leadership cadre within the organisation, and a day too soon for the British administration in Ireland. After the *Aud*/Casement developments, a decision had been made by the castle to arrest the leaders of the Volunteers. But its implementation was postponed until after Easter Monday. Pearse and his co-conspirators were probably little more than 24 hours away from incarceration. Instead the Rising took a badly prepared administration by surprise. The annual Easter race meeting at Fairyhouse had drawn away many of the military and administrative figures whose presence in Dublin was essential for a rapid and cohesive response to the military action of the Volunteers.

Although there was some rebel activity in Meath, Galway and Wexford the Rising was largely confined to Dublin. The failure to take Dublin Castle and, perhaps more crucially, to neutralise the communications hub of the Crown Alley Telephone Exchange, shortened the duration of the Rising but did not affect the eventual outcome. Command Headquarters, where Pearse, Connolly, Clarke, McDermott and Plunkett were based, was established in the General Post Office on Sackville Street (O'Connell Street today). The 1st Battalion of the Dublin Volunteers, was deployed on the north side of the city in the Church Street area and around the Four Courts. The 3rd Battalion, which would inflict the greatest number of casualties on the advancing British Army because of the engagement at Mount Street Bridge, was established in the south-east of the city around Boland's Bakery. It was under the command of Eamon de Valera. The 4th Battalion occupied positions in the south-south-west of the city, around the South Dublin Union, within a mile of Richmond Barracks. The Irish Citizen Army, commanded by Michael Mallin, with the often melodramatic assistance of Countess Markievicz, was set up around the Stephens Green/Harcourt Street area.

Taken by surprise, the British military response was sluggish at first. But the deployment of artillery and the gunboat, *Helga*, helped the military commander, Brigadier General Lowe, to regain the initiative. The arrival of reinforcements from the UK in the form of the Sherwood Foresters (some of whom assumed they had landed in France and were surprised to hear English being spoken) should have eased the situation still further. However, on a route march from Kingstown to the city centre, the Sherwood Foresters allowed themselves to be pinned down on Mount Street Bridge by seventeen Volunteers of de Valera's 3rd Battalion. They suffered casualties totalling 240 killed and wounded before they were able to advance.

By 29 April the shelling of Sackville Street and the GPO had made continued occupation of the building untenable. It was decided to evacuate to No. 16 Moore Street and from there Pearse surrendered unconditionally to General Lowe and issued a surrender order to all Volunteer units:

> In order to prevent the further slaughter of Dublin citizens, and in the hope of saving the lives of our followers now surrounded and hopelessly outnumbered, the members of the Provisional Government present at headquarters have agreed to an unconditional surrender, and the commandants of the various districts in the City and County will order their commands to lay down arms.[10]

The 'Sinn Féin' Rising, as it was erroneously dubbed by the British authorities and elements of the press, was over. There were undoubtedly a significant number of Sinn Féin members who had taken part but there was no formal connection between Arthur Griffith's political organisation and the Irish Volunteers. British military losses over the seven days of the conflict were first reported as 106 killed (later revised to 116) and 368 wounded. In addition 16 RIC and DMP constables were killed. Irish casualties amounted to 318 dead and 2,217 wounded. The vast bulk of the dead were civilians, though the official statistics failed to differentiate between Irish combatants and non-combatants. The Volunteers and Irish Citizen Army appear to have suffered between 60–4 dead.[11]

THE RESPONSE – 1–12 MAY 1916

On 26 April the British Cabinet had declared martial law throughout Ireland. The following day a military governor, General Sir John Grenfell Maxwell, was appointed. His selection was due, primarily, to his availability. His previous posting, in Egypt, had ended in March 1916. An alternative proposed to the Cabinet was the resurrection of the career of General Sir Ian Hamilton, the controversial commander of the Gallipoli campaign which had ended the previous December with the ignominious withdrawal of British, French and Australian forces from Turkey. Given the number of Irish deaths at Sedd el Bar and Suvla in 1915, presided over by Hamilton, it would have been richly ironic had he been appointed to the position of military commander of the country.

The army was in control of the military situation by the end of Easter week. Maxwell was given 'full authority to restore order, put down the rebellion and punish its participants'.[12] The Liberal chief secretary, Augustine Birrell, and the under secretary, Sir Matthew Nathan, were uneasy with the extent of the military governor's powers. They feared an adverse reaction to the subjection of peaceful parts of the country to martial law. Hence, Maxwell's relations with the civil authorities, who still retained control of the police, were tense from the outset. This became, temporarily, irrelevant with the resignations of Birrell on 1 May and Nathan two days later. By then the executions had begun. They were accompanied by a nationwide sweep of members of Sinn Féin and other Republican organisations. This resulted in the detention of more than

3,500 people. Both policies were assailed by John Dillon, deputy leader of the Irish Parliamentary Party, as parallel roads to political perdition for moderate nationalism. In the House of Commons on 11 May, Dillon warned the prime minister, Herbert Asquith, and the British Cabinet: 'You are letting loose a river of blood ... It is the first rebellion that ever took place in Ireland where you had the majority on your side. It is the fruit of our life work ... and now you are washing out our whole life work in a sea of blood'.[13] Dillon's famous speech would prove prophetic. In December 1918, he, and virtually his entire party, were condemned to political irrelevance in the sweeping general election victory of Sinn Féin.

The bulk of the rebels rounded up in Dublin on 29/30 April were despatched to prison camps in Britain. One hundred and eighty-seven 'ringleaders' were retained in Ireland for trial. These were to be undertaken by military courts martial under the terms of the Defence of the Realm Act (1914). However, the procedure adopted by Maxwell was closer to that of a 'drumhead' court martial of the type normally seen in the field, than to the 'emergency' due process envisaged by the provisions of the Defence of the Realm Act. This entailed the creation of a court with thirteen members, a professional judge and a legal advocate, with trials to be conducted openly. The Volunteer leaders were tried by three-judge military courts with no defence counsel. All trials were held *in camera* and there was no right of appeal. Maxwell's template might well have been permissible under martial law but it served, in retrospect, merely to give an impression of arbitrary procedure and summary execution. Even the British adjutant general conceded that, 'there is no legal justification for a Court Martial to be held in-camera, either in the Army Act, or in any regulation under the Defence of the Realm Act'.[14]

The courts martial took place in Richmond Barracks over a nine-day period with an unspecified number of trials taking place simultaneously. One of the prosecutors was 35-year-old 2nd Lieutenant William Evelyn Wylie, a Dublin-born, Northern-educated Trinity graduate and son of a Presbyterian minister. Wylie, who, despite his Dublin origins spoke with a Northern accent, had been called to the Bar in 1905 and became a king's counsel in 1914. He already had a thriving legal practice before the outbreak of the First World War. In 1915 he had joined the Territorial Army and during the Rising he had helped defend his old *Alma Mater* along with members of the Trinity College Officer Training Corps.

A short time after the unconditional surrender, Wylie was preparing to retire for the night when a military messenger arrived by motorbike instructing him to report to GHQ. In a 1939 memoir written for his daughter, the KC recalled:

> It was then after midnight, and I wondered whether I was going to be promoted or put in jail. I got on the back of the motor-bike and started for Parkgate Street. I was shown into a room and found a brass hat seated at a desk. It was General Byrne, who had just arrived from England as Assistant Adjutant-General.
>
> He said, 'Are you Wylie?'
>
> 'Yes, Sir.'
>
> 'Will you prosecute at the courts martial of the prisoners? Start tomorrow morning at nine at Richmond Barracks ...'
>
> I saluted and departed. Not much sleep for me that night.[15]

Thus began, for Wylie, a turbulent and disturbing ten-day period in which his Unionist sympathies and antipathy to the Rising would vie with his sense of fair play and legal training in the face of military authorities with little inclination towards the former and little expertise in the latter. Wylie would prosecute at the trials of most of the senior 1916 leaders. He did so in as professional a manner as possible. He was temperamentally disposed towards the exercise of the death penalty against a number of the leaders of the rebellion. Nonetheless even he quickly became disturbed at the cavalier disregard of due process he witnessed. There must be a suspicion, though there is no documentary evidence to this effect, that by the time of the belated courts martial of Seán MacDermott and the lame and severely ill James Connolly on 9 May, Wylie's attitude and advocacy was no longer altogether appreciated by his military superiors.

THE COURTS MARTIAL OF PEARSE AND MACDONAGH, 2 MAY 1916

After the surrender to General Lowe, Patrick Pearse was brought to Arbour Hill Military Detention Centre while most of the other leaders were taken to Richmond Barracks. In a letter to his mother written on 1 May, he revealed that before the final surrender he had advocated 'one more desperate sally before opening negotiations' but now accepted that this would have been wrong as it would have meant the deaths of 50–100 men. He told his mother:

> Our hope and belief is that the Government will spare the lives of all our followers but we do not expect that they will spare the lives of the leaders. We are ready to die and we shall die cheerfully and proudly. Personally I do not hope or even desire to live, but I do hope and desire and believe that the lives of all our followers will be saved including the lives dear to you and me[16] (my own excepted) and this will be a great consolation to me when dying. You must not grieve for all this. We have preserved Ireland's honour and our own. Our deeds of last week are the most splendid in Ireland's history. People will say hard things of us now, but we shall be remembered by posterity and blessed by unborn generations. You too will be blessed because you were my mother...

In what was either a naive and unguarded postscript, or a carefully contrived attempt to incriminate himself, he added 'I understand that the German expedition which I was counting on actually set sail but was defeated by the British'.[17] This was a reference to the aborted mission of the *Aud*. The letter was duly intercepted by the military authorities and was used against him at his court martial the following day.

On 2 May Pearse was transferred to Richmond Barracks. As 'Prisoner No. 1' he was court-martialled that afternoon. His was the first of nearly 200 courts martial. The president of the court, as was to be the case with most of the prominent leaders of the Rising, was Brigadier General C.G. Blackader, a 46-year-old career soldier who would shortly lead the 38th (Welsh) Division through the horrors of the Somme and the Third Battle of Ypres.

Shortly before Pearse was escorted into the court martial, William Wylie had introduced himself to the general. As he recalled, he had walked up to the table at which Blackader sat, and saluted:

> 'Well, what can I do for you?' the General had inquired.
>
> 'I have been detailed to conduct the prosecutions, sir.' He looked me over, ASC[18] badges and one pip. I could feel him saying 'My God' to himself.

'What are you in civilian life, may I ask?' he said.

'King's Counsel, sir.'

'Ah, that's better. Well, get in the first accused and we'll start.'[19]

Pearse, pleaded not guilty to the charge that he 'did take part in an armed rebellion and in the waging of war against His Majesty the King'. The first of three witnesses against him was 2nd Lieutenant S.O. King of the 12th Royal Inniskilling Fusiliers who told the court martial that:

> I was on duty at the Rotunda, Dublin on Saturday 29th April. The Sinn Fein [sic] was firing at the soldiers. The accused came from the neighbourhood from which the shots were being fired. The accused was in the same uniform in which he is now with belt, sword and revolver on and with ammunition. The accused surrendered to General Lowe.[20]

King had been a prisoner of the Volunteers and Pearse cross-examined him to establish that he had been properly looked after. King responded that he 'was very well treated'. The second witness, Constable Daniel Coffey of the DMP, told the court that: 'I was present when the accused Pearse was in custody at Irish Command HQ at about 5pm on Saturday the 29th April. I identify him as a member of the Irish Volunteers. I have seen him several times going through the city with bodies of men and acting as an officer'.

Pearse did not cross examine Coffey, or indeed the final witness, Sergeant G. Goodman, who identified the letter that Pearse had written to his mother as having been written by him. The letter itself was then produced in evidence. Wylie was favourably impressed at the demeanour of Pearse. More than twenty years later in his memoir to his daughter, he wrote:

> He was a schoolmaster, I believe and looked a decent chap. There was a lot of evidence against him, apart from the fact that he had been O/C of the rebels in the GPO. He had been in close touch with Casement, and letters were found on him showing this. When I had finished with the evidence against him, I asked him did he wish to make a statement. He said he did and made a very eloquent speech of which I always call the Robert Emmet type.

According to the official court martial transcript Pearse made the following short speech.

> My sole object in surrendering unconditionally was to save the slaughter of the civil population and to save the lives of our followers who had been led into this thing by us. It is my hope that the British Government who has shown its strength will also be magnanimous and spare the lives and give an amnesty to my followers. As I am one of the persons chiefly responsible, have acted as C-in-C and President of the provisional Government, I am prepared to take the consequences of my act, but I should like my followers to receive an amnesty. I went down on my knees as a child and told God that I would work all my life to gain the freedom of Ireland. I have deemed it my duty as an Irishman to fight for the freedom of my country. I admit I have organised men to fight against Britain. I admit having opened negotiations with Germany. We have kept our word with her and as far as I can see she did her best to help us. She sent a ship with men. Germany has not sent us gold.[21]

As transcribed it was dignified if somewhat disjointed valedictory. But posterity has also left an account of the speech that may have been written by Pearse himself in the hours before his execution. Whether he actually delivered the speech as written or as recorded by the military note-taker, it is the lengthier, more polished and more complete version that entered the public domain. In Pearse's own version of his address he reiterated the philosophy of continuity of purpose often expressed in his political and journalistic writings in the years before the insurrection. He concluded by insisting that the timing of the rebellion had been appropriate:

> we seem to have lost, we have not lost. To refuse to fight would have been to lose, to fight is to win, we have kept faith with the past, and handed a tradition to the future. I repudiate the assertion of the prosecutor that I sought to aid and abet England's enemy. Germany is no more to me than England is. I asked and accepted German aid in the shape of arms and an expeditionary force, we neither asked nor accepted German gold, nor had any traffic with

Germany but what I state; my aim was to win Irish freedom; we struck the first blow ourselves but I should have been glad of an ally's aid.

I assume I am speaking to Englishmen who value their own freedom, and who profess to be fighting for the freedom of Belgium and Serbia. Believe that we too love freedom and desire it. To us it is more desirable than anything else in the world. If you strike us down now we shall rise again and renew the fight. You cannot conquer Ireland; you cannot extinguish the Irish passion for freedom; if our deed has not been sufficient to win freedom then our children will win it by a better deed.[22]

The official record has a highly truncated appearance, as if it was a gallant effort at an accurate transcription rather than a comprehensive account. Pearse had more than one eye on posterity. He was probably disappointed that the proceedings were being conducted *in camera* and had ample time to prepare in advance the longer and more accomplished apologia. He may well have delivered a speech much closer to his own version than that of the official stenographer. Wylie's account of the address is not conclusive but suggests that Pearse spoke at greater length and in more detail than the official record allows. Writing a good 30 years before the release of the court martial transcripts, in a biography that interrogates sceptically the Pearse 'myth', Ruth Dudley Edwards maintained that 'As Emmet had inspired the framing of the proclamation of the Irish Republic, so Tone was the inspiration for Pearse's speech from the dock'.[23] However, there are similarities with the valedictory speech of the tragic revolutionary figure of 1803, not least the disavowal of an overweening dependence on Germany that echoed Emmet's disparagement of France. Perhaps the main similarity is that while the *spirit* of what both men said has been honoured in the account passed down to posterity neither may have been quoted entirely accurately.

After consulting briefly, the three officers of the court martial found Pearse guilty and condemned him to be shot at dawn the following morning. Although left with no choice, General Blackader appears to have greatly regretted the verdict. Later that night he dined at Elgin Road with Elizabeth, Countess of Fingall. She described him as 'a charming, sympathetic person, half French, very emotional and terribly affected by the work he had to do'. Lady Fingall found him very depressed and on inquiring as to the cause was told by the general: 'I have just done one of the hardest tasks I have ever had to do. I have had to condemn to death one of the finest characters I have ever come across. There must be something very wrong in the state of things that makes a man like that a Rebel. I don't wonder his pupils adored him'.[24]

As he waited execution, Pearse wrote a final letter to his mother. Probably assuming the note of 1 May would never find its way to her he repeated a point he had made in the missive produced at his court martial 'This is the death I should have asked for if God had given me the choice of all deaths—to die as a soldier for Ireland's freedom. We have done right. People will say hard things of us now, but later they will praise us'.[25] Pearse had expressed some concern that he and the other leaders of the Rising might be hanged rather than shot. But he suffered the fate he had sought, a soldier's death. On the same morning as Thomas MacDonagh and Thomas Clarke were executed, he was shot by firing squad in the stone-breaker's yard in Kilmainham Gaol sometime between 3.30 and 4.00 a.m. on the morning of 3 May. The Crown had extracted the ultimate penalty from Prisoner No. 1 and, in establishing such a precedent, had initiated a perilous process from which they were unable to extricate themselves. They had satisfied Pearse's own desire for martyrdom and validated his 'theology of insurrection'.[26]

The court martial of Pearse was quickly followed by that of another signatory of the proclamation, Thomas MacDonagh. A lecturer in English at University College Dublin, MacDonagh had been in command of the force that occupied the Jacob's Biscuit Factory. The transcript of his court martial is even briefer than that of Pearse. Once again Blackader presided (assisted, with some curious serendipity, by two colonels named German and Kent). MacDonagh pleaded not guilty to the charge of waging war against the king and a single witness was produced, Major Armstrong of the 1st Royal Inniskilling Fusiliers, who would later testify against MacBride. In response to questions from Wylie he told the court martial that

> I was present at St. Patrick's Park Dublin on 30 April 1916. There were British troops there and I saw them fired on. I was under fire myself. The shots came from the direction of Jacob's Factory. There were several casualties among the British troops. At a later hour I saw the accused coming from the direction of Jacob's Factory under a white flag. He made several journeys through our

lines—about 5pm he surrendered with over 100 others to General Carleton. He was acting as an officer when he surrendered. I made a list of the unarmed men and the accused was not on that list. He made a statement to me that he was a Commandant. He was subsequently sent under escort to Richmond Barracks.

MacDonagh briefly cross-examined Armstrong, called no witnesses and, according to the transcript, when asked did he have anything to say simply observed that 'I did everything I could to assist the officers in the matter of the surrender telling them where the arms and ammunition were after the surrender was decided upon'.[27]

Thanks to W.E. Wylie's memoir we know that much more actually occurred than was outlined in the bald transcript. Wylie, who saw MacDonagh as 'a poet, a dreamer and an idealist' had been a witness to his surrender and claimed to have been obliged to protect the members of the 2nd Battalion from angry crowds on the march to Richmond Barracks.[28] At MacDonagh's court martial there was, according to Wylie, always the diligent guardian of justice in his own narrative, a significant exchange which indicates that due process was not to be entirely overridden. After MacDonagh had been arraigned General Blackader asked Wylie if it was the case that there existed a proclamation of independence that had been signed by the prisoner. Wylie acknowledged that there was such a document and remarked that he had a copy in his pocket. Blackader, unversed in the laws of evidence, asked why it had not been cited. Wylie pointed out that the provenance of the document could not be established and, therefore, it was not admissible. Blackader, clearly puzzled, asked why this was the case and was informed that, as the proclamation was a printed document with certain names appended, it would be necessary to locate the original and confirm the signatures before it could be presented as evidence. He advised the three members of the court to 'obliterate all knowledge' of the proclamation from their minds.[29]

However, Wylie's account is at variance with the official court martial record. The prosecutor insisted in his memoir that when he had asked MacDonagh did he have anything to say the prisoner simply shook his head. Wylie claimed that MacDonagh, whose execution he described as 'particularly unnecessary', was the only prisoner who did not speak. The record asserts otherwise. That Wylie was mistaken is confirmed by the last letter of MacDonagh to his wife written on the night of 2 May. In retrospect the prisoner was clearly concerned at the complexion that might be placed on the remarks he had made to the tribunal. 'At my court martial,' he wrote, 'in rebutting some trifling evidence I made a statement ... on hearing it read after, it struck me that it might sound like an appeal. It was not such. I made no appeal, no recantation, no apology for my acts. In what I said I merely claimed that I acted honourably and thoroughly in all that I set myself to do.'[30]

William Wylie was greatly surprised in June 1916 when he noticed a pamphlet on sale in Dublin purporting to be the text of MacDonagh's address to his court martial. Twelve thousand copies had been printed, of which the authorities, deeming it subversive, seized just over three thousand. Like Pearse's 'amended' speech MacDonagh's was passionate and defiant. The text of the pamphlet has him concluding with a resounding call to arms in the florid, patriotic, and elitist, vernacular familiar from the style of Pearse and other nationalist writers:

> The generous high-bred youth of Ireland will never fail to answer the call we pass on to them—will never fail to blaze forth in the red rage of war to win their country's freedom. Other and tamer methods they will leave to other and tamer men; but they must do or die. It will be said that our movement was doomed to failure. It has proved so. Yet it might have been otherwise. There is always a chance of success for brave men who challenge fortune. That we had such a chance none knows so well as your statesmen and military experts. The mass of the people of Ireland will doubtless lull their consciences to sleep for another generation by the exploded fable that Ireland cannot successfully fight England. We do not profess to represent the mass of the people of Ireland. We stand for the intellect and the soul of Ireland. To Ireland's soul and intellect the inert mass, drugged and degenerate by ages of servitude, must, in the distant day of resurrection, render homage and free service—receiving in return the vivifying impress of a free people.
>
> Gentlemen you have sentenced me to death, and I accept your sentence with joy and pride; since it is for Ireland I am to die. I go to join the goodly company of the men who died for Ireland, the least of whom was wor-

thier far than I can claim to be, and that noble band are, themselves, but a small section of the great unnumbered army of martyrs whose Captain is the Christ who died on Calvary. Of every white-robed knight in all that goodly company we are the spiritual kin. The forms of heroes flit before my vision, and there is one, the star of whose destiny sways my own; there is one the keynote of whose nature chimes harmoniously with the swan-song of my soul. It is the great Florentine whose weapon was not the sword but prayer and preaching. The seed he sowed fructifies to this day in God's Church. Take me away, and let my blood bedew the sacred soil of Ireland. I die in the certainty that once more the seed will fructify.[31]

The rhetoric is bombastic and baroque and was certainly not spoken *ad libitum* at the conclusion of his court martial. If delivered at all it would have been from a prepared script. But was it actually written by MacDonagh for his trial or was it penned later by a sympathiser capable of mimicking his style? In the reference to the 'great Florentine' it reflects MacDonagh's interest in the works and personality of the Renaissance monk Savonarola who is referred to in his play *When the dawn is come*.[32] The executed leader's son, Donagh MacDonagh, has observed that 'there are several points of internal evidence which would seem to indicate that it was his work'.[33] At the trial of J.M. Butler, a newsagent and former *Freeman's Journal* employee who was fined for printing the offending pamphlet, the prosecutor was keen to scotch the notion that MacDonagh had ever actually made the speech. He insisted that

> The document, headed 'The Last and Inspiring Address of Thomas MacDonagh' purported to be no doubt a statement made by this person but it was pure fiction and no such statement, as far as he could gather was ever made by this man. The conduct of the defendant in having the document, which is absolutely bogus, printed and published by other persons for circulation could only be for the purpose of causing disloyalty and disaffection in the country at the present time ...[34]

However, while Robertson declared that *The last and inspiring address...*,[35] as printed, had never been spoken by MacDonagh at his court martial, he did not claim that it had not been written by him.

While it is entirely possible and indeed plausible that MacDonagh was the writer of the speech contained in the controversial pamphlet it is virtually certain that it was never actually delivered in the setting of a court martial. The speech begins with the prisoner addressing the court in the following terms. 'I choose to think that you have but done your duty, according to your lights, in sentencing me to death.' The fact is that, when asked by Wylie did he have anything to say, MacDonagh, although morally certain of the outcome, was not aware of the verdict of the court martial because the judges had yet to consider their verdict. As in the case of Pearse before him, and dozens of other prisoners subsequently, this was communicated to MacDonagh later.

There is also an additional piece of internal evidence, which, if Wylie is to be believed, suggests the speech may have been written, or amended, by someone other than MacDonagh. According to the published pamphlet, after an altercation between the prisoner and the court on the links between the Rising and Germany MacDonagh continued 'There is not much left to say. The proclamation of the Irish Republic has been adduced in evidence against me as one of the signatories'. [36] As Wylie noted in his memoir, the proclamation, because of the nature of the document, could not be adduced in evidence. Either MacDonagh was allowing himself a measure of poetic licence or the speech was written *ex post facto* by an able propagandist. However, this begs the question, if someone had gone to the trouble of fabricating an entire speech, why not attribute it to the much more celebrated Pearse?

There is no doubt as to the provenance of the last statement written by MacDonagh in the hours before his execution. It is a poignant document, dignified in the face of death but laced with regret at the consequences, financial and emotional, for his family. Like Pearse, MacDonagh expressed the conviction that his personal sacrifice would be viewed favourably by future generations.

> I, Thomas MacDonagh, [he wrote] having now heard the sentence of the Court Martial held on me today, declare that in all my acts—all the acts for which I have been arraigned—I have been actuated by one motive only, the love of my country, the desire to make her a sovereign independent state. I still hope and pray that my acts may have for consummation her lasting freedom and happiness. I am to die at dawn, 3.30 am, 3rd May. I am ready to

die, and I thank God that I die in so holy a cause. My country will reward my deed richly ... For myself I have no regret. The one bitterness that death has for me is the separation it brings from my beloved wife Muriel, and my beloved children Donagh and Barbara. My country will take them as wards, I hope.[37]

MacDonagh was shot by firing squad within minutes of the execution of Pearse and the oldest signatory of the proclamation, Thomas Clarke, on 3 May. The pervasive rumour in military circles was that most of the fifteen men eventually executed did not die in the initial volley of shots and had to be dispatched by the revolver of the officer in charge. After the death of each of the prisoners was confirmed an identifying label was fixed to their tunics and their bodies were taken to Arbour Hill Detention Centre. There, in accordance with instructions

The party will put the bodies close alongside one another in the grave (now being dug) cover them quickly with quicklime (ordered) and commence filling in the grave. One of the officers with his party is to keep note of the position of each body in the grave, taking the name from the label. A priest will attend for the funeral service.

Maxwell was insistent that the bodies would not be released to their families. He was of the opinion that 'Irish sentimentality will turn these graves into martyrs' shrines to which annual procession will be made'.[38] In that conjecture he was proven to be entirely accurate.

THE EXECUTIONS CONTINUE, 4–12 MAY

After the court martial of McDonagh, Wylie began a personal campaign to undermine the pace and partiality of the questionable legal process which Maxwell had initiated. He began a practice of consulting with prisoners about to face trial while the court was considering its verdict in a previous case. This was with a view to discovering whether they wished to call defence witnesses. Pearse and MacDonagh had been given no opportunity to produce any. In the case of Eamon Ceannt, at whose surrender Wylie had assisted, the prosecutor's preliminary intervention would lead to two adjournments as the DMP were sent to search for named witnesses.

Ceannt, tried on 3 May, also called MacBride to testify that he had not, as alleged, been stationed in Jacob's Factory. The ubiquitous Major Armstrong testified that Ceannt had been arrested there. This was indeed the case but Ceannt himself, as Commandant of the 4th Battalion, had been based at the South Dublin Union, closer to Richmond Barracks and well to the west of Bishop Street. He had also sought to call MacDonagh to testify to the same effect but was informed that the Commandant of the 2nd Battalion had been executed that morning.[39]

Wylie's intervention was, in part, responsible for Ceannt's court martial continuing into a second day where two more defence witnesses were produced. The prisoner himself argued cogently that 'there is reasonable doubt and the benefit of the doubt should be given to the accused'. A reading of the court martial transcript prompts the conclusion that, in an open criminal court with the customary level of evidential testing, the Crown would have failed to establish a *bona fide* case against Ceannt on the basis of the testimony presented. Ceannt, given the nature of the evidence against him, had an alibi. He was clearly not present during Easter week in the location where the prosecution placed him. This suspicion is reinforced by an opinion offered by the adjutant general, Sir Nevil Macready, on the issue of whether or not the accounts of the courts martial should be released. Publication had been promised by Asquith to the House of Commons in October 1916. Having consulted with Maxwell, General Macready wrote:

> publication is in my opinion a complete admission that there was no justification for trial *in camera* (which in itself is a grave reflection upon the discretion of Sir John Maxwell) and as I have reason to believe that in certain cases the evidence was not too strong the inevitable results of publication would be that a certain section of the Irish community will urge that the sole reason for trial *in camera* was that the authorities intended to execute certain of the Sinn Feiners whether there was evidence against them or not. This is an argument which in my humble judgment would be extremely difficult to meet successfully if, as I think, the evidence in some of the cases was far from conclusive.[40]

But the evidence presented against Ceannt satisfied the court martial judges who sentenced the 4th Battalion commandant to death. He was executed on 8 May. In one of the ironies that bedevil Irish history and were, for many years, omitted from the Irish historical narrative, Ceannt's brother, William, was killed on the Western Front on the first anniversary of the Rising.[41] Long before Ceannt's execution, Wylie, disturbed at the liberties being taken with due process, and despite his intense dislike of the man, visited the Irish attorney general, James Campbell, in his Dublin Castle office. There he asked the chief law officer to allow the appearance of defence counsel for the prisoners. Campbell refused and added that, personally, he would not be content until at least 40 of the prisoners had been shot. Wylie, in response, told the attorney general that it was his intention, while prosecuting, to defend the prisoners to the best of his ability. He later observed in his memoir 'It amuses me and is illustrative of politics to remember that Campbell, or Lord Glenavy as he became, was within a few years to be Chairman of the Free State Senate'. For his own part, within weeks of the Rising, Wylie was back at the Bar being briefed for an action on behalf of a Sinn Féin club in dispute with its landlord. Later, he became a High Court judge in the independent state created by the survivors of 1916.[42] Wylie also played a significant part in the fate of Eamon de Valera and a controversial role in the post-Rising narrative of Countess Constance Markievicz.

By the end of the first week in May tensions in Dublin were mounting as the executions continued. In London, Asquith was under pressure, in particular from John Redmond and John Dillon, to bring the judicial bloodshed to an end. In response he applied pressure of his own. Sir Nevil Macready, adjutant general recalled that:

> I was several times sent for by Mr. Asquith, the burden of whose complaint was the long-drawn-out tale of daily executions. I agreed, with wisdom learnt after the event, that it would have been better to have tried all the most conspicuous rebels at one time before several courts-martial—if, indeed, any form of trial other than a 'drumhead' court-martial was necessary for those taken in arms—executing those condemned to death in one batch.[43]

Asquith would, belatedly, travel to Ireland on 11 May to take control of the situation himself, having been unable to find, at short notice anyone willing to take on the job of chief secretary. He arrived in time for the final executions, of Connolly and MacDermott.

On 8 May Wylie had been hailed by Maxwell as he walked across the square of Richmond Barracks. The two men had built up a mutual respect in the course of a momentous week. Wylie remembered

> ... Maxwell was in a bit of a splutter.

> 'Read this' he said, handing me a telegram. It was from Asquith, the Prime Minister, and said that the executions must stop at once.

> 'Who is next on your list?' Maxwell asked.

> 'Connolly, sir,' I said

> 'Well I insist on him being tried.'

> 'But he's wounded, sir,' I said.

> 'The Court can be convened in the hospital.'

> I again demurred. I forget what I said, but it was to the effect that Connolly should not be tried until he was well again. Maxwell didn't reply, and the next I heard was that Connolly had been tried and condemned. I don't know who prosecuted.

This would imply that Wylie, who had prosecuted most of the senior Volunteer leaders, was adjudged to have 'gone native' and was not asked to be involved in the trial of the seriously wounded Irish Citizen Army leader. Maxwell appears to have been determined that Connolly and MacDermott, the only two proclamation signatories still alive, were to be shot at all costs, notwithstanding the political consequences for Asquith.[44] He had then asked Wylie which of the other acknowledged leaders had yet to be tried. Wylie responded:

> ' ... Someone called de Valera, sir.'

> 'Who is he?' said Maxwell. 'I haven't heard of him before.'[45]

> 'He was in command of Boland's Bakery in the Ringsend area.'

> 'I wonder would he be likely to make trouble in the future?' Maxwell went on.

> 'I wouldn't think so, sir, I don't think he is important enough. From all I can hear he is not one of the leaders.'[46]

In his memoir to his daughter, written on the eve of the Second World War, after seven years of Fianna Fáil government under de Valera, Wylie re-evaluated his assessment of the relatively anonymous 3rd Battalion commandant.

> I told the truth, what I knew it to be. But my God, I was far off the mark. But for Dev there would have been no split at the time of the Treaty, no Documents 1, 2, and 3, no Civil War, none of the burning of houses and destruction of property and life that took place in 1922 and 1923, and none of the bitterness, the dreadful bitterness and personal hatred which exists between the two parties in the country now, not to speak of the destruction of our relations with England.[47]

By his own lights, Wylie may have been right to upbraid himself for his wayward appraisal of de Valera's future, but it appears to have been more influential in the preservation of the future Taoiseach's life than his US birth. The court martial transcripts make no reference to de Valera having sought mitigation on the basis that he had been born in New York. But while Wylie's impromptu and wildly inaccurate assessment of de Valera's political potency may have played a part in the clemency afforded him it is more likely that, in the light of Asquith's telegram, he was saved by the timing of his court martial.

Wylie's memoir, simultaneously self-serving and relatively reliable, must be treated with some caution in his account of the court martial of Countess Markievicz. The often histrionic Citizen Army officer has become a colourful and iconic figure as a result of her participation in the Rising, though she has many capable detractors.[48] When being taken into custody, along with ICA Commandant Michael Mallin, she had, theatrically, kissed her revolver before surrendering it to the arresting troops. They were led, coincidentally, by the husband of one of her cousins, Captain Henry de Courcy Wheeler. Her fearsome reputation (she had once been convicted of assaulting a policeman) preceded her into her court martial on 4 May. Wylie, who was prosecuting, noticed that when her name was announced, Blackader, anticipating the worst, in a theatrical gesture of his own, placed his revolver on the table beside him. However, according to Wylie

> ... he needn't have troubled, for she curled up immediately.
> 'I am only a woman,' she cried, 'and you cannot shoot a

woman. You must not shoot a woman. You must not shoot a woman.' She never stopped moaning the whole time she was in the courtroom ... I think we all felt slightly disgusted. She had been preaching to a lot of silly boys, death and glory, die for your country, etc. and yet she was literally crawling. I won't say any more. It revolts me still.[49]

She was sentenced to death but the sentence was commuted by Maxwell, under orders from the Cabinet, 'to her intense chagrin',[50] according to 1916 chronicler, Max Caufield.

The trial record of the Markievicz court martial is totally at variance with Wylie's disparaging account. There she is recorded as having made a brief address, merely saying 'I went out to fight for Ireland and it doesn't matter what happens to me. I did what I thought was right and I stand by it'.[51] The fact that there is a disparity between Wylie's memory and the court record is of no great consequence. Such discrepancies, true in other instances, and internal evidence suggest that the prosecutor's account was often as likely to be accurate as the official record. Wylie's version of events has been described by one formidable commentator, who has chosen to accept the veracity of the court martial transcript, as a 'wilful and scurrilous distortion'.[52] However, Charles Townshend, author of perhaps the finest account of the Rising, concedes that if Wylie has distorted the record 'his motives are obscure'.[53]

Whatever the truth of the matter, rumours of the psychological breakdown of the countess spread quickly through the city. They were especially pervasive in Unionist and aristocratic circles where her perceived betrayal of her social class added piquancy to the retelling. Elise Mahaffy, daughter of the celebrated provost of Trinity College, Sir John Pentland Mahaffy, wrote of the countess that she was 'the one woman amongst them of high birth and therefore the most depraved ... she took to politics and left our class'.[54]

Markievicz, despite her affiliation to the socialist Irish Citizen Army and her previous reputation as a militant suffragette, did not exhibit much solidarity with her less fortunate sisters during her incarceration in Aylesbury Prison in England. She later told her sister that she had been imprisoned with 'the dregs of the population ... no one to speak to except prostitutes who had been convicted for murder or violence. The atmosphere is the conversation of the brothel'.[55]

The executions of James Connolly and Seán MacDermott, coming as they did after a four day hiatus and the commutation of the sentences on

Markievicz and de Valera, 'shocked public opinion as none of the others had' according to Max Caulfield.[56] Notoriously, in the case of Connolly, he was so badly wounded that he had to be propped up in a chair before being shot. Those within the military command structure, like Maxwell, who were determined that he should be executed must have been well aware that delay would probably prove fatal. Maxwell was conscious of the growing opposition to the continued executions both in Ireland and the UK. Even the Unionist leader, Edward Carson, spoke in the House of Commons against further retribution in its current form, warning the government that 'whatever is done, let it be done not in a moment of temporary excitement but in a moment of deliberation'.[57]

Connolly faced two charges, first, of taking part in an armed rebellion and, second, of attempting to cause disaffection amongst the civilian population. Four witnesses were produced against him, two of whom were soldiers who had been prisoners of the Volunteers in the GPO. Connolly would have stood out in Sackville Street, where he was surrounded by members of the Volunteers, owing to his Citizen Army uniform. One of the prisoners testified that he had been tied up in a telephone box and that when a Volunteer had sought permission from Connolly to move him to less cramped conditions he had been told 'I don't care a damn what you do with him'.[58] Also produced was a dispatch signed by Connolly that had been found on the already executed John MacBride. A statement from two doctors who had been treating the prisoner in a temporary medical post in Dublin Castle was read. They certified that 'during the entire period of James Connolly's detention as a patient in the Dublin Castle Hospital he has been perfectly rational and in complete possession of his faculties'.

Asked if he had anything to say before the court considered its verdict, Connolly replied:

> I do not wish to make any defence except against charges of wanton cruelty to prisoners. These trifling allegations that have been made in that direction if they record facts that really happened deal only with the almost unavoidable incidents of a hurried uprising, and overthrowing of long established authorities, and nowhere show evidence of a set purpose to wantonly injure unarmed prisoners.
>
> We went out to break the connection between this country and the British Empire and to establish an Irish Republic. We believe that the call we thus issued to the

people of Ireland was a nobler call in a holier cause than any call issued to them during this war having any connection with the war. We succeeded in proving that Irishmen are ready to die endeavouring to win for Ireland their national rights which the British Government has been asking them to die to win for Belgium. As long as that remains the case the cause of Irish Freedom is safe. Believing that the British Government has no right in Ireland, never had any right in Ireland, and never can have any right in Ireland, the presence in any one generation of even a respectable minority of Irishmen ready to die to affirm that truth makes that Government for ever a usurpation, and a crime against human progress. I personally thank God that I have lived to see the day when thousands of Irishmen and boys, and hundreds of Irish women and girls, were equally ready to affirm that truth and seal it with their lives if necessary.

In a somewhat capricious decision the court concluded that Connolly was not guilty of attempting to spread disaffection. On the principal charge he was found guilty. His death, perhaps more than any other, cemented the growing Irish disenchantment with the English military reaction to the failed rebellion.

The trial of Sir Roger Casement, August 1916

After the execution of the two surviving signatories on 12 May the Crown had one final score to settle with the leadership of the Rising. Sir Roger Casement, career diplomat, humanitarian and British civil servant, was the first of the leaders of the Rising to be arrested. He was the last to be tried and executed. Unlike his colleagues he was not given a soldier's death by firing squad. Lodged, with clear regard for symbolism, in the Tower of London, the Asquith government initially decided to deal with the man who had exposed the horrors of King Leopold's Congo in the same manner as his fellow rebels. He would be quickly court martialled and shot. But, according to one of his biographers, H. Montgomery Hyde, 'as the evidence appeared to build up against him, the Government began to be attracted to the idea of civil trial for treason'.[59] In the wake of the failed insurrection, opinion hardened against Casement in England. The man who had travelled from Germany to prevent the Rising from going ahead was to be tried as its instigator and *eminence grise*.

Casement, imprisoned in substandard conditions in the tower, was moved to Brixton to await trial. His defence was organised by George Gavan Duffy, a successful London solicitor in his mid-thirties, who was the son of the Young Ireland leader, Charles Gavan Duffy. The Casement trial would prompt him to abandon his London legal practice and become a Sinn Féin MP in 1918. For the authorities, the idea of putting Casement in the dock had the attraction of rehabilitation. Some of the international criticism drawn down on the heads of the Asquith government for the methods used to deal with the leaders of the Rising could be deflected by the presentation of a robust prosecution of Casement. A resounding government victory in a credible and open treason trial could be used, vicariously and retrospectively, to justify the verdicts and, by extension, the unsavoury process, of the Dublin courts martial. There was, however, an unfortunate corollary embedded in the governmental logic. Their forum for the *ex post facto* validation of Maxwell was Casement's platform for the justification of the Rising and the lionisation, implicit or explicit, of its leaders.

Duffy, with some difficulty, managed to engage the services of Serjeant[60] Sullivan (the son of the former owner of the *Nation* newspaper, A.M. Sullivan) to defend Casement. Sullivan was a Crown law officer in Ireland but he had been called to the English Bar and was, therefore, entitled to plead at the Old Bailey. Casement's desire was to conduct a defence based on an acceptance of the facts of the case. However, he emphatically denied that he was guilty of treason on foot of those facts. His contention was that what he had done was his duty to his country' His loyalty was to an Irish republic not to the English Crown. Sullivan, however, persuaded or browbeat his client into a more reductive line of defence. Casement was to be tried under the same treason statute of King Edward III as Emmet had been. This held that the crime of treason had been committed 'if a man be adherent to the King's enemies in his realm'. Sullivan would contend that Casement, in his dealings with the Germans, had not threatened the king in his own realm. As a credible line of defence it was as weak as that of Casement's. But, although Sullivan was under no illusions as to its prospects, there was a hopeful precedent in the case of Colonel Arthur

Lynch, who was a leader of the Irish Brigade during the Boer War. A similar defence had been entered in his case but he had been convicted and sentenced to death. Lynch, however, had been reprieved. Sullivan was hoping for similar treatment for Casement.

Casement shared Sullivan's view that, after the outcry over the Dublin executions, there was no official will to make a further example of him. He wrote to Duffy:

> The English mob and vast majority of the people would like to see me hanged and want it badly. The British government *dare not* hang me (they don't want to either—as individuals I think). They simply dare not. They would willingly bring back to life poor Sean MacDermott, Connolly, Pearse, Colbert (and the other victims of their military autocrats of Easter week) and they are assuredly not going to add to the roll of victims, me. They know quite well what the world would say of that, and what America would say of it.[61]

But there was another reason for acceding to Sullivan's insistence that his line of defence be adopted. Casement, famously, was a secret homosexual who had recorded many of his sexual exploits in a series of notebooks. These were in the possession of the prosecution. Adopting Sullivan's defence strategy, a plea based on a legal technicality, would not allow the prosecution to introduce the diaries in evidence. Prodigious use was made of the 'Black Diaries' covertly, both before and after the trial, but they were not produced in the Old Bailey.[62]

Casement's trial, which opened on 26 June, was presided over by the lord chief justice, Viscount Reading (formerly Sir Rufus Isaacs—along with Lloyd George he had only recently survived the Marconi financial scandal), the bilious Mr Justice Horace Avory and Mr Justice Thomas Gardner Horridge. Leading for the prosecution was Sir Frederick Smith, successor to Sir Edward Carson as attorney general and almost as inveterate an opponent of Irish nationalism at the time of the Home Rule crisis. Smith (later Lord Birkenhead) summarised the Crown case in a brief opening statement and concluded:

> I have, I hope, outlined these facts without heat and without feeling. Neither, in my position, would be proper, and fortunately, neither is required. Rhetoric would be

misplaced, for the proved facts are more eloquent than words. The prisoner, blinded by a hatred to this country, as malignant in quality as it was sudden in origin, has played a desperate hazard. He had played it, and he has lost it. Today, the forfeit is claimed.

Witnesses were called who had been prisoners of war in the German camps from which Casement had hoped to recruit for his Irish Brigade. All identified him but also acknowledged that they had been told that they would not be fighting for Germany but for Ireland. A number of witnesses identified Casement as having landed at Banna Strand. Sullivan's cross-examination was, essentially, a humorous and redundant five-finger exercise. He might attempt to ridicule them, but he was not going to shake their testimony. One of the Kerry witnesses, John McCarthy, a local farmer in Curraghane, told the court how he had found the boat which had brought the prisoner ashore, at 4.00 a.m. on Good Friday. At that point he had been, according to his own story, up and about for two hours.

SULLIVAN:	Do you usually get up at two o'clock in the morning?
McCARTHY:	No.
SULLIVAN:	Or had you been to bed at all?
McCARTHY:	Yes.
SULLIVAN:	What got you up so early?
McCARTHY:	I went to a well
SULLIVAN:	Thirsty?
McCARTHY:	No.
SULLIVAN:	What brought you to the well?
McCARTHY:	To say a few prayers.
SULLIVAN:	Were you ever saying your prayers at the well before?
McCARTHY:	No.
SULLIVAN:	Is it a long way from your house?

McCARTHY: Over a mile.

SULLIVAN: A dark night, a pretty dark night, was it not?

McCARTHY: It was when I was leaving.

SULLIVAN: You left in the dark, having got up at two o'clock in the morning to say prayers at a well you had never been to before?

McCARTHY: Yes.

SULLIVAN: ... All your life you had been living at Curraghane, had you not?

McCARTHY: Yes

SULLIVAN: What urged you, was it your conscience, to get up at two o'clock in the morning?

McCARTHY: It was to say a few prayers.[63]

Sullivan, having come full circle, had been unable to shake the pious McCarthy or plant any doubts in the minds of the jurors. He continued jousting, ineffectually, with the witness and attempted a similar line of inquiry with Mary Gorman, a servant girl who had seen Casement walk past the gate of the house where she was employed, at 4.30 a.m. When he asked was she usually 'out and about at that time of the morning' she put him in his place by pointing out that 'my usual hour is four o'clock'.[64] After further evidence from a variety of police witnesses, Sullivan rose to enter a motion to have the indictment quashed. He argued that the allegation of treason was bad in law and that in order to secure a conviction, it was essential that Casement should have been in the king's realm when he attempted to persuade the Irish POWs to change allegiance.

The judges ruled otherwise. They held that, despite the arguments of Sullivan to the contrary, a treasonable offence committed by one of His Majesty's subjects was liable to trial under Common Law wherever that offence was committed. Sullivan's strategy, unpromising from the outset, was in tatters. Since no defence witnesses had been called, Sullivan claimed the right to make the closing address to the jury. However, as in the Emmet trial, where Plunket had intervened, Sullivan was trumped by the insistence of the Crown on having the last word. However, before he began his address, Sullivan indicated that the prisoner had some remarks he wished to make on his own behalf.

Casement's unsworn statement (as opposed to his later speech from the dock after he had been found guilty) began, according to H. Montgomery Hyde, 'in a considerable degree of nervous excitement, but his reading, though at times inaudible, showed a mixture of diffidence and courtesy. His hands were seen to tremble as he turned over the pages of the paper he held ... '.[65] He first dealt with some of the wilder accusations made about his activities in Germany, namely that he had told POWs they would be asked to fight for Turkey against Russia or that he had caused the rations of recalcitrant Irish prisoners to be reduced to starvation level. He also denied, as had Pearse, the availability of 'German gold'. It had been offered but the offers had been rejected. 'The rebellion was not made in Germany and ... not one penny of German gold went to finance it.'[66]

Sullivan's address to the jury, in the light of the failure of his own defence strategy, now shifted towards that originally advocated by his client. He brought the jury back to the passage of the Home Rule Bill and asked them to consider how they might have felt had they seen such a boon snatched away from them 'because those who disliked it were arming to resist the King and Commons, and to blow the Statute off the book with powder? ... You may lie down under it, but, if you are men, to arms! When all else fails, defend yourself'.[67] Listening to this diatribe against the threats from Ulster Unionism of the likes of Carson and Craig, was one of their most bullish English supporters, the attorney general. Smith intervened and Lord Reading agreed that Casement was raising issues not germane to the proceedings. There then followed a bizarre sequence of events in which Sullivan apologised somewhat too profusely to the court after altercations on two points of law. He then began to show signs of physical and psychological strain before collapsing back into his seat with an almost inaudible 'My Lords, I regret to say I have completely broken down'.[68] The trial was immediately adjourned until the following day when Artemus Jones, Casement's other defence counsel (both were juniors) was obliged to continue in Sullivan's stead.

In his concluding remarks Smith addressed the attack on pre-war Unionism launched by Sullivan. He contended that, once Germany

> was trying to destroy this country and trying to make an
> end of this Empire ... what honest citizen was thinking or
> talking of whether or not there might at some future day
> be resistance to the Home Rule Bill? From the moment
> that Germany made her tiger spring at the throat of

> Europe, I say from that moment, the past was the past in
> the eyes of every man who wished well for England.[69]

After reiterating the Crown allegation that 'German gold' was behind the
rebellion Smith concluded: 'If those facts taken together, his journey to
Germany, his speeches when in Germany, the inducements he held out to
these soldiers, the freedom which he there enjoyed, the cause which he
pursued in Ireland ... satisfy you of his guilt, you must give expression to
that view in your verdict'.[70]

The direction by the lord chief justice to the jury left them with little
alternative but to convict Casement. Reading observed that

> it does not need a very vivid imagination to see that if
> Germany could introduce arms and ammunition into
> Ireland for the purpose of helping to create a rebellion
> there, or strife of a serious character, so as to occupy the
> attention of the British Executive, and also to necessitate
> the maintaining of a considerable number of His Majesty's
> soldiers in Ireland, that would be assisting Germany.[71]

The jury took less than an hour to find Casement guilty of treason.

Casement now took advantage of the opportunity that had been denied
Pearse, MacDonagh and Connolly. In a lengthy apologia for the entire
Republican movement, ignoring the injunction that he outline why the sentence of the court should not be passed upon him, Casement spoke with
dignity, passion and some degree of nervousness at first, about the objectives
of the leadership of the Easter rising. Speaking in the aristocratic accent of the
English diplomat, he began by making clear who he was really addressing:

> My Lord Chief Justice, as I wish my words to reach a
> much wider audience than I see before me here, I intend
> to read all that I propose to say. What I shall read now is
> something I wrote more than twenty days ago. I may say,
> my lord, at once, that I protest against the jurisdiction of
> this court in my case on this charge, and the argument,
> that I am now going to read, is addressed not to this court,
> but to my own countrymen.
>
> There is an objection, possibly not good in law, but
> surely good on moral grounds, against the application to
> me here of this old English statute, 565 years old, that
> seeks to deprive an Irishman today of life and honour, not

for 'adhering to the King's enemies', but for adhering to his own people.

When this statute was passed, in 1351, what was the state of men's minds on the question of a far higher allegiance—that of a man to God and His kingdom? The law of that day did not permit a man to forsake his Church, or deny his God save with his life. The 'heretic', then, had the same doom as the 'traitor'.

Today a man may forswear God and His heavenly kingdom, without fear or penalty, all earlier statutes having gone the way of Nero's Edicts against the Christians, but that constitutional phantom 'the King' can still dig up from the dungeons and torture-chambers of the Dark Ages a law that takes a man's life and limb for an exercise of conscience.

If true religion rests on love, it is equally true that loyalty rests on love. The law that I am charged under has no parentage in love, and claims the allegiance of to-day on the ignorance and blindness of the past.

I am being tried, in truth, not by my peers of the live present, but by the peers of the dead past; not by the civilization of the twentieth century, but by the brutality of the fourteenth; not even by a statute framed in the language of an enemy land[72]—so antiquated is the law that must be sought to-day to slay an Irishman, whose offence is that he puts Ireland first.

Loyalty is a sentiment, not a law. It rests on love, not on restraint. The government of Ireland by England rests on restraint, and not on law; and since it demands no love, it can evoke no loyalty ...

... If I did wrong in making that appeal to Irishmen to join with me in an effort to fight for Ireland, it is by Irishmen, and by them alone, I can be rightfully judged. From this court and its jurisdiction I appeal to those I am alleged to have wronged, and to those I am alleged to have injured by my 'evil example' and claim that they alone are competent to decide my guilt or innocence. If they find me guilty, the statute may affix the penalty, but the statute does not override or annul my right to seek judgment at their hands.

This is so fundamental a right, so natural a right, so obvious a right, that it is clear that the Crown were aware of it when they brought me by force and by stealth from Ireland to this country. It was not I who landed in England, but the Crown who dragged me here, away from my own country to which I had returned with a price upon my head, away from my own countrymen whose loyalty is not in doubt, and safe from the judgment of my peers whose judgment I do not shrink from. I admit no other judgment but theirs. I accept no verdict save at their hands. I assert from this dock that I am being tried here, not because it is just, but because it is unjust. Place me before a jury of my own countrymen, be it Protestant or Catholic, Unionist or Nationalist, Sinn Féineach or Orangemen, and I shall accept the verdict, and bow to the statute and all its penalties. But I shall accept no meaner finding against me, than that of those, whose loyalty I endanger by my example, and to whom alone I made appeal. If they adjudge me guilty, then guilty I am. It is not I who am afraid of their verdict—it is the Crown. If this is not so, why fear the test? I fear it not. I demand it as my right.

Casement then retraced the steps of Sullivan in his condemnation of British Conservative Unionism, ('an English party whose sole interest in our country lay in its oppression') its collaboration with loyalist intransigence in Ulster during the Home Rule crisis, and Liberal pusillanimity in the face of that combination. The perceived Unionist threat, in Casement's eyes, justified negotiation with Germany, 'it was our bounden duty to get arms before all else ... If, as the right honourable gentleman, the present Attorney-General, asserted in a speech at Manchester, Nationalists would neither fight for Home Rule nor pay for it, it was our duty to show him that we knew how to do both'. The money subscribed to this cause, he asserted, 'was Irish gold'.

His peroration was, arguably, the finest Republican valedictory since that of Emmet more than a century before:

We have been told, we have been asked to hope, that after this war Ireland will get Home Rule, as a reward for the lifeblood shed in a cause which, whoever else its success may benefit, can surely not benefit Ireland. And what will Home Rule be in return for what its vague promise has taken, and still hopes to take away from Ireland? It is not necessary to climb the painful stairs of Irish history—that treadmill of a nation, whose labours are as vain for her own uplifting as the convict's exertions are for his redemption, to review the long list of British promises made only to be broken—of Irish hopes, raised only to be dashed to the ground. Home Rule, when it comes, if come it does, will find an Ireland drained of all that is vital to its very existence unless it be that unquenchable hope we build on the graves of the dead.

We are told that if Irishmen go by the thousand to die, not for Ireland, but for Flanders, for Belgium, for a patch of sand in the deserts of Mesopotamia, or a rocky trench on the heights of Gallipoli, they are winning self-government for Ireland. But if they dare to lay down their lives on their native soil, if they dare to dream even that freedom can be won only at home by men resolved to fight for it there, then they are traitors to their country, and their dream and their deaths are phases of a dishonourable phantasy [sic]. But history is not so recorded in other lands. In Ireland alone, in this twentieth century, is loyalty held to be a crime. If loyalty be something less than love and more than law, then we have had enough of such loyalty for Ireland and Irishmen. If we are to be indicted as criminals, to be shot as murderers, to be imprisoned as convicts, because our offence is that we love Ireland more than we value our lives, then I do not know what virtue resides in any offer of self-government held out to brave men on such terms.

Self-government is our right, a thing born in us at birth, a thing no more to be doled out to us, or withheld from us, by another people, than the right to life itself— than the right to feel the sun, or smell the flowers, or to love our kind. It is only from the convict these things are withheld, for crime committed and proven, and Ireland, that has wronged no man, that has injured no land, that has sought no dominion over others—Ireland is treated today among the nations of the world as if she were a convicted criminal. If it be treason to fight against such an unnatural fate as this, then I am proud to be a rebel, and shall cling to my 'rebellion' with the last drop of my blood. If there be no right of rebellion against the state of things that no savage tribe would endure without resistance, then I am sure that it is better for men to fight and die without right than to live in such a state of right as this. Where all your rights have become only an accumulated wrong; where men must beg with bated breath for leave to subsist in their own land, to think their own thoughts, to sing their own songs, to garner the fruits of their own labours—and, even while they beg, to see things inexorably withdrawn from them—then, surely, it is a braver, a saner and truer thing to be a rebel, in act and in deed, against such circumstances as these, than to tamely accept it, as the natural lot of men.

My lord, I have done. Gentlemen of the jury, I wish to thank you for your verdict. I hope you will not take amiss what I said, or think that I have made any imputation upon your truthfulness or your integrity when I spoke and said that this was not a trial by my peers. I maintain that I have a natural right to be tried in that natural jurisdiction, Ireland, my own country, and I would put it to you, how would you feel in the converse case, or rather how would all men here feel in the converse case, if an Englishman had landed here in England and the Crown or the government, for its own purposes, had conveyed him secretly from England to Ireland under a false name, committed him to prison under a false name, and brought him before a tribunal in Ireland under a statute which they knew involved a trial before an Irish jury? How would you feel yourselves as Englishmen if that man was to be submitted to trial by jury in a land inflamed against him and believing him to be a criminal, when his only crime was that he had cared for England more than for Ireland?[73]

Casement's final speech would have a profound impact far beyond the Old Bailey and the Irish audience for which it was intended. The Indian nationalist and future dynastic leader Pandit Nehru described it as 'extraordinarily moving and eloquent ... it seemed to point out exactly how a subject nation should feel'.[74] The sentencing of Casement had a surreal quality to it. The length of the speech from the dock meant that the court tipstaffs who had been holding three black caps for the judges to wear when they pronounced sentence had grown tired on that hot June day. The black caps were, accordingly, set at inappropriately rakish angles when the time came for Reading to pass sentence. A failed appeal delayed Casement's execution and allowed a head of steam to build up in a campaign to have him reprieved. It was during this period that tactical use was made of the Black Diaries in order to influence newspaper coverage against Casement and dampen the enthusiasm of actual and potential supporters (such as John Redmond and George Bernard Shaw[75]).

Casement was hanged in Pentonville Prison on 3 August 1916. As with the other leaders of the Easter Rising, his body was buried in quicklime in the prison cemetery. In 1965, a year before the country commemorated the fiftieth anniversary of the Rising, Casement's body was repatriated and interred in Glasnevin Cemetery in Dublin. He was afforded a state funeral which was attended by President Eamon de Valera, the last surviving commandant of Easter week.

'A STREAM OF BLOOD COMING FROM BENEATH A CLOSED DOOR'[76]

It must, however, be borne in mind that from the moment the rebellion was crushed the question of punishment was a political and not a military question, and if the Cabinet had decided on a policy to counteract the feeble parody of government that had existed in Ireland for the past nine years, it was for them to inform and instruct the soldier who saved the situation for them.[77]

(Sir Nevil Macready, adjutant general,
Annals of an active life)

> I went down some of the back streets. Here and there
> people cursed me openly, frankly, and cursed all like me,
> strangers in their city.[78]
>
> (Canadian journalist, F.A. McKenzie, *The*
> *Irish rebellion, what happened and why*)

General Sir John Maxwell, became the sacrificial scapegoat[79] of the British government for military decisions made with tacit political approval. Because of the extreme reaction to the 1916 executions, which set in motion a sequence of events leading to independence in 1922, he has become known as 'The Man Who Lost Ireland'.[80] The invidious title belies the fact that Maxwell had few illusions about the long terms effects of his punitive measures. There were anecdotal examples and RIC evidence of a groundswell of support for the Rising around the country. This was reflected in an increased incidence of memorial Masses, a growth in sales of photographs of the leaders, the establishment of aid funds for families, the appearance of songs and ballads glorifying the conflict. A further and more significant straw in the wind, at least as far as the military was concerned, was that recruitment came to a virtual standstill other than in Ulster. This was also true of Irish communities in colonies like Australia.

Maxwell recognised that 'the first results of the punishments inflicted were good ... The majority of people recognised that they were not excessive ... [then] ... a revulsion of feeling had set in'.[81] Writing in June 1916, Maxwell, with a level of political sophistication and an historical perspective not universal among his peers (see Macready below), blamed the rebellion on the accommodation over a lengthy period of the demands of Carson and the Ulster Volunteers.

> It is becoming increasingly difficult [he wrote wistfully]
> to tell the difference between a Nationalist and a Sinn
> Feiner ... If there was a General Election, very few if any,
> of the existing Nationalist MPs would be re-elected so
> there is a danger that Mr. Redmond's party would be
> replaced by others perhaps less amenable to reason.[82]

However, to some degree, while Maxwell could discern the growing resentment of the population 'he was reluctant to attribute that antipathy to his own policies'.[83] The new chief secretary, Henry Duke[84] put a figure on the level of disenchantment on 19 September 1916 when he told the Cabinet ... 'three quarters of the population are more or less sore and embittered'.[85]

While Maxwell, as 1916 chronicler Charles Townshend puts it, 'has not received a good press, he cannot be held entirely responsible for British policy'.[86] He dealt in ineluctable facts (the guilt of Volunteers who had taken up arms with financial support from the German enemy) not in political nuance. The ramifications of his policies were of less concern to him than stabilisation of the military situation and avoiding a recrudescence of rebellion by wiping out the command structure of the rebels. Contrary to popular myth he was not a grim, blimpish martinet. While William Wylie expressed himself uncertain of Maxwell's status as a soldier 'he certainly was a clever man, broadminded and open to argument'.[87] The future president of the Executive Council (Taoiseach), William T. Cosgrave, who had fought at the South Dublin Union, accepted that 'there was probably not one "innocent" man brought up for Courtmartial'.[88] For the literal-minded Maxwell this constituted sufficient grounds for taking the action he did. But, as Roy Foster has put it, while 'the case in law, given the German connection, was conclusive for the death penalty ... in the circumstances of Ireland during 1916, the decision against commutation was inflammatory'.[89]

The least that can be said about Maxwell is that, despite his inadequacies, he displayed considerably more political *nous* than would have been the case with certain other potential military commanders. In 1929, in his autobiography, Sir Nevil Macready wrote that, as he saw it, there had only been two courses open to Britain after the defeat of the rebels,

> ruthless repression carried to a logical conclusion, or conciliation embracing the relinquishment of the death penalty coupled with the instant application of the Military Service Act to Ireland. Had the latter course been taken without hesitation, it would, so I have since been told by many Irishmen, have proved successful from a recruiting point of view, and have been accepted by the country at large.[90]

Intense Irish resistance to conscription in 1918, a campaign which united the Parliamentary Party and Sinn Féin, suggests that Macready was woefully misinformed by his many Irish friends.

According to the Canadian journalist, F.A. McKenzie, who had covered the Rising, support for the rebels did not just magically appear in the wake of the executions. 'I have read many accounts of public feeling in Dublin in these days,' he wrote in 1916 in *The Irish rebellion, what happened and why*, one of the first 'instant' insider books on the subject.

They are all agreed that the open and strong sympathy of the mass of the population was with the British troops. That this was so in the better parts of the city, I have no doubt, but certainly what I myself saw in the poorer districts did not confirm this. It rather indicated that there was a vast amount of sympathy with the rebels, particularly after the rebels were defeated. The sentence of the Courts Martial deepened this sympathy.[91]

While there was undoubtedly some support in the city for the 1916 rebels, most of the Dublin populace was at best ambiguous or simply downright hostile. Ernie O'Malley, later Officer Commanding (OC) the 2nd Southern Division of the IRA during the War of Independence, was a young medical student when hostilities broke out. The arc of his reaction was not untypical. He began with a mixture of curiosity and indifference but the executions filled him with a sense of vengeful rage. Before the courts martial and the executions 'The bitterness of the people against the Volunteers was tinged with a little admiration. They had fought well against the regular troops. Many hoped they would all be hanged or shot, and said so to everyone they met ... my friends were all hostile to the spirit of the Rising'.[92] But by the middle of May, especially in the wake of the execution of Connolly, he notes in his autobiography *On another man's wound* that 'Something strange stirred in the people, some feeling long since buried, a sense of communion with the fighting dead generations, for the dead walked round again'.[93]

Poetic hyperbole aside O'Malley was reflecting a growing volume of anti-English sentiment based not just on the execution of the leaders of the insurrection. There was anger in Dublin at incidents like the judicial murder of the pacifist and maverick Francis Sheehy Skeffington on the orders of a deranged British officer, Bowen Colthurst.[94] There was fury at allegations that soldiers had fired on and killed civilians on North King Street and at the perception of wanton and unnecessary infrastructural damage to the city.[95] In addition, the country-wide arrests, amounting to more than 3,000, and detentions, had, inevitably, included the arrest of a number of people whose connection to the Rising or the IRB was tenuous. There was also growing sympathy and admiration for the executed leaders. Much of this derived from the proliferation of rumours about the dignified manner in which they had gone to their deaths and the distribution of leaflets and pamphlets containing their, alleged, valedictory addresses to their courts martial. The tragic romance of the marriage of Joseph Plunkett to Grace Gifford in Kilmainham hours before his death, excited compassion in the same degree as the brutal nature of Connolly's death inspired nausea and resentment.

The growing consensus was neatly encapsulated in the writing of a distinguished exiled Dubliner, George Bernard Shaw:

> My own view is that the men who were shot in cold blood, after their capture or surrender, were prisoners of war, and that it was, therefore, entirely incorrect to slaughter them ... I remain an Irishman and am bound to contradict any implication that I can regard as a traitor any Irishman taken in a fight for Irish independence against the British government, which was a fair fight in everything except the enormous odds my countrymen had to face.[96]

However, the Rising had not just forced a reassessment of political attitudes on the part of a significant majority of the Irish people, it also led to a re-evaluation by the Volunteers of the feasibility and advisability of open, armed conflict. An order, in 1917, from the reconstituted executive of the organisation, which included a young IRB member and GPO veteran, Michael Collins, stipulated that the Volunteer leadership would 'not issue an order to take to the field until they consider that the force is in a position to wage war on the enemy with reasonable hopes of success. Volunteers as a whole may consequently rest assured that they will not be called upon to take part in any forlorn hope'.[97] It was a clear, posthumous, reproach to the leadership of the Rising who had, according to Collins 'bungled terribly, costing many a good life'. As prologue to the type of warfare that would characterise the War of Independence the utilitarian Collins had written that armed rebellion 'was not an appropriate time for memoranda couched in poetic phrases, or actions worked out in similar fashion'.[98] The Rising, had served its purpose, as a 'gesture of moral revivalism',[99] however, for the military pragmatists of 1919–21 it 'was to be revered but not to be repeated.[100]

In an ironic twist of nomenclature the rising, thanks to the manner in which it was reported and the ignorance on the part of the British military of the subtleties of Irish politics, became associated with Sinn Féin. That misapplication ultimately became a self-fulfilling and unifying phenomenon. Of course it was a quite different Sinn Féin from the pre-1916 model, now led by Eamon de Valera, which swept aside the Irish Parliamentary Party in the December election of 1918. Casement, for whom Sinn Féin was 'the cause closest to his heart'[101] had not been able to prevent Pearse from taking to the streets of Dublin on 24 April 1916. He had been excluded from the IRB cabal (his biographer, Brian Inglis refers to it as a'junta') that had planned the insurrection. But the undue credit gained from the event by Sinn Féin might have afforded his spirit a measure of grim satisfaction.

AFTERWORD

By Gor! 'tis the same law the whole time. The same dirty
English law. No change at all.[1]

(The Bull McCabe, in *The field*, John B. Keane)

'It is hereby declared that the ordinary courts are inadequate to secure the
effective administration of justice and the preservation of public peace and
order'.[2] A proclamation of William E. Forster perhaps? Or the sentiments
of Arthur Balfour as he grappled with agrarian unrest? Neither, as it
happens. The words are from Section 8(1) of the Criminal Justice
(Amendment) Act, 2009. The recently promulgated legislation is designed
to tackle the problem of criminal gangs in Ireland and introduce the new
offence of the direction of a 'criminal organisation'. The new law proposes
to dispense with jury trials in cases of gangland crime and replace them
with a special three-judge court. The stated object of this particular provi-
sion is to eliminate the possibility of jury tampering. As readers of this
volume will know, we have been here before. Forster and Balfour would
have approved wholeheartedly. They would also have applauded the
notion of a member of the Garda Síochána, of any rank, being allowed to
testify as to his or her 'opinion' regarding the existence of a criminal organisation.[3] However, Forster at least, might have doubted his ability to
shepherd such legislation intact through Cabinet and the House of
Commons in the late nineteenth century.

It is ironic that, in the light of such legislative measures as the Criminal
Justice (Amendment) Act, 2009, and of the findings of the Morris Tribunal
in relation to abuse of process by Garda officers in Co. Donegal, self-gov-
erned twenty-first century Ireland has little to teach its nineteenth century
equivalent, ruled from London, about civil liberties. From the perspective
of the guardians of the law there is precious little to choose between the
murderous gangs of modern, urban Ireland and the Ribbon/Fenian activists
of its rural, Victorian predecessor. The terminology of the 2009 legislation
could just as easily have been used to describe some of the informal agrarian secret societies of the Tithe or Land War eras. A 'structured group', i.e.
a gang, under the 2009 legislation, requires no 'formal rules or formal
membership, or any formal roles for those involved in the group'. Neither
does it require any 'hierarchical or leadership structure' or 'continuity of
involvement by persons in the group'.[4] Just as certain latter day criminal
elements are deemed ungovernable under ordinary law so were certain

unruly political and agrarian elements deemed to be out of control in the nineteenth and early twentieth centuries. As a consequence a set of actions deemed appropriate by the authorities was set in train. The ruler may have changed but the rules, it would appear, have not.

In 1843 the *Nation* commented starkly that, 'in no country is the law so hated as in Ireland ... A code enacted by foreigners, to be enforced by an alien aristocracy for their own profit, and for the protection of an unpopular church, was, and is, disrespected'.[5] It is a cliché, but a truism nonetheless, that disrespect for authority and the law has not entirely disappeared from the Irish psyche as we approach a century of legislative independence. In John B. Keane's play, *The field,* set in rural Ireland in the 1960s, the main protagonist, the Bull McCabe, heir to the Ribbon tradition and determined to secure a field of 'three acres, one rood and thirty-two perches' manifests his contempt for the law when he is questioned by the parish priest, the emblematic Father Murphy; and the local sergeant. The Bull rounds on these symbols of the authority of church and state. 'You have the law well sewn up, all of you ... all nice and tidy to yourselves,' he informs them.[6] To the Bull, the uniforms and the accents of the authority figures in his rural community may have been different to those of the nineteenth century but the song remained the same. The law still existed for the protection of the privileged. The disadvantaged were denied access or a proper hearing just as they were under the regime of the magistrates.

It is tempting to ascribe this sense of alienation to the folk memory of the incarceration of O'Connell, the hanging of the innocent Myles Joyce, the treachery of MacNally or the arrogance of the *Times*. The high profile cases discussed in the preceding pages left, no doubt, a lasting impact on the Irish collective memory. But the basis of Irish antipathy to laws framed in London at the behest of a power whose authority was contested, and often enforced by an aristocratic 'garrison', can be discerned at a much lower level than the Commission Court. Irish aversion to laws protective of a propertied and moneyed class began at entry level, at the Petty Sessions and Assizes, where their landlords became their judges.

During the 'long nineteenth century' Ireland was rarely a party to the politics of acquiescence. Containment rather than good governance was often a priority for British administrations. Ireland may have been an integral part of a legislative Union but it was frequently governed like an unruly colony. And, at crucial points during the 'long nineteenth century', it was precisely that. In the context of a properly functioning and fully consensual Union the ideal would have been the extension of the common law to Ireland, in spite of its roots in a radically different society. The reality was a legal structure characterised by legislative exceptionalism and procedural manipulation. It is hard to see how it could have been otherwise.

The current Irish coalition government, not to mention ordinary citizens living in fear in urban enclaves, might have some retrospective sympathy for British administrations attempting to manage the unmanageable. Once the issue of the contested legitimacy of British rule in Ireland is separated from the phenomenon of political/agrarian 'criminal' activities conducted under the Union, the circumstances, on some levels, are not dissimilar. While there is a world of difference between modern criminal gangs without altruistic or ulterior political motivation, and crimes that emanated more directly from a sense of social, economic, cultural or political oppression, the framers and enforcers of the law might well find it difficult to make that distinction. In the context of a challenge to the state and the rule of law by arrogant criminal elements, supporters of the Criminal Justice (Amendment) Bill, 2009, might well ask themselves would they have dealt much differently with the Whiteboys?

ENDNOTES

Introduction

[1] Oscar Wilde, *Ballad of Reading Gaol and other writings* (London, 1999).

[2] From a House of Commons speech by Burke given in 1775 see Edmund Burke, *On conciliation with America* (London, 1912).

[3] Matthias McDonnell Bodkin, *Famous Irish trials* (Dublin, 1918), x.

[4] The 'long nineteenth century' was defined by Eric Hobsbawm as 1789–1914.

[5] Clifford Lloyd, *Ireland under the Land League* (Edinburgh, 1882), 51.

[6] Lloyd, *Ireland under the Land League*, 43–4.

[7] Mark Finnane, 'Irish crime without the outrage', in N.M. Dawson (ed.), *Reflections on law and history: Irish Legal History Society discourses and other papers, 2000-2005* (Dublin, 2006), 204.

[8] Maurice Healy, *The old Munster circuit* (London, 1939), 13.

[9] Penny Bonsal, *The Irish RMs: the resident magistrates in the British administration of Ireland* (Dublin, n.d.), 17.

[10] Seán McConville, *Irish political prisoners, 1848-1922* (London, 2003), 3.

[11] E. Dwyer Gray, *The treatment of political prisoners in Ireland* (Dublin, 1889), 8— Gray should not be confused with his late father of the same name, also editor/proprietor of the *Freeman*.

[12] Gray, *Political prisoners*, 7.

[13] The Repeal Association leaders, Daniel O'Connell, Thomas Matthew Ray and Thomas Steele; and the newspaper editors John Gray, Charles Gavan Duffy (of the *Nation*) and Richard Barrett (of the *Pilot*).

[14] George H. Knott, *Trial of Sir Roger Casement* (Edinburgh/London, 1917), 200.

[15] Journalist and Chartist Feargus O'Connor was jailed for seditious libel in 1840 and John Frost, the Welsh radical, was sentenced to be hanged drawn and quartered for his part in a violent encounter in Newport, South Wales, in 1839. Like those of the Young Ireland leaders the sentence was commuted to one of transportation.

[16] R. Barry O'Brien, *Dublin Castle and the Irish people* (London, 1912), 146.

[17] Daire Hogan, *The legal profession in Ireland, 1789-1922* (Dublin, 1996), 3.

[18] As was the norm at the time the case, *Queen V Hynes*, had been transferred, under new coercion legislation, to Dublin in anticipation of the difficulty of securing a conviction in Clare.

[19] McDonnell Bodkin, *Famous Irish trials*, 157.

[20] Barry later presided over the Maamtrasna trials where there was no issue with judicial partiality but with the malfeasance of the Crown prosecutors.

[21] Healy, *The old Munster circuit*, 29.

[22] A generic name for members of an agrarian secret society.

[23] Patrick Geoghegan, *King Dan: the rise of Daniel O'Connell 1775-1829* (Dublin, 2008), 2.

[24] Frank Callanan, 'T.M. Healy: the politics of advocacy', in Dawson, *Reflections on law and history*, 56.

[25] Bonsal, *The Irish RMs*, 11.

[26] Bonsal, *The Irish RMs*, 11.

[27] Bonsal, *The Irish RMs*, 16.

[28] Ian Bridgeman, 'The constabulary and the criminal justice system in nineteenth century Ireland', in Ian O'Donnell and Finbarr McAuley (eds), *Criminal justice history: themes and controversies from pre-independence Ireland* (Dublin, 2003), 127.

[29] House of Commons Debates, vol. 72, cols 689–90, 13 February 1844.

[30] W. Torrens McCullagh, *Memoirs of the Right Honourable Richard Lalor Sheil* (2 vols, London, 1855), vol. ii, 340.

[31] State Trials Committee, *Reports of State Trials*, New Series (London, 1896) vol. VII 1848–1850, see Queen V Smith O'Brien.

[32] Thomas Keneally, *The great shame* (London, 1998), 179.

[33] Bridgeman, 'The constabulary and the criminal justice system', 127–8.

[34] *Freeman's Journal*, 25 January 1881.

Chapter one

[1] Thomas Moore, *Melodies* (London, 1808).

[2] Robert Southey, *Written immediately after reading the speech of Robert Emmet* (London, 1803).

[3] Thomas Bartlett, 'The life and opinions of Leonard MacNally (1752–1820): playwright, barrister, United Irishman and informer', in Myles Dungan (ed.), *Speaking ill of the dead* (Dublin, 2007), 11.

[4] Michael MacDonagh, *The viceroy's post-bag* (London, 1904), 396—as this gesture was, conveniently, to become 'the Judas kiss' many historians treat the veracity of the anecdote with caution.

[5] So described by Charles Phillips (biographer of Curran)—cited in Patrick Geoghegan, *Robert Emmet, a life* (Dublin, 2004), 19.

[6] MacNally's account of the conversation was self-serving and must be treated with more than a healthy dose of scepticism.

[7] W. Cobbett (ed.), *Cobbett's political register* (London, 1804), vol. v, 893.

[8] Marianne Elliott, *Robert Emmet: the making of a legend* (London, 2003), 102.

[9] *Annual register* (London, 1803), 211—House of Commons, William Windham in response to Lord Castlereagh.

[10] Oliver MacDonagh, 'Introduction—Ireland and the Union, 1801–70', in W.E. Vaughan (ed.), *A new history of Ireland* (9 vols, Oxford, 1989), vol. 5, xlvii.

[11] S.J. Connolly, 'Aftermath and adjustment', in Vaughan, *New history*, 8.

[12] Preliminary articles of peace followed in October 1801. The Treaty of Amiens was signed in March 1802. Anglo–French hostilities resumed in 1803. (Amiens St in Dublin was named to celebrate the treaty.)

[13] M. MacDonagh, *Viceroy's post-bag*, 254.

[14] M. MacDonagh, *Viceroy's post-bag*, 253.

[15] Geoghegan, *Robert Emmet*, 70.

[16] Geoghegan, *Robert Emmet*, 63.

[17] R.R. Madden, *The United Irishmen, their lives and times* (New York, n.d.), 297.

[18] M. MacDonagh, *Viceroy's post-bag*, 279—the description was obtained by Major Sirr from Thomas Elrington, Emmet's maths tutor at Trinity College Dublin.

[19] Miles Byrne, *The memoirs of Miles Byrne* (2 vols, Dublin, 1907), vol. 1, 263.

[20] Byrne, *Memoirs*, vol. 1, 264.

[21] Byrne, *Memoirs*, vol. 1, 269.

[22] Emmet met the first consul and Talleyrand in Paris in 1801.

[23] M. MacDonagh, *Viceroy's post-bag*, 278.

[24] M. MacDonagh, *Viceroy's post-bag*, 273.

[25] M. MacDonagh, *Viceroy's post-bag*, 279.

[26] M. MacDonagh, *Viceroy's post-bag*, 281–2.

[27] Geoghegan, *Robert Emmet*, 154.

[28] National Archives of Ireland (NAI), Rebellion papers, 620/12/155/5.

[29] M. MacDonagh, *Viceroy's post-bag*, 291.

[30] NAI, Rebellion papers, 620/11/134.

[31] Described by one chronicler as 'one of the most humane dispensers of the law in a rather brutal age' (M. MacDonagh, *Viceroy's post-bag*, 293).

[32] Geoghegan, *Robert Emmet*, 182.

[33] Byrne, *Memoirs*, vol. 1, 285.

[34] Oliver MacDonagh, *The hereditary bondsman: Daniel O'Connell 1775–1829* (London, 1988), 94. As a member of the Lawyers Artillery Corps, O'Connell was called up to assist in yeomanry searches for rebels after 23 July 1803.

[35] Elliott, *Robert Emmet*, 103.

[36] Alexander Marsden to Lord Pelham, 23 July 1804, in M. MacDonagh, *Viceroy's post-bag*, 294.

[37] Lord Hardwicke to Charles Yorke, 24 and 26 July 1803, in M. MacDonagh, *Viceroy's post-bag*, 302.

[38] Yorke to Hardwicke, 2 August 1803, in M. MacDonagh, *Viceroy's post-bag*, 303.

[39] *Annual register* (1803), 210–11.

[40] Thomas Bartlett, '"The cause of treason seems to have gone out of fashion in Ireland": Dublin Castle and Robert Emmet', in Anne Dolan, Patrick Geoghegan

and Darryl Jones (eds), *Reinterpreting Emmet: essays on the life and legacy of Robert Emmet* (Dublin, 2007), 16.

[41] M. MacDonagh, *Viceroy's post-bag*, 339.

[42] M. MacDonagh, *Viceroy's post-bag*, 340.

[43] NAI, Rebellion papers, 620/11/132.

[44] M. MacDonagh, *Viceroy's post-bag*, 347–51 and NAI, Rebellion papers, 620/11/132.]

[45] Sarah Curran would only outlive Emmet by five years. Letters sent to friends in Cork (Anne and Bessie Penrose) towards the end of her short life refer to her 'fruitless grief over a past sorrow' and the birth and early death of her only child in January 1808. (National Library of Ireland (NLI), MS. 8,326/1, Sarah Sturgeon to Anne Penrose)—she herself died of TB in May 1808.

[46] M. MacDonagh, *Viceroy's post-bag*, 389–90

[47] Geoghegan, *Robert Emmet*, 214.

[48] Thomas Russell had, unsuccessfully attempted to raise a convincing force in Antrim and Down. He was subsequently executed.

[49] Geoghegan, *Robert Emmet*, 226.

[50] Ruán O'Donnell, in his biography of Emmet, claims that Burrowes was also circumscribed by his attempt to distance himself from his defence of United Irish suspects and was a low-level agent of the castle. Given MacNally's record, therefore, 'the government possessed two excellent, cross referenced sources as to Emmet's planned defence and his comments relating to the trial' (Ruán O'Donnell, *Robert Emmet and the Rising of 1803* (Dublin, 2003), 155.

[51] Geoghegan, *Robert Emmet*, 229.

[52] Maeve Ryan, '"The reptile that had stung me": William Plunket and the trial of Robert Emmet', in Dolan *et al.*, *Reinterpreting Emmet*.

[53] William Ridgeway, *A report of the proceedings in cases of high treason in a court of oyer and terminer* (Dublin, 1803), 11–33.

[54] R.R. Madden, *The life and times of Robert Emmet* (New York, 1896), 178–84.

[55] Ridgeway, *Cases of high treason*, 79–92.

[56] The definition of treason under a statute of King Edward III.

[57] Ryan, 'William Plunket and the trial of Robert Emmet', 78, 80.

[58] Ridgeway, *Cases of high treason*, 79–92.

[59] Geoghegan, *Robert Emmet*, 241.

[60] Ryan, 'William Plunket', 83.

[61] M. MacDonagh, *Viceroy's post-bag*, 398.

[62] Ryan, 'William Plunket', 81.

[63] Ridgeway, *Cases of high treason*, 95.

[64] For an analysis of the different versions in circulation through the nineteenth century see R.N.C. Vance, 'Text and tradition: Robert Emmet's speech from the dock', *Studies* 71 (1982), 185–91.

[65] Vance, 'Text and tradition', 186.

[66] As with the other speeches some minor changes, cosmetic and grammatical, have been made in punctuation and layout. The speech has also been edited (where shown) for reasons of space.

[67] Where text within the trial extracts is added by this author it is denoted in italic enclosed in square brackets. Comments/asides present in the original edition remain in roman.

[68] Christopher Temple Emmet, known in the family as 'Temple' who died at the age of 27.

[69] Trinity College Dublin.

[70] Ridgeway, *Cases of high treason*, 96–100.

[71] Madden, *Robert Emmet*, 191–2.

[72] Ridgeway, *Cases of high treason*, 101.

[73] Madden, *Robert Emmet*, 192–4.

[74] R.R. Madden, *The life and times of Robert Emmet* (New York, 1896), 178–84.

[75] Writing to his brother, now home secretary, Hardwicke observed that 'He was more than once interrupted by the Judge, and was prevented from proceeding to the conclusion of his speech, which appeared rather calculated to excite the indignation than the pity of those who were present' (M. MacDonagh, *Viceroy's post-bag*, 398).

[76] Elliott, *Robert Emmet*, 96.

[77] NLI, MS. 4,597, R. Rainey to 'Frank', 18–20 September 1803.

[78] Geoghegan, *Robert Emmet*, 266.

[79] Elliott, *Robert Emmet*, 98.

[80] See note 57 above.

[81] Adrian Hardiman, 'The trial of Robert Emmet', in Dolan *et al.*, *Reinterpreting Emmet*, 238.

[82] Hardiman, 'The trial of Emmet', 239.

[83] Hardiman, 'The trial of Emmet', 238–40.

[84] Elliott, *Robert Emmet*, 78.

[85] Hardiman, 'The trial of Emmet', 227.

[86] See note 73 above.

[87] Hardiman, 'The trial of Emmet', 228.

[88] Ridgeway, *Cases of high treason*, 78.

[89] Two other treason trials had ended in acquittal as a consequence of vigorous cross-examination by defence counsel (Hardiman, 'The trial of Emmet', 237).

[90] Hardiman, 'The trial of Emmet', 236.

[91] See Ruán O'Donnell on Burrowes above *Robert Emmet and the Rising*, 155.

[92] Elliott, *Robert Emmet*, 104.

[93] Elliott, *Robert Emmet*, 113–14.

[94] As recounted by Patrick Geoghegan in his prologue, *Robert Emmet*, xix.

Chapter 2

[1] Alexander Andrews (ed.), *Chapters in the history of British journalism* (London, 1998), 5.

[2] Tobias Smollett, *The expedition of Humphrey Clinker* (London, 1771; repr. Oxford, 1998), 205.

[3] *Dublin Evening Post*, 16 July 1813.

[4] Donal McCartney, *The world of Daniel O'Connell* (Dublin, 1980), 2.

[5] Geoghegan, *King Dan*, 47.

[6] S.J. Connolly, 'The Catholic question: 1801–12', in Vaughan, *New history*, vol. 5, 26.

[7] O. MacDonagh, *The hereditary bondsman*, 93.

[8] Connolly, 'The Catholic question', 26.

[9] O. MacDonagh, *The hereditary bondsman*, 113.

[10] [Denys Scully], *A statement of the Penal Laws which aggrieve the Catholics of Ireland* (2 vols, Dublin, 1812).

[11] *The trial of John Magee, proprietor of the Dublin Evening Post, for publishing an historical review of the duke of Richmond's administration in Ireland* (Dublin, 1813), xxxiv.

[12] The *Dublin Journal* at its lowest ebb.

[13] The *Correspondent* in its heyday when it had untrammelled access to the government 'expresses'.

[14] Brian Inglis, *The freedom of the press in Ireland, 1784–1841* (London, 1954), 114.

[15] Stephen J.M. Brown, *The press in Ireland* (New York, 1971), 21–3.

[16] Brown, *Press in Ireland*, 23.

[17] Inglis, *Freedom of the press in Ireland*, 121.

[18] Inglis, *Freedom of the press in Ireland*, 113.

[19] Inglis, *Freedom of the press in Ireland*, 115.

[20] Stephen Koss, *The rise and fall of the political press in Britain* (London, 1981), 33.

[21] Inglis, *Freedom of the press in Ireland*, 128.

[22] Inglis, *Freedom of the press in Ireland*, 129.

[23] Hugh Oram, *The newspaper book: a history of newspapers in Ireland, 1649–1983* (Dublin, 1983), 40.

[24] Inglis, *Freedom of the press in Ireland*, 120.

[25] Inglis, *Freedom of the press in Ireland*, 134.

[26] *Dublin Evening Post*, 5 January 1813.

[27] O. MacDonagh, *The hereditary bondsman*, 120.

[28] *Dublin Evening Post*, 3 June 1813.

[29] Robert Dunlop, *Daniel O'Connell and the revival of national life in Ireland* (London, 1900), 61.

[30] O. MacDonagh, *The hereditary bondsman*, 118.

[31] C.M. O'Keeffe, *Life and times of Daniel O'Connell* (2 vols, Dublin, 1864), vol. 1, 297.

[32] O'Keeffe, *Life and times of O'Connell*, vol. 1, 309/10.

[33] Geoghegan, *King Dan*, 84.

[34] Inglis, *Freedom of the press in Ireland*, 136.

[35] Dunlop, *Daniel O'Connell*, 63.

[36] O'Keeffe, *Life and times of O'Connell*, vol. 1, 284.

[37] *The trial of John Magee*, 58.

[38] *The trial of John Magee*, 60–73.

[39] Geoghegan, *King Dan*, 126.

[40] Geoghegan, *King Dan*, 127.

[41] O'Keeffe, *Life and times of O'Connell*, vol. 1, 309.

[42] Seán O'Faoláin, *King of the beggars* (Dublin, 1980), 165.

[43] *The trial of John Magee*, 73–153.

[44] *The trial of John Magee*, 171.

[45] O'Faoláin, *King of the beggars*, 156.

[46] O. MacDonagh, *The hereditary bondsman*, 119.

[47] NLI, MS. 13,647, 'E.B' to O'Connell, 28 July 1813.

[48] *The trial of John Magee*, xxiv.

[49] O'Keeffe, *Life and times of O'Connell*, vol. 1, 297.

[50] O'Faoláin, *King of the beggars*, 156.

[51] The *Post* had written of it 'we suspect the wolf, though dressed in sheep's clothing' (Inglis, *Freedom of the press in Ireland*, 124).

[52] O'Keeffe, *Life and times of O'Connell*, vol. 1, 302.

[53] O'Keeffe, *Life and times of O'Connell*, vol. 1, 305—the pamphlet would lead to further legal action against the *Post*.

[54] O'Keeffe, *Life and times of O'Connell*, vol. 1, 301.

[55] O'Faoláin, *King of the beggars*, 155.

[56] Geoghegan, *King Dan*, 125.

[57] O. MacDonagh, *The hereditary bondsman*, 122–3.

[58] *The trial of John Magee*, xxviii.

[59] William Fagan, *The life and times of Daniel O'Connell* (2 vols, Cork, 1847–8), vol. i, 89.

[60] The man who would be King George IV was unhappy that the *Post* had published a speech of O'Connell to which he took exception.

[61] Inglis, *Freedom of the press in Ireland*, 139.

[62] Robert Peel to Lord Desart, 10 August 1813 cited in O'Faoláin, *King of the beggars*, 179.

[63] O'Faoláin, *King of the beggars*, 180.

[64] Geoghegan, *King Dan*, 63.

[65] O. MacDonagh, *The hereditary bondsman*, 123.

[66] O'Faoláin, *King of the beggars*, 181.

[67] Geoghegan, *King Dan*, 136.

[68] M.R. O'Connell, *The correspondence of Daniel O'Connell* (8 vols, Dublin, 1972–80), vol. i, 347.

[69] O'Faoláin, *King of the beggars*, 181–2.

[70] Inglis, *Freedom of the press in Ireland*, 140.

[71] Inglis, *Freedom of the press in Ireland*, 141.

[72] O. MacDonagh, *The hereditary bondsman*, 124.

Chapter 3

[1] *The Quarterly Review*, December 1844.

[2] William Joseph O'Neill Daunt, *Eighty-five years of Irish history, 1800–1885* (London, 1888), 250.

[3] Michael MacDonagh, *The life of Daniel O'Connell* (London, 1903), 344.

[4] Oliver MacDonagh, *The Emancipist: Daniel O'Connell 1830–47* (London, 1989), 247.

[5] Charles Gavan Duffy, *My life in two hemispheres* (London, 1898), 94.

[6] Another accused priest, Fr James Tyrrell from Lusk, Co. Dublin, died before the case came to trial.

[7] M. MacDonagh, *Daniel O'Connell*, 342–3.

[8] M. MacDonagh, *Daniel O'Connell*, 343.

[9] Charles Gavan Duffy, *Young Ireland: a fragment of history, 1840–1850* (London, 1880), 491.

[10] *Freeman's Journal*, 3 June 1844.

[11] Duffy, *Young Ireland*, 492.

[12] Oliver MacDonagh, 'The age of O'Connell, 1830–1845', in Vaughan, *New history*, vol. 5, 167.

[13] *Annual register* (London, 1844), 307.

[14] O. MacDonagh, *The Emancipist*, 220.

[15] O. MacDonagh, *The Emancipist*, 228.

[16] O. MacDonagh, *The Emancipist*, 221.

[17] Professor Kevin Whelan, RTÉ Radio 1—*Reputations: Daniel O'Connell*, July 2005.

[18] O. MacDonagh, *The Emancipist*, 230.

[19] Keneally, *The great shame*, 97.

[20] *Shaw's authenticated report of the Irish state trials* (Dublin, 1844), 19.

[21] *Shaw's authenticated report*, 74.

[22] *Shaw's authenticated report*, 33.

[23] O. MacDonagh, *The Emancipist*, 234.

[24] Duffy, *My life in two hemispheres*, 92.

[25] *Nation*, 7 October 1843.

[26] R.F. Foster, *Modern Ireland: 1600–1972* (London, 1988), 313.

[27] Duffy, *My life in two hemispheres*, 93.

[28] Duffy, *Young Ireland*, 408.

[29] Duffy, *Young Ireland*, 411.

[30] NLI, MS. 433, Smith O'Brien Papers, Memo from John O'Connell to William Smith O'Brien—O'Connell points out that if a page had been 'dropped' from the list both Catholics and Protestants with the same initial and from the same Dublin parish would both have been omitted. He demonstrates in the case of St Andrews parish that this was not the case—'Thomas Maguire—Joshua McCormick—Bernard Martin—Nicholas Martin and Thomas Murray were in the same *list*—the same *sheet*—the same *letter* ... yet the three last mentioned names being Catholics were dropped, and the other two being Protestant were secured'.

[31] One of the members of the jury was English.

[32] Duffy, *Young Ireland*, 392.

[33] Duffy, *Young Ireland*, 433—as Duffy observed 'with a benevolence none of which it reserved for the benefit of the traversers'.

[34] Duffy, *Young Ireland*, 420.

[35] Duffy, *Young Ireland*, 403.

[36] O. MacDonagh, *The Emancipist*, 244.

[37] *Shaw's authenticated report*, 5–8.

[38] Duffy, *Young Ireland*, 399.

[39] *Shaw's authenticated report*, 22.

[40] *Shaw's authenticated report*, 22.

[41] *Shaw's authenticated report*, 23.

[42] *Shaw's authenticated report*, 33.

[43] *Nation*, 20 January 1844.

[44] Clifden, Co. Galway, 17 September 1843.

[45] Duffy, *Young Ireland*, 423.

[46] Such as the Mullaghmast resolution—'Resolved—That this meeting hereby declare its devoted loyalty to the person and throne of her gracious Majesty Queen Victoria, Queen of Ireland, and its determination to uphold and maintain inviolate all prerogatives of the crown as guaranteed by the constitution'.

[47] *Shaw's authenticated report*, 89.

[48] *Shaw's authenticated report*, 91–2.

[49] French left-wing politician Alexandre Auguste Ledru Rollin who spent twenty years in exile after the 1848 revolution in his country. He was a supporter of repeal of the Act of Union and other radical causes.

[50] *Shaw's authenticated report*, 237.

[51] McCullagh, *Richard Lalor Sheil*, vol. 2, 333.

[52] *Shaw's authenticated report*, 275–7.

[53] McCullagh, *Richard Lalor Sheil*, vol. 2, 336.

[54] *Shaw's authenticated report*, 311–12.

[55] *Annual register* (1844), 325.

[56] William Henry Curran, *Sketches of the Irish Bar* (2 vols, London, 1855), vol.1, 173.

[57] *Shaw's authenticated report*, 467–8.

[58] *Shaw's authenticated report*, 473.

[59] *Shaw's authenticated report*, 477–80.

[60] *Shaw's authenticated report*, 515.

[61] Duffy, *Young Ireland*, 432.

[62] *Shaw's authenticated report*, 615.

[63] *Shaw's authenticated report*, 617.

[64] *Shaw's authenticated report*, 618.

[65] Duffy, *Young Ireland*, 436.

[66] Duffy, *Young Ireland*, 440.

[67] NLI, MS. 13,649, Letter from Ralph Lawrenson, 25 March 1844.

[68] *Nation*, 17 February 1844.

[69] O. MacDonagh, *The Emancipist*, 246.

[70] McCullagh, *Richard Lalor Sheil*, vol. 2, 342.

[71] Letter to Charles Buller, 9 January 1844, in O'Connell, vol. viii, 237.

[72] Letter to Richard Lalor Sheil, 19 June 1844, in O'Connell, *Correspondence*, vol. vii, 256.

[73] NLI, MS. 433, Smith O'Brien Papers, O'Connell to Smith O'Brien, 23 March 1844, fol. 1152.

[74] Duffy, *My life in two hemispheres*, 94.

[75] McConville, *Irish political prisoners*, 12.

[76] O'Connell to Betsy fFrench, 1 August 1844, in O'Connell, *Correspondence*, vol. vii, 261.

[77] Duffy is referring to himself (he was aged 28) and Gray (aged 30). John O'Connell, at 34, was the only other prisoner who could be described as 'young'.

[78] Duffy, *Young Ireland*, 492.

[79] Duffy, *Young Ireland*, 494.

[80] M. MacDonagh, *Daniel O'Connell*, 354.

[81] NLI, MS. 13,660, O'Connell to Margaret O'Mara, 21 June 1844.

[82] Duffy, *Young Ireland*, 531.

[83] O'Connell, *Correspondence*, vol. viii, 165.

[84] Seán O'Faoláin, *King of the beggars* (Dublin, 1980), 349.

[85] M. MacDonagh, *Daniel O'Connell*, 347.

[86] M. MacDonagh, *Daniel O'Connell*, 348.

[87] *Freeman's Journal*, 7 September 1844.

[88] O. MacDonagh, *The Emancipist*, 251.

[89] M. MacDonagh, *Daniel O'Connell*, 349—though the prospect of having his house returned to him after three months might have been just as dizzying.

[90] O'Faoláin, *King of the beggars*, 350.

[91] Michael Doheny, *The felon's track: a narrative of '48* (New York, 1867), 21.

[92] McConville, *Irish political prisoners*, 45.

[93] M. MacDonagh, *Daniel O'Connell*, 349.

[94] Doheny, *The felon's track*, 21.

[95] *Freeman's Journal*, 7 September 1844.

[96] Doheny, *The felon's track*, 22.

[97] M. MacDonagh, *Daniel O'Connell*, 351.

[98] O'Faoláin, *King of the beggars*, 351.

[99] M. MacDonagh, *Daniel O'Connell*, 352.

[100] O'Connell, *Correspondence*, vol. vii, 235.

[101] Duffy, *Young Ireland*, 532.

[102] O'Faoláin, *King of the beggars*, 336.

Chapter 4

[1] [Anon.], *Lamentable lines on the execution of the Maamtrasna murderers* (1880s).

[2] Taken from Joyce's 1907 article 'Ireland at the Bar', see Kevin Barry (ed.), *Occasional, critical, and political writing* (Oxford, 2000), 146.

[3] Michael Davitt, *The fall of feudalism in Ireland* (London, 1904), 110.

[4] *Annual register* (London, 1881), 27—the total was 2,590. The *Register* points out that Forster accepted that just over half that number consisted of threatening letters

as opposed to acts of physical violence. They were more than ten times the figures for 1877. Evictions were more than five times higher in 1880 than three years before.

[5] *Freeman's Journal*, 20 September 1880.

[6] The generic term applied to the agrarian violence perpetrated by Irish secret societies. The Ribbonmen was the name of one of the better known of these fraternities. Activities ranged from sending threatening letters, through physical intimidation, to murder.

[7] A health warning. Historians differ as to the real significance of the eviction figures. Although there is no denying the five-fold increase over a three-year period, it should be pointed out that a large percentage of evictions were of a 'technical' nature, i.e. tenants were served with eviction orders but were left on their farms as caretakers.

[8] *Annual register* (1881), 28.

[9] *Annual register* (1881), 29.

[10] A study of the evidence to the Parnell Commission (1888/9) and a reading of the correspondence and writings of Special Magistrate Clifford Lloyd bear out this contention.

[11] *Special Commission on Parnellism and Crime* (11 vols, London, 1890), vol. I, 76.

[12] *Special Commission on Parnellism and Crime*, vol. 1, 75/6.

[13] An accord whose existence was denied by both sides. Gladstone could not be seen to have negotiated with the agents of the Land League (hence the use of Captain William O'Shea as intermediary) while Parnell incensed even some of his more moderate supporters (Tim Healy) by appearing to have made concessions in order to secure his freedom.

[14] *Annual register* (London, 1882), 102.

[15] Sometimes spelt Leyden or Louden.

[16] Jarlath Waldron, *Maamtrasna: the murders and the mystery* (Dublin, 1992), 10.

[17] The murder of the Huddys (above) is a case in point. Their bodies were recovered in Lough Mask.

[18] Andrew Dunlop, *Fifty years of Irish journalism* (Dublin, 1911), 187–8.

[19] *Times*, 21 August 1882.

[20] *Times*, 22 August 1882.

[21] Because of the number of Joyces and Caseys who play a major part in this narrative, many of whom with the same first names, an attempt will be made to distinguish between each.

[22] This was about three to four hundred yards from the house of John 'Maolra' Joyce.

[23] The RIC conducted their own experiments and concluded that what the Maolras heard, in this instance, were the fatal shots.

[24] *Freeman's Journal*, 14 November 1882—It has been pointed out that in fact the Maolras did not approach the police until Saturday, 19 August. This has been used to suggest that they required a considerable amount to time to concoct and rehearse their story.

[25] Lord Spencer to Lord Granville, 17 September 1882, in Peter Gordon (ed.), *The*

Red Earl: the papers of the Fifth Earl Spencer, 1835–1910 (2 vols, Northampton, 1981 and 1986), vol. 1, 221.

[26] As noted in the introduction to this book, O'Brien was popularly known as 'Peter the Packer' based on his perceived expertise in identifying jurors sympathetic to the prosecution cause and 'packing' the jury accordingly

[27] The youngest Maolra, Paddy, son of John, identified nine of the gang members.

[28] *Freeman's Journal,* 14 November 1882.

[29] Which included a jeweller, a stockbroker, a retired army officer, a lodging-house keeper, a saddler, a wine merchant, a landowner and a bank manager.

[30] *Freeman's Journal,* 14 November 1882.

[31] *Freeman's Journal,* 15 November 1882.

[32] *Freeman's Journal,* 16 November 1882.

[33] *Freeman's Journal,* 18 November 1882.

[34] His age, according to different sources, has been given as anything from his late forties to late fifties.

[35] *Freeman's Journal,* 18 November 1882.

[36] *Freeman's Journal,* 20 November 1882.

[37] Timothy Harrington, *The Maamtrasna massacre: impeachment of the trials* (Dublin, 1884), 35.

[38] Lord Spencer to Sir William Harcourt, 23 November 1882, and Harcourt to Spencer, 24 November 1882, in Gordon, *The Red Earl,* 226.

[39] Lord Spencer to Queen Victoria, 11 December 1882, in Gordon, *The Red Earl,* 229.

[40] Waldron, *Maamtrasna,* 142/3.

[41] Lord Spencer to Judge C.R. Barry, 19 December 1882, in Gordon, *The Red Earl,* 231/2.

[42] Harrington, *The Maamtrasna massacre,* vi.

[43] North of Lough Mask the parish included the village of Tourmakeady and the townland of Glensaul where Thomas Casey lived.

[44] Harrington, *The Maamtrasna massacre,* 3.

[45] It was facing in the wrong direction.

[46] Newton Brady—one of the original investigators (see above).

[47] Harrington, *The Maamtrasna massacre.*

[48] T.M. Healy, *Letters and leaders of my day* (2 vols, New York, 1928?), vol. 1, 187.

[49] NLI, MS. 8,584, Fr McHugh, CC, Claremorris, to Timothy Harrington, 3 November 1882, fols 14–15.

[50] L.P. Curtis Jr., *Coercion and conciliation in Ireland, 1880–1892: a study in Conservative Unionism* (Princeton, 1963), 43.

[51] 17 January 1980.

[52] R.V. Comerford, 'The politics of distress, 1877–82', in Vaughan, *New History,* vol.6, 51.

[53] Comerford, 'The politics of distress', 52.

Chapter 5

[1] John Adye Curran, *Reminiscences of John Adye Curran* (London, 1915).

[2] Joseph Mullet, diary entry, 6 May 1882, in *Dublin Commission Court, depositions in Phoenix Park murders* (Dublin, 1883), 228.

[3] It would be a mistake to overestimate Mallon's importance in the general scheme of things—most of the more egregious crimes of the 1880s were taking place outside his jurisdiction, in rural Ireland.

[4] R. Barry O'Brien, *The life of Charles Stewart Parnell* (London, 1910), 237–40.

[5] Katharine O'Shea, *Charles Stewart Parnell: his love story and political life* (London, 1914), 117.

[6] *Annual register* (1882), 45–6.

[7] Discussed in Myles Dungan, *The captain and the king: William O'Shea, Parnell and late Victorian Ireland* (Dublin, 2009), 90–115.

[8] Land League secretary.

[9] Tom Corfe, *The Phoenix Park murders: conflict, compromise and tragedy in Ireland, 1879–1882* (London, 1968), 135.

[10] Who despite being dubbed 'Number 1' was probably little more than a glorified go-between.

[11] Fenian and Invincible (and approver) Patrick Delaney in his evidence to the *Times* Commission (see following chapter) agreed with counsel for Parnell, Charles Russell that the Fenians were not an assassination society. Pledged to open rebellion they would only assassinate informers. When asked were they different from the Invincibles he replied 'different altogether'— *Special Commission*, vol. 3, 552.

[12] Curran, *Reminiscences*, 159.

[13] Parnell ended this facility by insisting on the need for multiple signatures before future disbursements could take place. This was in June 1882, a month after the murders. Egan resigned as treasurer in October of that year.

[14] Corfe, *Phoenix Park murders*, 138.

[15] A 'Centre' was the effective commander of an IRB unit.

[16] Corfe, *Phoenix Park murders*, 140.

[17] Corfe, *Phoenix Park murders*, 143.

[18] *Depositions, Phoenix Park murders*, 211.

[19] Corfe, *Phoenix Park murders*, 26.

[20] Senan Molony, *The Phoenix Park murders: conspiracy, betrayal and retribution* (Dublin, 2006), 28.

[21] *Freeman's Journal*, 8 May 1882.

[22] Molony, *Phoenix Park murders*, 33.

[23] Molony, *Phoenix Park murders*, 45.

[24] Mary Gladstone, *Mary Gladstone (Mrs. Drew): her diaries and letters*, ed. Lucy Masterman (New York, 1930), 248.

[25] *United Ireland*, 13 May 1882.

[26] *Freeman's Journal*, 8 May 1882.

[27] *Times*, 8 May 1882.

[28] Healy, *Letters and leaders*, vol. 1, 159.

[29] *Times*, 9 May 1882.

[30] Healy, *Letters and leaders*, vol. 1, 160.

[31] *Times*, 9 May 1882.

[32] The legend surrounding his nickname is that he had slaughtered and skinned a pet goat in order to raise money to buy alcohol.

[33] Frederick Moir Bussy, *Irish conspiracies: recollections of John Mallon, the great Irish detective* (London, 1910), 80.

[34] See Dungan, *The captain and the king*, 146–55.

[35] *Special Commission*, vol. 3, 539

[36] *Special Commission*, vol. 3, 548.

[37] Bussy, *Mallon*, 81/2.

[38] P.J. Tynan, *The Irish National Invincibles and their times* (New York, 1894), 427.

[39] Tynan, *Invincibles*, 450.

[40] NLI, MS. 5,449, Report of John Adye Curran, 3.

[41] Bussy, *Mallon*, 84/5.

[42] *Freeman's Journal*, 22 January 1883.

[43] Tighe Hopkins, *Kilmainham memories: the story of the greatest political crime of the century* (London, 1896), 65.

[44] Corfe, *Phoenix Park murders*, 244.

[45] Bussy, *Mallon*, 89.

[46] Bussy, *Mallon*, 93–109.

[47] Curran, *Reminiscences*, 181.

[48] J.B. Hall, *Random records of a reporter* (Dublin, *c.* 1910), 177.

[49] Bussy, *Mallon*, 93.

[50] *Freeman's Journal*, 19 February 1883.

[51] Dudley W.R. Bahlman, *The diary of Sir Edward Hamilton, 1880–1885* (Oxford, 1972), 400.

[52] Corfe, *Phoenix Park murders*, 246.

[53] Hall, *Random records*, 179.

[54] *Freeman's Journal*, 12 April 1883.

[55] Hall, *Random records*, 179/80.

[56] Curran, *Reminiscences*, 172.

[57] Healy, *The old Munster circuit*, 12.

[58] Confederate officer of the American Civil War. His first visit to Ireland was for the Fenian rising. Captured and released in 1870 and immediately rearrested. Tim Healy speculates in *Letters and leaders* that he may have been he may have been 'the chief pursuer of revenge' (vol. 1, 50).

[59] *Report of the trials at the Dublin Commission Court (April and May, 1883) of the prisoners charged with the Phoenix Park murders* (Dublin, 1883), 26/7.

[60] *Report of the trials*, 33.

[61] NLI, MS. 5,449, Report of John Adye Curran, 6.

[62] Hall, *Random records*, 181.

[63] *Freeman's Journal*, 17 April 1883.

[64] *Freeman's Journal*, 17 April 1883.

[65] *Report of the trials*, 137–9.

[66] *Freeman's Journal*, 18 April 1883.

[67] *Report of the trials*, 217–19.

[68] Bussy, *Mallon*, 138.

[69] Bussy, *Mallon*, 137.

[70] Hall, *Random records*, 181.

[71] Corfe, *Phoenix Park murders*, 255.

[72] Bussy, *Mallon*, 131.

[73] Hall, *Random records*, 184.

[74] Bussy, *Mallon*, 129.

[75] A killing in Barbaville, Co.Westmeath.

[76] Molony, *Phoenix Park murders*, 278–80.

[77] Corfe, *Phoenix Park murders*, 257.

[78] Hopkins, *Kilmainham*, 71.

[79] Hopkins, *Kilmainham*, 81.

[80] Hopkins, *Kilmainham*, 94.

[81] *Freeman's Journal*, 10 June 1883.

[82] Earl Spencer to Queen Victoria, 4 June 1883, in Gordon, *The Red Earl*, 248/9.

[83] Hopkins, *Kilmainham*, 74.

[84] Bussy, *Mallon*, 149.

[85] Hall, *Random records*, 185.

[86] Davitt, *The fall of feudalism*, 454.

[87] Tynan, *Invincibles*, 492–3.

[88] *United Ireland*, 11 August, 8 September, 15 September 1883.

[89] *Depositions, Phoenix Park murders*, 2.

[90] *Special Commission*, vol. 3, 544.

[91] *Special Commission*, vol. 3, 545.

[92] *Special Commission*, vol. 3, 561.

[93] Henri Le Caron, *Twenty-five years in the secret service: the recollections of a spy* (London, 1892), 209.

[94] Le Caron, *Twenty-five years in the secret service*, 228/9.

[95] Curran writes of having police protection for eight years after the investigation concluded.

[96] Healy, *Letters and leaders*, vol. 1, 181.

[97] Hopkins, *Kilmainham*, 74.

[98] T.D. Sullivan, *Recollections of troubled times in Irish politics* (Dublin, 1905), 206.

[99] *Hansard*, CCLXXVI, 722–5, 23 February 1883.

[100] Corfe, *Phoenix Park murders*, 256.

[101] Named after the inquisitorial procedure instituted in Tudor times, and established under the Crimes Act, it allowed Curran to question suspects and potential

witnesses who might otherwise not have been obliged to co-operate with his investigation.

[102] Corfe, *Phoenix Park murders*, 257–8.

Chapter 6

[1] Sir Charles Russell, *The Parnell Commission: the opening speech for the defence* (London, 1889), 8.

[2] *Special Commission*, vol. 1, 41.

[3] *Special Commission*, vol. 1, 354.

[4] The name given to the uneasy alliance of Whigs and radicals, led by Lord Hartington and Joseph Chamberlain, who had split from the Liberal Party over Home Rule in 1886.

[5] Though rumoured at the time to be Patrick Egan, a Fenian and influential Land League treasurer.

[6] *Times*, 7 March 1887.

[7] The two men, who had never entirely trusted each other, had first fallen out in 1885 over local government proposals advanced by Chamberlain as an alternative to Home Rule.

[8] Prompting (unproven) allegations that he was a stalking-horse for the government and/or the *Times* itself.

[9] Curtis, *Coercion and conciliation* (London, 1963), 279.

[10] Ironically, the Whig leader, Lord Hartington, although far closer to the political philosophy of the Conservatives than was Chamberlain, advised the government against the course of action it was taking (Curtis, *Coercion and conciliation*, 280).

[11] Curtis, *Coercion and conciliation*, 280.

[12] Margaret O'Callaghan, *British high politics and a nationalist Ireland* (Cork, 1994), 114.

[13] O'Callaghan, *British high politics*, 280.

[14] Patrick Egan to Henry Labouchere, 2 December 1888, in Algar Labouchere Thorold, *The life of Henry Labouchere* (London, 1913), 346.

[15] John Macdonald, *Diary of the Parnell Commission* (London, 1890), 1/2.

[16] See Dungan, *The captain and the king*, 284–322.

[17] *The history of the Times: the twentieth century test, 1884–1912* (4 vols, London, 1947), vol. 3, 43.

[18] Macdonald, *Diary of the Parnell Commission*, 150.

[19] *Special Commission*, vol. 5, 443–501.

[20] Who wrote under the pseudonym Owen Roe.

[21] Macdonald, *Diary of the Parnell Commission*, 155.

[22] *Special Commission*, vol. 5, 484.

[23] Sir Alfred Robbins, *Parnell: the last five years* (London, 1926), 87.

[24] In his biography of Russell, R. Barry O'Brien claims that Pigott 'looked well and pugnacious' under examination. It should be pointed out that the 'breaking' of a

more composed Pigott would have reflected even more credit on O'Brien's subject.

[25] Robbins, *Parnell*, 88.

[26] Said in conversation with his biographer R. Barry O'Brien. However he also observed that 'All that we have ever got from England we got by lawlessness and violence', in R. Barry O'Brien, *The life of Lord Russell of Killowen* (London, 1901), 218.

[27] O'Brien, *The life of Lord Russell*, 216.

[28] Of both Russell and Parnell.

[29] This can be taken with a pinch of salt. The attorney general had just concluded his examination of Pigott. As soon as he had finished Russell commenced his cross-examination without allowing Pigott to leave the stand.

[30] O'Brien, *The life of Lord Russell*, 229–30.

[31] *Special Commission*, vol. 5, 501.

[32] Robbins, *Parnell*, 89.

[33] *Special Commission*, vol. 5, 502–07.

[34] Robbins, *Parnell*, 88.

[35] Robbins, *Parnell*, 91.

[36] *Special Commission*, vol. 5, 515–17.

[37] Pigott had already been given £200 by Egan to moderate the attacks in his newspapers against the Parnellites.

[38] *Special Commission*, vol. 5, 530–35—the gist of the correspondence was subsequently made public in the *Freeman's Journal* in December 1881.

[39] The reference may be to a Galway tenants' rights activist, Michael M. O'Sullivan, who spoke at the Irishtown meeting in April 1879. Davitt, Andrew Kettle and Thomas Brennan were Land League secretaries at its inception in October 1879.

[40] *Special Commission*, vol. 5, 536–9.

[41] *Special Commission*, vol. 5, 545.

[42] *Special Commission*, vol. 5, 550–2.

[43] Macdonald, *Diary of the Parnell Commission*, 161.

[44] Macdonald, *Diary of the Parnell Commission*, 161.

[45] Macdonald, *Diary of the Parnell Commission*, 161.

[46] Davitt, *The fall of feudalism*, 581.

[47] F.S.L. Lyons, *Charles Stewart Parnell* (London, 1977), 420.

[48] *Special Commission*, vol. 6, 31/2.

[49] Macdonald, *Diary of the Parnell Commission*, 168.

[50] *Special Commission*, vol. 6, 33.

[51] Lyons, *Parnell*, 422.

[52] *Times*, 4 March 1889.

[53] Captain O'Shea to Joseph Chamberlain, 9 March 1889, in Dungan, *The captain and the king*, 321.

[54] Amassed by Michael Davitt and contained in his 'Notes by an amateur detective' notebook (Trinity College Dublin (TCD), Davitt Papers, MS. 9,551).

[55] Even the existence of this correspondence, not to mention the familiar and chatty tone, is curious. Under cross-examination by Russell, O'Shea had barely admitted even being vaguely acquainted with Houston.

[56] Edward Caulfield Houston to Captain O'Shea, 6 March 1889, in Dungan, *The captain and the king*, 318.

[57] *History of the Times*, vol. iii, 89.

[58] Whose total fees for the twelve months of the Special Commission were £3,300— O'Brien, *The life of Lord Russell*, 259.

[59] Lyons, *Parnell*, 429.

[60] *A popular and complete edition of the Parnell Commission report* (London, 1890), 146.

[61] O'Callaghan, *British high politics*, 113.

[62] *The collected poems of Rudyard Kipling* (London, 1994), 238.

Chapter 7

[1] [Canon Charles O'Neill], *The foggy dew* (1919).

[2] Ernie O'Malley, *On another man's wound* (Dublin, 1979), 52

[3] W.B. Yeats, *Easter 1916* (Dublin, 1916).

[4] Charles Townshend, *Easter 1916: the Irish rebellion* (London, 2006), 179.

[5] Piaras F. Mac Lochlainn, *Last words: letters and statements of the leaders executed after the Rising at Easter 1916* (Dublin, 1990), 60.

[6] Fintan O'Toole and Shane Hegarty, *The Irish Times book of the Rising* (Dublin, 2006), see www.irishtimes.com/focus/easterrising/aftermath/ (last accessed 30 July 2009).

[7] Brian Barton, *From behind a closed door: secret court martial records of the 1916 Easter Rising* (Dublin, 2002), 225–7.

[8] Hobson was 'arrested' by fellow IRB members favourable to the Rising on 21 April in order to prevent him from interfering with the plans of the Military Council (Townshend, *Easter 1916*, 136).

[9] John Devoy, *Recollections of an Irish rebel* (New York, 1929), 458–65.

[10] Mac Lochlainn, *Last words*, 14.

[11] Townshend, *Easter 1916*, 393 fn.

[12] Barton, *From behind a closed door*, 45.

[13] Townshend, *Easter 1916*, 269.

[14] Tim Pat Coogan, *1916: the Easter Rising* (London, 2005), 157.

[15] Léon Ó Broin, *W.E. Wylie and the Irish revolution: 1900–1921* (Dublin, 1989), 20–1.

[16] This was a reference to his brother, Willie, who, uniquely, pleaded guilty at his own court martial and described himself as an *aide-de-camp* to his brother. Like 89 other prisoners, Willie Pearse was sentenced to death. However, Maxwell's confirmation of the sentence was undoubtedly based on his relationship to Patrick Pearse.

[17] Mac Lochlainn, *Last words*, 14.

[18] Army Service Corps.

[19] Ó Broin, *Wylie*, 21.

[20] Ó Broin, *Wylie*, 21.

[21] Barton, *From behind a closed door*, 116–17.

[22] Max Caulfield, *The Easter rebellion* (London, 1963), 359.

[23] Ruth Dudley Edwards, *Patrick Pearse: triumph of failure* (London, 1977), 317.

[24] Elizabeth, Countess of Fingall, *Seventy years young* (Dublin, 1991), 376.

[25] Barton, *From behind a closed door*, 111.

[26] Foster, *Modern Ireland*, 483.

[27] Barton, *From behind a closed door*, 127.

[28] Ó Broin, *Wylie*, 19–20—It should be noted that other observers refer to the rebels being cheered as they approached Richmond Barracks—Frank Robbins, *Under the starry plough* (Dublin 1977), 127.

[29] Ó Broin, *Wylie*, 22.

[30] Barton, *From behind a closed door*, 127.

[31] Mac Lochlainn, *Last words*, 56.

[32] Thomas MacDonagh, *When the dawn is come* (Dublin, 1908).

[33] Mac Lochlainn, *Last words*, 59.

[34] Mac Lochlainn, *Last words*, 57.

[35] [Thomas MacDonagh], *The last inspiring address of Thomas MacDonagh* (Dublin, 1916).

[36] Caulfield, *Easter rebellion*, 361.

[37] Mac Lochlainn, *Last words*, 60–6.

[38] Barton, *From behind a closed door*, 60.

[39] Barton, *From behind a closed door*, 194–7.

[40] Coogan, *1916*, 156–7.

[41] O'Toole and Hegarty, *Irish Times book of the Rising*.

[42] He died in 1964, two years before the fiftieth anniversary celebrations.

[43] Sir Nevil Macready, *Annals of an active life* (2 vols, London, 1924), vol. 1, 241.

[44] Asquith had not actually insisted that the executions cease, he told Redmond that he had written to Maxwell asking that he desist 'unless in some quite exceptional case'—a case could be made convincingly by Maxwell that the cases of Connolly and MacDermott were 'exceptional'.

[45] It must be deemed highly unlikely that Maxwell would have been unaware of de Valera's command of the 3rd Battalion.

[46] Ó Broin, *Wylie*, 30–2.

[47] Ó Broin, *Wylie*, 32–3.

[48] See Ruth Dudley Edwards, 'Mrs. Markievicz', in Dungan, *Speaking ill of the dead*, 87. 'Beautiful and flamboyant, Constance Markievicz was all style and no substance. Along with other uncompromising green harpies of her generation ... she became a role model for generations of women who mistook pitilessness and intransigence for principle.'

[49] Ó Broin, *Wylie*, 27.

[50] Caulfield, *Easter rebellion*, 362.

[51] Townshend, *Easter 1916*, 286.

[52] Barton, *From behind a closed door*, 80.

[53] Townshend, *Easter 1916*, 286.

[54] Barton, *From behind a closed door,* 81.

[55] Barton, *From behind a closed door,* 82.

[56] Caulfield, *Easter rebellion,* 362.

[57] Caulfield, *Easter rebellion,* 362.

[58] Barton, *From behind a closed door,* 295–8.

[59] Brian Inglis, *Roger Casement* (London, 1974), 333.

[60] A legal designation—he too was Alexander Martin Sullivan.

[61] Inglis, *Casement,* 349.

[62] Although some still maintain that the diaries are forgeries and the work of the British Intelligence Service, the consensus is that they are genuine. After a forensic examination of the diaries in 2002 Dr Audrey Giles, an acknowledged expert in the field of document forensics, concluded that Casement had written the diaries. Jeffrey Dudgeon, in his study *Roger Casement: the black diaries—with a study of his background, sexuality and Irish political life* (Belfast, 2002) proceeds from the premise that the documents are genuine. The same is true of the recent Séamas Ó Síocháin biographical work *Roger Casement: imperialist, rebel, revolutionary* (Dublin, 2008).

[63] H. Montgomery Hyde, *Famous trials: Roger Casement* (London, 1960), 96–7.

[64] Hyde, *Famous trials,* 98.

[65] Hyde, *Famous trials,* 101.

[66] Hyde, *Famous trials,* 102.

[67] Inglis, *Casement,* 356.

[68] Hyde, *Famous trials,* 106—Inglis ascribes the collapse of Sullivan to a concern for his future at the English Bar. He alleges that Sullivan realised he had gone too far in reminding Smith of his pre-war activities on behalf of Ulster Unionists and pulled back. Hyde, more charitably, describes it as 'nervous exhaustion'.

[69] Hyde, *Famous trials,* 109.

[70] Hyde, *Famous trials,* 112.

[71] Inglis, *Casement,* 359.

[72] The original statute had been written in French.

[73] George H. Knott, *Trial of Sir Roger Casement* (Edinburgh/London, 1917), 197–206.

[74] Inglis, *Casement,* 261.

[75] Inglis, *Casement,* 373–4.

[76] Countess of Fingall, *Seventy years young,* 375.

[77] Macready, *Annals,* 241.

[78] F.A. McKenzie, *The Irish rebellion: what happened and why* (London, 1916), 104.

[79] Before the end of 1916 he was banished to an obscure command in the north of England.

[80] The title of a TV documentary made by Mint Productions, scripted and directed by Darragh Byrne and transmitted as part of the *Hidden history* series in March 2006.

[81] Barton, *From behind a closed door,* 87.

[82] Coogan, *1916,* 169.

[83] Townshend, *Easter 1916*, 302.

[84] Asquith had succeeded in getting someone, in this instance a Unionist, to take the job.

[85] Barton, *From behind a closed door*, 87.

[86] Townshend, *Easter 1916*, 300.

[87] Ó Broin, *Wylie*, 29.

[88] O'Toole and Hegarty, *Irish Times book of the Rising*.

[89] Foster, *Modern Ireland*, 485.

[90] Macready, *Annals*, 242.

[91] McKenzie, *The Irish rebellion*, 105–06.

[92] O'Malley, *Another man's wound*, 47.

[93] O'Malley, *Another man's wound*, 48

[94] The 'popular and saintly' Sheehy Skeffington had been a witness to Bowen Colthurst shooting an unarmed boy. Found guilty but insane, Bowen Colthurst was released after the war and ended his life as a bank manager (Foster, *Modern Ireland*, 484).

[95] Connolly had been well wide of the mark in his conviction that capitalists would not destroy property.

[96] Clair Wills, *Dublin, 1916: the siege of the GPO* (London, 2009), 100.

[97] O'Toole and Hegarty, *Irish Times book of the Rising*.

[98] Townshend, *Easter 1916*, 254.

[99] Foster, *Modern Ireland*, 480.

[100] O'Toole and Hegarty, *Irish Times book of the Rising*.

[101] Inglis, *Casement*, 337.

Afterword

[1] John B. Keane, *The field* (Cork, 1987),

[2] Criminal Justice (Amendment) Bill 2009 – Section 8 (1), see www.oireachtas.ie/documents/bills28/bills/2009/4509/b4509d.pdf (last accessed 30 July 2009).

[3] Criminal Justice (Amendment) Bill, 2009—Section 71B (1), see www.oireachtas.ie/documents/bills28/bills/2009/4509/b4509d.pdf (30 July 2009).

[4] Criminal Justice (Amendment) Bill, 2009—Section 3 (1) (b), see www.oireachtas.ie/documents/bills28/bills/2009/4509/b4509d.pdf (30 July 2009).

[5] *Nation*, 7 October 1843.

[6] Keane, *The field*, 74.

BIBLIOGRAPHY

Manuscript Sources

NATIONAL ARCHIVES OF IRELAND

Rebellion Papers
NAI, 620/12/155/5
NAI, 620/11/134

NATIONAL LIBRARY OF IRELAND

Harrington Papers
NLI, MS. 8,584

O'Connell Papers
NLI, MS. 13,649
NLI, MS. 13,660

Smith O'Brien Papers
NLI, MS. 433

Additional material
NLI, MS. 4,597
NLI, MS. 5,449

TRINITY COLLEGE DUBLIN

Davitt Papers
TCD, MS. 9,551

Newspapers

Dublin Evening Post
Freeman's Journal
Irish Times
The Times
United Ireland

Printed sources

Annual register various dates London. J. Dodsley.

Court of King's Bench, Ireland 1883 *Dublin Commission Court, depositions in Phoenix Park murders.* Dublin. HMSO.

Courts of Oyer and Terminer and General Gaol Delivery 1803 *A report of the proceedings in cases of high treason in a court of oyer and terminer.* Dublin. John Exshaw.

Parliament of Great Britain various dates *House of Commons Debates (Hansard).* London. Hansard.

Report of the trials at the Dublin Commission Court (April and May, 1883) of the prisoners charged with the Phoenix Park murders 1883 Dublin. Alex Thom.

Russell, Sir Charles 1889 *The Parnell Commission: the opening speech for the defence.* London. Macmillan & Co.

Shaw's authenticated report of the Irish state trials 1844 Dublin. H. Shaw.

Special Commission to Enquire into Charges and Allegations Against Certain Members of Parliament and Others 1888–90 *Special Commission on Parnellism and Crime*, vols 1, 3, 5 & 6. London. George Edward Wright.

Special Commission to Enquire into Charges and Allegations Against Certain Members of Parliament and Others 1890 *A popular and complete edition of the Parnell Commission Report.* London. The Liberal Unionist Association.

State Trials Commission 1896 *Reports of state trials*, New Series, vol. VII 1848–1850—Queen V Smith O'Brien. London. HMSO.

The trial of John Magee, proprietor of the Dublin Evening Post, for publishing an historical review of the Duke of Richmond's administration in Ireland. 1813 Dublin. John Magee.

Primary sources (memoirs/diaries/letters)

Bahlman, Dudley W.R. 1972 *The diary of Sir Edward Hamilton, 1880–1885*. Oxford. Clarendon Press.

Byrne, Miles 1907 *The memoirs of Miles Byrne, two volumes*. Dublin. Maunsel.

Bussy, Frederick Moir 1910 *Irish conspiracies: recollections of John Mallon, the great Irish detective*. London. Everett & Co.

Curran, John Adye 1915 *Reminiscences of John Adye Curran*. London. E. Arnold.

Curran, William Henry 1855 *Sketches of the Irish Bar* (2 vols). London. Hurst & Blackett.

Davitt, Michael 1904 *The fall of feudalism in Ireland*. London/New York. Harper & Bros.

Devoy, John 1929 *Recollections of an Irish rebel*. New York. Chas P. Young.

Doheny, Michael 1867 *The felon's track: a narrative of '48*. New York. Farrell & Son.

Dunlop, Andrew 1911 *Fifty years of Irish journalism*. Dublin. Hanna & Neale.

Gladstone, Mary 1930 *Mary Gladstone (Mrs. Drew): her diaries and letters* (ed. Lucy Masterman). New York. E.P. Dutton & Co.

Gordon, Peter (ed.) 1981 and 1986 *The Red Earl: the papers of the fifth Earl Spencer, 1835–1910* (2 vols). Northampton. Northamptonshire Record Society.

Hall, J.B. *c.* 1910 *Random records of a reporter*. Dublin. Fodhla Printing.

Harrington, Timothy 1884 *The Maamtrasna massacre: impeachment of the trials*. Dublin. Nation.

Healy, Maurice 1939 *The old Munster circuit*. London. Brown & Nolan (Richview Press).

Healy, T.M. 1929 *Letters and leaders of my day* (2 vols). New York. Frederick A. Stokes.

Hopkins, Tighe 1896 *Kilmainham memories: the story of the greatest political crime of the century*. London. Ward, Locke & Bowden.

Le Caron, Henri 1892 *Twenty-five years in the secret service: the recollections of a spy*. London. W. Heinemann.

Lloyd, Clifford 1882 *Ireland under the Land League*. Edinburgh. William Blackwood.

Macdonald, John 1890 *Diary of the Parnell Commission*. London. T.F. Unwin.

McKenzie, F.A. 1916 *The Irish rebellion: what happened and why*. London. C.A. Pearson Ltd.

Ó Broin, Léon 1989 *W.E. Wylie and the Irish revolution: 1900–1921*. Dublin. Gill & Macmillan.

O'Malley, Ernie 1979 *On another man's wound*. Dublin. Anvil Books.

Robbins, Sir Alfred 1926 *Parnell: the last five years*. London. Thornton Butterworth.

Sullivan, T.D. 1905 *Recollections of troubled times in Irish politics*. Dublin. Sealy, Bryers and Walker/Gill.

Thorold, Algar Labouchere 1913 *The life of Henry Labouchere*. London. Constable.

Tynan, P.J. 1894 *The Irish National Invincibles and their times*. New York. Irish National Invincible Publishing Co.

Secondary sources

Barton, Brian 2002 *From behind a closed door: secret court martial records of the 1916 Easter Rising*. Dublin. Blackstaff Press.

Bonsal, Penny 1997 *The Irish RMs: the resident magistrates in the British administration of Ireland*. Dublin. Four Courts Press.

Brown, Stephen J.M. 1971 *The press in Ireland*. New York. Lemma.

Caulfield, Max 1963 *The Easter rebellion*. London. Holt, Rinehart & Winston.

Coogan, Tim Pat 2005 *1916:The Easter Rising*. London. Phoenix.

Corfe, Tom 1968 *The Phoenix Park murders: conflict, compromise and tragedy in Ireland, 1879–1882*. London. Hodder and Stoughton.

Curtis, L.P. 1963 *Coercion and conciliation in Ireland, 1880–1892: a study in Conservative Unionism*. Princeton. Princeton University Press; Oxford University Press.

Dawson, N.M. (ed.) 2006 *Reflections on law and history: Irish Legal History Society discourses and other papers, 2000–2005*. Dublin. Four Courts Press.

Dolan, Anne, Geoghegan, Patrick and Jones, Darryl (eds) 2007 *Reinterpreting Emmet: essays on the life and legacy of Robert Emmet*. Dublin. University College Dublin (UCD) Press.

Dudgeon, Jeffrey 2002 *The black diaries—with a study of his background, sexuality and Irish political life*. Belfast. Belfast Press.

Duffy, Charles Gavan 1898 *My life in two hemispheres*. New York. The Macmillan Co.

Dungan, Myles (ed.) 2007 *Speaking ill of the dead*. Dublin. New Island Books.

Dungan, Myles 2009 *The captain and the king: William O'Shea, Parnell and late Victorian Ireland*. Dublin. New Island Books.

Dunlop, Robert 1900 *Daniel O'Connell and the revival of national life in Ireland*. London. G.P. Putnam's Sons.

Dudley Edwards, Ruth 1977 *Patrick Pearse: triumph of failure*. London. Littlehampton Books.

Elliott, Marianne 2003 *Robert Emmet: the making of a legend*. London. Profile Books.

Countess of Fingall, Elizabeth 1991 *Seventy years young*. Dublin. Lilliput Press.

Fagan, William 1847–8 *The life and times of Daniel O'Connell* (2 vols). Cork. J. O'Brien.

Foster, R.F. 1988 *Modern Ireland: 1600–1972*. London. Allen Lane.

Geoghegan, Patrick 2004 *Robert Emmet, a life* Dublin. Gill & Macmillan.

Geoghegan, Patrick 2008 *King Dan: the rise of Daniel O'Connell 1775–1829*. Dublin. Gill & Macmillan.

Gray, Edmund Dwyer 1889 *The treatment of political prisoners in Ireland*. Dublin. Freeman's Journal.

Hogan, Daire 1986 *The legal profession in Ireland, 1789–1922*. Dublin. Incorporated Law Society of Ireland.

Inglis, Brian 1954 *The freedom of the press in Ireland, 1784–1841*. London. Faber and Faber.

Inglis, Brian 1974 *Roger Casement*. London. Coronet Books.

Keneally, Thomas 1998 *The great shame*. London. Chatto & Windus.

Knott, George H. 1917 *Trial of Sir Roger Casement*. Philadelphia. Cromarty Law Book Co.

Koss, Stephen 1981 *The rise and fall of the political press in Britain*. London. Hamish Hamilton.

Lyons, F.S.L. 1977 *Charles Stewart Parnell*. London. Collins.

McCartney, Donal 1980 *The world of Daniel O'Connell*. Dublin. Mercier Press.

McConville, Seán 2003 *Irish political prisoners, 1848–1922*. London. Routledge.

McCullagh, W. Torrens 1855 *Memoirs of the Right Honourable Richard Lalor Sheil* (2 vols). London. Hurst and Blackett.

MacDonagh, Michael 1903 *The life of Daniel O'Connell*. London. Cassell.

MacDonagh, Michael 1904 *The viceroy's post-bag*. London. J. Murray.

MacDonagh, Oliver 1988 *The hereditary bondsman: Daniel O'Connell 1775–1829* London. Wiedenfield and Nicolson.

MacDonagh, Oliver 1989 *The Emancipist: Daniel O'Connell 1830–47*. London. Wiedenfield and Nicolson.

McDonnell Bodkin, Matthias 1918 *Famous Irish trials*. Dublin. Maunsel.

Mac Lochlainn, Piaras F. 1990 *Last words: letters and statements of the leaders executed after the Rising at Easter 1916*. Dublin. Stationery Office.

Macready, Sir Nevil 1924 *Annals of an active life* (2 vols). London. Hutchinson & Co.

Madden, R.R. [nd] *The life and times of Robert Emmet*. New York. Kenedy.

Molony, Senan 2006 *The Phoenix Park murders: conspiracy, betrayal and retribution*. Dublin. Mercier Press.

O'Brien, R. Barry 1901 *The life of Lord Russell of Killowen*. London. Smith, Elder & Co.

O'Brien, R. Barry 1910 *The life of Charles Stewart Parnell*. London. T. Nelson & Sons.

O'Brien, R. Barry 1912 *Dublin Castle and the Irish people*. London. K. Paul, Trench, Trübner & Co.

O'Callaghan, Margaret 1994 *British high politics and a nationalist Ireland*. Cork. Cork University Press.

O'Connell, M.R. 1972–80 *The correspondence of Daniel O'Connell* (8 vols). Dublin. Irish University Press.

O'Donnell, Ian and McAuley, Finbarr (eds) 2003 *Criminal justice history: themes and controversies from pre-independence Ireland*. Dublin. Four Courts Press.

O'Donnell, Ruán 2003 *Robert Emmet and the Rising of 1803*. Dublin. Irish Academic Press.

O'Faoláin, Seán 1938 *King of the beggars*. Dublin. Viking Press.

O'Keeffe, C.M. 1864 *Life and times of Daniel O'Connell*. Dublin. J. Mullany.

Oram, Hugh 1983 *The newspaper book: a history of newspapers in Ireland, 1649–1983*. Dublin. MO Books.

O'Shea, Katharine 1914 *Charles Stewart Parnell: his love story and political life*. London. Cassell.

Ó Síocháin, Séamas 2008 *Roger Casement: imperialist, rebel, revolutionary*. Dublin. Lilliput Press.

O'Toole, Fintan and Hegarty, Shane 2006 *The Irish Times book of the Rising*. Dublin. Gill & Macmillan.

The Times 1947 *The history of the Times: the twentieth century test, 1884–1912*. London. The Times.

Townshend, Charles 2006 *Easter 1916: the Irish rebellion*. London. Penguin.

Vaughan, W.E. (ed.) 1989 *A New History of Ireland*, vol. 5. Oxford. Oxford University Press.

Waldron, Jarlath 1992 *Maamtrasna: the murders and the mystery*. Dublin. Edmund Burke Publishers.

Wills, Clair 2009 *Dublin, 1916: the siege of the GPO*. London. Profile Books.

Articles

Bartlett, Thomas 2007 'The cause of treason seems to have gone out of fashion in Ireland': Dublin Castle and Robert Emmet. In Anne Dolan, Patrick Geoghegan and Darryl Jones (eds), *Reinterpreting Emmet: essays on the life and legacy of Robert Emmet*, 9–25. Dublin. UCD Press.

Bartlett, Thomas 2007 The life and opinions of Leonard MacNally (1752–1820): playwright, barrister, United Irishman and informer. In Myles Dungan (ed.), *Speaking ill of the dead*, 10–24. Dublin. New Island Books.

Bridgeman, Ian 2003 The constabulary and the criminal justice system in nineteenth century Ireland. In Ian O'Donnell and Finbarr McAuley (eds), *Criminal justice history: themes and controversies from pre-independence Ireland*, 113–41. Dublin. Four Courts Press.

Callanan, Frank 2006 T.M. Healy: the politics of advocacy. In N.M. Dawson (ed.) *Reflections on law and history: Irish Legal History Society discourses and other papers, 2000–2005*, 51–66. Dublin. Four Courts Press.

Connolly, S.J. 1989 The Catholic question: 1801–12. In W.E. Waughan (ed.), *A new history of Ireland*, vol. 5, 24–47. Oxford. Oxford University Press.

Finnane, Mark 2006 Irish crime without the outrage. In Dawson, *Reflections on law and history* 203–22.

Hardiman, Adrian 2007 The trial of Robert Emmet. In Dolan *et al.*, *Reinterpreting Emmet*, 227–41.

Ryan, Maeve 2007 'The reptile that had stung me': William Plunket and the trial of Robert Emmet. In Dolan *et al.*, *Reinterpreting Emmet*, 77–101.

Vance, R.N.C. 1982 Text and tradition: Robert Emmet's speech from the dock. *Studies* 71, 185–91.

INDEX

Page numbers in italic refer to illustrations

H

Hall, J.B., 91, 192, 200, 206–07, 210, 272

Hanlon, Joseph, 188, 196–7, 206, 209, 215, 216

Hannen, Sir James, 225, 261

Harcourt, Sir William, 133, 154–5, 169–70, 186–7, 191, 273

Hardiman, Adrian, 42, 43

Hardwicke, Lord, 7, 11–12, 14, 43, 52, 55

Harrington, Timothy, 147, 158, 160–2, 168, 169, 215

Hartington, Lord, 176, 182

Healy, Maurice, xiv, xix, 193

Healy, T.M., xiv, 168, 184, 213, 226, 230

Home Rule

Home Rule League, 223

leadership, 130

opposition to, 225, 263, 295, 300

support for, 213, 229, 301, 302

Home Rule Bill (1886), 220, 221, 263, 298

Hopkins, Tighe, 189, 208, 209, 211, 213

Horridge, Justice Thomas Gardner, 295

Houston, Edward Caulfield, 229–31, 233, 245, 258, 260

Huddy, John, 133, 139

Huddy, Joseph, 133, 139

Hynes, Francis, 186, 215

I

ICA. *see* Irish Citizen Army (ICA)

ILPU. *see* Irish Loyal and Patriotic Union (ILPU)

Inglis, Brian, 59, 84, 309

Invincibles. *see* Irish National Invincibles

IRB. *see* Irish Republican Brotherhood (IRB)

Irish Citizen Army (ICA), 271, 272, 273, 274, 289, 290–1

Irish Loyal and Patriotic Union (ILPU), 229, 230, 231

Irish Magazine, 44, 56

Irish National Invincibles

botched assassination attempts, 179–80

formation of, 177–9

Phoenix Park murders, 181–2

investigation of, 187–90

members of, 173

Parnell's links to, 251, 261

trial. *see* Phoenix Park murders: trial

Irish National League, 225, 261, 262

Irish Parliamentary Party, 130, 160, 178, 214, 223–4, 261–3

Irish Republican Brotherhood (IRB), 176, 213, 267, 271

Military Council, 271, 272

Supreme Council, 176, 271

Irish Volunteers, 267, 269, 271, 272, 274, 278

Irishman, 226, 231

J

James II, xviii, 49

Johnson, Constable, 140, 141, 142, 160

Joyce, Anthony 'Maolra', 136–8, 146, 148, 160, 164–65, 167–9

Joyce, Bridget, 135

Joyce, John, 134–41, 148, 157, 160, 163–64

Joyce, Maolra, 138, 140, 147

Joyce, Margaret, 135, 225, 262

Joyce, Martin 'Seán', 136, 138, 143, 144, 169

Joyce, Michael, 135, 141, 160

Joyce, Myles 'Seán', 129, 136–40, 143–5, 153–4, 156–60, 167–70

Joyce, Paddy 'Maolra', 136–7, 138

M

Y